KATHARINE HEPBURN
A REMARKABLE WOMAN

"Meticulously detailed . . . Hepburn fans should be delighted."
                                        —*Cosmopolitan*

STREISAND
A BIOGRAPHY

"Edwards has made a specialty of the well-researched biography . . . books characterized by their fast-moving story lines [and] profusion of gossipy insights mixed with hard facts."
                                        —*Biography*

"Unusually thorough and perceptive . . . Veteran celebrity biographer Edwards walks the tightrope of fairness with remarkable ease and grace."
                                        —*Kirkus Reviews*

ALSO BY ANNE EDWARDS

BIOGRAPHY
SONYA: THE LIFE OF COUNTESS TOLSTOY
VIVIEN LEIGH: A BIOGRAPHY
JUDY GARLAND: A BIOGRAPHY
ROAD TO TARA: THE LIFE OF MARGARET MITCHELL
MATRIARCH: QUEEN MARY AND THE HOUSE OF WINDSOR
A REMARKABLE WOMAN: A BIOGRAPHY OF
KATHARINE HEPBURN
KATHARINE HEPBURN: A BIOGRAPHY (UK title)
EARLY REAGAN: THE RISE TO POWER
SHIRLEY TEMPLE: AMERICAN PRINCESS
THE DeMILLES: AN AMERICAN FAMILY
ROYAL SISTERS: ELIZABETH AND MARGARET
THE GRIMALDIS OF MONACO: CENTURIES OF
SCANDAL/YEARS OF GRACE
THRONE OF GOLD: THE LIVES OF AGA KHANS
STREISAND

NOVELS
LA DIVINA
THE SURVIVORS
SHADOW OF A LION
HAUNTED SUMMER
MIKLOS ALEXANDROVITCH IS MISSING
THE HESITANT HEART
CHILD OF NIGHT (UK title RAVEN WINGS)
WALLIS: THE NOVEL

AUTOBIOGRAPHY
THE INN AND US (with Stephen Citron)

CHILDREN'S BOOKS
P. T. BARNUM
THE GREAT HOUDINI
A CHILD'S BIBLE

EVER AFTER

DIANA AND THE LIFE SHE LED

ANNE EDWARDS

St. Martin's Paperbacks

EVER AFTER: DIANA AND THE LIFE SHE LED

Copyright © 1999 by Anne Edwards.
Jacket photograph by © Terence Donovan/Camera Press/Donovan

First published in Great Britain as *Diana: And the Rise of the House of Spencer* by Hodder and Stroughton, a division of Hodder Headline

ISBN: 0-312-97873-1

Printed in the United States of America

St. Martin's Press hardcover edition / May 2000
St. Martin's Paperbacks edition / May 2001

St. Martin's Paperbacks are published by St. Martin's Press, 175 Fifth Avenue, New York, NY 10010.

10 9 8 7 6 5 4 3

FOR CATHERINE SADLER GRILL
WITH LOVE

CONTENTS

Photo Credits

Edward John Spencer *Camera Press* by Fayer
Edward John Spencer and Frances Fermoy *Hulton Getty* Photo by Lee
Diana's maternal grandparents, Lord and Lady Fermoy *Hulton Deutsch*, Keystone
The Honourable Diana Spencer's first birthday *Hulton Getty*
Diana at age three on a visit to Althorp *Camera Press*
Althorp, in Northamptonshire circa 1840 *Mary Evans Picture Library*
Sarah Churchill, 1st Duchess of Marlborough *Mary Evans Picture Library*
Diana and younger brother Charles at Park House, 1967 *Camera Press*
Diana on holiday in the summer of 1970 *Camera Press*
A Spencer family portrait circa 1972 *Hulton Deutsch*
The 8th Earl Spencer and Countess Raine Spencer *Camera Press* (The Times)
Diana at West Heath School of 1970 *Camera Press*
Diana the kindergarten teacher *Camera Press* Charles De La Court
Diana, a favourite to marry the Prince of Wales *Rex Features* by Richard Young
Kanga the Australian *Rex Features* by Philip Ide
Camilla Parker Bowles *Rex Features* by Darien Fletcher
Diana's Grandmother, Lady Fermoy *Camera Press*
Diana and Prince Charles face the press as a couple *Hulton Deutsch*
Diana the bride and her father at St. Paul's Cathedral *Camera Press* by Tony Drabble
The bride and groom share a moment *Camera Press*
The new Princess of Wales and her groom on their way to Buckingham Palace *Camera Press* by Lionel Cherruault
Earl Spencer shares a carriage with the Queen *Keystone Press*
Diana with Princes William and Harry in Majorca *Camera Press* by Glenn Harvey
Diana the loving mother *Camera Press* by Glenn Harvey

Harry's first day at school *Popperfoto* by Peter Skingley

Diana's riding instructor, James Hewitt *Rex Features* by Richard Young

Diana on tour in the Middle East *Colorific!* by David Levenson

Dancing on stage with Wayne Sleep *Rex Features*

The crowds loved Diana *Camera Press* by Richard Gillard

Diana dedicated herself to children's charities *Camera Press* by Nigel Hinkes

Dr. Hasnat Khan *Mirror Syndicate*

Diana in Pakistan *Rex Features* by David Hartley

Rose Monckton, Diana's friend *Camera Press* by Srdja Djukanovic

Diana and the Princes join Mohammed al Fayed on his yacht *Popperfoto*, Reuters

Dodi Fayed *Rex Features* by Richard Young

Mohammed and Dodi al Fayed *Rex Features*

Happy days for Diana and Dodi *Rex Features*, Sipa Photo by Sipa Press

Princes William and Harry march with their father, Prince Philip and Earl Spencer behind their mother's coffin *Camera Press*

Earl Spencer, Prince William, Prince Harry and Prince Charles *Rex Features* by Peter Nicholls

Diana's funeral at Westminster Abbey *Camera Press*

Earl Spencer *Rex Features* by Simon Walker

Diana's last ride to Althorp where she is buried *Magnum* by Peter Marlow

ACKNOWLEDGMENTS

A GOOD BIOGRAPHY requires fresh archival material, witnesses with intelligence and sensitivity, and gossip. In approaching the life of Diana, Princess of Wales, I found there was a plethora of all of these. My aim from the beginning of my work on this book has been to place Diana in historical context. I came to my subject without prejudice and/or hagiography. She was a young woman who could inspire great impatience. She squandered much and turned manipulation into an art form. Yet I firmly believe, having spent several years digging in dusty archives and talking to a hundred or more people who figured in her life, that Diana is one of a small group of women in this century to have effected change, both in the British monarchy and its subjects. She was the reality of a Grimms' fairytale—for a young woman to marry a prince does not mean that either of them will live happily ever after. But that does not stop them from contributing a great deal to our society.

I could not see how Diana's life could be presented without digging deeply into her ancestral background. The Spencers are an important family in the history of Great Britain, but Diana also had American roots. One great-grandmother was Frances Work, an American heiress, and a multi-millionaire great-great-grandfather was a friend of such American dynamos as Vanderbilt and Rockefeller. I am told I am the first person to have delved into the archives of the Work family from Chilicothe, Ohio, later of New York City. I am tremendously grateful for the help given me by the various libraries and archives in those two cities.

I was fortunate in writing this book, which had its origins before her tragic death, in having the insight and recall of many of Diana's close friends, staff and others who knew her at different stages in her life. As happens often in biographies of this nature, where power and conflicting loyalties exist, there were many true witnesses to Diana's life who would not allow me to interview them unless I agreed not to disclose their names. I respect their requests and want them to know how grateful I am for the assistance they did extend to me. Those personal reflections, retelling of known incidents, and the filling in of so many details, have contributed greatly in my being able to present a full and more accurate portrait of Diana, Princess of Wales. Those who were gracious enough to lend their names I have mentioned in the text and in my chapter notes, but I thank them here once again.

Also, I want to extend my gratitude to two of my peers, Andrew Morton and Anthony Holden, who generously gave me the benefit of their many years on the "Royal Run."

I have been fortunate in having Roland Philipps at Hodder & Stoughton as my English editor, and Cal Morgan at St. Martin's Press as his American counterpart. My life has been a divided one: I have spent half my time in England, where I came as a young woman and remained for twenty-one years, and half in the States. This has afforded me the benefit of good friends on both sides of the Atlantic. Among them I would like to mention a few who have helped in some way to the realization of this book: Sally Carr, Terence McCarthy, Ion Trewin, Sally Ann Howes, Mitchell Douglas, Gill Coleridge, Eric S. Askanase, Roseanne Boyle, and Hazel Orme.

My deepest gratitude goes to my husband, Stephen Citron, who has been by my side during every phase of this book as he has in all others written during our twenty-five years of exceptional togetherness. A master biographer on his own, he always takes time away from his work to discuss the multitude of problems that come up during my endeavours, reads and rereads my many, many revisions, and always can be counted on for a lively and accurate assessment.

EVER AFTER

DIANA AND THE LIFE SHE LED

PROLOGUE

A Visit to Althorp
1964

I

AT THE AGE of three Diana Spencer was taken on a rare visit to see her paternal grandparents, the Earl and Countess Spencer, at Althorp House in Northamptonshire, on what was intended to be an occasion of great celebration. Her mother had produced a healthy male heir for the House of Spencer, which had featured prominently in the history of England since the mid-sixteenth century. The young heir, her infant brother Charles, was screaming in his nanny's arms unaware that one day he would inherit a substantial fortune, an earldom—granted originally by Charles I—and the massive estate whose noble halls, on this crisp autumn day in 1964, echoed to his bawling cries. Diana knew there was something special about Charles that made him more important to her parents than either she or her two older sisters, Sarah and Jane: since his birth there had been an air of jubilation in their home, Park House near King's Lynn.

After the rail journey, the family was met at Northampton station by the Earl's dark green Rolls-Royce, adorned with the Spencer crest, and driven the remaining six miles to Althorp. The splendid Tudor mansion, with its vast acreage, had been home to the Spencer family since 1508. The current Earl was vigorously protective of his cars so the chauffeur drove slowly along the Northampton-Rugby road, through small villages whose inhabitants had been reliant for generations upon the successive masters of Althorp for their livelihood.

At last the car passed through the gates of Althorp and continued on beneath an arch of ancient oaks to the front entrance where the Earl and Countess were standing. Upon arrival, Diana's mother Frances, a tall, lean, blonde woman, pushed forward the little girl at her side and let go of her hand. "This is Diana, the shy one," she announced.

Diana gazed up at the gruff, unsmiling face of her grandfather, Albert (Jack) Edward John Spencer, the 7th Earl Spencer. Later she recalled being too terrified to speak as he grunted something at her, then turned his back and walked away.

A moment later her grandmother, Cynthia, bent down, took her hand and said, "Well, Diana, you certainly have grown into a lovely big girl." These words, with minor revisions appropriate to Diana's passage from childhood to adolescence, were repeated on all her future visits to Althorp until her grandmother's death.

Diana adored her grandmother, in whose presence she always felt protected. She was still lovely, with softly waved silver hair and deep blue eyes, and a warm, genuine smile. It was she who kept the peace between her rather brusque husband and his family.

On that day, Cynthia led Diana across the black and white checkered marble floor of the hall, up the deep steps of the grand, balustered staircase. They went along a wide corridor hung with portraits of men in uniform, swords at their sides, and bejewelled women, until eventually Countess Spencer opened a door into "a soft blue and delicately flowered" sitting room. "This was my favourite book as a child," she said as she retrieved a book with a brightly coloured cover from a glass-fronted cabinet. "I would like you to have it now." It was an illustrated edition of *Grimms' Fairy Tales*, which Diana treasured for the rest of her life.

Diana never knew her grandfather well, for Jack Spencer had little interest in his family. Althorp was his passion and he had great pride in his Spencer heritage which he considered, because of its solid English roots, of a higher order than that of the Windsors. That dynasty had been founded by the Hanoverian George I in 1714, four centuries after William Spencer, an English sheep-farmer, had become a prominent landowner. Jack Spencer had one son, Diana's father Edward John—Johnnie—Viscount Althorp, for whom he had small regard. Johnnie lacked intellectual curiosity, and he had little respect for the history of the earldom that he would one day inherit. Neither could he manage his income. He drank heavily, and family rumour ran that he had struck Frances more than once.

Diana was fascinated by the family portraits, so much so that it would not take too many years before she would be well-schooled in her family history. She made a practice of interweaving the basic facts about the Spencers with those she learned about the kings and queens of England. For instance it was Sir John Spencer (1533–99) who had built Althorp and founded the family fortunes during the reigns of Henry VIII and Elizabeth I. His son-in-law Thomas Sackville, Earl of Dorset, Lord Treasurer and Lord High Steward had been given the awesome task in 1587 of informing Mary Queen of Scots that she had been sentenced to death, and in 1600 had presided over the trial for disobedience of the Earl of Essex.

More than a hundred portraits and paintings, by Van Dyck and Gainsborough among others, hung in Althorp's spectacular Long Gallery. Diana came to know the history of most of their subjects. There were also portraits of many of the estate's illustrious royal guests: Queen Anne, James I's consort; King Charles I and his queen, Henrietta Maria; King Edward VII; King George V and VI and their queens, Mary and Elizabeth; and the Empress of Austria were only a few among the many who enjoyed its ambience, hunt parties and fine library.

Among Diana's antecedents were ambassadors, privy councillors and Knights of the Garter. There were intellectuals, politicians, poets and philosophers—philanderers and Philistines too. She was related to Charles II, seven American presidents, and the distinguished Suffolk, Sunderland, Shaftesbury, Marlborough, Abercorn, Seymour, Halifax, Devonshire, Peel, Baring and Churchill families. Through the Suffolks the Spencers were directly descended from King Henry VII. They could also claim descent from Sir Robert Walpole, usually regarded as the first prime minis-

ter, the great Duke of Marlborough and the ill-fated Lady
Jane Grey. Diana was proud of her Spencer ancestry and
when at times she faced confrontation, she would say to
herself, "Remember, Diana, you are a Spencer."

Diana took away from her first visit to Althorp the warm
memory of Grandmother Spencer, and a sense of apprehension when she thought of her grandfather, whose oppressive
personality pervaded the great house. Later in life she said
she could feel his presence minutes before he entered a
room. Of that visit she also recalled that her parents had
abruptly gathered together their children and departed hur-
riedly, her father's face red and unsmiling, her mother silent
until they were on their way home to Park House. Then
there was a row. Diana never knew what had been the
cause, but it left her with a sense of foreboding that shad-
owed her childhood and followed her throughout her life.

PART ONE

A SPENCER CHILDHOOD

2

DIANA'S GRANDFATHER DEVOTED his life to the preservation of Althorp. He had little time for frivolity and had no patience with fools or children. A blunt man, "he would say and do precisely what he thought true and right without the faintest regard for the reaction his words or deeds might produce."

Educated at Harrow and Trinity College, Cambridge, he had been wounded in the shoulder and leg in the First World War. His experiences at the front and the brutality of battle marked him for life. His wounds, though not life-threatening, had caused him considerable and lasting pain and might have accounted in part for his frequent ill-humour. He became the 7th Earl Spencer in 1922, aged thirty, on the death of his father, Charles Robert, Earl Spencer, three years after he and Cynthia were married, and two years before the birth of his son and heir, Diana's father.

When he was eight Johnnie Spencer was sent away to board at St. Peter's Court School in Broadstairs. The regime was strict, the dormitories unheated, curtainless and grim. Parents were allowed to visit only once a term. Johnnie recalled that his mother made these trips alone or with his older sister Anne. At thirteen, in the summer of 1937, he went on to Eton. He was not popular there, perhaps because he liked playing tricks on his fellows—he once put a worm in another boy's food.

In his senior year, as was customary, he had a "fag," a younger boy who had to do chores for him. "He wasn't as fierce as some one heard about," said John Bovill, "and didn't beat me much. I had to light the fire in his room, make his toast for tea and run his errands. There was a tuck shop where you could get some fried bread, which we called rafts, with an egg or sausage on it. In wartime,

though [coal and sticks were scare and a fire was difficult
to start]—woe betide you if you didn't get it going . . .
Toast was cooked in front of the fire, and when on one
occasion I burned it, Johnnie gave me six of the best with
a leather belt."

After Eton, Johnnie went to Sandhurst for a year before
joining the Army in 1942 at eighteen. After his initial training he received his commission and, in the spring of 1944,
joined the Royal Scots Greys. He fought in Normandy with
the Tank Corps, a traumatic experience. "We have been
existing in a world of noise, ruin and the choking dust of
a boiling summer," he wrote in his diary. "Evil sights and
the stench of burned flesh have become more and more
commonplace." In August 1944, when his regiment was
fighting near Caen and overcoming German forces, he recorded, "Everywhere in ditches, in carts, in streams and on
the roads lay scattered hundreds of German bodies rapidly
decaying under the August sun." Like many others, he tried
to obliterate the haunting images in heavy drinking.

He fought hard and well, but even so he was unable to
win the admiration of his company. "He had all the signs
of never having been given his head," his senior commanding officer confessed. "He was very nice but very stupid,
very slow and lacking in go . . . It was all squashed out of
him by a domineering father. He had beautiful manners and
was always correct, but was one of the stupidest officers I
had at that time met. I recall a private soldier remarking to
me that you could set his trousers on fire and it would be
ten minutes before he realized his bun was burning—
though the word used, needless to say, was not bun."

During the war, Althorp was used by the armed forces
as temporary headquarters for soldiers about to be sent to
France. The park was a mass of tents and although Jack
Spencer considered himself a patriot, he was not pleased at
the presence of the troops. He claimed they blocked his
view of his estate and demanded that the men run past
windows that faced the best vistas.

His father's wartime injuries and their shared experience

of war might have brought Johnnie Spencer closer to his father, but they were always at loggerheads. The Earl was a domineering father and Johnnie never seemed able to please him. Jack Spencer was accustomed to having his own way.

In the early 1950s, when Jack Spencer heard that the family vault under St. Mary's Church in Great Brington, which adjoined the Althorp estate, was overcrowded and that many of the coffins were disintegrating, he cremated the remains of his ancestors, to the disapproval of "his more conventional neighbours." The villagers felt he had committed an act of desecration. However, Earl Spencer dismissed their objections as misguided.

One of the few amusing stories told about Jack Spencer had to do with his penchant for dark green Rolls-Royces. His chauffeur had strict orders "never to turn his head when the Earl was in the car, but to start the car and move off when he heard the door slam." One day Jack was being driven to Buckingham Palace, in his official attire as honorary sheriff of Northampton. On the return journey he ordered the chauffeur to stop near some thick bushes by the roadside and got out to relieve himself. A strong wind was blowing, the car door slammed shut and the chauffeur drove off, "leaving the Earl stranded and he had to hitch a lift in full regalia from a passing motorist." The story became part of family lore but was never repeated in front of the Earl himself.

Another anecdote recalls how Jack once entered the Long Library at Althorp where his cousin Winston Churchill was researching a book on the Duke of Marlborough. On finding Churchill smoking a cigar, the Earl "ripped it right out of his mouth": he allowed no one to smoke there for fear of damage to Althorp's wealth of rare books.

Cynthia's soft nature did not offset her husband's gruffness, but it did contribute to his social acceptance. More importantly, in personal terms, it had given her son, Johnnie, who she tried desperately hard to protect from his father's ill-temper without much success, a home where love and warmth was accessible and where Jack Spencer's authoritarian rule could be somewhat modified, if only in small ways, by her intervention. But she had long ago given up trying to mediate between her grown son and her aging husband. Rather, Cynthia turned her attention to her grandchildren who she sensed, with great sadness, were presently caught between two warring parents.

The Honourable Diana Frances Spencer was born in her parents' bedroom at Park House on 1 July 1961, as the sun was setting and shadows falling across the vast rear lawns and the open fields where her father's cows grazed. Her mother had been in labour since early that morning. Diana was her third daughter; her only son, John, born eighteen months earlier, had lived just ten hours. Frances knew that unless she could deliver a son, Althorp, the Spencer fortunes and the title would pass on Johnnie's death to his nephew.

Her first words to the midwife who had attended Diana's birth were, "Is it a boy?"

When she was told she had a girl, weighing seven pounds twelve ounces, it is claimed she said, "Johnnie will be so disappointed." And, indeed, although he loved his three daughters, Viscount Althorp badly wanted a son.

"Diana wasn't many hours old," Ray Hunt, the former groundsman at Park House recalled, "[When] Viscount Althorp sent for me and asked if I would put the lounge television in the bedroom for his wife so that she could have a telly to watch in bed. [He] and I carried this monstrous console television up the staircase and put it in the bedroom. Lady Althorp was in bed with Diana and said to me, 'Come have a look at the little brat, right?' She was laughing because she didn't mean it and I went over and had a look—and she was beautiful, a beautiful baby."

Shortly after Diana's birth, Frances visited a series of Harley Street specialists to undergo tests to determine why she could not deliver a healthy boy. In the early sixties it was not yet commonly known that a child's sex is determined by its father. It was a painful and humiliating experience for her, compounded by post-natal depression. Johnnie and Frances quarrelled endlessly, their raised voices echoing through Park House, and Frances suffered constantly from migraine headaches, which made the sound of her three children at play unbearable.

Before her marriage to Johnnie Spencer, the eighteen-year-old Frances Roche, daughter of Lord and Lady Fermoy, had been free-spirited, cheerful, attractive and popular with her "set." She was a skilful dancer, but not gifted in any of the arts—a disappointment to her mother who was a talented musician.

It was in 1953, at a dance at Holkham Hall, the nearby home of the Earl and Countess of Leicester, that Frances met Johnnie Spencer, Viscount Althorp. He was slim and tanned, his red hair slicked back to frame his high forehead and his well-defined features. He had recently completed a tour of duty as equerry to Queen Elizabeth II and the Duke of Edinburgh, and was at Sandringham for the weekend as a guest. He was about to become engaged to Lady Anne Coke, eldest daughter of the Leicesters. Anne had been a maid of honour to the Queen at her coronation and there was much excitement in the county over her expected betrothal.

However, from the moment Johnnie set eyes on Frances as she whirled around the dance floor in her escort's arms he was drawn to her. At one point she caught him staring at her, came over and asked if he wanted to dance with her. He accepted and hardly left her side for the rest of the evening.

"It was a terrible scandal when Johnnie Spencer ran out on Lady Anne," a contemporary recalled, and added, "The Fermoys were nothing"—at least, not in comparison with the Leicesters, who had held their earldom since Elizabeth I had granted it to Robert Dudley. However, Johnnie was smitten and had never before been pursued in quite the same fashion. In fact, until he had met Anne, who was far more reserved than Frances, he had not had much success

with women. Now thirty, twelve years older than the im-
petuous Frances, he was being urged by his father "to settle
down with a girl of good stock and raise a family, to include a male heir." Johnnie proposed a few months after
their fateful meeting.

Frances was the youngest bride to be married at Westminster Abbey since the turn of the century. Only two or
three weddings are held there each year: to qualify for the
privilege you must be either a member of the Royal Family,
or closely connected with it, a holder of the Order of the
Bath, or have served the Abbey in some capacity. At Lady
Fermoy's request, the Queen agreed that the wedding could
be held at the Abbey, most likely because Frances was marrying the future Earl Spencer. His family, after all, had
served monarchs for centuries.

Lady Fermoy devoted her time for the next three months
to directing the wedding preparations, like a general preparing for battle. Her headquarters were at her London home
in Wilton Place, Belgravia. Seventeen hundred people were
invited to the service but only eight hundred to the reception. Weeding out the unlucky nine hundred without of-
fending some of England's "best" families was Lady
Fermoy's hardest task.

Frances and Johnnie were married on 1 June 1954, in
the presence of nine members of the Royal Family—the
Queen, the Duke of Edinburgh, the Queen Mother, Princes
Margaret, Marina, Duchess of Kent, Princess Alexandra,
the Duke and Duchess of Gloucester, and the Princess
Royal.* The *Daily Mail* called it "the wedding of the year,"
and Lady Fermoy watched proudly as her daughter signed
the register just two pages after Princess Elizabeth and
Lieutenant Philip Mountbatten.

Frances looked young and ethereally lovely in a white
faille wedding gown embroidered all over with crystals,

---

*The Princess Royal (1897–1965) was Mary, the younger sister of
Edward VIII and George VI. She married Henry, Viscount Lascelles,
6th Earl of Harewood.

which were interspersed with small floral sprays of hand-cut diamonds on the bodice. The magnificent Spencer diamond tiara held her veil in place. Bride and groom walked under the raised swords of a guard of honour mounted by Johnnie's regiment, the Royal Scots Greys. The reception was held at St. James's Palace. Lady Fermoy was bursting with pride: her daughter had married one of the country's most eligible men.

Lady Fermoy, née Ruth Sylvia Gill, was the daughter of an Aberdeenshire landowner. She was a talented pianist and as a young woman had been accepted as a student by the piano virtuoso Alfred Cortot. After four years' study at the Paris Conservatory under his personal instruction, she returned to Great Britain and began what appeared to be a promising career with a performance at the Royal Festival Hall in the presence of King George V and Queen Mary. Shortly afterwards, however, she met Maurice Burke Roche, the 4th Baron Fermoy, who was considered somewhat exotic, having been raised in New York City by his American mother, the divorced heiress Fanny Work.

Frank Work, Fanny's father, was one of America's wealthiest entrepreneurs. He was born on 10 February 1819, in Chillicothe, Ohio, the son of John Work, a civil engineer, who died when Frank and his younger brother, Clinton, were still in their teens. Frank had three great loves: horses, swimming, and an overriding ambition to make enough money to move his mother from Dogsburg, the poorer section of Chillicothe, and make all the towns-folk sit up and take notice. He also loved to shock the town elders.

As a young boy, he would gallop naked astride a gaunt grey horse the length of the main street of Chillicothe on his way home from swimming in the river. As he passed the market house, people would throw fruit and vegetables at him, but the barrage never slowed him down. When a teacher at his school whipped him for his behaviour, Frank took his small savings and ran away from home. He never saw his mother again—she died before he had made his fortune.

He went to New York where he found a job in a gas fittings store and ended up owning the company. As soon as he began to make money, he bought horses, which led to his friendship with Commodore Cornelius Vanderbilt. During the panic of 1873, the old Commodore lent Frank money to keep his business afloat, then persuaded him to sell out and operate in stocks under his guidance. Within five years his fortune was estimated at $15 million. Frank was now an eminent member of New York society.

He married Ellen Wood, also from Chillicothe, and had two striking daughters, Fanny and Lucy. Nothing was too good for his girls, but Frank set down certain rules for them. Besides their presidential connections, one of his wife's ancestors had been the American Revolutionary War hero Nathan Hale, who was hanged by the British as a spy and whose last words had been, "I regret that I have only one life to give to my country." The American flag flew proudly over the Work mansion on Fifth Avenue and his daughters warned that they must marry American men or lose their rights to their inheritance.

Fanny, a lively young woman with luxuriant auburn hair and "amazing brown eyes," was a childhood friend of Jennie Jerome Churchill, Winston Churchill's American mother. On a four-month tour of Europe and Great Britain with her sister and her mother in 1879, Fanny was introduced by Jennie, at one of her large social gatherings at her London home, to the impoverished heir of the Irish barony of Fermoy, James Boothby Burke Roche. James had both seductive charm and devilishly good looks. Fanny fell wildly in love and accepted Fermoy's proposal shortly before the family's scheduled departure for New York. Despite her parents' objections and warnings from friends that James would never settle down they were married in 1880.

The voices of doom proved right. James was both a philanderer and a spendthrift, and lost his wife's money in extravagance and gambling. After eleven years of marital disharmony, when their son Maurice was eight Fanny returned to New York and divorced her husband. Frank Work reinstated her in his will. Fermoy's attempt to win a large settlement for himself so infuriated Frank that he added a codicil stating that his grandson might inherit his fortune only if he never again set foot in Great Britain.

In 1903 Fanny, as great a rebel as her father, shocked society again by choosing as her second husband Aurel Batonyi, the Hungarian who managed her father's stables. Once again Frank cut her out of his will, but reinstated her three years later when she divorced Batonyi, after he lost what money she had given him in poor investments and high living. Frank Work died in 1911 leaving Maurice heir to millions.

In 1929 the father Maurice had not seen since childhood died, making Maurice 4th Baron Fermoy, a title he relished although it came with no great house, property or income. Despite Frank's stricture that none of his heirs leave the United States, Fanny went to Paris and became prominent in the "fast" international set of wealthy foreign divorcees and pleasure-seekers, while Maurice returned to Britain to adopt his impoverished barony.

Ruth Gill met Maurice Fermoy in 1930. She was twenty-two while he was forty-five and still considered one of Britain's most eligible bachelors. Ruth was dazzled by his wealth, title and royal connections. One of his closest friends was the Duke of York, the future King George VI, and King George V, as a favour to his son, granted the new Lord Fermoy the lease on Park House, close to Sandringham. Ruth was so thrilled at the prospect of becoming Lady Fermoy and moving into this enchanted circle that she agreed to give up her musical career to marry Maurice. With her support he became Conservative MP for King's Lynn, then mayor of the ancient coastal town.

Widowed at forty-six, which was too late for her to return to the concert stage; Lady Fermoy gave her time and energy to establishing an annual music festival at King's Lynn with distinguished musicians like Yehudi Menuhin,

Benjamin Britten, Peter Pears and Gerald Moore, with appearances by theatrical greats such as Dame Edith Evans, Dame Sybil Thorndike and Emlyn Williams. She inaugurated monthly noonday concerts in the town and contributed some of her collection of paintings to start the Fermoy Art Gallery, in what is now the King's Lynn Guildhall. She always remained a close friend of Queen Elizabeth, the Queen Mother.

The lease of Park House, which Lady Fermoy found too large after her husband's death, was given to Frances and Johnnie, who were then living in Gloucestershire. Lady Fermoy, as Woman of the Bedchamber to the Queen Mother,* travelled back and forth at various times of the year between the royal residences: Clarence House in London, Balmoral in Scotland, Sandringham in Norfolk and Windsor. She had small but comfortable private quarters on the Sandringham estate, and retained her London home where she entertained, when time permitted, with musical evenings.

Diana never knew her maternal grandfather, but Lady Fermoy was an important figure in her life. Like her older sister Sarah, Diana displayed an aptitude for the piano, which Lady Fermoy encouraged. She helped Diana with her early lessons, and played Mozart to her. As a treat she would take her grandchildren into King's Lynn for tea at Ladyman's—"the place to go for such an outing. Not too fancy, very homestyle," recalled Elsie Byre, who worked there as a waitress. "There was a large balcony where the children liked to sit. There would be a big fuss if a child threw something down, even though it happened frequently. You know, one child would throw something over the railing—a wad of paper, something like that—and another would follow suit. Lady Fermoy came fairly regularly with

*Woman of the Bedchamber is an honorary position in the Households of the Queen and the Queen Mother. It involves some minor secretarial duties, writing letters or notes, and accompanying the Queen to public events, on tours, or simply as a companion.

the girls. She would order buns to go round. Diana—she was the youngest—always begged for and got a cream-filled bun when I would be taking their order."

"I always felt different from anyone else," Diana once said. "It was a very unhappy childhood. Parents were busy sorting themselves out. Always seeing my mother crying. Daddy never spoke to us about it [and] we never asked questions."

It wasn't long before food became both solace and re-ward.

PARK HOUSE, DIANA'S home, was a ten-bedroom Victorian country house with staff cottages, stables and a tennis court. Although it was four miles inland, easterly winds brought the scent of salt to remind the occupants of the area's seafaring history. The somewhat inelegant facade of the house was concealed from the main road to King's Lynn by trees and shrubs, and stood at the end of short, curved, grey gravel drive just beyond Sandringham church. A weathered brick wall separated Park House from the Sandringham estate. On the Queen's side of the wall was the graveyard where Lord Fermoy and the infant John, Diana's older brother, were buried side by side.

The exterior of the house was a dingy sand-brick and, as few windows faced the drive, it had a bleak, almost institutional aura, lightened only by the green of the parkland. The one hint that children lived in this house was a small windmill, partially hidden by shrubs and built, as its Lilliputian size would indicate, as a playhouse.

Park House had not been conceived as a one-family residence and it lacked cohesion. There was no one room at the heart of the house. Instead there were several reception rooms constructed to give courtiers privacy to entertain guests. The walls were hung with portraits of royalty and their distinguished countrymen and women. The furniture was mainly Victorian, of dark mahogany, sturdily built, and had come with the house when it was first leased by the Fermoys.

During Frances's childhood, there had been a more formal atmosphere at Park House. The Fermoys did a good deal of entertaining and Lady Fermoy held musical evenings in the front drawing room, which housed her prized Bechstein piano. Life was more relaxed in Frances and

Johnnie's early married life when their children were small. Johnnie occasionally went shooting with the Duke of Edinburgh. However, the romantic haze that had enveloped Frances at the start of her marriage soon faded. She and Johnnie were not well matched. Frances was bursting with curiosity, and needed to spread her wings. Johnnie seldom wanted to leave Park House, where he felt entirely comfortable. Whatever their disagreements Johnnie and Frances shared a love of horses and dogs. Frances had several keeshonds—a large Netherlands breed, with thick greyish-black hair—Johnnie had his gun dogs and the children all had their own pets. Diana was especially fond of Gitsy, one of her mother's dogs, but generally preferred hamsters, rabbits and guinea pigs. She also had a bad-tempered ginger cat called Marmalade who purred contentedly when little Diana stroked him but hissed at almost everyone else.

Sarah, Jane and Diana banded together to offset the tension created by their parents, both of whom drank heavily. Of the two older girls, Jane was the practical one and Sarah, the eldest, the leader and a daredevil. On being given a new pony for her birthday, she rode it straight into the kitchen to the consternation of staff and family, especially Lady Fermoy who happened to be visiting at the time.

The immense nineteenth-century kitchen with its stone-flagged hearth and floor had a stove that predated the First World War. Next to the kitchen was a dark green laundry room that always smelled of bleach, and next to that the former butler's pantry, now converted into a schoolroom for the sisters. It overlooked the south lawn and was wallpapered in a pattern of leaves and balloons. The shelves held books and stationery, and a blackboard faced the door. The kindly, persevering Gertrude Allen, called Ally by her young charges—who included five or six local children—presided over their studies.

Ally had been Frances's governess and had only been parted from her during the years Frances spent at West Heath and at Downham School near Bishop's Stortford in Hertfordshire. As one observer noted, "[Ally] was one of

the fast-fading breed of spinster ladies who devoted her life
to looking after other people's children." Ally was a family
fixture and Diana was close to her: Frances had never entirely recovered from her post-natal depression after Diana's birth, and turned over the care of her third little girl
to the nanny and Ally, who found her "a serious little girl
who tried hard, who was fond of history, and [as she grew
older] loved stories of kings and queens not of battles."

Charles's birth eased the tension between the Althorps,
but only temporarily. Having delivered the son and heir,
Frances, still only twenty-eight, realized how little she and
Johnnie had in common. He was dull, without personal
drive, and Frances had neither the physical stamina nor the
desire to push him. Nor could she conceive of life continuing as it was. Deeply resentful of his past abuse and impatient with his often foolish behaviour, she grew
increasingly restless. (He enjoyed cricket and once, to his
wife's fury, offered any member of the Sandringham
Cricket Club five pounds if he could hit a ball through a
window at Park House which was fifty feet from the pitch
and, when no one took up his offer, proceeded to attempt
it himself.)

As they continued to grow apart, Johnnie spent more
time drinking alone in his study while Frances stayed in
London, shopping, going to the theatre or visiting old
friends. The children saw less and less of their parents. In
1966, when Diana was five and Charles two, Jane, now
nine, and Sarah, eleven, were sent to West Heath boarding-
school. They came home only at half-terms and in the
school holidays. Diana was desolate: she worshipped her
eldest sister, who had been like a surrogate mother to her.
She was terrified of the dark and it had been Sarah who
had sat beside her in the cream-coloured nursery until she
fell asleep. "In my bed," Diana later recalled, "I'd have
twenty stuffed animals and there would be a midget's space
for me, and they would have to be in bed every night. That
was my family. I hated the dark and had an obsession about
[it], always had to have a light outside my door until I was

at least ten." She felt that she was the child her parents had not wanted. "[They] were crazy to have a son and heir and there comes a third daughter." It was in 1966 too, at a Christmas party in London, attended by both Frances and Johnnie, that they met Janet Munroe Shand Kydd, an artist, and her husband Peter, heir to a wallpaper fortune. Tall, dark and good-looking, Peter had impeccable manners and a light-hearted air. He was fun to be with and Frances was charmed by him. They began to meet secretly during her trips to London.

Diana was too young to understand the change in her mother but she told her nanny, "I'm glad Mummy isn't crying so much any more." However, a short time later her mother's sobs began anew, and Diana came to fear that somehow she might have been the cause.

Diana was on her way through the deserted drawing room from the kitchen, where she had gone to visit her menagerie of pets, when she heard raised voices in the hallway. She hid behind the open door and kept very still. Through the narrow crack where the hinges were she could see her parents. Her father was grasping her mother's arm and tugging at it.

Terrified, but unable to move, she crouched in her hiding-place long after she saw her mother break away and run up the stairs, and her father storm off. Her mother's sobs were obliterated momentarily by the slam of her father's study door. Then a member of staff discovered her: "She thought she had seen her father hitting her mother. It was possible. Their rows had led to violence before."

Life at Park House became a minefield of emotional outbursts. Then, suddenly, in the summer of 1967, when Diana was six, they seemed to stop. Her mother was gone more often—"shopping in London," Ally told the children. But when Frances was at home she was happier. Also, Johnnie was hardly drinking. Park House had been emptied of alcohol and new bottles were not allowed in the house. This seemed to have been the result of a pact between Johnnie

and Frances, for Johnnie confided as much to a close friend.
He also enjoyed telling the story of how one day the Queen
Mother, who was known to "love a tip of the bottle,"
dropped in unexpectedly with Lady Fermoy when there was
nothing but a bottle of cooking sherry to offer her. It was
poured into a crystal decanter and presented to the royal
guest.

Now that Sarah and Jane were at West Heath, Frances
spent more time with Diana and little "Charlie." Diana was
glad of the attention and the lessening of tension at home,
but it was not to last.

Frances was deeply involved with Peter Shand Kydd and
had taken a small, elegant flat in Cadogan Place, a short
walk from Sloane Square and King's Road, Chelsea. She
and Johnnie had agreed to a trial separation. Everything
seemed amicable. Johnnie did not believe that Frances
would actually leave him. He thought that what she needed
was breathing space. She had had too many pregnancies
too close together, and was going through "a woman thing."
He did not realize that his wife and Shand Kydd had been
lovers for over six months.

A former naval officer, Shand Kydd had been educated
at Marlborough and Edinburgh University. He had married
Janet in 1952 when they were both still in their early twenties. With the birth of their children, Adam, Angela and
John, he had gone unenthusiastically into his family's business. After eleven years he withdrew from the firm, leaving
it under the directorship of his younger brother. He then
bought a sheep farm in the outback of Australia and moved
his family into a comfortable but plain-built farmhouse
many miles over dusty roads from the nearest town, Canberra, Australia's capital. They were, however, close to the
beach at Mollymook, where the children could surf in the
clear blue waters of the Tasman Sea. There was a hardware
and a grocery store nearby but no air-conditioning in the
house to combat the intense heat of the summer months.

Janet, though, was used to the sophisticated life of London's Knightsbridge, and the strain of rural existence in a

place so distant from her home was too much for her. Three years later the Shand Kydds returned to England. By now their marriage was in trouble, but they were trying to hold it together. Within months of their arrival back in England, they had met the Althorps and the two couples had hit it off. For Frances, the Shand Kydds hit just the right spark in her own failing marriage. Janet was bright and talented, Peter entertaining. Johnnie was relaxed in their company and enjoyed Peter's vivid stories. In late February 1967 they went to Switzerland, without the children, on a skiing holiday. It was during this ten-day vacation that Frances and Peter realized they were in love.

It was in September that Johnnie found out about the affair. What followed was a row that Diana never forgot.

Diana and Charlie were upstairs in the nursery when they became aware that their parents were quarrelling. A short time later they heard the click of their mother's high heels as she descended the stone steps of the front staircase. There was more shouting. The children made their way downstairs, Diana holding her little brother's hand. The front door was ajar. Outside, on the gravel forecourt, they could see their father loading their mother's suitcases into the boot of her car. More harsh words were exchanged. The car door slammed, the engine revved and, with a sharp screech of tyres, the vehicle turned on to the road. For a moment there was silence. Then their father came in, passed the children without a word, and disappeared into his study. Diana remembered little Charlie, who was only three, crying softly, not knowing what had happened, and clinging to her for comfort.

Their mother had been so upset when she left the house that she had not said goodbye to Diana and Charlie, which formed the basis of the story that she had "bolted" and deserted her children. That was not what she had intended, but her sudden, unexplained departure scarred all her children.

Diana thought she would never see her mother again. There were no telephone calls, and she was afraid to ask questions, for when Johnnie came out of his study he wore a forbidding expression and said nothing to her. She began to believe that somehow she had made her parents so unhappy that they didn't want to be with her. At night, with her stuffed animals surrounding her, and the landing light on, she could hear Charlie "crying in his bed, down at the other end of the house, crying for my mother . . . It was always very difficult. I never could pluck up the courage to get out of bed [and go to comfort him]," she remembered. It was a source of guilt throughout her childhood and youth that she had deserted Charlie when he had needed her most.

One cold, grim October morning, three weeks after her mother had left, Ally came into Diana's room and told her to get dressed. Her mother had found a lovely apartment and she and Charlie were going to take the train to London that day. Violet Collinson, a housemaid and long-time employee at Park House, would accompany them.

Diana and Charles got ready for the journey. When they were standing in the hall, their coats buttoned, their father came out of his study. "I will see you next weekend," he promised, took them in his arms and kissed them. One of the staff drove them to the station and Ally waved to them from the platform. Charlie had a slight cold and sniffled throughout the two-hour ride. Diana put her arm protectively around his shoulders, and they sat like that for most of the journey to Liverpool Street station.

When they arrived Frances was waiting for them and took them back to her flat. She was delighted to be reunited with her two youngest children. Plans were made for outings and Violet went into the kitchen to prepare a tea that included Diana's favourite cream buns.

"Frances was a passionate and devoted mother," a close relative insists. "The idea of abandoning her children for any man, or for any other reason, would have been unthinkable. It has been particularly galling for her that the world believes, to this day, that she just upped and left, dumping the children like compost in a storage shed. She did not."

She brought them to London, and "fully expected to have them for ever."

Indeed, Diana was enrolled at a small school near her mother's home and both children quickly adjusted to their new living conditions. Charlie did not cry at night any more and the three enjoyed feeding the ducks on the Serpentine and trips to London Zoo where Diana particularly liked the penguins and amused Charlie by copying the way they walked. The children loved having tea at the fifth-floor restaurant in Peter Jones, which overlooked Sloane Square and where Diana ordered peanut butter and banana sandwiches. Charlie remembered their father's weekend visits as unsettling interruptions in an otherwise pleasant nursery schedule, and that they invariably ended with his mother "sobbing" and his father "forlorn."

As Christmas 1967 approached, Diana and Charlie were promised that the whole family, including their mother, would be reunited at Park House. They set off from Liverpool Street, their mother and Violet loaded with shopping-bags, and were met at King's Lynn by Johnnie's chauffeur. The two older girls and Lady Fermoy were waiting at Park House to greet them.

It was the last time they were together as a family, and it was fraught with tension. Their father and mother hardly spoke to each other during the first few days and it was apparent that the marriage could not be saved. Behind closed doors divorce was discussed. "Best you don't knock," Gertrude Allen warned. "Mummy and Daddy are having a serious discussion."

When the holiday was over, Johnnie adamantly refused to allow Diana and Charlie to return to London with their mother, and eventually Frances left, promising the children that they would soon be back with her in Cadogan Place, and threatening Johnnie that she would sue for custody of all four. It was Sarah who tried to explain to Diana what divorce meant, not that she fully understood it. For Diana it always meant the loss of a parent, the sense of being different, the fear of somehow being at fault.

Park House was lonely again when the older girls returned to West Heath. Diana and Charlie were enrolled at Silfield School, Gayton Road, in King's Lynn, Charlie in the nursery class. On the first day Jean Lowe, the headmistress, noted how edgy Diana was. "Is anything wrong?" she asked.

"Is Charlie all right?"

"Would you like to go and see?"

"Yes, please."

Diana "trotted off and came back quite happy."

Silfield School was approached along a narrow tree-lined drive. The school was a short distance on the left, while straight ahead was the Principal's house. Charlie attended in the mornings only, while Diana stayed for the afternoon until someone from Park House came to collect her. Jean Lowe was strict but not unapproachable, and she was sensitive to her pupils' moods. The building that housed Diana's class looked a bit like an elves' cottage from the outside and was simple but cosy inside. No class had more than eight children, and red and grey uniforms were worn. Diana was not immediately happy at Silfield: the news of the impending divorce and the scandal it seemed likely to engender had shocked the conservative families of King's Lynn. It set Diana and Charlie apart and made Diana aware that they were "different." "She was the only girl who I knew whose parents were [separated or] divorced," Delissa Needham, another Silfield student, remembered. "Those things just didn't happen then."

"Everything in Diana's tormented psyche turned on what happened to her at the age of six," a latterday friend commented.

Diana was slow to make friends, but when she did she was tremendously loyal. She became close to Alexandra Loyd, the daughter of the Queen's land agent at Sandringham and one of the children whom Frances had brought to Park House for classes with Ally.

Without the laughter and energy of her sisters to fill it, Park House was a large, echoing place, frightening at night when the wind rattled the windows and mice could be heard scampering across the attic floor above her bedroom. Diana sorely missed Sarah and Jane, and when they were at home on holiday, she ran errands for Sarah, helped to tidy her room, and followed her about. Charlie was still a toddler, unable to enter into the games she so enjoyed when Sarah and Jane were at home, especially since Ally had been relieved of her position with the family because of her allegiance to Frances.

At home, the children spent the majority of their time in their nursery at the top of the house under the care of a series of nannies. One woman remembered how seriously affected both Diana and Charlie were by their mother's departure. "[Diana], always so willing to please anyone she liked, started showing signs of churlishness and rebelliousness . . . She took to locking the maids in the bathroom, throwing their clothes out of the house, and chattering, for the first and only time in her life, non-stop."

On the other hand, she took on the role of surrogate mother to Charlie. She "would take him firmly but lovingly in hand," a close relation recalled, "making him tidy up his room, pack up his books at school, and do the myriad things little boys are meant to but often do not. She became a real little mother hen."

With Charlie at her heels she would go "over the wall" to Sandringham where they placed flowers they had picked from the garden at Park House on the graves of their dead brother and their grandfather, neither of whom they had known. "At first it seemed a strange place for little children to come alone," a gardener at Sandringham reflected, "but they seemed very comfortable as they knelt there on the grass arranging their small offerings."

Their father, bitter over the breakdown of his marriage, remained in the sanctity of his study, submerging himself in the minutiae of his work for the National Association of Boys' Clubs and his farm. He blamed most of his problems on his relationship with his father, who continued to hold tightly to the Spencer purse strings. The improvements

made to Park House since he and Frances had moved in
had been paid for out of the inheritance she had received
on the death in 1947 of Fanny, her American grandmother,
which had worried Frances and fuelled Johnnie's anger towards his father.

"When I saw Johnnie [during this time]," Lord Warding-
ton, a close friend, recalled, "I got a sense of his great
frustration that his father was still alive. He was waiting to
take over. I don't think he had any respect for his father.
He felt frustrated that he was in Norfolk in a small house
on the Sandringham estate and felt that his children should
be growing up in Althorp."

Occasionally, their father came up to the nursery to see
Diana and Charlie at tea-time. These were strained events,
for Johnnie was no more at ease with children than Jack
Spencer had been. His grim demeanour darkened further
when on 10 April 1968 Janet Shand Kydd sued her husband
for divorce on grounds of adultery, naming Frances as co-
respondent. The story was headlined in the salacious tabloid
press, which reported in lurid detail their early trysts in a
South Kensington hotel.

Lady Fermoy was distraught. During the period between
these revelations and her daughter's custody battle for her
children, the staff at Park House noted her frequent visits,
during which she confined herself mostly to private talks
with her son-in-law. "She did not seem at all like her old
self," one of the staff remembered. "She was a woman in
crisis. She would hurry in and out and spend very little
time with the children, and several times I could see that
she had been crying."

Of course, Lady Fermoy was disturbed at the plight of
her grandchildren. However, her main concern was with
how her daughter's "unacceptable" behaviour would reflect
on her own standing with the Royal Family, and the future
position of her grandchildren. Frances's liaison was common gossip, a scandal. While extramarital indiscretions
were not unknown in the lives of Park House's Sandringham neighbours—rumours abounded that Prince Philip had

had numerous mistresses—they were never made public. Frances had been "caught out," which was unforgivable. In 1968—a decade before the break-up of Princess Margaret's marriage—a divorced couple were still excluded from royal society.

Therefore Lady Fermoy set out to convince Johnnie to fight his wife for custody of the children. Any loyalty to her daughter was put aside in the interests of "privilege and social cachet." Lady Fermoy was also determined not to lose her close friendship with her son-in-law, who would one day become Earl Spencer. The Spencers were, and would remain, in the upper echelons of the aristocracy and there was no doubt that society would support Johnnie in this scandal. She offered to swear on oath in court that Frances was not a fit mother. This, she argued with Johnnie, who had not been inclined to fight for custody, would exonerate him from any guilt in the marital breakdown, making him the injured party, and would lessen any social repercussions for the children. It seems that no thought was given to how the children might suffer from losing close contact with their mother, or how their grandmother's action would affect Frances then and the children in the future.

It was the ultimate betrayal of a daughter by her mother: Lady Fermoy knew that Frances dearly loved her children. And Lady Fermoy's infamy did not stop there. Next she convinced Jean Rowe to agree to be a witness against Frances. Frances would be described as "uncaring," as not having discussed her children's progress or conduct with the school staff, not attending school functions, and not replying to letters sent to her by the school about the children, all charges Frances refuted to no avail. That she was in constant contact with her husband about such matters was not mentioned; neither were her pleas to him to allow the children to live with her in London.

Frances knew nothing of the plan to take her children from her. She went ahead with her custody petition believing that no British court, which automatically granted custody to a mother, unless she was proven to be abusive, would deny it to her. She entered the private hearing room in the Family Division of the High Court in September 1968, thinking that she would be reunited almost immediately with all four children. She had even reserved places for Diana and Charlie at the London school they had previously attended.

It could not have been easy for Lady Fermoy to speak against Frances in front of her, but it was a devastating blow to her daughter, one from which she never truly recovered. When the judge accorded custody to Johnnie, she collapsed.

In Britain, custody is settled before a divorce petition is granted. Frances laid all her hopes on a reversal of the earlier ruling when her petition was heard. On 12 December Diana's parents were back in court with Frances suing for divorce on the grounds of cruelty. Johnnie, however, had cross-petitioned, citing her adultery with Peter Shand Kydd, which had already been proven in Janet's case. He won his action, which made him the aggrieved party and vindicated him in the eyes of society and his peers.

Diana and Charlie were now in their father's custody and neither child understood why they could only see their mother on special visits.

DIANA MISSED HER mother deeply, but with Charlie to look after she could not express her own grief. Everything in her life had changed. Although she still lived at Park House it was a different place without her mother. She tried to hold on to the memory of Frances coming into the nursery at night, smelling of verbena cologne, the gay vases of flowers she had placed around the house, the barking of her dogs as they followed her about, even her crying, which had made Diana want to hug her until she was happy again. With her father so distant and sad, Park House was a grim place.

Nannies came and went. Diana and Charlie hated most of them. Their father always interviewed the applicants and chose the most attractive one. The children devised tricks that they hoped would drive the intruder away. After heavy rain, one nanny's clothes were tossed from the nursery windows into the puddles below. Another sat in a chair where the tip of a safety-pin pointed upward.

But nothing they could do brought their mother home, and on 2 May 1969, their parents' divorce became absolute. A month later, Frances and Peter Shand Kydd were married. Peter moved into the flat in Cadogan Place and they purchased a pleasant, unpretentious cottage in Sussex. They were apparently happy, but Frances "suddenly seemed to have aged. She was far more serious, almost sombre. How shall I describe it?" a close friend mused. "She walked with an air of recent sorrow."

Diana was haunted by all elements of the divorce. Once a teacher had called her into her office to tell her that a judge was coming to the school to ask her whether she wanted to live with her mother or her father. She was overcome with terror at the prospect of earning the wrath of whichever parent she rejected. The judge did not come and Diana never had to make such a choice, but she worried when her father was accorded custody that her mother would *believe* she had chosen to live with him.

She did not understand what had taken place between her mother and Lady Fermoy. Yet she was aware of the chilly atmosphere between them. In this her loyalty was with Frances: memories of her grandmother's visits just before the divorce reinforced her sense that Grandmother Fermoy had had something to do with the loss of her mother. Diana felt betrayed by both her parents *and* her maternal grandmother—and somehow responsible for it all. The guilt increased as their father spent even less time with Charlie and her. She yearned for his love and attention and fought for it the only way she knew how: by making small disturbances and trying to push the nannies into leaving. But Johnnie Spencer was too involved in his own grief at the death of his marriage to recognize his children's needs.

There were respites, "cool-water oases," one friend called them. At Easter in 1969, her father took all four children to Althorp, where Grandmother Spencer's kindness eased the pain and confusion of Diana's days at Park House. She organized an Easter-egg hunt and had presents for all the children. Diana adored her, clung to her, and was never brushed aside. "You must remember that you are special," Cynthia told her.

"Why?" the child enquired.

"Because you are a Spencer," her grandmother replied.

Diana attended the Easter services at the small church in Great Brington with her grandparents, father and siblings, in seats next to the chancel where, with a side-glance, she could see the stone effigies of her Spencer ancestors. Once she asked a nanny if when you died you were turned to stone. "Of course not," the woman replied. "You become dust." That idea intensified her fear of the dark, which she equated with death.

This visit to Althorp was most memorable to Diana because of Grandmother Spencer's affection. On one rainy day she took Diana and Charlie to the vast attic where they opened trunks filled with grand uniforms and lovely gowns that had once been worn by Althorp's former occupants. Cynthia told them stories of the balls that had been held there, the coronations at which their ancestors had participated, royal weddings they had attended.

Shortly after the holiday, Diana and Charlie went to London to meet their stepfather for the first time. Peter Shand Kydd was waiting at the station with Frances when they arrived. He won them over almost immediately: he had a natural affinity with children and showered them with presents. He was also far more permissive than either of their parents.

A competition ensued between Johnnie and Frances for their children's love. On Diana's seventh birthday her father gave a party for her at Park House at which the main attraction was a camel called Bert from nearby Dudley Zoo. A platform was built for the young guests to climb on to Bert's back for a bumpy but exciting ride.

In September 1970 Diana was sent to Riddlesworth Hall, a boarding-school in Thetford, Norfolk. She was only nine and would be separated for the first time from Charlie. She worried that he would be lonely without her, which he was. Also, her father had just emerged from his depression and had become altogether warmer and brighter. Separation from both parents, Charlie and Park House worsened Diana's sense of instability. Park House and King's Lynn were where she was rooted and she was terrified to leave. She cried and pleaded with her father to change his mind about sending her away, but to no avail.

After a tearful parting with Charlie, the current nanny accompanied her by train to her new school. Labels had been sewn into all her clothes and while the nanny took care of the luggage Diana held tightly to a small cage containing one of her pet guinea pigs, which she had been assured would have a place in the school's pet corner. A car met them at the local station and drove them to the school where the nanny delivered Diana into the hands of the headmistress, Elizabeth Ridsdale.

Diana was assigned a narrow metal bed in an austere dormitory. The girls were allowed to have some personal possessions, and Diana had brought with her a select number from her menagerie of stuffed animals.

Riddlesworth Hall was a large, neo-classical house set in a rather dull, flat landscape. About seventy-five girls, ranging in age from seven to eleven, attended the school and one of the reasons Riddlesworth had been chosen for Diana was that Alexandra Loyd was also going there. Her presence helped ease Diana's homesickness over the first few weeks. Once again the school uniform was red and grey. Gloves, a bowler hat and sensible black shoes were to be worn to Sunday church services and on all other outings.

Once Diana had settled in and made friends, she was relatively happy. One of the games the girls in her dormitory played was "the Water Jump." This involved leaping over one bed after another—including the one that its occupant wet each night. Usually this brought a school prefect quickly to the door to insist they stop what they were doing. Immediately.

Elizabeth Ridsdale, or Riddy, as she was known to the girls, believed in learning by rote. The girls chanted their multiplication tables, had to ask permission to turn a page in an exercise book before continuing, and library books were kept in locked cases. Their manners were constantly scrutinized and they were reminded daily of the respect due to their elders. It was not an agenda that lent itself to the enquiring mind or welcomed debate.

Diana was unexceptional in the classroom, but turned her energy to sport—she swam like a water sprite and won a cup for diving in her first term—and the piano. She loved to play and got on well with her teacher. Lessons and practice were a joy to her. "She showed talent and curiosity, always wanting to do the next lesson before she had finished what we were working on," her teacher said. She also

enjoyed dancing, and had lessons in tap and ballet, but ballet music drew her to the more classic form of dance and
a lifelong devotion to Tchaikovsky's work. She dreamed of
becoming a ballerina and of dancing in the *Nutcracker*,
Sleeping Beauty and *Swan Lake*.

She enjoyed being in school plays but only if she had a
non-speaking part. In one production she was made up as
a silent Dutch doll. She hated being called "Di," which
remained true throughout her life, and as every girl at
school had a nickname, she became known as "Duch" for
the impressive mime she gave as the Dutch doll.

To her surprise and delight, when she returned to Park
House for her summer break, a swimming-pool had been
built on the south side of the house. Warm, sunny days
were spent in joyous water-play with her siblings and Alexandra Loyd. In a wildly extravagant moment, her father had
had the pool imported in sections from the United States
and constructed on site. The American pool, he claimed,
was better made and safer than any British product. She
took tennis lessons with a Mrs. Lansdowne, but was not as
keen on the court as she was in the pool where she performed back flips off the side and was proud of her ability
to dive with perfectly straight legs.

The train rides to London or Sussex to see her mother
at weekends during the summer were a time of painful recollection. She and Charlie usually travelled together, and
there would be tearful partings from Frances: she would
cry and declare that she could not bear them to leave. On
their arrival back at Park House their father complained that
their mother and Peter spoiled them and made things more
difficult for him. On their journeys between parents, both
children were filled with apprehension at what they would
have to deal with at their destination.

Where her parents were concerned, whatever Diana did
she never seemed to get it right. And when she felt most
confused she would raid the refrigerator. Her bad eating
habits escalated when she returned to Riddlesworth Hall. "I
ate and ate and ate," she admitted. "It was always a great

joke—let's get Diana to have three kippers at breakfast and six pieces of bread. And I did all that."

Throughout these eating binges she never knew, of course, that she was starved of affection. Neither Frances nor Johnnie were inclined to hug or kiss their children, but Diana would often embrace Charlie and he would cling to her—they were "stuck together," she would often say. She rarely saw Sarah and Jane, whose term dates were different from hers and who therefore "drifted" in and out of her life: both parents found it easier to have just two of their children with them at a time.

At Christmas, though, the four siblings gathered together at Park House. The cold weather kept them mainly indoors where they spent many hours in Sarah's room exchanging confidences. Diana sat wide-eyed at Sarah's feet as her sister told stories of life at West Heath. There were shared giggles, a sense of comradeship, of belonging.

Each year, a month before Christmas, Diana and Charlie were given a catalogue from Hamley's, London's largest toy shop, and told to put a tick beside the toys they would like. On Christmas morning they would find them prettily wrapped beneath the tall tree that stood in the hall. The element of surprise—as well as the personal touch—was missing from their father's presents but there were imaginative gifts from their mother and stepfather—a new saddle for Sarah, a musical box, whose lid lifted to reveal a ballerina twirling on one foot to music by Tchaikovsky for Diana, an admiral's hat for Charlie. Lady Fermoy could be relied upon for book tokens and Grandmother Spencer for pretty jumpers and frocks.

Lady Fermoy joined the children and their father at Park House for the holiday and accompanied them to services at St. Margaret's Church. "I remember Diana used to sit on the fifth pew on the right-hand side next to her father," Wendy Twight recalled. "I was one of the bell ringers and sat opposite them. [Her father] was a churchwarden. I remember her in a lovely hat and coat. . . . She was a very shy, retiring little girl, very fond of animals and quite a delightful little character."

"She had a sweet singing voice and liked to join in when the hymns were being sung. It was common talk that her mother had left her children," another of the church staff remembered. "It was a shocking thing. We all felt sorry for the father but much more saddened for the little ones. You couldn't help but notice that Diana was playing the role of mother to her younger brother. She would sit between him and her father at services and whisper to him from time to time and when they got up to leave she always had him tight by the hand."

For years the Royal Family had spent Christmas at Sandringham. In 1964, though, they went to Windsor.* However, there was still much activity on the estate as the staff and workers remained. Sandringham House, though labyrinthine and containing 365 rooms—Queen Mary described them as having been laid out much like a rabbit warren—is one of the Queen's private homes. The main rooms are not on such a grand scale as in her other houses, and were decorated in a less grandiose style by their first occupants, the future King Edward VII and Queen Alexandra, when they married in 1863. The children's wing is especially comfortable and there is a small cinema where the family gathers to see the latest movies.

With spring's arrival, invitations to Sandringham were extended occasionally to Diana and Charlie. Later she complained they were "shunted over" to Sandringham three years in succession to watch *Chitty Chitty Bang Bang*, starring Sally Ann Howes and Dick Van Dyke—it was then Prince Andrew's favourite film—with Princes Andrew and Edward, their cousins David and Sarah Armstrong-Jones, Princess Margaret's two children, and the children of Sandringham estate workers. All the young guests viewed an invitation to Sandringham to see a film as a command, and

*In 1989 the Royal Family reverted to their earlier agenda and have spent Christmas at Sandringham ever since.

knew they had to curtsy to the princes and wear their best clothes.

All the children felt that they were expected to be grateful for inclusion in this lofty circle. Prince Andrew was a terror, a handsome youngster, arrogant and overbearing, who enjoyed imitating farting noises then looking in an accusatory manner at someone else. ("Talk about spoiled!" one of the other young guests to these Sandringham children's parties recalled. "He had the *most* outrageous toys— a shiny grey miniature Aston Martin convertible, perfect in every detail and with JB 007 for James Bond on the licence-plate. He could really drive it around the grounds but we were not allowed to touch it!") Edward, who was Charlie's age, was inhibited, afflicted with a rather "rabbity nervousness" and seemed to resent being forced to watch the film and play host to children he only saw at gatherings organized by the Queen's staff.

Diana would "kick and scream" that she did not want to go, and one of the staff would run for her father who would demand angrily that she dress immediately: one did not refuse to attend an invitation from a member of the Royal Family, he insisted. It was rude, unacceptable behaviour. She always gave in. Other children among the twenty or so guests at these gatherings say they felt much the same about them. One described Diana as "painfully shy. She kept her head down quite a lot and stayed very close to her little brother's side. He seemed to idolize her. Great big eyes, I remember, always looking her way."

At this time Prince Charles and Princess Anne were away at school. Diana had seen them fleetingly at Sandringham on various visits, but that was all. Usually at the end of one of the Sandringham children's gatherings, the Queen would make a brief appearance and shake everyone's hand. What impressed Diana was that on these occasions the Queen wore gloves even though she was indoors. She saw less of Prince Philip, but the few glimpses she had were of a tall, brusque, good-looking blond man who seemed not to like children. The young guests sensed it and everyone "kind of froze up when he appeared."

During the Christmas holiday Lady Fermoy always took the children to King's Lynn so they could do their own shopping for presents. Afterwards they went to Ladyman's for tea. Diana was conscious of the attention they attracted. People of Lynn, as the townsfolk called themselves, felt sorry for them. "We all knew who the children were," one shopkeeper said, "and about the scandal. It was a sad thing. 'What in God's name is their poor father to do with all those little ones?' was the question most asked. The boy was one thing, but three girls? We expected he would re-marry. *Who*, was the mystery everyone wanted to see solved. He used to come in my store alone, do his shopping himself about once a week. He was all alone in that big house once the children went off to boarding-schools. Must have been pretty lonely in that rattling old Victorian place they lived in."

Johnnie Spencer's emotional state had not improved since the divorce. Once again he was considered a good catch, but after the failure of his marriage he was wary. He had also begun drinking again. With the children he was short-tempered and remote, and ruled his household with a rod of iron. Charlie recalled that his father's voice was always the last to be heard. He did not allow his children to eat with him until they were nine or ten. Instead he occasionally came up to the nursery to have tea with them.

Diana and Charlie were happiest at Park House when Sarah and Jane were there too. Sarah, with her shock of red hair and expressive eyes, was growing into a beautiful young woman. She was still mad about horses but she also talked a lot about boys. She had to watch her weight and was already on a diet. "You mustn't eat so much," she warned Diana. "One day soon you'll be sorry. It's not good to be fat. Boys don't like fat girls."

Sarah was having severe emotional problems, although no one in her family had recognized how serious they were. She, too, had suffered from her parents' divorce, yet as the oldest child she had been expected to bear up and set an example for the others. She held in much of the turmoil she experienced. She was desperate for a steady boyfriend but in her cloistered life as a schoolgirl there was little opportunity to meet a young man. She had already had a teenage battle with alcohol. She has admitted that she drank anything she could lay her hands on—"whisky, Cointreau, sherry or, most usually, vodka," because she believed the latter could not be detected on her breath. She hid the bottles in her underwear drawer at school and disposed of the empty ones when she went out. Her addiction made her more daredevil than ever, but somehow she was able—for a while, at least—to keep her drinking undetected, although it is doubtful that Jane was unaware of it.

Sarah and Jane were independent of outsiders but co-dependent on each other. Their characters had been moulded by the way in which they had been forced to use their own resources. Like Diana and Charlie they stuck together. However, the younger pair at least had a parent close by, albeit self-absorbed, during the crisis period. "Their father was a very distant man," admitted Jean Rowe. "He came of the generation and background where parents lived quite separate lives from their children." That was true certainly, but he also had about him a vulnerability that promised more affection than he could give. All the children lived in hope of a time when he would reach out to them.

Diana remained in awe of Sarah. "I used to do all her washing when she came back from school. I packed her suitcase, ran her bath, made her bed, the whole lot. I did it all and I thought it was wonderful." Sarah, loving and appreciative of Diana's slavish attention, often stopped what she was doing to hug her. The only other person who hugged Diana was Grandmother Spencer, whose visits to Park House were infrequent.

During the spring of 1972, Johnnie took Diana and Charlie to Althorp while Sarah and Jane went to their mother. Despite their fear of their grandfather, and frequent reminders not to touch this or that, the children had a marvellous time. Their special kingdom remained the long range of attics where, besides the trunks of old clothes, "they discovered such fascinating and forgotten objects as chamber-pots, and piles of old diaries and albums." Teatime was always special, with tiny sandwiches cut in unusual shapes and Grandmother Spencer telling them stories about the people whose pictures they had found in the attic.

Diana remembered this visit in vivid detail because it was the last she made to Grandmother Spencer. Shortly afterwards, Cynthia died of a brain tumour, aged seventy-five. Diana had difficulty in controlling her sobs during the memorial service held at the Chapel Royal in St. James's Palace. But Sarah realized how lonely her grandfather would be in that vast estate by himself and began a correspondence with him which, for the first time, exposed the softness that was hidden beneath his gruff exterior. "The shine is gone from my life," he said, after his wife's death. He withdrew from most of his former activities and became "a solitary man, living on memories."

Frances and Peter Shand Kydd had recently bought a house on the Isle of Seil, near Oban off the coast of Scotland. All four Spencer children joined them there with Peter Shand Kydd's three children in August for a carefree holiday filled with boating, fishing and setting lobster-pots. It was followed by a family upset: Sarah was caught drunk at school and was asked to leave West Heath. After numerous family conferences it was decided that in September she would be sent abroad to study the piano at a conservatory in Vienna, which pleased Lady Fermoy more than it did Frances, who was still not speaking to her mother.

Diana celebrated leaving Riddlesworth with an excellent report. In September, she would go to West Heath, where Jane would be in her final year. It would be the first time that she had ever been at school with one of her sisters and she was looking forward to it.

West Heath was in Kent, a short distance from Sevenoaks, where Jack Cade's rebels defeated Henry VI's army in 1450. With its half-timbered facades, steep gables, mellow bricks, and its near proximity to London—just twenty-five miles—and to two of the largest and most historic homes in England, Knole House and Hever Castle, the childhood home of Anne Boleyn, tourists crowded the streets and its shops and restaurants during all but the most inclement days. But West Heath was surrounded by rolling hills and verdant countryside. It was a small school of some 120 girls, well known for the élite families of its students. Eighty-five years earlier, the Queen's grandmother, Queen Mary, when she was Princess May of Teck, had been a pupil.

Ruth Rudge, the Australian headmistress, recognized Diana's musical talent and encouraged her to continue her piano and dance lessons. To begin with Diana threw most of her considerable energy into these fields, to the detriment of her other studies. She also accepted "dares"—perhaps hoping to gain friends—such as night-time raids of the school larder. She was soon in trouble with Miss Rudge, who perhaps feared she had another Sarah on her hands, but Diana soon settled in and got on with her schoolwork.

She slept in a long, narrow, ten-bed, sparsely decorated dormitory. There were portraits of the Royal family on the walls, one of the Queen and, prophetically, one of Prince Charles, in his investiture robes as Prince of Wales, over her bed. As always, she had brought with her some stuffed animals and photographs, of Charlie, her mother and Peter Shand Kydd, and a snapshot of the three sisters taken just before she left for school. She also had one of her father holding her as a small child.

At West Heath all the girls had to do community work in Sevenoaks. At weekends, Diana helped an old lady with light cleaning until she was moved into hospital. Then she visited handicapped children at a nearby home, and later spent many hours at Derenth Park, a large psychiatric hospital. This was frustrating work that disturbed most of the other girls, but Diana got great satisfaction from eliciting smiles from her patients and never tired of visiting them.

Her life at West Heath was not entirely happy: she worried constantly about Charlie. She felt guilty that she was not with him to help him through his loneliness at Park House, his inability to communicate well with his father, and then being sent at six to boarding-school. Neither could she come to terms with the way she kept growing. At twelve she was over five foot ten, and her ballet teacher had told her that now she could never become a ballerina. Her height caused other problems: all her peers, male and female, were shorter. She hated attending parties as she felt awkward and out of place.

"It was queer about Diana," one of her schoolfriends said. "She could have been the most popular girl in the class. She was one of the prettiest and, although she hated her height and was always hunching herself up to look shorter, or flopping down, cross-legged on the floor in a group instead of standing or sitting in a chair, I thought it [her height] made her look even more attractive. She never seemed to trust people. Most of us confided the most personal things to each other. It formed a bond. Diana was never able to do that, although she had a few close friends. She had a great sense of humour. Rather flip, very sharp, very fast. And she read a lot. Always had her nose in a book when we had time to ourselves. Romance novels mostly. She had fallen off a horse, she told me, when she was younger and was afraid of them and so she never was involved with riding, which was an important aspect at West Heath."

Her passion for the piano remained and for a time she fantasized about becoming a concert pianist. Her tennis remained passable, but she won several medals for swimming and diving. Mathematics, French and English grammar were her downfall, and she had trouble keeping up her marks. A friend recalled, "I remember how much she liked pretty clothes. She always looked trim and rather stylish, an almost impossible task during the early teens. Maybe it was her height. But I don't think that was it. She had what

I guess you would call an eye. She knew what looked well on her.

"She was somewhat compulsive about her clothes, always ironing them to get out every wrinkle, and she had a way with her hair. None of us were allowed to wear makeup, but her lovely colouring saved the day. Those startling blue eyes. And I seem to remember that her hair was rather reddish then. Yes, certainly auburn, not true blonde. Whenever we did something against the rules—had food in our rooms, or the light on too late, or were late too many times to class—Miss Rudge gave us yard work to do as a punishment. Diana seemed to relish this. She would weed like a crazy person. The rest of us hated it."

Carolyn Pride was also in this dormitory of West Heath's youngest girls and the two became fast friends. They shared not only many interests but were both children of divorced parents, which was still a rarity.

Diana had grown from "a very quiet, reserved child to being a self-reliant, loving, domesticated person," Albert (Bertie) Betts, Johnnie's butler at Park House, noted of her return home during the Christmas break of 1974. "She washed and ironed her own jeans and did all her own chores. She was always immaculate. My wife Elsie [the cook-housekeeper] used to make her a lot of raspberry and strawberry ice cream. Diana was very fond of lemon soufflé and loved chocolate cake with butter icing, which my wife used to make for her tuck-box before she went back to school."

In the summer of 1975, just before her fourteenth birthday, her grandfather Earl Spencer died aged eighty-three. The old gentleman's death changed her life dramatically. Her father was now the 8th Earl Spencer, she was Lady Diana Spencer, Charlie, at eleven, had become Viscount Althorp, and the family was to take up residence at Althorp House, set in a 600-acre park on an estate of 13,000 acres. There was also Spencer House in London (which was leased to the Economist Intelligence Unit), the fabulous Spencer library, works of art, antiques and family jewels.

Her father was now a very wealthy man, no longer dependent on his father for support. Speculation was rampant as to when he might remarry.

He claimed that until this time he "had fought shy of any emotional commitment. . . . I just wanted to bring up my children and it was very hard alone. . . . I had my chances with the girls. I took out one or two but in London, never at home, but somehow they didn't seem, well, suitable."

"Well, of course," one of these ladies said, "Johnnie Spencer was eminently eligible. He would one day—sooner or later—become Earl Spencer and have a great house and money. He was not the most fascinating company, though. Travel, the world, even gossip did not seem to interest him much. No wonder when he was once mentioned as a possible husband for the Princess Elizabeth before she became engaged to Philip she crossed him off her list. Although they could well have discussed dogs and horses, I should think. He was good-looking and from a great family, but he lacked charisma. And after Frances left him he also had four children who were not that easy to deal with, from what was being said about them, and in addition, Johnnie was a man of high and low moods. He had impeccable manners, and—I don't mean to shoot him down too much—he could be good company. But then he would suddenly grow silent—long, morose silences. I was wary, and I guess not as hungry for the splendours and responsibility of an estate like Althorp as some women might have been."

Enter Raine, Countess of Dartmouth, mother of four, daughter of the legendary romantic novelist Barbara Cartland. Raine's parents had divorced when she was young and she had had difficulty in adjusting to her mother's new husband and her step-brothers. From her youth she had seemed determined to make a grand success of her life and to upstage her famous, flamboyant mother. With her marriage, she acquired a title, which her mother did not have, but Raine was bored with her husband and disappointed that his title did not come with a great house.

Raine possessed an indomitable will and had personally accomplished a great deal. After a tough campaign she had been elected to the London County Council to represent West Lewisham, and then Richmond-on-Thames. She became chairman of the Historic Buildings Board, the Covent Garden Development Committee and a member of at least a dozen more important committees. She appeared on television and radio, gave lectures, and became well known for her trim figure (5'8", 36-24-34), and her immaculately coiffed bouffant hairdo. She was not a great beauty, but she was a woman of striking vitality and an astute business sense. She enjoyed the company of men, and knew how to win them over.

She had only met Johnnie Spencer at an occasional dinner until they both attended a Kensington garden party in the summer of 1974. "It was a hot day and everyone was in the garden," she recalled. "When I went inside there was only one person there—John. 'I haven't seen you in twenty years,' he said. 'Things are so coincidental aren't they?' I replied."

From that moment on, Raine channelled all her energy into Johnnie. Her impact on him was enormous, for Johnnie liked having his life directed for him. A colleague of Raine described her as having "an iron hand in an iron glove, which is so beautifully wrought people don't realize that even the glove is made of iron until it hits them." Another exclaimed, "She's absolutely wonderful, you know. If you brief her properly, she will take everything in and once she has the bit between her teeth she'll never let go!"

By the time Diana and her siblings arrived home for the summer in 1975, Raine was in full charge. Their father explained that Countess Dartmouth had kindly offered to help him move from Park House to Althorp. Decisions had to be taken as to what furniture and art should go with them and, more importantly, what work needed to be done at Althorp to accommodate its new occupants.

On Diana's arrival at home, boxes and crates were everywhere. She took the deep stone stairs two at a time to make sure her bedroom had been left untouched. Empty packing cases stood outside the door but as yet nothing had been moved. She put on a bathing suit, locked the door and went for a swim. Although she had realized that when her grandfather died they would move to Althorp, she had not been prepared for the sudden reality of it. Park House had been the only home she had known and it was frightening to be leaving it, especially as Althorp had overwhelmed her with its vast magnificence.

That evening her father had arranged for his four children to meet Countess Dartmouth for the first time. Nothing was said then of any serious relationship between Raine and Johnnie, and in any case the Countess was married to someone else. That night, apparently, her husband had commitments in London, which was why he would not be joining them.

Raine arrived at Park House at about half past six that evening in a chauffeur-driven car, wearing a floral chiffon dress, a blinding diamond pin and a rather large picture hat. Diana and Sarah exchanged a look as she entered the room on their father's arm. Raine had done her homework and knew quite a lot about them all, their interests, what they had been doing lately, and she found something on which to compliment each of them. Diana loathed her immediately, although she was impressed that she was the daughter of Barbara Cartland, one of her favourite authors.

They went in Raine's limousine to the Duke's Head Hotel, the only venue in King's Lynn for an elegant dinner. Diana and Charlie insisted on sharing the front seat with the chauffeur. The party was whisked inside and upstairs to a private room that overlooked the ancient Tuesday Marketplace, which had recently been modernized for use as car parking. Across the square was the old Corn Exchange and beyond that the historic port.

Diana would have preferred to eat in the dining room, which seemed jollier than this lacklustre room, but it was soon evident that this was to be a special dinner and that their father did not want them to be exposed to curious eyes. As the dinner was served, Raine carried the burden of conversation. They would be driving to Althorp the following day with Raine, who had supervised the redecorating. Johnnie kept insisting how kind of her it was to take so much time from her important work to help them, and how grateful they should be. After dinner, the children were driven back to Park House while their father remained at the Duke's Head "for a short talk with Raine."

Sarah had immediately dubbed the Countess "Acid Raine" and not one of the four young Spencers was inclined to accept her intrusion into their lives without a struggle.

5

THE MOVE TO Althorp in the summer of 1975 was traumatic for the Spencer children. The house was vast, the grounds seemingly endless. None of them had visited it since the death of their grandmother in 1972, and Althorp without Cynthia Spencer was like a museum. It did not help that Raine had chosen which bedroom suite each child would occupy and that it was she, in her crinoline skirts, who greeted them on their arrival.

Raine had been brought up in a mode that had been all but swept away, and she was a prisoner of past mores. "When you think of today's women," the historian Sir Roy Strong explained, "Raine was a throwback. She has a very good mind, but it has somehow been encompassed by the aspirations of being a countess with a large house and changing your clothes ten times a day. She has a very candy exterior but underneath it a very acute mind."

The problem for the young Spencers was that Raine cut such a ridiculous figure, despite her enormous energy and the hard work she had put in to prepare Althorp for Johnnie and his family. They could not take her seriously and resisted anything she did for them.

Diana had been given the old night nursery on the first floor, which had been unoccupied since she had slept there as a toddler. It had the advantage of being simpler in design than the rooms in the rest of the house, and the windows had an unobstructed view across the magnificent rear gardens. Raine had removed the old furniture and refurbished the rooms in what she considered teenage chic—white-painted furniture, a comfortable couch in a flowered pattern, bulletin boards and bookshelves. There were twin beds, one of which Diana covered almost entirely with her stuffed animals. From the window near her bed she could see the lush green summer grass and a lily pond. But it seemed strange to be in this house without her grandparents. She acutely missed the familiarity of Park House and King's Lynn and she had always thought of herself as a Norfolk person. Here they were isolated: the little village of Great Brington, which bordered the estate, had only a pub and a post office, and she had been warned that at summer weekends visitors were allowed to view the grounds and some of the rooms in the house. Diana hated that idea even though she was aware that the money taken in entrance fees was needed for the upkeep of the house. That year, even the Queen had opened Sandringham to the public.

But it was Raine's presence above all that Diana disliked. However, lest she displease her father, she fought to hide it. Raine, she recalled angrily, would "accidentally find us [the four children] in places and come and sit down and pour us with presents, and we all hated her so much because we thought she was going to take Daddy away from us but actually she was suffering from the same thing. She wanted to marry Daddy and that was it." Raine was frightened that if his children resisted strongly enough Johnnie would back off.

Johnnie and Raine did not hide their attachment to each other. Her position as adviser to him on the refurbishment of Althorp gave her a cover, outside the family, for her adulterous affair, but it did not fool Diana or her siblings. Raine and Johnnie would walk through the rooms at Althorp holding hands as they surveyed his palatial domain—which was, according to Raine, filled with exquisite antiques, dazzling art treasures and architectural wonder but in dire need of a makeover. It would be a formidable undertaking.

At last Johnnie was master of Althorp, but he had also to find £2 million in inheritance tax, and £100,000 per year to run Althorp. Although fabulously wealthy in possessions and property, the Spencer estate was suffering an extreme cash-flow problem. Johnnie had no private funds as he had never held a salaried job that might have allowed him to invest the money he drew from his trust as Viscount Althorp. He did not own Park House and Jack Spencer had not been generous to him over the years. Johnnie made his financial situation clear to Raine. She knew that something had to be done quickly and he gave her the go-ahead to act, which she did, but never without his agreement to what she was doing.

First they gave notice to twenty members of staff, who had spent their lives in service of Althorp and its occupants. Those who remained were much overworked and unfairly blamed Raine, as had many of the staff at Park House who, like Bertie Betts and his wife Elsie were given only a month's notice, during which time they were to pack whatever Spencer possessions had not been moved to Althorp. There was a rush to empty Park House to return it to the Queen so that it could be refurbished for use by Princess Anne and her family at Christmas. Park House had two basements and they were filled with decades of accumulated bits and pieces, from both the Fermoy and Spencer families, as well as a full cellar of wine Johnnie had bought after his abstemious period ended with his divorce. When the Bettses had not completed the task by the end of the month, Johnnie had the heating turned off. The former butler and his wife had to resort to "boiling water in a saucepan to wash." "I feel very bitter now," Betts wrote in his diary, "after giving my whole life to private service. I was treated very badly by this great lord. Everyone thinks he is so charming but there is another side of him that the public don't see."

Soon after the move to Althorp had been accomplished, Charlie, now twelve, returned to his prep school, Maidwell Hall, in Northampton, Diana to West Heath, and Sarah, who was now twenty-one, to London where she shared a flat. Jane, nineteen, had just returned from studying art history in Florence for six months. At the age of eighteen the two older girls had each come into about £60,000 from the estate of their American great-grandmother, Frances Work. Diana would inherit a similar amount at the same age.

By now Sarah had abandoned any musical aspirations and Jane was learning shorthand and typing. Neither girl had decided upon a particular career, which did not worry their father who had grander visions for his daughters than for them to become working women. He wanted them to make prestigious marriages, an idea Raine encouraged—perhaps one might even win the marriage sweepstakes and become Princess of Wales. This was not an idle dream: Sarah and Jane were friends of Princess Anne and had known Prince Charles since childhood. Recently he had shown interest in Sarah, who was now a handsome young woman with a vivacious personality.

Spencers had tried unsuccessfully for over two centuries to wed their daughters to a Prince of Wales. In 1729, one such antecedent, Sarah Jennings, Duchess of Marlborough (known as the "fiery Duchess Sarah"), had been determined to marry her granddaughter, another Lady Diana Spencer, to Frederick Louis, Prince of Wales, son of George II and Queen Caroline. However, as she was not on good terms with the King and Queen, she had been forced to plot a secret alliance. Frederick Louis was at great odds with his father, who had cut off his allowance. The Duchess, an enormously wealthy woman, offered the young Prince the astronomical sum of £100,000 as a dowry. As Lady Diana was a great beauty, Frederick was more than willing. A date was set for a secret wedding but when the all-powerful First Lord of the Treasury, Sir Robert Walpole, got wind of the scheme he scotched it.*

There was no portrait of Diana's distant namesake in Althorp's great gallery, but there was one of the Duchess

---

*Frederick Louis, Prince of Wales, married Princess Augusta of Saxe-Coburg. He died in 1751, nine years before his father's death. His eldest son became George III. In 1731 Lady Diana Spencer married John Russell, brother and heir to the Duke of Bedford. Just one year later his brother died and Diana became Duchess of Bedford and mistress of the great house at Woburn. Tragically, she died in 1735 at the age of twenty-six of a disease diagnosed as galloping consumption.

of Marlborough, and Diana read fascinating stories of the power the Duchess came to exert on Queen Anne, younger daughter of James II, who reigned from 1702 to 1714. Rumour was substantiated by the discovery of Queen Anne's voluminous letters to Sarah: they were "real, loving, at times passionate and poured from a full heart."* Historians have agreed that Queen Anne was deeply in love with the charismatic Duchess, whom she addressed for the sake of privacy as Mrs. Freeman. (Sarah addressed her letters to Mrs. Morley.) "Mrs. Morley has a constant heart, loves you tenderly, passionately and sincerely," the Queen wrote in one letter to Sarah, "and knows the world too well (if she were of a fickle temper) ever to be charmed with anybody but your dear self. . . . I hope I shall get a moment or two to be with my dear Mrs. Freeman that I may have one dear embrace which I long for more than I can express."

Such romantic tales that hinted of the possibility of a lesbian affair between a queen and one of her ancestors, intrigued Diana, and she learned as much as she could about all the Spencer women whose portraits graced the great gallery. There was Dorothy, Duchess of Sunderland, a woman of such beauty and wit that the poet and politician Edmund Waller wrote many passionate, if jejune, poems about his love for her. Then there was the devoutly religious Georgiana Poyntz, who secretly married John Spencer in 1755 at Althorp in his mother's dressing room—she feared her parents might object as she was only sixteen—while 500 guests were gathered downstairs at a gala Christmas ball. Georgiana's great passion was education: she founded many schools and sometimes supervised and taught in them. She gathered around her a group of the most

---

*An unopened love letter from Lady Cecily Cornwallis to the future Queen Anne was found by Anne's mother, the Duchess of York, in her daughter's bedside table. Cecily was banished from court, but about "a thousand letters full of the most violent professions [of love]" survived long enough to have been seen by the Duchess of Marlborough.

brilliant men of the time, Dr. Johnson, David Garrick and
Sir Joshua Reynolds among them, and kept up a regular
correspondence with Garrick, which Jack Spencer later edited and published. Georgiana had a daring side to her nature: she was a compulsive gambler—"a Bible on the table,
the cards in the drawer," one of her contemporaries said of
Althorp and Spencer House during her occupancy. Another
claimed that Althorp resembled "nothing so much as a gambling house," especially at Christmas time when the large
parties assembled there would sit up until the small hours
playing for alarmingly high stakes.

An idealized portrait by Sir Joshua Reynolds of Georgiana, Countess Spencer, holding her young daughter and
namesake, Lady Georgiana Spencer (later the infamous
Duchess of Devonshire who gambled away a fortune),
while a small dog attempts to divert the mother's attention
from her child, was one of Diana's favourites. Then there
was the beautiful Charlotte Seymour, who married the 5th
Earl Spencer and became a close friend to the Prince and
Princess of Wales, later King Edward VII and Queen Alexandra, whom she entertained lavishly at Althorp.

But the portrait Diana treasured most was of Grandmother Spencer by William Nicolson. It had been painted
shortly after she came to Althorp as a young bride, and her
clear blue eyes seemed to beckon her granddaughter as she
approached and to follow her on her daily walks through
the great gallery. Later Diana claimed that her grandmother
("so divine") came to her "very clearly," and looked after
her from the spirit world.

Diana was incurably romantic and continued to seek
love and recognition from her father, who was now besotted with Raine. Her mother had recently converted to Roman Catholicism and was obsessed with religion and the
rural life in Scotland she shared with Peter Shand Kydd.
Her sisters were involved in their London lives, and Charlie
was of an age when he was embarrassed to be "mothered."

Diana began the autumn term at West Heath in a state
of confusion. Now that her father was Earl Spencer she

detected a difference in the way in which she was addressed by staff at Althorp and at school. She had stopped growing but still towered over the other girls in her form. Looking back, Diana observed, "All my friends had boyfriends but not me, because I knew that I had to keep myself tidy for whatever was coming my way."

"I think she had a crush on Prince Charles even at the age of fourteen," one of her friends said. "She fantasized a great deal. She was a dreamer. 'Some day' she would start a story to me about a premonition she had about her future—that she would marry one of the most famous men in the world, that she was fated to do wonderful things. She would save the children and sufferers all over. Things like that. I thought she was just rationalizing her lack of boyfriends and making up stories. But there is always the possibility that she had some sort of ability to see into the future. She exaggerated things a lot and she read these awful romance novels of Barbara Cartland."

Many of Diana's teachers and even her brother have mentioned her tendency to "tell stories." Perhaps she was having difficulty in grappling with the real world, and escaping from it into dreams. At other times she escaped into romantic books. "She had dozens of them in her room," an ex-roommate ventured. "It seemed odd since Barbara Cartland was Raine's mother and she hated Raine so, but I think Raine gave her the books as presents. She was a compulsive reader and always kept a flashlight under her pillow and would read by its light after we had the lights off. She also liked books like *Pride and Prejudice* and *Little Women*— stories about sisters and romance—they were her theme. Now that I look back I believe she was trying to find herself in these books—or, maybe, just a role she could play in life."

Diana was a troubled young woman. She was already binge-eating and adopting fad diets, and her marks at school had declined. She had difficulty in sleeping and was unable to concentrate or sit still for any length of time. Her school reports reflected her uneasy state of mind. "Diana has a defeatist attitude where her weaknesses lie . . . She tends to be quarrelsome [with her teachers]. She must try to be less emotional."

"I believe Duch [Diana] felt she should be at Althorp," a schoolfriend speculated. "She talked about this terrible woman who was after her father and how he was 'unprotected' as all of them [her brother and sisters and herself] were not right there on the spot to ward her off. I never heard her refer to her future stepmother as 'Acid Raine' or I think I would have remembered it. But I do remember her calling her 'the dragon lady' a couple of times."

The picture of the Prince of Wales still hung over Diana's bed. "She laughed about the portrait and said maybe one day he would be her brother-in-law. She adored Sarah, that was obvious. She talked about her a lot—how beautiful she was, how popular and how she envied her free life in London," Diana's former schoolfriend added.

"I wasn't any good at anything, I felt a failure," Diana confessed later. Yet her teachers at West Health talked of how good she was at history and English, and how she wrote insightful essays on Jane Austen and Henry James. It appears that, like so many of us, Diana was only good at the subjects that interested her.

"When Diana talked about a book she had read, it was with much understanding and deep involvement. Then when test time came she appeared to draw a complete blank. It was as though she wanted to fail," one teacher said. "I spoke privately to her about it, that I believed she was one of the smartest girls in my class and yet she was failing all the exams. She vowed she would do better, but at the next test time she in fact did worse. Finally, she was not to pass even one O-level. It was shocking. She was troubled, I sensed that. But it was not my place to mention this in my year-end note to Earl Spencer. At West Heath the staff would never venture to involve themselves in the family matters of our students."

Dancing remained her secret passion and at dead of night, after lights out, Diana would slip barefoot down the front staircase to the hall used for ballet classes. By moonlight, she would warm up at the *barre* and then, with a whisper of sound from a record turned to its lowest decibel, she would dance for hours, whirling and leaping until the tension left her and she was exhausted enough to go to bed. "It was like a mysterious rite, very private, a secret we, her roommates, felt must be honoured. I don't think any of us ever told on her," one of her concealed watchers ventured.

She continued to win trophies for diving, and her father built a swimming-pool at Althorp so that she could keep up her training at home.

Now that Johnnie had Althorp and Raine in his life he was a different man. He laughed more, appeared confident, had regained control of his alcohol consumption. He was drawn sexually to Raine as he had not been to any woman since Frances's departure. Raine was now redecorating his bedroom suite with the help of interior designer David Laws, which gave her a socially acceptable reason for being at Althorp for several days at a time. She occupied the exotic India Silk Bedroom, which was directly across the first-floor corridor from Johnnie's suite.

It is difficult to believe that neither Lord Dartmouth nor Raine's own four children—William, Lord Lewisham, thirty-one, Rupert, twenty-nine, Charlotte, eighteen, and Henry, twelve—were ignorant of her affair with Earl Spencer. Rumours had been leaked to the press shortly after the Spencers had moved into Althorp. Sarah was especially vitriolic about Raine's brazen liaison with her father. That same month, she picked up the telephone to be confronted by a reporter wishing to confirm the romance and the prospect of a divorce in the near future for Countess Dartmouth. Could he please speak to Lord Spencer?

Sarah replied, "Lord Spencer is in bed with Lady Dartmouth and I don't want to disturb them." Then she hung up. To another such enquiry she snapped, "Since my grandfather died just last June and we moved from Sandringham to Althorp, Lady Dartmouth has been an all-too-frequent guest."

Diana did not express her dislike of Raine as boldly as Sarah did. It was said that when Raine was "visiting" she and Charlie would walk up and down the corridors together singing, "Raine, Raine, go away, Don't come here another day," but Diana claimed they did this out of her hearing. Sarah, though, made sure that Raine could hear her when she yelled on the telephone, "I'd sooner take up residence in Lenin's tomb, cuddling his corpse for warmth, than have Raine Dartmouth as my stepmother."

Life at Althorp gave Diana an even greater pride in her heritage, but Raine's presence seemed somehow to endanger it. There were three places on the estate where she went to escape. Her favourite on warm days was the tiny island in the middle of the lake that was reached in less than five minutes by a rowing-boat tied up at the bank. Charlie joked about the possibility of buried treasure on it but Diana had no such fantasy. She would row out in the early mornings to gather greenery for the housekeeper to mix with the fresh flowers that brought life to Althorp's vast rooms, or to read and sun herself. She never took anyone to the island: it was as though she had claimed it for herself. She found solace in the portrait gallery, and in the huge old kitchen, with its massive stove and shelves lined with glowing copper pans, the air moist with the aroma of freshly baked bread and hearty stews. The kitchen was always her second stop on coming home from school—the first was her bedroom to change into a pair of jeans. In the kitchen she would catch up on local gossip with Betty Andrews, Althorp's cook. She chatted standing up, a glass of milk in one hand, perhaps, a biscuit in the other. She knew the names of all the staff, their children's names, health problems, and the romantic attachments of the single ones. Occasionally she would walk into Great Brington to post some letters and buy chocolate. "Oh, she was very fond of chocolate," Christine Whiley, the postmistress, recalled. "She was really one of us. Never uppity. She was the only one of the Spencers who did come by. Usually one of the staff did the posting."

Althorp "would burst into life" with the arrival of the Spencer siblings, Betty Andrews remembered. "One by one they used to run into the house, drop their things, then come rushing into the kitchen to find something to eat. They were not fussy eaters and often Diana or Charles would do their own cooking. Diana even used to cook for the staff. She loved to make bread-and-butter pudding for us and rice or milk pudding for herself. She also did her own washing and often Charles's too. She would put his things in the washing-machine and then iron them for him. She was lovely with him. She was also quite tidy. You didn't have to do much tidying up after her."

She possessed a wild streak that would "just peek through" at times and would "often fly down the seventeenth-century front staircase on a tea-tray or practise her dancing in the black-and-white marble entrance hall, known as Wootton Hall. She had great elevation and her leaps were often accompanied by whoops of delight [a vocal reaction she could not indulge in at school]."

In the spring of 1976 Lord Dartmouth finally acknowledged that his wife was having an affair with Johnnie Spencer, whom he referred to as a friend from schooldays. The tabloids had discovered that Johnnie had suffered a mild stroke during a tryst with Raine at the Dorchester Hotel. She had called an ambulance and never left his side until he was safely out of danger and back at Althorp. Her presence in the suite was kept out of the press reports, but it was soon common gossip among her social and political acquaintances and enemies.

Within weeks of Johnnie's stroke, Lord Dartmouth sued for divorce on the grounds of his wife's adultery. Ironically, Johnnie was saved the humiliation he had inflicted upon Frances: his name was never revealed publicly as corespondent. In his case there were mitigating circumstances: he was reputed to be a dutiful and loving father.

After the divorce, Raine was certain that Johnnie would propose to her. When he did not, she went to her eldest son Lord Lewisham for advice. He told her to take a two-week cruise—alone. She did. Her absence did the trick, and on 14 July 1976, in a private ceremony at Caxton Hall Register Office in Victoria, London, Raine became the Countess Spencer. No member of the Spencer clan was present; neither were her children nor her mother. Only her brother Glen was there as a witness.

"It was such a quiet wedding that even I didn't go," Barbara Cartland rationalized later to the press. "They rang me immediately afterwards and just said, 'Hello. We're married.' When it's a second marriage I don't think you should have a reception," she added.

"She is not allowed to interfere [with my life]," Raine commented tersely when asked later what her mother felt about the register-office wedding.

Barbara Cartland has said that the Spencer sisters told their father he could marry anyone but Raine when the subject of his possible remarriage came up. "But Johnnie and Raine had a passion, which in the end he found irresistible," Cartland declared, sounding much like a heroine of one of her many hundreds of romantic novels.

None of the Spencer siblings was told in advance of their father's wedding. Neither did the newlyweds contact them with the news before leaving on a honeymoon cruise. Diana and Charlies learned of their father's remarriage from their respective school principals. Diana contained herself until she reached her room. Then, according to one of her classmates, she threw herself down on the bed: "Nothing will ever be the same again," she wept.

She was right.

When Diana arrived at Althorp for the summer holiday, Raine—just back from honeymoon—had already begun to make changes. She had been working on plans to enhance Althorp's money-making potential. Although the estate had been partially open to the public for some years, it had not adapted itself as successfully to visitors as had other great estates, such on Woburn, Blenheim and Longleat. While Johnnie's inherited fortune was estimated at over £12 million, most of it was in property and cash was in short supply.

That summer workers scurried all over the estate readying the house, outside buildings and grounds in the first step of Raine's renovation—to which Johnnie had readily agreed. Once Raine became his wife, Johnnie was happy to turn over the financial side of managing Althorp House to her, and as a start she opened a souvenir shop and tea room in the stables.* "As I entered the gift shop," Linda Sutherland, an American visitor, said, "I witnessed the Countess, who sells tickets of admission, being extremely rude to an American girl, who expressed concern [when her handbag was taken from her upon entering] over parting with her passport. Her handbag was considered by the Countess to be large enough to hold three machine-guns and a hand grenade. The Countess then went on, in a most undignified manner, to explain that no British person would want [to steal] an American passport. I was nonplussed . . . I was greatly disillusioned. Then the Earl of Spencer helped to lift this feeling when he walked across the courtyard, and was engaged in conversation by a young Oriental couple, who asked to have their photo taken with him. He gladly consented."

In fact, Johnnie much enjoyed his position as master of Althorp and often led tour groups himself, rather too swiftly for his followers, while he told his own version of his family's history and that of Althorp House.

As November 1977 approached, bringing with it the prospect of the shooting season, the new châtelaine of Althorp prevailed upon her husband to host a ball, the first

---

*The stables at Althorp had been built in the early 1700s by the noted architect Roger Morris for Charles, 3rd Earl of Sunderland (1675–1722) during his marriage to Lady Anne Churchill. At the time the stable block was considered "the finest piece of architecture at Althorp." It remained one of the handsomest buildings on the estate, with its classic Georgian lines and four-columned front entry. In 1998 the stables were renovated and restructured to accommodate the new Princess Diana Museum.

such lavish affair to be given on the estate in over fifty years, and to invite the Prince of Wales as a weekend guest and participant in a shooting party to precede it. When Charles accepted, Raine, who had never entertained a member of the Royal Family before, went into a state of mad excitement. She was hoping, she told friends, that the Prince of Wales and Sarah might get "better acquainted." In fact, he was already seeing quite a lot of Sarah, and there was speculation in the press that his interest seemed more than simple friendship.

At the time Diana was just sixteen, and Charles had not seen her since she had come as a child to holiday gatherings at Sandringham. Later Diana recalled that Charles had arrived at Althorp with his Labrador of whom he was extremely fond and protective. "My sister [Sarah] was all over him like a bad rash . . . God, what a sad man, I thought." When she met the Prince on the ploughed field of Nobottle on the grounds of Althorp mid-way through the shoot, when a picnic lunch was being served,* Diana was wearing jeans, boots, and an oversized sweater. She was conscious that she must appear "a fat, pudgy, no-makeup, unsmart lady, but I made a lot of noise." Charles took notice of her and came over to where she stood. She recalled saying something that made him laugh, then Sarah interrupted "and whisked him away."

That evening Diana wore her first evening gown, of dotted, blue organza with a low neckline that revealed the softly swelling curves of her young breasts. Around her neck was a gold heart on a chain, a present from her father on her sixteenth birthday. She had only lately taken a greater interest in her clothes and was aware that the dress enhanced her looks and drew attention to her deep blue eyes and her fair complexion.

Charles was seated at a table with Sarah, while Diana

---

*Women seldom joined the men on a shoot, unless it was to trail behind them to pick up the game they had bagged. But it was ritual for women to supply lunch before the men returned to their shooting.

was on the opposite side of the hall. But she was aware of his presence and was certain that he was aware of hers. "He came up to me after dinner and we had a big dance and he said, 'Will you show me the gallery?' and I was just about to show him the gallery and my sister Sarah comes up and tells me to push off and I said, 'At least let me tell you where the switches are to the gallery because you won't know where they are,' and I disappeared. And he was charm himself and when I stood next to him the next day, a sixteen-year-old, for someone like that to show you any attention—I was just so sort of amazed. Why would anyone like him be interested in me? And it *was* interest."

There seemed little chance that anything more would develop between them: he was Sarah's friend and closer to her age. Diana knew that her father was hoping that a Spencer woman would become Princess of Wales and one day queen consort, and that her future son would become king. He also had high hopes for Diana. "All her life, [her father and Lady Fermoy] had Diana earmarked for Prince Andrew. They were quite open about it, and it didn't seem at all unlikely. They'd known each other since they were children. Andrew and Edward used to go over to Park House to swim in the pool. They were all pretty chummy. But no one envisaged her for the Prince of Wales. It was just, well, inconceivable," said one of Sarah's contemporaries.

Inconceivable to everyone, that was, except Diana.

6

FROM AN EARLY age Diana felt she could foresee her future, and all her self-prophecies concerned being loved by a man. Through this man she would also fulfil an important mission in life. By marrying "up" and bringing more honour to the family, she would win her father's love and approval. The truth was that Earl Spencer had an especially soft spot for Diana, who to him had seemed motherless from such an early age. However, it was Sarah upon whom his hopes of a prestigious union were centred, Sarah who had one of the most lavishly extravagant coming-of-age parties since before the Second World War, and Sarah whose growing friendship with the Prince of Wales had filled him with pride.

Much has been written about Diana but she remains an enigma unless it is understood how strongly the idea of marrying well had been impressed upon her as a young woman, how conditioned she was to the concept that her husband's status would be the measure of her significance. Also, she was "the girl who was supposed to be a boy" and her sex had disappointed her parents. Her musicality had impressed neither Frances nor Johnnie, nor were they unduly concerned about her poor scholastic achievement. Her swimming and diving proficiency had won her father's praise when she was younger, but Diana was obsessed with the idea that if she did not marry a man of some consequence he would be disappointed in her and she would lose his love.

Diana was in conflict with herself: one half of her believed she was fated for great things, the other that she was unworthy of love, especially from her parents, for she was the third daughter they never wanted. Her self-loathing manifested itself in her belief that Sarah, Jane and Charlie were more worthy than her of parental approbation and in her need to perform for her siblings the most menial tasks. She did not express this attitude with her friends at West Heath. She was popular with the other girls because "one felt Diana sincerely cared about you."

In Prince Charles she had perceived something in the way he looked at her, the timbre of his voice, the touch of his hand on her shoulder, on the night of the hunt ball at Althorp, that signalled his attraction to her. With this realization came an overwhelming sense of guilt, for she knew that Sarah was anticipating a more serious relationship developing between Charles and herself.

Diana returned for her last term at West Heath severely troubled. Her headmistress, Ruth Rudge, recalled that she had been disturbed about her new stepmother. "Life will never be the same for any of us [the Spencer children]," she complained. A girl in her form said, "She seemed confused. She told me, 'I don't want to leave here because I don't know what will happen to me then.'"

Her piano teacher, Penny Walker, found added passion in the way Diana threw herself into her playing. She seemed able to work through some of her emotional conflict in these sessions. After a lesson or practice session, she would be much more herself, giggling, taking the stairs in West Heath's handsome entrance hall two at a time, or on occasion sliding down the grand, old, highly polished banisters. When caught in the act she was contrite. "She was a most polite girl, inclined to tales of fancy that one really could not call lies. They were often told to cover her true feelings and not to hurt someone else, I thought," a teacher said.

The one place she appeared at ease was when she was helping out with a group of disabled children in a nearby hospital. She learned quickly that it was important to sit or crouch so that she could look a child straight in the eye, and these children would smile if she touched them or let them play with her hair or hold her hand. She understood the need for physical contact with another person.

Sarah, Jane and Charlie had all done well at school and Diana felt unable to compete. Her parents thought of her low self-esteem as just "Diana's shyness," which she would outgrow. She blushed easily, giggled nervously, would lower her head and glance downward at any compliment. "Sarah is the pretty one in our family," she would say. "I'm just pretty hopeless." But, in fact, she was growing into quite an attractive young woman with a slow, winning smile that could warm an unheated room on the coldest day.

A compulsive reader, she did not like to finish a book without there being another to begin. Romantic fiction remained a favourite, but she enjoyed English history, and especially since moving to Althorp. ("So much to learn. So much to learn," she told a schoolfriend, who commented on the stack of books on her bedside table.) Also despite her shyness, she had an amazing command of *bon mots* and a sometimes surprising natural wit: at sixteen, when accused of being too naïve, she replied, "I'm too tall for much to go over my head and too well bred to admit I know what you're talking about."

In December 1977, she resat and again failed her O-levels. University was out of the question, and her parents were in a quandary as to what should be done with Diana. They decided to send her to the Institut Alpin Videmanette, a finishing school in Rougemont, Switzerland. A few days after Christmas at Althorp, she boarded a plane for Geneva. On arrival she was met by a representative of the school and, with several other girls returning to Videmanette after the holiday, took the overheated mountain train through the narrow Alpine passes to their destination.

Although it was only a short distance from the glitzy, international resort of Gstaad, Rougemont, which was in a French-speaking canton, had a rural feel. There were fewer boutiques and outdoor cafés, and no grand hotels like Gstaad's Palace to draw the rich, famous and infamous. The British film star David Niven and the American writer and political pundit William Buckley both owned chalets in

Rougemont, but Gstaad was where people went for glamour and excitement, where the Aga Khan hosted lavish parties, heiresses had affairs with ski instructors, and Elizabeth Taylor and Richard Burton made headlines as they fought and made up in endless rotation.

Gstaad was also the winter home of Le Rosey, one of the world's most prestigious private boys' schools, often called the School of Kings. The Institut Alpin Videmanette consisted of a series of charming, dark-wood chalets and was almost its female equivalent. At Videmanette, students were prepared for their social débuts and to become good wives and hostesses. Few went on to university or into professional careers, but a large number married extremely well.

The winter sun was strong and its reflection on the shiny-fresh snow was dazzling as the train trundled up the tracks to Rougemont. Diana's companions chattered away to each other in French and made no effort to speak to her in English. Her French was haphazard and her accent poor. The girls were clannish and she felt a complete outsider, even more so when they arrived at the school. She was one of the few new "older" girls, and one of only nine English-speaking students out of an enrolment of seventy-two. French was the language of communication at Videmanette, and Diana was told that she would be given a crash course in the language. She shared a room with three girls who were honour-bound not to speak English with her and not to answer her unless she spoke to them in French. The idea was that her desire to communicate would help her to conquer the language barrier. It was a method that often worked—but not in Diana's case.

Her room, though accommodating four, was small, low-beamed and smelled of aged wood and wax polish, a sweet smell like dried flowers. Her bed was tucked under an eave and the bathroom ceiling was so low that she was unable to stand erect in it. She suffered episodes of claustrophobia whenever she was in her room and kept out of it as much as she could. She made one good friend in Sophie Kimball.

French took up the greater part of their class time, and they also had courses in cooking, dressmaking and the social graces—table-setting, writing invitations and thank-you notes.

The school had a lodge higher up the mountain where the girls were given ski instruction and allowed free time to practise the sport. Diana treasured the time she spent on the slopes, breathing in the cool, crisp air. She said that, so high up, she experienced something close to a true religious awareness. She could hear the sound of her own breath and she felt at one with the vastness that surrounded her. She mastered the basics of skiing and was moved to a more advanced group.

Skiing gave her a sense of freedom, but as soon as she returned to the classroom she was miserable. Videmanette had no music or dance classes and little access to English books. However, on Saturday afternoons, she took the train into Gstaad and walked from the station down the village's bustling main street, cowbells echoing from the surrounding snow-covered hills, to Cadanau's, a stationery and bookstore that stocked English books, magazines and newspapers.* She spent most of her weekly allowance at Cadanau's, and on chocolate and a sweet bread that was a speciality of the area. The remainder went on postage. "I wrote something like 120 letters in the first month I was there," she later recalled of Videmanette. "I was so unhappy there I just wrote and wrote," to her mother and stepfather, to her father (almost always marked "personal" and never co-addressed to Raine), to Sarah and Jane and her grandmother, Lady Fermoy. All the letters mentioned her unhappiness, and impressed upon the recipients her need to come home, that she "felt out place," that it was "just too claustrophobic," and, worse, boring.

---

*Heidi Yersin, the headmistress at the Institut Alpin Videmanette added that, "Diana only ever went to the cinema [on Saturday afternoon] with the girls. They were allowed to go into Gstaad and meet up with the boys [from Le Rosey] but Diana never accompanied them."

Diana rose in the icy dawn and with the other girls had yogurt, muesli and hot chocolate every morning. Then, weather permitting, they went up on the slopes to ski. In the afternoon there were cooking, dressmaking and French classes, which she thought a waste of money. School fees, she complained, were astronomical. "I've learned how to make eight different kinds of potatoes," she wrote to a former nanny, "all of them with gobs of butter and cream." She was not actually homesick. After all, she had been living away from home for years and in a society of youngsters who were all separated from their families and accepted it as the norm. She simply hated the school and she envied Sarah and Jane, now an assistant editor at *Vogue*, who lived such exciting lives in London.

In fact, Sarah had been going through a difficult period. Her early flirtation with the Prince of Wales had come to nothing. She had then entered into a relationship with Gerald Grosvenor, soon to be the 6th Duke of Westminster, one of Britain's most eligible bachelors, but just when she had been expecting a proposal, he had become engaged to the beautiful Natalia Phillips.

Sarah was devastated, and during the summer and autumn of 1977 struggled with the onset of anorexia nervosa. Eventually she went of her own accord to a nursing home in Regent's Park where she was placed under the care of Dr. Maurice Lipsedge, a specialist in eating disorders.

Anorexia may be an unconscious cry for help. It is also brought on by feelings of extreme guilt and self-loathing. Sarah had lost first the interest of Prince Charles and then was rejected by a man she had been certain was about to propose. She looked on this as a terrible failure on her part. The idea that she must marry "up" had been stressed even more to Sarah, as the oldest daughter, than to her two younger sisters. Eating disorders often emanate from a feeling of having no control over one's life. Food—bingeing and denying oneself its pleasure and sustenance—is something the individual can control. At the moment Sarah was rudderless and desperately in need of a stabilizing influence, a way of putting order back in her life.

After several months under Dr. Lipsedge's intensive care, she began to feel better. Her eating disorder had not disappeared, but she had gained enough control over it to leave the clinic. Shortly afterwards she went to watch Prince Charles play polo at Smith's Lawn. Her dramatic weight-loss had given the fine-boned contours of her face a haunting beauty, and Charles found himself still attracted to Sarah. Their friendship rekindled and they began to see each other again. The Prince was certainly aware of Sarah's recent medical history, but when Sarah told him she was cured, he found no reason to doubt her.

In February 1978, while Diana was writing pleading letters from Videmanette, Sarah joined the Prince of Wales and the Duke and Duchess of Gloucester* on a skiing holiday to Klosters, Switzerland. Sarah and the Prince had been an "item" in the international press for several months and there was much excitement at Diana's school about the possibility of her having Prince Charles as a brother-in-law. Apparently Sarah had expected a proposal during this holiday and when it did not come she was disappointed. "If Prince Charles asked me to marry him, I would turn him down," she vowed impetuously to a reporter on their return to London. And then added—disastrously, "I wouldn't marry a man I didn't love, whether he was a dustman or the King of England."

It was an extraordinary public statement, and Charles was wounded. Sarah's chance to make a marital connection with the Royal Family had ended. "Sarah had well and truly blown it," one observer comments. "She had humiliated the Prince and broken quite a few upper-class taboos in one fell swoop. Never frighten the horses. Keep things within your circle. Keep your mouth shut in public. And never, but never, speak to the press."

---

*Richard, Duke of Gloucester: only surviving son of Henry, Duke of Gloucester, who was brother of King Edward VIII and King George VI. The present Duke of Gloucester is married to the former Birgitte van Deurs.

She might have been brashly indiscreet and highly emotional, but she was also a canny young woman and there
were things about Charles that set up an alarm signal in
Sarah. At the same time as he was with her he was receiving several calls each day from a close woman friend, the
glamorous Australian, Dale, Lady Tryon, who had been in
love with him since they had first met aged twenty-five—
and not at a Geelong Church of England Grammar School
dance in Victoria, South East Australia, aged eighteen, as
has been written elsewhere.

"We met at a Buckingham Palace reception which Anthony [Tryon] took me to in 1973. It was love at first sight
for me." Kanga, as Charles called Dale, was the daughter
of Barry Harper, a wealthy Australian publisher, notably of
Vogue. Charles later claimed that she was the one woman
who truly understood him, and she had strong influence
over some of his personal decisions.

Fresh and fun and not in the least awed by him, Kanga
was ten months older than Charles, blonde, vital, with a
mature, curvy body, and a flashing smile. She had suffered
a painful childhood: born with a mild form of spina bifida,
she had been unable to walk until she was nine and spent
three years in hospital. She was a valiant survivor and
seemed now to be making up for all the time she had lost
as a child. But the Prince was not ready for marriage and
she subsequently married Tryon (a merchant banker and
Old Etonian friend of Prince Charles, known as Lord
Ummm for the way he finished sentences), and remained
in England. Two years after their wedding Charles was
godfather to their first son, also named Charles. Kanga and
the Prince remained for years the best of friends. The
Tryons' marriage produced four children and began to
founder. Sarah concluded that Kanga's strong feelings for
Charles were the underlying cause and that he was not im-
mune to the attractive Lady Tryon's overtures. Sarah knew
she would only be second best if their relationship continued—so publicly rejected him.

Diana, of course, knew only that Sarah was going

through a difficult time, and that she might be able to help if she was closer to her. This gave Diana yet another reason to return home. Finally, she convinced her parents that Videmanette was (1) a total waste of money, (2) that she was learning only how hurtful and snobbish her peers could be, and (3) that as they served so many fattening things she had gained an enormous amount of weight in the short time she had been there and would probably end up obese if she stayed. That did it. In April, after only one term at the Alpine finishing school, she returned to London and her mother's flat as the family prepared for a great event.

Jane was to be married to Robert Fellowes, fifteen years her senior. William Fellowes, his father, had been the Queen's land agent at Sandringham and Johnnie and Frances had known their future son-in-law since his youth. Robert had been secretary to Prince Charles and was now assistant secretary to the Queen. It was not the prestigious marriage that Johnnie would have chosen for his twenty-one-year-old daughter, although Robert's future, if lacking an old title and a grand house, looked promising.

"We have known each other all our lives," Jane told the press on the announcement of their engagement, "and have gradually grown closer." Diana was surprised at her sister's choice, for Fellowes was rather stiff, conservative in his attitudes and dress, and had been described by an American friend as "a consummate company man." But she was thrilled at the prospect of being a bridesmaid and pleased that Jane seemed so happy.

The couple's wedding, in the Guards' Chapel at the Wellington Barracks in central London, was a grand affair with a reception at St. James's Palace attended by the Queen Mother, who arrived with Lady Fermoy, the Duchess of Kent, and the Duke and Duchess of Gloucester. Although Jane was too caught up in the excitement of being a bride to notice, Diana was distressed by the hostility displayed between her parents, and by Raine's overbearing presence and insistence on being included in all the family photographs. There was one nasty moment when Raine's voice grew defiantly loud when she was asked by a photographer to step aside "as Peter Shand Kydd had gracefully done," for a picture of the wedding couple and their parents. (She finally obliged.)

After the wedding Diana went to Althorp, but living in a house where Raine was mistress grew increasingly difficult for her, and although Johnnie had given the newlyweds a cottage on the Althorp estate as a wedding gift, Diana did not feel she could intrude on Jane and Robert so soon after their honeymoon. Finally, it was decided that she could stay at her mother's flat in Cadogan Place. Frances and Peter were in Scotland, but Violet Collinson would be there to look after her and Sarah was close by. She was given six weeks in which to decide what she would do next.

By the end of that time she had chosen to work as a mother's help to six-year-old Alexandra Whitaker, daughter of Major Jeremy Whitaker and his wife Philippa, who were friends of the Shand Kydds. They had a charming house in Hampshire, called Land of Nod, and Diana loved caring for Alexandra, playing with her, ironing her clothes and generally being a good companion. However, when the summer came and with it, on 1 July 1978, her seventeenth birthday, she renewed her pleas to be allowed to live in London, perhaps with Sarah. Her older sister did not think this was a good idea.

The sister whom Diana had idolized throughout her life now saw her as a nuisance *and* a threat, for Diana was maturing into an attractive young woman. She took Sarah's rejection to heart: "She very much wanted to move in with Sarah and her flatmate, Lucinda Craig-Harvey," a friend says. "She was willing to do anything to make it happen— even took on the job as a char for her at a pittance. She worked for them three days a week—scrubbing floors, washing dishes, cleaning lavatories, ironing and straightening closets. Not that Sarah was ever mean to her in any way. But she did take advantage of her good nature and slavey instincts—which Diana did nothing to discourage. It was not an easy time for her—but, then, when was there

such a time for Diana? I've known her since our days at
Silfield. She always felt like a piece of flotsam, in the way
of everyone she loved, and Diana's need to give love was
even greater than her need to receive it."

She spent the summer working at a series of odd jobs—
nannying, house-cleaning for Sarah and some of Sarah's
friends, moving back and forth between London, where she
stayed at her grandmother's or her mother's flat, and Althorp where Raine was immersed in turning the estate into
a lucrative enterprise. Raine came at her job with a driving,
tireless passion and iron will that during her years in politics had caused co-workers, friends and enemies to compare
her with Margaret Thatcher, who was now leading the Conservative Party. Raine had "the same iron self-discipline,
same determination, same dauntless energy, same blithe
disregard for opposing views," wrote Russell Miller, *The
Times* correspondent.

Johnnie was especially glad that Raine had dealt with
the inheritance tax liability for him. She had sold, by agreement with the Inland Revenue in lieu of the debt, four Van
Dycks, several portrait drawings by Gainsborough (commissioned by the 1st Earl Spencer), furniture from Spencer
House in London and twenty pieces of porcelain (distrib-
uted to eight different museums).* Now she was ruthlessly
sorting through Althorp's other great paintings to select a
number for sale to pay for the refurbishment of Althorp,
which was opened to the public every weekend during the
summer.

As châtelaine of Althorp, Raine had a vast, rich archive
at her disposal. Beside paintings, furniture and porcelain
worth many millions, there was a rare cache of silver and

*The Van Dycks were sold individually to the Tate Gallery, *Albert
de Ligne, Prince of Brabaçon and Arenberg*, to the National Gallery,
Viscountess Andover and Lady Elizabeth Thimbleby, to the York City
Art Gallery, *Penelope Wriothesley, wife of William, 2nd Lord Spencer*,
and *Rachel de Ruvigny*, to the Fitzwilliam Museum, Cambridge. The
Gainsborough portrait drawings were sold to a private collection.

gold, a collection of original manuscripts by Mozart and Beethoven, drawings, rare books and property. During the next decade Raine sold treasures from all these categories. Even the Spencer family archives were sold, by private treaty, to the British Library for £1 million.

As yet, the children did not know how far their step-mother would go in her sell-off of Althorp's treasures, but Diana was deeply hurt to see the great family portraits that she so loved dispersed, and Raine's inclination towards gold trimmings and scarlet velvet offended her. Of the four Spencer siblings she was, however, the only one to contain her anger. "Sarah resented me," Raine told newspaper columnist Jean Rook, "even my place at the head of the table, and gave orders to the servants over my head. Jane didn't speak to me for two years, even if we bumped in a passageway." Then she added, "Diana was sweet, always did her own thing." Charlie had a penchant for cruel jokes, once taking a bet that he could throw Raine into the swimming-pool at a dance at Althorp when she was wearing a magnificent ball gown. Raine just managed to slip out of his grasp inches from the pool and ran into the house shaking and furious. The four felt that Raine was making Althorp look too gaudy—"just like a summer pudding." But Johnnie approved of everything she did and believed that the children and the press were being unfair and vindictive towards her. "He was as besotted with Raine as Edward VIII was with Wallis Simpson," an observer said at the time. "He could see no wrong in anything she did. And she *was* treated unfairly. Yes, art that had been part of a great collection for over two hundred years had been sold off. And yes, the house had a gaudy look to it. But people forget that when Althorp was built, gold gilt and deep-pile red and purple velvet were all the style. Raine was restoring it according to the fashion of its original state."

Earl Spencer revelled in showing off Raine's work in the house to visitors and would greet paying guests at weekends and show them round, giving personal comments

as he went along. "These rooms are best in the evenings,"
he often said, "when they are candle-lit. Quite marvellous!"
The house had been opened first in 1954 and there is little
doubt that it needed a good refurbishing: Jack Spencer had
refused to change or replace anything, and almost no major
repairs had been done in decades. "We decided to put up
the scaffolding very soon after [we married]," Raine told
Nicholas Wapshott of *The Times*. "We got the show on the
road right away, no hanging about."

Diana bristled at Raine's brash way of putting things and
her cloyingly coy manner with her father. "Johnikins!"
Raine would say and glance at him seductively. *His* children and hers were seldom in the house as the same time,
but when they were there was no love lost between them.
Barbara Cartland visited frequently, powdered, perfumed
and permed, wearing extraordinary clothes, mostly in bright
pink. Mother and daughter resembled each other: both had
a strong personality, both were high achievers—but the
mother had a softer way with her, born of another and more
gentle age perhaps. Diana still read her books and was
pleased to see her.

In mid-September 1978, Diana spent the weekend near
Sandringham at the family home of her childhood friend
Caroline Harbord-Hammond, the daughter of Lord Suffolk.
On Monday morning, 18 September, when all the guests
were gathered for breakfast in the dining room, someone
casually asked after Diana's father.

Something mysteriously overcame Diana and she replied, "I've got this strange feeling that he's going to drop
down and if he dies, he'll die immediately otherwise he'll
survive." The room grew silent.

"Surely that can't be so," the woman said nervously.

Diana looked so upset that the subject was dropped.
"Next day the telephone rang," Diana told Andrew Morton,
"and I said to the lady, 'That will be about Daddy.' " It
was. He'd collapsed. I was frightfully calm, went back up
to London, went to the hospital, saw Daddy was gravely
ill." She was told that he was going to die, but she clung

to her premonition that he would survive as he had not died immediately.

When he woke on that Tuesday morning Earl Spencer had not felt well. He was alone in his bed as Raine had gone into London to do some shopping and to meet her mother for lunch at Claridges. He had a violent headache and took two Disprin, followed by a simple breakfast of tea and toast, then dressed and walked over to his office, which was in another building about a hundred yards from the house. Walking was no longer easy for him as he had gained an enormous amount of weight recently, which was dangerous, he knew, with his high blood pressure, and the remembered warnings of Dr. Dalgliesh. He made some phone calls and signed a few cheques. Still not feeling well, he told Richard Stanley, who managed the estate, that he was going back to the main house. He had not gone more than a few yards when he collapsed. Stanley ran to him. Johnnie was ashen and having trouble breathing. Stanley said he would go for help, but Johnnie would not hear of it, so Stanley helped him to his feet. The two struggled towards the house. The butler seeing them approach ran to assist and Dr. Dalgliesh was called.

Johnnie had suffered a major stroke, and was taken to Northampton general hospital, a fifteen-minute journey by ambulance. On arrival he was unconscious. Within an hour Raine was by his side as doctors fought to save his life.

All four children converged on the hospital: Diana arrived from Norfolk, Charlie from Eton, and Sarah and Jane from London, to find Raine in full charge. By the next morning Johnnie had declined into a deep coma. His condition was complicated by the onset of pneumonia. Raine had him moved by ambulance to the National Hospital in London, where great advances with stroke patients had been made. Johnnie was placed on a life-support machine, and then had immediate, delicate and risky brain surgery.

He survived the four-hour operation and was returned to his room, but a discordant, tense atmosphere had settled on his family. He was still unconscious, in a critical condition, and Raine blocked the door to his room, refusing to let anyone enter. She took a bed at the hospital and was by his side constantly willing him to pull though. Their exclusion made the children furious, but Raine would allow no one but medical staff to enter his room, convinced that any outside influence would adversely affect him.

"She wouldn't let us see Daddy," Diana remembered. "[Sarah] took charge of that and went in sometimes to see him. Meanwhile, he couldn't talk because he had a tracheotomy so he wasn't able to ask where his other children were. Goodness knows what he was thinking because no one was telling him."

Raine only once said anything negative that related to Johnnie's condition, and that was addressed to a hostile, teenage Charlie who had been exceedingly curt with her. "If your father dies," she told him, "I will be out of Althorp completely, the next morning." Then she disappeared back into her husband's room and the door closed with some finality behind her.

Still unable to communicate, Johnnie was transferred to the intensive-care unit at the Brompton Hospital in South Kensington where it was believed he might receive better long-term care. He was on the critical list for three weeks, unconscious and on life support. Once again Raine ordered that his children should not be allowed into his room. She claimed to friends that "The girls [the sisters] used to shout at her" at Johnnie's bedside, and she "did not need teenagers throwing tantrums." Diana insisted this had never occurred. But the damage done to family relationships with Raine during this time would be irreparable.

For several months Johnnie was unable to speak. Raine would sit by his bed, holding his hand, "hour after hour, week after week," Johnnie later recalled, "holding my hand and talking about our holidays and my photography, things she knew I liked . . . She used to shout at me sometimes, bless her. "Can you hear me?" she'd yell. I nodded because I couldn't answer. She was always there at my side and I could feel her great strength, her determination that I should

live even when the doctors said she must lose me. Raine
won."

Diana was devastated by this tragic family drama. Never
as verbal in her anger as her sisters and brother, she contained her deep resentment of Raine. By November, though
her father had begun to show signs of improvement, he still
could not speak and remained in the Brompton Hospital.

Before her father's stroke, Diana had started cooking
classes at a school in Wimbledon with no particular idea
of how she would use what she learned. It had been at her
mother's suggestion and the classes were attended by other
daughters of wealthy parents who were looking for something to occupy their time until the right marriage proposal
came along. The other alternative had been a secretarial
course, which Diana thought she would hate. The choice
was obvious to her: she liked cooking and eating, and especially loved rich cream sauces—and was fined for constant sampling of the dishes she was preparing.

While her father remained in hospital, Diana stayed in
London at her mother's flat, commuting to the cooking
school and returning each evening to the hospital to sit
outside her father's room. None of the family had attended
any social gatherings during the first weeks of his illness,
but in October Diana had received an invitation to a party
in honour of Prince Charles's thirtieth birthday, on 14 November, to be held at Buckingham Palace. Sarah was also
to attend; her romance with Charles was over but the two
remained friends. Sarah was puzzled as to why Diana had
been invited and Diana herself could not explain it. She
knew only that she had been thrilled to receive an invitation.

Fearful that she would anger Sarah by accepting, Diana
asked her sister if she would mind. Sarah reluctantly agreed
that she could go. It never seemed to have occurred to Diana that she had been sent her own invitation apparently
because the Prince had wanted her to be present and that
Sarah had no right to make that decision for her. She had
no escort for the dance, and as she had gained weight be-

tween the cooking classes and the junk food she had eaten keeping vigil in the hospital, she had no dress that fitted. She went on a crash diet for a week but when she realized she had lost only two pounds, she grew desperate, terrified that her "pudgy look" would embarrass Sarah, that no dress could cover the ugliness of her body. Yet, somehow she knew that, despite her weight and her father's precarious condition, she must go to the party. For the next two weeks she dieted, lost weight and got into the dress she had worn for a party to celebrate Jane and Robert's engagement.

Diana was not exactly Cinderella going to the ball, but the evening had a romantic, prophetic tinge. She claimed she "wasn't at all intimidated by the surroundings," although she thought Buckingham Palace "an amazing place."

It is, indeed. In many ways it is a monstrous, antiquated museum with interminable, unheated corridors. But there is a cold magnificence to it, a sense of history, of a privileged world. The state apartments and banquet rooms were all on the ground floor, which even so had to be reached by an imposing stone staircase, overlooking the rear gardens. There were 350 guests and well over thirty liveried footmen ministering to them. Massive floral arrangements surrounded the dance-floor. When Diana entered with Sarah and her escort, she was greeted by Prince Charles, who stood flanked by his equerries. At his side was his current ladyfriend, the blonde, bubbly film actress Susan George, who exuded a kind of kittenish sexiness as she glanced at him.

Charles seemed pleased to see Diana. He stared quite boldly at her daring neckline as she curtsied. "You've grown," he said, and smiled.

"Oh, I hope not, sir," Diana is reported to have replied.

There was no further contact between them during the evening, but Diana danced with several unattached young men. She had a true grace and a way of making her partners seem far better dancers than they were. "Had a very nice time at the dance," she later commented. "Fascinating." She had fallen under the spell of majesty.

Charles remembers her at this time as a bouncy, fun-loving teenager. His life, in contrast, had become highly pressured. The Queen, his country and the media were expecting him to find a bride as he had said he would by his thirtieth birthday.

The difficulty was that Charles was in love with one married woman and unable to live without another.

DIANA'S KNOWLEDGE OF Charles and his set was mostly culled from the *Daily Mail*. The stories she read were often accompanied by photographs of the Prince with a "new friend"—usually someone blonde, busty and pretty. There had been a parade of beautiful young women before and after Sarah's unfortunate royal romance. As each candidate came and went the media elected a new future Princess of Wales: Davina Sheffield, Sabrina Guinness, Lady Cecil Kerr, Lady Jane Wellesley and the fiery Anna Wallace all acquired brief fame as a possible royal bride.

Sarah did not discuss with Diana her past relationship with Charles. Neither did she say anything about the two married women—Kanga Tryon and Camilla Parker Bowles—who dominated his private life but were seldom photographed with him unless others were present. It is doubtful that Sarah fully understood the pressure and confusion that Charles suffered because of his bachelorhood, and Diana had no idea of it whatsoever: she saw him as a dashing figure. He had been dubbed "Action Man" by the press because of his sporting prowess, and because he could pilot a fighter aeroplane, skipper a mine-sweeper, perform as a paratrooper. He skied, sailed, surfed, hunted, fished and had even been known to race camels. He played polo and was an excellent horseman. He was always in demand and forever in the public eye. Diana sensed in him a sadness, which increased his appeal.

Charles's bachelor status placed him in an intolerable predicament: there was deep concern inside and outside the Royal Family as to when and who he would marry. But unlike any other man, he could not marry a woman for love alone. At this time he was emotionally and sexually torn between his feelings for Kanga, who "understood" him, and

for Camilla, who "excited him as no other woman had."
Either would have to divorce her husband to marry him.
For any union he would need the approval of the Queen
and Parliament, and it would not be forthcoming in either
of these instances. The Church of England teaches that marriage is indissoluble, so it stood to reason that a Prince of
Wales, who on succeeding to the throne would also become
supreme Governor of the Church of England and Defender
of the Faith, could not marry a divorcee.

Charles had been warned that such a decision on his part
would spell disaster for his family and his country. "You
must remember Uncle David [Edward VIII, Duke of Wind-
sor]," was the message. Uncle David's notorious affair and
subsequent marriage to the twice-divorced Wallis Simpson
had precipitated his abdication and brought his younger
brother, George VI, to the throne. Perhaps if "Uncle David"
could have kept Mrs. Simpson as his mistress and married
another woman he might have held on to his throne. After
all, Edward VII, Charles's great-great grandfather, had always had his mistresses. His favourite, Alice Keppel, was
Camilla's great-grandmother, of which Camilla had reminded Charles at their first meeting in 1972, adding, it is
said, "So how about it, then?"

He was serving in the Navy at the time and Camilla
Shand was dating his polo friend Andrew Parker Bowles,
and had previously dated Princess Anne. Camilla was not
only direct, she was fun to be with, a good sport and sports-
woman. She loved to hunt, and had none of the artifice of
the young débutantes he generally met. Prince Charles felt
comfortable with her. They fell instantly in love and she
dropped Parker Bowles, and entered into an affair with
Charles. But Camilla, who was a commoner and "a woman
of experience," as one courtier euphemistically referred to
her, was not considered acceptable by the Queen or the
Prince's advisers as a future Princess of Wales. He was
given no option but to cast aside the idea of marrying Camilla and look elsewhere for a more suitable prospective
wife.

Charles heeded the advice and saw a number of other young women. Camilla made no public statement, but retaliated by marrying Parker Bowles. When he became godfather to her son, Charles realized he had lost the woman he loved. It was not long before he and Camilla were once again lovers. His one hope was that she would remain his mistress and that whoever he took as his bride would be tolerant of his alliance.

However, finding the right young woman, whether or not he had a mistress, was difficult. By the Act of Settlement of 1701, she could not be Roman Catholic. She must be capable of bearing children, pass a stringent investigation into her past to make sure there were no dark scandals lurking there, and be approved by the Queen. She should preferably be English of impeccable ancestry. This last was not an absolute, but he was discouraged from dating eligible foreigners, for the Queen and the government were convinced that the British people would not react favourably to a non-British future queen.

"I don't know why any sane girl would ever want to take me on," Charles once said. Diana had been right to identify in him a deep, inner sadness. He had been hurt throughout his life, bullied in childhood by his father, who continued to snipe at and belittle him in public. "The two could hardly bear to be in each other's company," one observer noted.

Prince Philip's resentment towards his son was due partly to the disparity between their personalities. Charles had developed into an able sportsman—he could ride, shoot, ski and surf with the best—but he was not inclined towards locker-room jokes and much preferred the company of women and older men, like his uncle Earl Mountbatten or Laurens van der Post, the South African-born writer, explorer and mystic, who, when Charles was in his early twenties, had begun to counsel him on spiritual matters. On their first meeting van der Post had told Charles that there was "a missing dimension" in the atmosphere created around him by his father, which immediately drew the younger man to him.

Under van der Post's influence Charles developed a strong spiritual side, while Philip was a pragmatist. An even greater barrier for father and son to surmount was Charles's position as heir to the throne. The family structure would always prohibit a closeness between them, which Charles missed and his father did not.

At Charles's birth on 18 November 1948, the fountains in Trafalgar Square were made to run blue in honour of his sex, for Britain now had a male heir to the throne. The knowledge that he would one day be king dawned on him slowly, he once claimed, but "in the most inexorable sense." He was only three when his mother became Queen. Her first duty and responsibility had to be to her subjects, not to him. He was taught to bow when she entered a room where he was, even if it was his own nursery. He was warned never to run to her, or grab at her, or to kiss her before she kissed him. Other people bowed to him and called him sir, and there was an unseen barrier between him and all others that he did not know how to penetrate.

An appointment had to be made to see either of his parents. Sometimes they appeared with their children in public, occasions for which both Charles and his sister Anne were carefully prepared. Private family gatherings with his parents at this time were marked by an edge of hostility that signalled the marriage difficulties they were experiencing. Disharmony had existed almost from Elizabeth's accession when she did not rename Britain's ruling house Mountbatten-Windsor, a great blow to Philip and his uncle Lord Mountbatten.*

Philip was furious. "I'm just an amoeba—a bloody

---

*Lord Louis Mountbatten, Earl of Burma (1900–1979), British admiral, great-grandson of Queen Victoria and Prince Philip's uncle through his mother. He was governor-general of India in 1947-8. It was Mountbatten who engineered the marriage of his impecunious nephew to Elizabeth when she was heir to the Throne.

amoeba!" he shouted, in the presence of several members of the Palace staff. Time did not placate his rancour. There were a number of years of near estrangement between him and his wife. Elizabeth was young—only twenty-five in 1952 when she became queen. The first five years of her reign were exceptionally hard as she learned to deal with the intricacies of monarchy and the intrigues and machinations of her courtiers. She loved her children but could only spend limited time with them, while Philip searched in frustration and futility to find a niche for himself. When he could not, he philandered and spent much of his time touring the world with his recently divorced, Australian seafaring friend, Michael Parker, who also enjoyed the intimate company of beautiful women.

Philip rankled at being a consort without a job and no power to make any independent decisions. He was still thought of as "Philip the Greek"* by court xenophobes and he was conscious of their suspicion of his motives. His love for his wife chilled even further by her refusal to grant him the title HRH Prince Philip, until 1957, when he was "grafted into the British royal tree." His children, however, retained the surname Windsor.

Charles was twelve when his brother Andrew was born in 1960, and had spent four years boarding at Cheam, where his father, then an impoverished Greek prince in exile who spoke only rudimentary English, had also been sent at eight.

Philip's mother, whose brother was Lord Louis Mountbatten, had been unhearing from childhood and turned to a

---

*Prince Philip, although born in Greece and the son of Prince Andrew of Greece, was a great-great grandson of Queen Victoria on his mother's side. His parents both had strong Germanic roots. Greece won independence in 1832, but had to accept a Bavarian prince (Otto I) as King. Prince Andrew was his descendant. Philip's mother, Alice, (1885–1969) known as Princess Andrew, was Mountbatten's sister. Their parents were both German and their mother's sister became the Empress Alexandra of Russia. So Prince Philip owed less to his Greek than his German roots.

religious order for solace. His father, Prince Andrew of Greece,* had escaped with his life in time to avoid being put on trial for treason as a royalist by the Revolutionary Committee that assumed the country in 1923, during Greece's turbulent Civil War, when Philip was just two years old. Philip had been "the poor relation" of his mother's family for the majority of his young life, having always to live on their generosity (mainly his two English-based uncles—Mountbatten and George, 2nd Marquis of Milford Haven), as did his parents and sisters.† His Viking good looks were his one tangible asset, and he used them to great advantage. With his uncle, the wildly ambitious Mountbatten, behind him, Philip began a deliberate, and highly successful, wooing of Elizabeth when she was a shy, chubby, insecure fourteen-year-old girl. George VI, who adored his daughter, never completely trusted Philip, and the Queen's decision to fashion her dynasty as the House of Windsor and her reluctance to grant him the title of HRH Prince Philip, surely had their roots in her father's wariness and her increasing knowledge of his "wandering eye."

Spartan in his beliefs, Philip had felt that the rigour of life at Cheam had made a man of him and would do the same for his son. But the lonely young Prince found his five years at Cheam "a misery." He did not make friends easily. His status formed a barrier between himself and his classmates, although it did not buy him immunity from the headmasters' (there were two at Cheam) rod when he misbehaved—which wasn't often as he had a terror of corporal punishment.

*Prince Andrew of Greece (1882–1944). After Philip went to England, Prince Andrew was stateless and impoverished. He lived an empty life in exile in the South of France supported by women who were impressed by his title and charmed by his manner.
†Philip had three older sisters each of whom lived in Germany and were married to German princes who had served under Hitler during the Second World War. This had been a sticky public relations problem when Elizabeth and Philip were first engaged, but it somehow got brushed under the carpet.

From his earliest memory Charles had been surrounded in public by the intrusive cameras of the over-zealous press. They waited for him at the school gates when he arrived each term, and were there when he left. It was drilled into him that he must be polite, no matter how difficult the circumstances, and often the press and public pressures were intense.

He left Cheam "subdued and withdrawn, serious to the point of solemnity." His father found his demeanour irksome. He would publicly rebuke Charles "for inconsequential behaviour." At times he would mock him so cruelly that Charles "seemed to be foolish and tongue-tied in front of friends as well as family."

To the "distress and embarrassment" of other members of the Royal Family and courtiers who were close to them, the young Prince was frequently brought to tears by his father's inexplicably harsh, bantering gibes. Charles had artistic ability and could draw well; he was also interested in music, literature and botany. Philip believed such interests unmanly and never lost an opportunity to put down his son's accomplishments in these areas. When Charles was ten or eleven, an observer remembers, there was "a whole table of people present. The tears welled into his eyes . . . and I thought how could [Philip] do that." Charles realized the contempt in which his father held him and it cut him deeply. What hurt him even more, perhaps, was his mother's disregard of the humiliation to which his father subjected him. She did nothing to counteract her husband's verbal abuse of their son.

The Queen had made a personal compromise. Since Philip had little to do with her public role, in the matter of their children she would "submit entirely to the[ir] father's will." There was great inequality in this regard. Philip's favourite offspring was his only daughter Anne, and since she was a born horsewoman they had much in common. Charles on the other hand had no one to champion him.

After Cheam Charles was dispatched to Gordonstoun in northeast Scotland, which Philip had also attended. Later he regarded his years there as his "time of imprisonment." A contemporary at Gordonstoun was the author William Boyd, who wrote a coruscating essay about his time at the school.* Life there, he claimed, was hard, and a "casual brutality" existed during the day. At night "a gang of thugs roamed the house beating up smaller boys, extorting food and money, pilfering, and creating an atmosphere of genuine terror." Another former Gordonstoun pupil bitterly remembered the custom "to greet a new boy by taking a pair of pliers to their arms and twisting until the flesh tore open." He added, "Boys were regularly trussed up in one of the wicker laundry baskets and left under the cold shower sometimes for hours." Charles was no exception and was subjected to cruelties by older boys that were malicious "and without respite." Otherwise he was left much alone. "Even to open a conversation with the heir to the throne," Jonathan Dimbleby, Charles's official biographer, has written, was "to face the charge of 'sucking up' and to hear the collective 'slurping' noises that denoted a toady and sycophant."

His pleading letters to the Queen and his sister that life was "absolute hell . . . I simply dread going to bed because I get hit in the head all night long," did not win him a reprieve. Although he had great respect for Dr. Eric Anderson, a young Gordonstoun master who encouraged him to perform in the school's Shakespearean productions, his only confidant during the five years he spent at Gordonstoun was a sympathetic art teacher, Robert Waddell, who recognized his talent. Working under Waddell's instruction, Charles developed into quite a good ceramicist. He also found that he could work with Waddell out of school hours, away from his tormentors.

Classical music appealed to him. He had heard little at home as his parents' taste ran to patriotic, show and choral music. He made an unsuccessful attempt to play the trumpet in the school orchestra and then took up the cello. When

*School Ties, Penguin, 1985.

at Sandringham in 1965, he visited Lady Fermoy and performed a piece for her. "He could have been a very good
cellist," she commented later, "because he's such a sensitive musician and he made a lovely sound. At the end he
said, 'I'm hopeless.' "

"Not at all, sir," she replied, adding diplomatically, "It
takes much time to be a good cellist and you have so many
other important matters to attend to."

In February 1966, amid tremendous media coverage,
Charles arrived in Australia to attend a new school, Timbertop, an outback offshoot of Geelong Church of England
Grammar School in Victoria, a hundred miles to the north-
east in the foothills of the Great Dividing Range and "a
very long way from home." He was there for one term.
During his stay he performed over fifty engagements, as
well as keeping up with a physically strenuous daily routine. He appeared officially at sheep-shearing events, film
openings, polo matches, and was seen panning for gold,
mustering cattle, chopping wood for war widows, and
lunching at Government House.

It was a killing schedule, but he took to Australia and
Timbertop, where he was not harassed or beaten and where
he made friends. He returned to Gordonstoun in the autumn
of 1966 for his final year, a time he looked to with despair
and foreboding. But in actual fact Gordonstoun did not
prove to be as dismal as the previous years. He sang with
the choir, went on with his painting and potting, and he
was given his own study-bedroom adjoining the flat occupied by the sympathetic Robert Waddell. None the less, he
had no regrets when he finally left Gordonstoun for the last
time a year later, and began what was to be a far more
rewarding and fearless four terms at Trinity College, Cambridge.

His time at Trinity was interrupted by a term at the University College of Wales at Aberystwyth, a political decision on the part of Buckingham Palace. This was a time of
fractious relations between Britain and Wales. Charles's arrival was greeted with placards declaring "Go Home Char-

lie" in Welsh. A week later a bomb exploded in the street outside police headquarters in Cardiff.

The portrait of Charles that hung over Diana's bed when she was at West Heath pictured him at his investiture as Prince of Wales on 1 July 1969 at Caernarfon Castle. He was nearly twenty, and the twenty-first Prince of Wales descending from a line that had begun with the future Edward II, who was invested as Prince of Wales in 1301. "For me," Charles wrote in his diary that same day, "by far the most moving and meaningful moment came when I put my hands between Mummy's and swore to be her liege man of life and limb and to live and die against all manner of folk—such magnificent medieval, appropriate words, even if they were never adhered to in those old days."

What followed shortly thereafter was "a crash course in royal diplomacy and the function of the monarchy." He made official visits to Australia and to the United States to meet President Nixon. Then he did a five-month stint with the Royal Air Force, followed by an attachment to the Royal Navy where he served first on the nuclear submarine HMS *Churchill* and then on HMS *Norfolk*. Nothing about his time in the Navy was normal: he had extra protection, and special arrangements were made to guard his clothes, his letters, his diary. A line of communication was set up between the Admiralty and the Palace in case a problem should arise. He was called "Prince Charles" by those of equal naval rank, and "sir" by those who weren't. No matter what their rank, upon first meeting everyone had to bow and call him "Your Royal Highness."

Once again, he was set apart and, isolated and alone, he began an intimate exchange of letters with Lord Mountbatten, whom he called "Grandpapa," although Mountbatten was his great-uncle. The warmth he never received from his father came to him from Mountbatten, who had two daughters but no son and whose relationship with Philip had soured over the years. Philip was anything but happy about Mountbatten's influence over Charles, sensing that

"Uncle Dickie" might manipulate his son as once he had manipulated him.

After five years in the Navy and his affair with Camilla, Charles had been transformed into a more self-assured young man. But one problem took precedence over any other. As he had said poignantly in his graduation address from Cambridge University, "I do not really know what my role in life is . . . but somehow I must find one." He was still looking for it. He remained deeply in love with Camilla but confused as he had also formed a close relationship with Kanga.

Diana was oblivious to the sophisticated arrangements of Charles's private life. From what she read in the press, he dated one beautiful young woman after another and she told a friend, "If I'd had the chance Sarah had [with Prince Charles] I never would have blown it." She remained girlishly romantic, yet with an underlying strength of purpose to her fantasizing.

Although the Spencers were no longer neighbours of the Royal Family, Robert Fellowes made the seasonal migrations with Jane from London to Windsor to Sandringham to Balmoral as a member of the Queen's staff. And in January 1979, the same week that Lord Spencer came out of hospital after his stroke, Diana joined her sister and brother-in-law at Sandringham for a shooting weekend. Prince Charles was also present. They saw each other only briefly. He seemed happy to see her again, but also "as if wrestling with some private matter that deeply affected him."

Even so, Charles never had the remoteness that marked his mother. Diana always had the feeling that the Queen was not truly interacting when there was an exchange between them, not that she ever had more than a few words at a time in conversation with her. Her questions were always innocuous and seemed rehearsed. "I hope your father is coming along well," she once said.

"Yes, thank you, ma'am," Diana replied.

"I understand you've been attending cooking school. What a good idea."

"Well, it was really my mother's suggestion, but I am enjoying it."

A royal nod and the Queen turned away. Diana understood from Jane that the Queen enjoyed "unmalicious" gossip, but as royal reporter Anthony Holden comments, "Years of avoiding controversy have rendered her conversation rather bland. To meet her even briefly is to encounter someone so distinctly from another world that she might as well be a temporary (and very reluctant) visitor from Mars."

On Diana's eighteenth birthday, 1 July 1979, she received her inheritance from her great-grandmother Frances Work, and the wherewithal to buy her own flat in London. Her father had returned to Althorp but not in the best of health and was still having problems with his speech. Diana felt that he had "basically changed character. He was one person before and he was certainly a different person after [his long illness]." He had remained "estranged but adoring" she was to say, unaware of the contradiction within her statement. She bought a pleasant three-bedroom flat at 60 Coleherne Court, off the Old Brompton Road, for £60,000 and, with her mother's help, began to improve and decorate it in a bright, modern style. She took as flatmates her old friends Carolyn Pride, Sophie Kimball and Philippa Coaker. A month later Sophie and Philippa moved out to be replaced by Anne Bolton and Virginia Pitman.

Her flatmates paid her £18 a week, shared the food and household expenses, and rotated housekeeping tasks. Diana tacked a sign to her bedroom door that read "Chief Chick" and, according to Carolyn, "always had the rubber gloves on as she clucked around the place." Still unaware of what she wanted to do, Diana felt that although she was in limbo it would not be long before Mr. Right took her by the hand and led her into the future they were always meant to share. But she had to find something to occupy her time and supplement her income that would be more rewarding than cleaning the lavatories and ironing the sheets at Sarah's flat.

She had not truly given up the idea of establishing a

place for herself in the world of dance. With this in mind, she contacted Madame Betty Vacani, who ran the Vacani Dance School in South Kensington where many members of the Royal Family—the Queen, Princess Margaret, Prince Charles and Princess Anne—had taken lessons as children. Madame Vacani had once judged a dance contest at West Heath, which Diana had won. She was given an audition, interviewed and hired to teach the youngest class of pre-schoolers and accompany them on the piano.

She began work in mid-January 1979, and found it rewarding. She loved the children, and her ability to use her two main skills—piano and dance—productively gave her a new sense of self. For the next three months she was happier than anyone had seen her in a very long time. In March, she joined an old Norfolk friend, Mary-Ann Stewart-Richardson, for a weekend skiing in the French Alps, where she fell and tore the tendons in her left ankle. For three months she was in and out of plaster casts.

When she recovered, she went to see Victoria Wilson and Kay Seth-Smith, who knew her sister Jane and who ran the Young England Kindergarten in Pimlico, near Victoria station. They were impressed with the instant rapport she showed with the youngsters and hired her part-time. On Monday, Wednesday and Friday she would teach drawing, a little dancing and organize games and play times. Also Seth-Smith knew an American couple who needed a part-time nanny for Patrick, their toddler son. Diana was hired to work for the Robertsons on Tuesdays and Thursdays.

She was enjoying herself immensely. She had a place of her own, flatmates who were good company, and she was dating, mostly Old Etonians she had met skiing or at the family homes of friends. She never forgot her instinct that she must remain chaste. Rory Scott, one of her male friends during this period, says, "She was sexually attractive and the relationship was not a platonic one as far as I was concerned, but it remained that way. She was always a little aloof, you always felt there was a lot you would never know about her." Scott was in the Army, a tall, attractive young man, who had appeared in a BBC documentary on Trooping the Colour. Diana laundered and ironed his shirts, proud that there was never a wrinkle to be seen.

But it was to the children at the kindergarten and Patrick that she gave her full attention and love. They made her feel needed, and prepared her for the family life she knew would one day be hers.

IT WAS AUGUST, London was experiencing a heatwave and strong sunlight streamed through the open windows of Diana's bedroom. Carolyn knocked at the door and called that it was time she got up for work. On the bedside table was an unfinished letter she had been trying to write before she fell asleep the previous evening. It was a letter of sympathy to Prince Charles.

Late yesterday the world had learned that IRA terrorists had murdered Lord Mountbatten and his fourteen-year-old grandson Nicholas in a bomb attack aboard the family's fishing boat, *Shadow V*, on the west coast of Ireland. Mountbatten's daughter Patricia, her husband John Brabourne, his mother and Nicholas's twin, Timothy, were all in critical condition. The young Irish boatman, Paul Maxwell, was also dead.

At the time of the tragedy, Charles was in Iceland where he had gone the previous day prior to a private fishing holiday. Kanga had accompanied him on the Royal Flight. "We awoke," she recalled, "when the plane had landed to see a reception committee, including a band, outside. He [Charles] had just a couple of minutes to shave and dress. Apart from the crew, we were the only people on the plane." A short time later Charles was called to the telephone and told about the bombing of the *Shadow V*. "Desperate emotions swept over" him—"agony, disbelief, a kind of wretched numbness." As soon as he collected himself he called "Mummy to find out exactly what had happened." The Queen told him all that she knew and suggested he return to London, but not before extra precautions had been put in place for his own safety.

As he waited for instructions, Charles wrote in his journal, "I still can't believe what has taken place and continue, vainly, to imagine that he will somehow revive and prove to everyone that he has yet again survived . . . I have lost someone infinitely special in my life; someone who showed enormous affection, who told me unpleasant things I didn't particularly want to hear, who gave praise where it was due as well as criticism; someone to whom I knew I could confide anything and from whom I would receive the wisest of counsel and advice. In some extraordinary way he combined grandfather, great-uncle, father, brother and friend and I shall always be eternally grateful that I was lucky enough to have known him for as long as I did." Then he added: "Life will *never* be the same now that he has gone and I fear it will take me a very long time to forgive those people who today achieved something that two world wars and *thousands* of Germans and Japanese failed to achieve. I only hope I can live up to the expectations he had of me and be able to do *something* to honour the name of Mountbatten."

He left Iceland late the next afternoon feeling "supremely useless and powerless." Charles had always dreaded Mountbatten's death, but had not expected to be faced with it so soon, so abruptly and in such a monstrous fashion. But there was no time for private grieving: from the moment his plane landed he would be on public display.

That day Diana bought almost all the papers, of which each one carried a photograph of Charles. "Oh, God," she told one of her flatmates, "he looks so awfully sad."

The Mountbatten tragedy awakened a political awareness in Diana—she began to read about the history of Ireland and the IRA—and also made her realize the precarious position of people in the public eye, like Mountbatten and the Royal Family. She talked about this to friends and about the death of Mountbatten's grandson, Nicholas: "He was only fourteen years old. It's so unfair."

Meanwhile her job at Young England was going well. The kindergarten was housed in a small building in a church complex at the corner of St. George's Square and Lupus Street in Pimlico. The church grounds were screened from the converging roads by thick foliage so that the children played in privacy, their laughter and trilling voices rising in bell-like joy above the high hedges and leafy trees. The little ones took to Diana immediately. They ran to her when she arrived each day. They clung to her legs until she lifted them up and gave them a hug.

When she wasn't working, she enjoyed jazz, tap and keep-fit classes at the Dance Centre in Covent Garden. She was dating George Plumptre, eight years her senior, the third son of Lord Fitzwalter, and they went to the cinema together, attended parties, or she cooked dinner on occasion. She now owned a car and usually spent her weekends at friends' country homes. Her mother had sold the Cadogan Place flat and was living full-time in Scotland, and she spoke to her father every few days, but spent as little time as possible at Althorp.

Although Johnnie was making slow progress, he credited Raine with saving his life. He believed that his children had not been as attentive as they should have been during his ordeal. Raine was more protective and watchful of her husband than ever: his illness had made her recognize the vulnerability of her situation. If Johnnie died, Charlie would inherit Althorp and she would have to leave almost as soon as she was widowed. The selling of Althorp's treasures accelerated.

To Diana's surprise, Sarah began a serious romance with Raine's cousin, Neil McCorquodale, a former Coldstream Guards officer, quite a few years older than her and now a landowner and farmer. As usual with Sarah, the relationship did not go smoothly. The wedding date was set, broken and eventually rescheduled for May 1980, at St. Mary's Church, Great Brington, with Diana as a bridesmaid. Sarah came slowly down the narrow aisle of the ancient church holding her father's arm securely so that he did not stumble, as his balance was bad and his step shuffling. A reception followed at Althorp with Frances an uneasy guest while Raine and Barbara Cartland smiled like Cheshire cats.

Two of Johnnie's girls were now married, and he was

also a grandfather: Jane had given birth to her first child, Laura, the previous year. But neither daughter had made the marriage he had hoped she would. Now it was up to Diana to unite the House of Spencer with another great British family.

In early July 1980, Diana received an invitation from Philip de Pass to join him as a weekend guest at Petworth House, in West Sussex. He was a good friend of the current occupants, Max and Caroline Egremont. This extraordinary house had been built by Charles Seymour, 6th Duke of Somerset (a very distant cousin of the Spencers), in the seventeenth century. The great English artist J. M. W. Turner had had a studio there where he painted many of his best-known landscapes and interiors. The magnificent deer park had been landscaped in the eighteenth century by Lancelot "Capability" Brown.

Diana drove to Petworth early on a Saturday morning. The estate was on the edge of a small village with narrow streets that knotted around a charming little marketplace. She was given a pleasant room towards the rear of the second floor, then taken by Philip on a personal tour of the state rooms, which contained most of Petworth's fabulous art collection, and the famous Carved Room, decorated by Grinling Gibbons. Then she went with him and other house guests to watch Prince Charles play polo for his team Les Diables Bleus at nearby Cowdray Park. Charles was passionate about the game; his Uncle Dickie had not only championed but had written a definitive book on the sport, published in 1931 which went through seven editions, and one of Charles's greatest thrills was when his Uncle Dickie presented him with an award in August 1979, shortly before his death. Polo is a sport that totally envelops a player. It takes quick thinking and is both dangerous and humbling. Ben Johnson once wrote, "Princes learn no art truly, but the art of horsemanship: the reason is, the brave beast is no flatterer. He will throw a Prince as soon as his groom." Charles had been thrown more than once and received some bad knocks. But he continued to get back on the field.

Although confusing for a first-time spectator like Diana, she was impressed with Charles's courage and prowess, and yet somehow not quite involved, her own fear of horses returning to her. She often looked away, certain and fearful that a horse and rider would fall and be seriously injured.

Afterwards, she returned to her room, and got ready for the big barbecue that evening. She dressed casually in jeans and a white blouse then joined the rest of the guests outdoors where bales of hay had been laid about in quasi-rusticity for people to sit on. She was seated next to Philip when Charles, to whom she had spoken briefly at Cowdray, appeared. "He was all over me again and I thought it was very strange," Diana told Andrew Morton. "I thought, well, this isn't very cool. I thought men were not supposed to be that obvious. I thought this was very odd."

It was not just odd, it had been planned. Charles was now thirty-two. He had recently moved into Highgrove, a beautiful house in Gloucestershire, and Camilla's country home, Bolehyde Manor, was only a fifteen-minute drive away. The Queen had given Andrew Parker Bowles the position of Commander-in-Chief of the Household Cavalry, and he and his wife were included in parties at Balmoral and Windsor. The Queen knew of the liaison between her son and Camilla, but was keeping up appearances. None the less, she had let Charles know that his duty was to marry, whatever his relationship with Camilla, and that the public were getting restive about the comings and goings of his ladyfriends.

Charles was well aware that his duty was to marry and produce an heir, and that he had to do so soon. He turned to Camilla for advice. She met with Kanga, and the women drew up a list of girls they thought might do. Diana's name headed the list.* She had the right background for a Prin-

---

*It has been said, but not confirmed, that Kanga and Camilla drew up their list by narrowing bridal candidates from a rather long list of something like twelve to fifteen names Charles had been given by the Palace. The young women on the list had already been checked for

cess of Wales, and she was naïve, not too bright and rather shy. Camilla and Kanga thought she would be thrilled just to be a princess, to please her father, and wear a tiara. She would do nothing, the pair decided, to upset their position with Charles—Camilla as his mistress, Kanga as his "best, good friend." All very civilized, all neatly conceived to allow Charles to do his duty to the monarchy without disturbing their own relationship.

That evening, when Philip de Pass stood up, Charles took his place on the bale with this "bouncy, young teenager" who, as it happened, he found both refreshing and attractive. She told him how sad he had looked at Lord Mountbatten's funeral (which she had watched on television), how much she had empathized with his loss, and of her uncompleted letter. Diana had an uncanny ability to convey a depth of emotion with her eyes fixed and on the person to whom she was talking, her hand gently pressuring theirs. Charles took this as encouragement and, to her surprise, moved closer, appearing about to make a pass.

She kept him "at bay." They talked for a long time until Diana drew back, somewhat fearful that he had received the wrong message. She had so desperately wanted his attention. This was the culmination of her lifetime fantasy, that the Prince of Wales would be drawn to her. But she wanted him to understand that she could never be a short-term girlfriend.

Charles was not turned off by her sudden coolness but asked her to go back to London with him the next day and to Buckingham Palace where he had some work to do. She gracefully refused: it was going too fast and she wanted to be sure she could deal with it. She did not want to place herself in a situation that might be embarrassing to both of them. This was a clever move.

---

background and eligibility. Kanga and Camilla were said to have narrowed this list to five names with Diana as the top choice. Who the other four women were remains unknown, although Kanga hinted to friends that they were all English.

Although he had been gently rebuffed, Charles did not go off straight away to mix with the other guests as Diana had feared he might, but spent most of the evening talking to her—what she had been doing over the past year, what she liked, music, art, sport. At the end of the evening he commented that they certainly had a number of shared interests. She returned to London late on Sunday afternoon still dazzled from her royal encounter, and waited anxiously for him to make the next move.

On the following Friday, in rather a last-minute gesture, he invited her to the Royal Albert Hall, apologizing for the lateness of the invitation but he had only just realized, he said, that they would be playing Verdi's *Requiem*, and that he recalled her saying it was one of her favourite pieces. He added that he had already spoken to Lady Fermoy, who had kindly agreed to accompany them.

She had only a short time to dress. Her flatmate Carolyn came in at about six o'clock. "Quick, quick, I've got to meet Charles in twenty minutes," Diana cried, as Carolyn helped her wash and dry her hair. A car arrived from the Palace to drive Diana and Lady Fermoy to the Albert Hall, where Charles met them in a private room, a few steps from the royal box, where drinks and hors d'oeuvres were laid out.

She regarded their evening at the concert as a rather important and indicative sign of his interest in her, but an anxious fortnight passed before Charles called again. This time he asked her to join him the next weekend at Cowes on the *Britannia*: a jolly group of people were going too and she might enjoy it. His cousin Lady Sarah Armstrong-Jones, daughter of Princess Margaret and Lord Snowdon, whom he understood Diana knew, would be among them. Diana had always liked Sarah, but it was Charles she most wanted to see. She accepted with enthusiasm.

Boarding the *Britannia* was an awesome experience for Diana: she had never seen anything to equal its seafaring luxury. The topmost deck was where the royal suite was situated. Directly below was the veranda deck and the elegant state apartments designed by Sir Hugh Casson. Diana's suite on this deck, twice the size of her London apartment, had a fireplace in the living room, magnificent French rugs and large, colourful chintz sofas. The antique furniture of highly polished mahogany caught the light of the crystal wall sconces. The twin bedroom had a super-luxurious *en suite* bathroom.

Over the weekend on which Diana was a guest, there were eighteen passengers and 277 crewmen, all of whom wore rubber-soled shoes and communicated to each other with hand signals so that their presence would not be intrusive. There was a swimmingpool, two tennis courts, five smaller boats for excursions and a garage for a Land-Rover and a Rolls-Royce, whichever might be needed when *Britannia* was in dock and her passengers required land transport. There was a bar by the pool and a sumptuous outdoor luncheon buffet on sunny days for those guests who wished to remain on deck. Dinner was a more formal affair in the private dining room (there was also a state dining room) which gleamed with polished silver and the gold of the royal crest emblazoned on the wall facing the entrance doorway. Diana later said she felt intimidated by being younger—except for Sarah Armstrong-Jones—than the other guests. Also she was not a member of Charles's inner circle or his family and she did not know who the others were talking about, or what was behind a particularly snide remark. Neither could she reconcile their ignoring her when Charles was not around with their attentiveness when he was. "Someone," she said later, "must have talked."

However, having recognized that the Prince of Wales was interested in her, Diana determined to make him fall in love with her. The other guests watched as she sunned herself seductively on deck, stretching her long legs and arching her torso invitingly as Charles glanced in her direction. Then she showed off her mastery of diving and swimming at a time when all eyes, including his, would be on her performance. Most of all she was sympathetic, a good listener when he was talking, laughing at his jokes, answering him with her natural wit. There was even something intimate in the way she addressed him as "sir," as everyone had to. ("Even his wife?" she had asked someone years before. "Yes, even his wife." "I do hope she says "Sir-darling," she had giggled in response.)

There is no doubt that Charles was intrigued by this lithe girl and beginning to feel that Camilla and Kanga had been both sensitive and astute in their advice. Still, he was unsure if he should press on with a young woman who was unquestionably a virgin, and whose family were trusted courtiers. As one of his adored grandmother's closest friends, Lady Fermoy's feelings especially had to be considered. Sarah had broken off their relationship, and that had been one thing, but if he were to hurt Diana he would be held accountable.

To Diana's confusion and disappointment, Charles's interest seemed to cool after Cowes. However, Lady Fermoy was staying with the Queen Mother at Birkhall, her home in Scotland. She suggested that perhaps it would be a nice idea to invite Diana to Balmoral at the same time as Prince Charles was to be there. The Queen Mother, who thought Diana "a jolly girl," agreed and in early September 1980, Diana arrived at Balmoral, where not only her grandmother but her sister Jane and her family were also ensconced, and where Charles had joined his family the previous day. Diana stayed in a cottage on the estate with Jane, Robert and Laura, while Lady Fermoy remained at Birkhall.

The Queen Mother liked to fish for trout and salmon on the River Dee during the day, and although Lady Fermoy was not an angler, she often accompanied her. In the evenings, everyone gathered at Balmoral for cocktails, dinner and whatever other entertainment had been planned. The great house, set in forty thousand acres, had seen remarkably few changes since Prince Albert had bought and rebuilt it in 1848. The white-granite, castellated mansion, designed in the Scottish baronial style, stands on the south bank of the Dee, backed by the mountains and high valleys of Lochnagar. A solid stone bridge leads directly to the castle gates. Outside, the glow of the facade's glittering white stone and the lush green of the background give the castle a brightness, but inside it is formidably dark and dismal, reflecting Prince Albert's heavy Germanic tastes. Although the Queen had now occupied the castle for over twenty-five years, there remained "a masculine odour in the corridors, a smell of wood fire, stags" heads (many shot by preceding monarchs), rugs and leather."

Diana confessed later that on her first visit, "I was terrified. I was frightened because I had never been to Balmoral and I wanted to get it right."

She was fearful that Charles would pay little attention to her, that perhaps he wasn't as drawn to her as she had supposed. She relaxed almost immediately when he telephoned her a few minutes after her arrival and asked if she would like to go for a walk. "Yes, please!" she replied. And from that point she remained as available as she could. She sat on the bank of the river as he fished and watched him adoringly, for she had fallen in love.

She had not been at Balmoral for more than forty-eight hours when a trio of press photographers using binoculars and long-range lenses spotted her and Charles across the river where they were having a picnic. The moment they became aware of the intruders, Diana jumped to her feet and hid behind the centuries-old trunk of a nearby tree.

That week was a teenage girl's fantasy come true. There were barbecues and Scottish dancing in the gardens. Dress for dinner, as it had been for decades, was kilt, jacket and jabot for the Scottish gentlemen and dinner jackets for the others, with the women in appropriate dress. "Grouse, slightly high, but delicious, was on the menu most evenings . . . and a dozen of the Queen's pipers would march round the dining table to the moving and deafening wail of Scottish airs."

The Queen seemed relaxed. As reported by one courtier, there was one moment when Prince Philip and Charles had a sharp exchange but the Queen turned a hard, cold eye on her son, who immediately walked away.

Besides the Queen, Prince Philip, the Queen Mother and Prince Charles, most of the Royal Family were present at some time during Diana's stay. Princess Margaret was in especially good form and after dinner one evening went to the piano to accompany herself in a couple of her favourite Noel Coward songs. Prince Edward and Prince Andrew arrived at the weekend, bringing high spirits with them. And there were members of Charles's usual coterie—the Parker Bowleses most prominent among them. Diana still felt an outsider but she remained smiling, cheeks flushed with excitement—and always just a few paces behind Charles.

It was clear to all present that Diana adored Charles. Whether her feelings were reciprocated was not yet apparent. He did pay her great attention, though, and seemed to enjoy her company.

Just three months earlier, while Andrew Parker Bowles had been in Rhodesia as aide-de-camp to the last governor, Lord Soames, Charles had taken Camilla to the fashionable Annabel's, and the two had been seen kissing passionately on the dance-floor. A few weeks later, shortly after Parker Bowles's return, Camilla accompanied Charles to Rhodesia as his official escort where he was to represent the Queen at the ceremonies marking the country's independence as Zimbabwe. The Foreign Office was further appalled when he took Camilla to one of the ceremonies. "The hauling down of the British flag was a humiliating enough circumstance without everyone knowing the Royal Family's envoy had brought his popsy along with him," a Foreign Office employee complained. While Camilla was with Charles, Parker Bowles was at Bolehyde, entertaining Charlotte, the daughter of Lord Soames . . .

On the morning that Diana was to leave Balmoral, Camilla telephoned her and asked her to come to Bolehyde the following weekend. Diana, with no knowledge of Charles's torrid feelings for Camilla, or of Camilla's motive, was flattered. Camilla's invitation intimated to her that she was now being looked upon seriously as the woman Charles might marry and, therefore, his friends wished to know her better. She was happy to accept, never dreaming that Camilla's motives were far more disingenuous.

DIANA STOOD ON the threshold of a new life, a new world and she had no intention of letting the rich, fresh earth give way beneath her feet. There was no one upon whom she could rely to give her the advice she needed. She had never wanted anything more in her life than she now wanted Charles, but not for a fling, or an affair: it had to be marriage. However much she had criticized Raine, Diana had been a first-hand observer of her deliberate, successful campaign to get Johnnie to propose. She may not have liked Raine, but she admired her strength of purpose, her ability to get what she wanted and, amazingly, remain feminine and seductive.

The one flaw in Raine's crusade was the fairly public knowledge that beneath her soft, womanly curves and doting manner she was made of tempered steel guaranteed to survive, and could twist to her advantage anything that stood in the path of her achieving her goal. Diana, on the other hand, had a most deceptive persona. People thought of her as guileless, vulnerable, naïve. That was what Camilla and Kanga supposed and Charles believed. What Charles and his camp-followers did not see was the quiet desperation that had always undermined Diana's life, the gnawing need for love and attention, and the determined belief that she would succeed where Sarah had failed and marry Charles. That was the sort of thing that happened in the book of fairytales given to her so long ago by Grandmother Spencer: always the unfortunate young woman, the one least likely to appear to others as a princess, would win the prince's hand in marriage, and always she was a young woman with secret charms and innate goodness that the prince recognized where others did not. Diana saw herself in that light and created herself in that image.

The best fiction is often how we interpret our own lives and what we see as our common due. It is created usually as a means of avoiding reality which, if seriously considered, might negate our ability to strive for what might seem the impossible. Diana believed herself to be less bright than Jane, less talented than Sarah, less important than Charlie. In the mirror she saw a too-tall, somewhat plump girl, whose parents expected little of her in personal achievement. In any case, she was a Spencer: that was her greatest asset; she also had good breeding, impeccable manners, and although she was not really beautiful, she was certainly attractive when "done up." All those qualities would be an advantage in her making a good match. Prince Andrew had been the height of Lady Fermoy's ambitions for Diana, but he had matured too wild and raunchy to be a suitable husband for her less adventurous, youngest Spencer granddaughter.

Diana knew nothing of life outside the archaic society into which she was born. Her schooldays had been spent with others from that same world. When she worked as a cleaner it was for Sarah and her friends. She went to a cooking school that taught débutantes with nothing else to do, tended the children of family friends in grand houses and was never treated as hired help.

She felt a deep loneliness and a sense of disconnection so extreme it verged on dread. She yearned for warmth, a sense of belonging, a feeling that she was *someone*. She believed these needs would be satisfied only in the protective arms of the right man. That man, she thought, was the Prince of Wales. What had begun as a fiction of the mind now became an endeavour of will.

Lady Fermoy, although confused at Charles's sudden interest in her granddaughter ("She does seem rather young and unaccomplished to warrant the Prince of Wales's attention," she told a confidante), wasted little time in promoting her granddaughter's cause. Lady Fermoy was wise in the ways of the court: she had had the Queen Mother's confidence for years; she knew Camilla was Charles's mistress but kept her silence lest Diana was frightened off.

Charles had a standing arrangement to see his grand-mother, usually for tea, once a week. He adored the Queen Mother and particularly liked hearing her stories of past times. She was a fount of family history—not so much what had been recorded but what she had actually witnessed. She recalled with bitterness all the problems that had ensued over Edward VIII's affair with Mrs. Simpson and urged Charles to find an acceptable wife quickly.

"The Queen Mother's fear," one courtier says, "was that Camilla might divorce Parker Bowles and Charles decide to marry her, which would have been a ghastly replay of the Edward-Wallis débâcle, and could have ended with Andrew as heir to the throne. She had little confidence in Andrew's ability at this time or of the public's acceptance of a situation so similar to that in the past."

In a discussion with the Queen Mother about Charles and his over-long bachelor status, Lady Fermoy gracefully suggested what a fine young woman Diana was—trustworthy, pure, no gossip, adored children and was so pleasant. She added what a lovely couple they made and how in harmony they seemed. The Queen Mother listened, and the next time she saw Charles she repeated what she had heard about Diana. Charles, who greatly respected his grand-mother, was now almost convinced that Camilla and Kanga had been right, but was still far from ready for commitment. He certainly found Diana attractive, but he was not in love with her.

Duty had been drummed into Charles since infancy, and his duty now was to get married and produce an heir. Duty meant that should Camilla divorce Parker Bowles, Charles still could not marry her. He was the Prince of Wales and materially had almost anything he could wish for, but he did not have freedom of choice. That was the price he had to pay for his status, and he had come to a point in his life when he was willing to compromise. If not Camilla, than why not the jolly, bouncy Diana, untouched and unsophisticated? She was a Spencer and her family had been trusted courtiers for centuries. It was also obvious to him that Diana was in love with him.

Still, Charles was not sure. "He was afraid he would be unable to face a future without Camilla," a courtier confided. "Before he could even consider proposing marriage to Diana, he had to be sure that Camilla would not desert him."

What Charles had missed was Diana's uncompromising romanticism and her strength of character. She possessed a strong, inner spirit, an "I'll show you!" attitude born of the knowledge that she had been unwanted as a baby, that she had failed at almost everything she had attempted so far, that no one gave her credit for having a brain. She kept it all so well hidden beneath her "bouncy" exterior that Camilla, Kanga and Charles were misled.

However, at a luncheon around this time, Barbara Cartland declared to a table partner, "Diana is *not* shy. She tends to look down and bend over, but she does that because she's so tall. It's nothing to do with shyness. She has a distinct personality, and is not a person, whether she speaks or not, who can be ignored."

Certainly the press did not ignore Diana. The photos of her and Charles taken by the Dee at Balmoral appeared in the papers before her return to London, and when she arrived back at her flat her entrance was blocked by a corps of newsmen and photographers. They stuck cameras in her face and asked bold questions: "Are you in love with the Prince? Is the Prince in love with you?"

She kept her eyes down and said nothing.

Charles telephoned her and they made plans for her to come to Highgrove that weekend. He suggested that to foil the press she should drive herself to Camilla's home from which someone would bring her the rest of the way. Then he spoke of how terrible the past week had been for Camilla, three or four newsmen outside her door, expecting her to have some news they could wangle from her. Ghastly. Poor Camilla.

That should have alerted Diana to trouble ahead. Why

poor Camilla? She had far more reporters at her door, she was the one who was being followed, had cameras and microphones thrust in her face, and her car blocked. Her telephone rang incessantly and had to be answered by one of her flatmates: "No comment. Sorry." Yet Diana remained uncomplaining to Charles, for fear of rocking the boat.

Charles's valet, Stephen Barry, said later that Diana went after Charles with "single-minded determination. In all my years, I've never seen anyone as tricky or as determined as she was." Ironically, in this she was placing herself exactly where Charles, Camilla and Kanga wanted her. Even her demeanour with the press was spot on. She was well mannered, vulnerable and winning their sympathy at the same time as she derided their obtrusive behaviour. And she was drawing public interest and admiration.

Never had one of Prince Charles's romances garnered quite as much press attention. The public took to Diana instantly and newspaper sales soared. Unlike the sophisticated social butterflies and publicity-loving actresses Charles had previously romanced, Diana's public image was that of an ingenuous teenager, a nursery teacher, a working girl. She was someone with whom her peers, their mothers, fathers and grandparents could identify.

Diana was being driven by instinct as well as intellect. Truman Capote once wrote, "The brain may take advice, but not the heart, and love having no geography knows no boundaries." And there was no doubt that Diana was in love and that as this was the first time, she was in uncharted country.

The romance progressed through secret meetings. Once, when Diana and Charles were going to spend the weekend at the Mountbatten estate, Broadlands, she tied sheets together in her flat and, holding her suitcase, slid down the makeshift rope from a rear window to the deserted alley, walked a block, hailed a taxi then telephoned one of her flatmates to bring her car to her, avoiding the press men. "I was constantly polite, constantly civil. I was never rude. I never shouted," Diana recalled. "I cried like a baby to the four walls. I just couldn't cope with it. I cried because I got no support from Charles and no support from the Palace press office. They just said, 'You're on your own,' so I thought, Fine."

At Bolehyde Camilla was having second thoughts. She no longer believed that Diana was as naïve as she had at first assumed. She could see too that Charles was attracted to Diana, that he was looking at her with covetous glances, that a familiarity had formed between them. Camilla was anxious now that she and Kanga had miscalculated. She attempted to dissuade Diana from encouraging Charles to propose. Diana began to wonder why and how Camilla seemed to know so much about Charles and herself.

In fact, Charles spoke on the phone to Camilla several times a day. There was little she did not know—what was said in his conversations with Diana, how much Diana was in love with him, how zealously she was defending her honour, what she wore, and on and on. Armed with this inside information, Camilla implied to Diana that she was making a fool of herself, that her schoolgirl gush was embarrassing Charles. Camilla had sensed that the game she had started was now outside her court and she was fighting to bring it back in.

Having championed Diana to Charles in the beginning, Camilla was unable to reverse her position without losing credibility. She tried another tactic. She became dismissive of Diana and arranged more meetings for herself with Charles. But he was now intrigued by Diana's youthful ardour and instead chose to spend weekends with Diana at Broadlands.

Broadlands is a magnificent Elizabethan manor with exquisite Robert Adams interiors. The Queen and the Duke of Edinburgh had spent their honeymoon there so the place had a romantic history. At that time the press and overzealous well-wishers had hidden in trees and long grass to catch a glimpse of the royal couple. This time Diana and Charles had outwitted the press, who thought they were at Balmoral. They walked in Broadlands' lush gardens, and exchanged confidences before a glowing fire in the study.

Diana felt great compassion for Charles. They talked of their families, their love of nature, their unhappiness at school. Diana sensed that Charles needed mothering, but kept her distance. They sat up late talking—nothing intellectually challenging, Diana said later, and added that Charles had "a besotted look in his eyes." If it was lust, Diana did not recognize it: she wanted to believe that what she saw was love.

They had separate bedroom suites and Charles's staff, including his valet, Stephen Barry—an ally of Camilla and suspicious of "the Virgin child," as he called Diana—were also present. Diana returned to Coleherne Court in a romantic fervour, certain that Charles would soon propose.

Lady Fermoy, aware of Camilla's significance in Charles's life, began to have second thoughts about Diana's romance with the Prince of Wales. "You must understand that their [the Royal Family] . . . lifestyle is very different. I don't think it will suit you," she warned. But it was too late for such advice.

Diana spent Christmas at Althorp while Charles was at Sandringham. Raine was all over her, her stepdaughter's past coolness forgotten. She was free with her advice and took completely the opposite stance to Lady Fermoy. She and Barbara Cartland comforted and cheered Diana on. Raine claimed she wanted to be "a refuge" for her during this time of "momentous" decision. However, the decision was not Diana's to make. She and the Spencers waited anxiously for Charles to take the next step.

Diana continued her work at Young England, but the press dogged her every step. It was gruelling, terrifying, and sometimes she simply broke down and cried. Several reporters took pity on her and began to shield her from the unrelenting news-greed of the others. She joked with these few favourites, and in return gave them exclusive shots.

January was bleak. The skies were slate grey, a penetrating damp pervaded the city and Prince Charles had escaped to Klosters with a group of his friends, including the

Parker Bowleses, for a skiing holiday. Diana had not been invited to join them—too dangerous an announcement of intention, which Charles was not yet ready to make. Before leaving for Switzerland and the home of Charles and Patty Palmer-Tomkinson, where he would be staying, Charles had spoken with his mother about Diana and his indecision about the future of their relationship. The holiday was to give him time to consider his options.

By law Charles had to have the Queen's permission to marry, in accordance with the Royal Marriage Act of 1772, as must all close members of the Royal Family. Where Diana was concerned the Queen had been in a quandary. She was worried about Diana's age, the instability of her childhood, her lack of common interests with Charles. Hunting and polo were an integral part of Charles's life but Diana was terrified of horses. Charles was a probing, intelligent, highly educated man. Diana's education had been limited. Could she be expected to meet and talk with world figures as a Princess of Wales must? It did not seem that the pair would be compatible for long. And there was Camilla. The Queen believed that Charles could not give up that relationship and that Diana did not have the forbearance to put up with it. Perhaps most important, the Queen was a caring mother: she wanted her son to be happy and she did not believe that he was in love with Diana. She was convinced that he was being pressured into making a compromise that he would ultimately regret.

There were a number of reasons why she finally agreed that the marriage could take place. First, the news coverage the romance was attracting meant that Charles could not delay his decision much longer. To do so "would cause everlasting damage to Diana Spencer's reputation, which in any case was in danger of being compromised" by their "secret meetings" which the press reported.* Prince Philip

---

*James Whitaker of the *Daily Mirror* had reported that he had seen Diana enter a carriage of the royal train, where Charles was waiting for her, and had spent the night. The story was not verified by any

told his son that he must either become engaged to Diana or end the relationship. Charles viewed his father's words as an ultimatum and it was this decision that he was struggling with in Klosters.

The Queen also gave Charles strong reasons why he *should* propose to Diana. If he ended this relationship, with a young woman who had won public affection, the country might feel that he, an older, more experienced man, had been exploiting an innocent teenage girl—they would think of their sisters, their daughters, their granddaughters. There was little doubt that the public wanted the Prince of Wales to get married—and soon—or that Diana was a popular choice and would make a beautiful bride.

The country had also endured an extended period of inflation, joblessness, strikes, and severe problems in the National Health Service. The Queen could not help but recall how her own wedding in 1947 had brought the nation such great joy after so many years of war and sacrifice. Also, not to be forgotten was the boon to the economy that it had generated.

On Monday 2 February Charles rang Diana from Klosters. His voice was warm and confiding. "I've got something to ask you," he said. "Not now, when I return." He was to join HMS *Invincible*, the Royal Navy's latest aircraft carrier, for manoeuvres on Thursday, 5 February, and would meet her on Friday the sixth at Windsor.

Diana spent the rest of the week in a state of agitation. Was he going to propose? He must be. Then shards of doubt would stab at her. He might want to tell her he had decided they were wrong for each other, a kiss on the cheek and goodbye and that would be it. She went about her usual schedule at Young England, was silent in the face of queries from newshounds, and spent her evenings "in with the girls."

---

other witnesses and there was speculation that the "woman on the train" might have been Camilla Parker Bowles, but this was at a time when Camilla's name was not linked in the media with Charles's.

On Friday morning she had her hair done at Headlines, in South Kensington, where Kevin Shanley had been her stylist for the last three years. Later, on that winter afternoon, her hair shiny and neat, her legs freshly waxed, she barrelled her way through the press corps and drove out to Windsor. She arrived around five o'clock, and was immediately rushed inside by security guards.

Charles came to greet her, took her hand and ordered tea. Then he led her on a short tour of the family's private rooms in the castle. When they entered the nursery she shivered slightly and he put his arm about her. Then he proposed. Diana had been waiting so anxiously to hear this, but the question did not seem real. She laughed nervously, then accepted him. Charles reminded her that marriage to him meant that she would one day be queen, and she said she understood the responsibility involved.

He kissed her lightly then said, "I must call Mummy," and was gone.

Diana sat in shock for a long while. The Prince of Wales had proposed and she had accepted. It dawned on her then that Charles had never said he loved her. None the less she believed that he had just been too overcome to say the words.

She returned to her flat that night convinced ("in my immaturity") that Charles was in love with her. She went into her room, sat down on her bed and called in her three flatmates.

"Guess what?" she said, a mischievous look in her eye.

"He asked you!" yelled the three in unison. "What did you say?"

"Yes, please."

The girls screamed with delight. It was one a.m. The press had abandoned their posts and gone home for the night. The girls piled into Diana's car and circled Hyde Park several times. They talked, and talked, and *talked*. Diana told them that Charles wanted to wait three or four weeks before publicly announcing their engagement, to give her time to think about it and feel sure she had made the right decision. As soon as it was made public, she would have to move into rooms at either Clarence House or Buckingham Palace so that she would be under close security guard. Everyone cried and hugged each other. It meant the end of life as they knew it at Coleherne Court, but Diana was to be Princess of Wales. Once back at the flat they toasted Diana in Coca-Cola—she had never liked alcohol.

The next morning Diana telephoned her father. He told her that Charles had already rung up. "Can I marry your daughter? I have asked her," he quoted the Prince, "and very surprisingly she has said yes." Earl Spencer replied, "Well done," and told him he was delighted for the two of them. That had been only moments before her call. "Diana, you must marry the man you love," he said. "That's what I'm doing," she replied. Then she telephoned her mother, who was also thrilled and suggested that as it would be weeks before an official announcement was made, perhaps she would join Peter and herself in Australia where she could enjoy the sun and rest.

Two days later, she was on her way Down Under for three weeks. The English press was puzzled. Was this the end of Diana's romance with Charles?

When Diana reached the Shand Kydds' remote farmhouse she also became puzzled. Charles did not telephone her and when she rang him he was out and never returned her call. His neglect disturbed her, she was unable to eat and lost over ten pounds.

She returned to London on Sunday, 22 February, tanned and slim, her mother's wedding list in hand. Her father and Raine met her at the airport. Security police led them through a private exit to where their car was waiting. Her father wanted her to go back to Althorp with them, but Diana said she had left a message for Charles that she would be at Coleherne Court.

Shortly after she got home a member of Charles's staff arrived with a bouquet—but no personal note. Later that day, the Prince's private secretary, the Hon. Edward Adeane, telephoned to tell Diana that she would be collected in the morning and taken to Clarence House where she would stay as a guest of the Queen Mother, and that the following day, Tuesday, 24 February, an official announcement of her engagement to the Prince of Wales would be made. Less than an hour after Adeane's call, Chief Inspector Paul Officer was stationed at the flat. "I just want you to know," he told Diana, "that this is your last night of freedom ever for the rest of your life, so make the most of it."

Clarence House had been the first residence of Princess Elizabeth and the Duke of Edinburgh and had been renovated at that time. When George VI died, and his daughter succeeded him, she moved into Buckingham Palace while the Queen Mother went to Clarence House.

When Diana arrived with her one suitcase, packed—she was sure—with all the wrong things, there was only a curt member of the Queen Mother's staff to greet her. "It was like arriving at a strange hotel," she said. She was shown to her suite, where she found a large bouquet from Charles with a note to say that he would see her that evening. On her pillow lay an envelope. It was a letter from Camilla, dated two days earlier: "Such exciting news about the engagement. Let's do have lunch when the Prince of Wales goes to Australia and New Zealand. He's going to be away three weeks. I'd love to see the ring. Love, Camilla."

Diana was perplexed. Charles had not mentioned an impending trip, and since her engagement ring was as yet only a drawing of a sapphire with eighteen diamonds encircling it, Camilla's wish to see it seemed premature. And how had Camilla known two days ago that she was going to be at Clarence House when Diana herself had not yet been informed of it? Camilla's letter unsettled her.

Also she was at a loss to know what to do with herself: no one had offered a tour of the house so she remained in her room while an elderly maid helped her unpack. Finally, Lady Fermoy telephoned to congratulate her and to say that she would be expected in the Queen Mother's sitting room for tea and that she would join her there. Someone would come to her rooms to escort her. "Wear something simple," she was informed, "and don't forget to curtsy."

Lady Fermoy's presence was meant to ease the tension at tea, but her grandmother was unusually restrained. Diana had always though of the Queen Mother as friendly, but today she felt as if she were undergoing a clinical inspection. Happily, Charles soon joined them. She curtsied. "Good to see you, sir." He grinned and she relaxed. He kissed his grandmother's cheek, then Diana's lightly.

When they had finished tea, a man from Garrard's, the Crown jewellers, joined them. He carried a case and had come on the pretext that it was soon going to be Prince Andrew's twenty-first birthday. The case supposedly held signet rings so that the Queen Mother could choose one as a gift for her grandson. The case actually contained nine or ten huge sapphires for Diana to select the one she wanted as the central stone for her engagement ring. She chose the largest and bluest. (Its rumoured price was £28,000.)

None of this was how Diana had pictured her engagement and, like Alice in Wonderland—not an unlikely comparison, for she felt suddenly very small and very frightened—things grew *curiouser and curiouser*.

CHARLES HAD LEFT early. Diana was alone once again in her unfamiliar bedroom, with no television, record player or radio. The telephone sat silently by her bed. She yearned to call the girls at Coleherne Court, but didn't like to. In parting, Charles had said she must get some rest so that she would be prepared for the next day when the announcement would be made. She did not want him to leave when he did, but was too intimidated by their surroundings to speak out.

Diana felt, she later said, as if she were being "swept into a concealed abyss." Her role was still unclear, although Adeane had warned her not to speak to the press unless it was under his aegis. She and Charles would make their first public appearance together before the cameras and she would wear the bright blue suit with the Eton jacket and the blue and white print blouse that she had purchased at Harrods the previous day. Blue had always suited her. She was attuned to colours; different ones created different moods for her. Blue was a romantic, peaceful colour in all its shades, for it reminded her of the sea and the sheltering sky.

The bed was turned down, a pair of pyjamas draped across it. On the bedside table was the novel she had been reading before leaving the flat and had taken with her. She fell asleep with the lamp on. When she awoke it was morning, the light was out and the curtains had been drawn back. It was nine a.m. and the day did not look promising. There was a tea tray on the bureau and the elderly maid was beside her bed with several of the morning papers. There was also a crested envelope.

The letter was from Adeane informing her that an announcement by the Queen and Prince Philip of her en-

gagement to His Royal Highness would be made by Lord
Maclean, the Lord Chamberlain, at exactly eleven o'clock
that morning. A news release had also been prepared and
would be delivered to television, radio and press at the pre-
cise same time. However, *The Times* had somehow managed to scoop the Palace. The maid had placed it on top of
the papers. The front-page headline was the engagement
news and there were photographs of Charles and herself.

A short schedule was enclosed in Adeane's letter with
the advice that Young England would be notified as soon
as the announcement was made that she would not be returning to resume her duties. A car would take her from
Clarence House to Buckingham Palace at eleven fifteen
where she would meet with His Royal Highness for forty-
five minutes. At twelve, they would attend a press conference where she would be expected to answer some
questions. She would be advised about this beforehand.

The sun broke through the clouds just before she left for
Buckingham Palace. She was escorted there by Paul Officer
who, she learned, was to be her personal bodyguard. He
was an experienced policeman, well educated and rather
philosophical.

"Do you have a gun?" she asked him.

"Yes, ma'am."

"Am I in danger?"

"I hope not. But it's best not to second-guess those
things," he replied.

Charles was less reserved than he had been the previous
night. He slipped his arm around her waist, told her she
looked lovely, that all she had to do was be herself during
the interview, but not to venture much more than a simple
answer to questions presented directly to her. They were
joined in his office by Adeane and Charles's secretarial assistants—Jenny Allen, Claire Potts, Pauline Pears, Julia
"Lulu" Malcolm, Sonia Palmer and Philippa Tingey. Pink
champagne was brought out to toast the newly engaged
couple as Charles slipped on Diana's engagement ring, the
sapphire she had selected now encircled by diamonds. It

was the first piece of jewellery he had given her and she kept looking at it with amazement.

The press conference was held on the garden steps of Buckingham Palace. Diana smiled winningly for the camera, but Charles was stiffer.

"Are you in love?" the BBC interviewer asked.

"Of course!" Diana asserted.

"Yes. Whatever love is," Charles modified.

If Diana was taken aback by Charles's qualified answer, she managed to hide it. As the week progressed she had to hide an increasing sense of fear, puzzlement and insecurity. To add to this, she had been horrified when she saw herself on the BBC interview. She looked chubby, her blue suit was all wrong and she had been photographed at unattractive angles that made her look shorter than she was, to accentuate Charles's height.

Less than a fortnight after the announcement of their engagement, Charles departed on what he later termed a "much regretted" expedition, for it had not been the right time to leave Diana to face the press alone. The night before he left Diana was in his study with him when his private telephone rang.

It was Camilla, and Diana was unnerved by Charles's long, muffled conversation with her. His conspiratorial tone alarmed her: something was going on, but she was not sure what it was and was afraid to confront him.

She sat quietly, her eyes avoiding his, but the incident caused her great anguish.

The next day, wearing a bright red coat (red for courage), Diana went to see Charles off and could not control her sobs. The press thought she couldn't bear to be parted from him but it had more to do with the intimacy with which he had spoken to Camilla the previous night. Diana felt now that she was losing Charles before they could reach the altar.

This was not so. Charles was committed to their future together. But something alarming had occurred. For several years both Camilla and Kanga had been his mistresses, but his relationship with Camilla, whom he now realized was his true love, had intensified since his proposal to Diana— who could not help but sense a change in Charles. He still believed, though, that he would be able to have the best of both words with Camilla as his mistress and a compliant Diana as his wife.

Diana was not yet certain that Charles and Camilla were lovers, just that Camilla was exerting all her seductive powers over him to make it happen. This, Diana tried to convince herself, was something she would put a stop to. It seemed to her that she held the high cards in playing out her hand. Camilla was much older, married, a mother, and not nearly as attractive as herself. She could not accept that Camilla held the trump card: her sexual hold on Charles.

While Charles was away, Diana worked hard to overcome her anxieties. She kept herself busy with the wedding plans. However, as time passed and Charles rarely telephoned, she conveyed her feelings to one of her former flatmates, who was alarmed at how thin Diana had grown since the announcement of her engagement.

"She confirmed to me that she was fighting bulimia," her friend says. "I told her she had to be more frank with Charles, tell him his lack of attention disturbed her. I knew nothing about Camilla and she did not mention that there was another woman in his life. I just thought he must be a terribly cold person, and as I knew how needy Diana was, I did not come away with a good feeling about their future together."

In the final days of his tour, Charles flew to Venezuela to discuss the establishment of a new United World College. His last stop was Williamsburg, Virginia where he gave a speech at William and Mary College, referring in it to the marriage of his forebears, William and Mary. The latter, when told she was to marry this man twelve years her senior, collapsed into tears. "There is also a twelve-year gap between myself and my fiancee, but there, ladies and gentlemen," he emphasized, "the similarity comes to an abrupt halt."

His official biographer, Jonathan Dimbleby, writes of Charles's state of mind at the time of the Australia-United States tour, "If his betrothal to Diana Spencer was hardly the love match for which his friends had hoped, that she had perhaps wanted and which the nation certainly assumed, he was determined that their marriage should succeed."

Shortly before Charles's departure Diana had been moved from Clarence House to rooms in Buckingham Palace. They looked much like a grand suite in one of the old hotels, like Claridges or the Ritz, except for the family portraits that graced the walls. If Diana had thought that proximity would bring her closer to the Queen, or that the Palace would now help her adjust to her new situation, she was wrong. She was, as she later said, "just pushed into the fire," left much to her own devices and basically alone, except for Paul Officer and members of Charles's staff who answered the hundreds of daily letters she received.

London was already in a state of royal wedding fever. Diana received up to thirty requests a day from reporters who wanted to interview her. Whenever she left the Palace, a troop of photographers and journalists thrust microphones and cameras at her. She yearned for the comfort and privacy of Coleherne Court, and for the friends with whom she felt safe and in whom she could confide. She involved herself in the design of her wedding gown, and chose her trousseau, which she found depressing because she felt "as fat as butter." Staff at the Palace noted that she was not eating and David and Elizabeth Emanuel, who were designing her dress, had to keep taking it in as her weight fell.

Seamstress Nina Missetzes was present for all the fittings. "She was so sweet, so shy," Missetzes recalled. "When she first came to see me, she didn't want to take off her clothes so I could take her measurements. I told her if she didn't, the dress would be too big, so she did what I asked. As I was pinning the pattern to her, I could tell it was very new to her to be fitted." So was living in a palace

where everyone had their own suites, seldom met even in
the corridors, and had to make appointments to see each
other. It took Diana a full five minutes to walk from her
suite to the gardens. And wherever she went Detective Officer accompanied her.

The Queen and Prince Philip did not invite her to tea,
nor did they include her in any intimate family dinners. She
saw them rarely, although the Queen asked after her, generally through a staff member, every few days. Her accommodation did not contain a kitchen. Food was brought up
from the kitchens through the maze of corridors and re-
heated on warming plates at mealtimes when she was in.

Carolyn Pride became alarmed when she saw her: Diana's waistline had narrowed by six inches in six weeks.
"She went to live at Buckingham Palace and then the tears
started," Carolyn recalled. "The little thing got so thin I
was worried about her. She wasn't happy, she was suddenly
plunged into all this pressure and it was a nightmare for
her."

Spring came suddenly and prematurely at the beginning
of March, and there was a fortnight of almost summer heat.
The trees came into leaf, and all London seemed a-quiver
with the preparations for the wedding, now scheduled for
29 July. Diana felt frightened, suddenly trapped.

She had decided to meet Camilla for lunch. This did not
prove easy to arrange, for the restaurant had to be made
secure. Finally, a small Italian restaurant in Sloane Street
was chosen. When Diana arrived Camilla was waiting for
her. At thirty-two, Camilla seemed older than her years, a
country matron, while Diana looked like the teenage deb-
utante she might have been.

After Camilla had examined Diana's engagement ring
and they had ordered lunch, she leaned across the table.
"You are not going to hunt, are you?" she asked.

Diana was startled. It seemed a strange question.

"You are not going to hunt when you go and live at
Highgrove, are you?" Camilla asked again.

"No," Diana answered.

Camilla sat back in her chair. "I just wanted to know," she said, suddenly at ease. Hunting was the sport Camilla shared with Charles, and she was making certain that they would still be able to meet without Diana's interference at the various hunts that took place in Gloucestershire.

When Charles returned from his tour Diana's fears dissipated. Fully informed by his staff of the nerves that had engulfed his fiancée once she was alone, he spent as much time as he could with her, and was gentle and forbearing. But his commitments left him less free time for her than either of them would have wanted. To his credit, he now saw how vulnerable she was and he became somewhat fatherly towards her, which seemed to calm her. He was, perhaps, more in love with her during this period than he ever had been or ever would be.

Lady Susan Hussey, a lady-in-waiting to the Queen and a trusted confidant of Charles, was recruited to help acquaint Diana with royal protocol. Oliver Everett, a career diplomat at the Foreign Office who had been assistant private secretary to the Prince of Wales from 1978 to 1980, sacrificed his own advancement in the Foreign Office to advise and instruct Diana further in the business of being royal. Charles forfeited some of his office space at the Palace so that Frances Shand Kydd could come in on three afternoons a week to help Diana with some of the wedding details and, with Anna Harvey of *Vogue*, her new wardrobe needs.

The bride's guest list was constantly redrawn, with some names added, others removed. There was a crisis over the inclusion of Barbara Cartland's: Frances found Raine's flamboyant mother "distressing," and in the end, Diana's step-grandmother was not invited, which left a new chill between Raine and Diana. "If Johnnie had spoken to Diana about this, I am sure she would have rescinded this snub to his wife's mother. But he was prone not to intervene in any of the wedding arrangements," a member of the family said.

The Palace was having its own problems with the wedding list, which had to be kept down to 1,500 guests (later it would extend to 2,500). There were some diplomatic situations regarding which heads of state must or could not be invited. There were the courtiers, some of whom would be greatly offended if they could not be accompanied by their husband or wife. And there were those who had served the Royal Family through the years, the Prince of Wales's staff and personal friends, Wales and Duchy of Cornwall representatives, and the limited number, but very important and a difficult choice, of ordinary men and women of the realm whose work had earned them the honour of attending the wedding.

The Queen would pay for most of it. Charles was responsible for the flowers and the music. The Spencers would pay for the wedding gown and Diana's wardrobe. The government covered various ceremonial expenses, which included fireworks on the night beforehand. There was a huge debate over whether they should be married at Westminster Abbey (the Queen's choice) or St. Paul's (Charles and Diana's). The last time a Prince of Wales was married in St. Paul's Cathedral had been in 1501 when Arthur, eldest son of Henry VII, married the fifteen-year-old Katharine of Aragon.

"I've always longed to have a musical wedding," the Prince of Wales told the BBC's Angela Rippon. "One of the reasons I particularly wanted to be married in St. Paul's is that . . . the whole acoustic is so spectacular with ten or eleven seconds after sound, after note."

The selection of the music was something that Diana could share with Charles, and she insisted on having one hymn special to her, "I Vow To Thee My Country." Sir David Willocks, director of the Royal College of Music, worked with them in choosing the rest of the music. Charles made one demand, that the music to which they would walk up the incredibly long aisle of St. Paul's should be something stirring and dramatic, "Because if you have something rather quiet you start hearing your ankles cricking." There would be three orchestras, the Bach choir and the great

Maori soprano Kiri Te Kanawa. Thinking of the emotional impact of all that glorious music in such a grand and historical cathedral, Charles added, "I shall, I think, spend half the time in tears." Diana had been advised to let Charles do most of the talking and so she was almost monosyllabic in her responses. Nowhere in the interview did Charles acknowledge her unusual musical knowledge. She appeared not to notice.

Diana was trying desperately hard to avoid any show of emotional feeling. Now that she was active she was in happier spirits and eager to please. She worked diligently every day with Lady Susan Hussey on the royal wave, how to enter and leave a room, to exit from a car, sit on a podium, smile sedately, look at people with steady regard—"the royal gaze." She also practised walking down the aisle of St. Paul's without stumbling on her train.

Oliver Everett taught her how to address heads of foreign states and suggested she study English royal history, on which he gave her daily tests. For the first time she learned her husband-to-be's full name—HRH Prince Charles Philip Arthur George Prince of Wales and Earl of Chester, Duke of Cornwall, Duke of Rothesay, Earl of Carrick and Baron of Renfrew, Lord of the Isles and Great Steward of Scotland—and she was made to write "Diana" over and over again to develop a stronger signature. To relieve the tension she asked if a former piano teacher, Lily Snipp and her ballet mistress, Wendy Vickers, from her West Heath days, could give her lessons at the Palace. "She lived for ballet," Miss Snipp explained, and these lessons became escape from the pressures of life at the Palace as a soon-to-be royal bride.

But Diana had a strong mind of her own, which showed in her insistence on having a say in her clothes. The Emanuels were working on her wedding gown and also designing the gown she was to wear at her first formal appearance with Prince Charles at Goldsmiths Hall for a traditional charity gala in aid of the Royal Opera House. Diana was determined to make a distinctive mark here as a mature, fashion-minded woman. Against the Emanuels' instincts she selected a black silk taffeta, strapless gown with a plunging *décolletage*. She had insisted that the gown be a surprise for Charles. When she appeared at his study door moments before they were to depart, he was furious. The Royal Family, he told her, may wear black only to a funeral, a lesson Lady Susan Hussey had overlooked. And they *never, ever* appeared in public with that amount of cleavage on display. He told her to change.

"I haven't another to wear," she protested, "so I either wear this gown or I don't go."

Charles had to back down.

When he stepped out of their limousine at Goldsmiths Hall ahead of Diana, he said to the waiting press, "Wait till you get an eyeful of this." There was a shocked silence as Diana was helped out of the car then stood erect, looking unbelievably glamorous and unexpectedly seductive. Perhaps not acceptably royal by Windsor rules but extraordinarily regal. At one point in the evening, Princess Grace of Monaco accompanied her to the ladies' room where Diana confided how horrified she was by her *faux pas*. "Don't worry," Monaco's movie-star princess replied, "it will get a lot worse."

It did.

As the pressures of the wedding mounted, Diana became increasingly edgy. Her twentieth birthday on 1 July was celebrated with a small party in Charles's apartment. He gave her a beautiful matched set of leather luggage ornamented with the fleur-de-lis and "Princess of Wales" in gold. The following day Camilla fell ill and Diana learned through one of Charles's staff that he had sent her flowers with a warm greeting, and that they always used the initials G, for Gladys, and F, for Fred, when they corresponded. Diana could not avoid the implications of that.

She confronted Charles and insisted that Camilla's name be taken off the invitation list to the ball the Queen was giving two nights before the wedding, the service at St. Paul's *and* the wedding reception. He refused. Camilla, he explained, was an old and close friend (he had not admitted that they had been lovers) and her husband was a loyal courtier and in charge of the wedding route to St. Paul's and back to the Palace. Charles was adamant that the Parker Bowleses attend everything. Diana left his study in tears. Jane, who was staying with her, tried to calm her down.

"I don't think I can go through with it," Diana cried.

"Well, bad luck, Duch," Jane replied. "Your face is already on the tea towels so you're too late to chicken out!"

The next day Lily Snipp wrote in her daily journal, "Lady Diana looking very tired . . . counting how many days of freedom are left to her. Rather sad. Masses of people outside of Palace . . . Lady Diana said, 'In twelve days I will no longer be me.' "

On 24 July, Diana was in the office she shared with Charles's finance officer, Michael Colbourne, when a package arrived from the royal jewellers addressed to HRH The Prince of Wales. Certain that it was a gift for her, she begged Colbourne to open it while she was there. Colbourne refused quite firmly. Diana picked it up and opened it herself.

Inside was a gold bracelet with a blue enamel disc and the letters F and G entwined. No sooner had she lifted it out of the box than Charles entered the room. There was a terrible scene; and Charles asked one of his female staff to see "Lady Diana to her rooms." He added something about pre-wedding stress. That afternoon she had her last session with Nina Missetzes. The gown had to be taken in another inch and the fitter recalled, "Lady Diana got very emotional and cried."

Diana was now feeling the full pressure of royal life. There was hardly a moment in the day that was not scheduled. "One minute you've got the King and Queen of Sweden coming to give you their wedding present of four brass candlesticks, the next minute you get the president of somewhere else," she explained. And every night there was a dinner party in honour of some visiting royal relative.

On Thursday afternoon, 23 July, Charles and Diana had

been at a Palace garden party for 3,500 disabled people and
their helpers. Diana came alive. These were people with
whom she fully empathized and were easy to talk to. The
clouds burst with a torrential summer shower shortly after
they arrived and the Queen and other members of the Royal
Family were guided to shelter. But Diana insisted that she
and Charles press on, noting that their guests did not have
any shelter other than an umbrella and that for them this
was one of the great moments of their lives. She shook
hands and joked with their guests: she commiserated with
a one-armed veteran on how difficult it must be to take a
bath, especially when the soap slipped. Her Palace guard
turned pale, but the old soldier was greatly moved. "You
understand," he said.

"Something should be invented to help you. I'll work
on that," she said, and smiled.

She was the undoubted star of the show. On the following morning she and Charles arrived separately at Tidworth
Garrison in Hampshire to visit the Cheshire Regiment, of
which the Prince was colonel-in-chief. While he went off
to look at machine-guns, Diana talked with Army wives
and their children. The next day she did much the same
with Navy families near Petersfield. At lunch she and
Charles attended the annual reunion of survivors of HMS
Kelly, the destroyer once commanded by Earl Mountbatten.

After lunch, they drove in Charles's open-top Aston
Martin to a polo match where he was to play for the Navy
against the Army. Thirty or forty photographers were present, some with telephoto lenses that "resembled naval guns
from Jutland," concentrating on taking photographs of her.
As they pressed closer, she leaped up from her seat and,
head down, walked quickly to the back of the stables.
Charles rushed to her and led her to his car, where they
were joined by Lady Penelope Romsey. Diana burst into
tears, and the two women were driven to Broadlands.

With the wedding arrangements, her full immersion into
public life and the continuing personal drama over Camilla,
it was no wonder that Diana was on edge. The Queen and

the Queen Mother were not unaware of problems between Charles and Diana, and the royal apartments at both Clarence House and Buckingham Palace were astir with concern that Diana might bolt. Equal care was taken to ensure that the media did not discover that anything was wrong. It was made plain to them that Lady Diana was suffering the pre-wedding nerves of most brides.

On the Sunday, three days before the wedding, Diana walked hand in hand with Charles to the paddock at Smith's Lawn, Windsor, where he was playing polo for England against Spain. She looked pale, but was on her best public behaviour. She gave a well-practised wave to the 20,000-strong crowd as they applauded her arrival in the Royal Pavilion, then turned to Charles to give him a good-luck peck on the cheek as he rode off to play.

That afternoon, at the private chapel in Windsor Castle, Princess Anne's baby was christened Zara Anne Elizabeth. Among her godparents were Camilla and Andrew Parker Bowles. There was some consternation that neither Diana nor Charles attended the christening, but it was explained that they could not fit it into their overcrowded schedule.

A few hours later the bridal couple arrived at St. Paul's Cathedral for the wedding rehearsal. Diana donned a mock veil of old net curtaining and practised her slow march up the aisle, which would not be easy due to the weight of the dress and its train and the fact that she would be taking the walk with her father who was still not too steady on his feet. When Charles arrived he appeared to be in a buoyant mood as he waved nonchalantly at the massive crowds who were waiting to see him. Then, he missed his footing and tripped on a step, to be grabbed and kept from falling by a bodyguard.

Inside, a television camera crew was setting the lights for the filming of the wedding. The glare was blinding, the heat stifling. Diana appeared edgy as Elizabeth Emanuel placed the mock veil over her head, and she started slowly down the aisle to the magnificent altar. She repeated this about six times, while cameramen showed her where their

cameras would be located, and clergy told her where she
must stand at the altar and when she must speak. She managed her part of the rehearsal, then retreated to a corner of
the cathedral where she collapsed in sobs. Sarah
Armstrong-Jones rushed to her side, followed by Charles,
and she calmed herself before leaving hand in hand with
him.

That night the Queen gave a dinner at Buckingham Palace for ninety guests, mostly members of the Royal Family
and foreign dignitaries. Afterwards there was a reception
and dance for 1,500 guests with music played by the Three
Degrees, Charles's favourite pop group. Diana was in high
spirits: Camilla and her husband were not there. She did
not know, of course, that Prince Philip had elicited a vow
from his son that he would not see Camilla for five years
after he and Diana were married and that he would be a
true husband to Diana. Charles had undertaken to do this
and had told Camilla. She had agreed to suspend their physical relationship, but did not see how they could avoid seeing each other as friends—or why they should.

Diana danced and danced. She wore a magnificent shell
pink ball gown, with an exquisite pearl and diamond neck-
lace, an engagement gift from the Queen. Princess Margaret
attached a balloon to her diamond tiara, "Prince Andrew
tied one to the tails of his dinner jacket." Charles Spencer,
just down from Eton, recalled bowing at a uniformed waiter
because "there were so many royal people there, I was in
automatic bowing mood. I bowed and he looked surprised.
Then he asked me if I wanted a drink."

"Everybody got terribly drunk [but not the Queen,
Charles or Diana, and certainly not First Lady Nancy Rea-
gan]," recalled a guest. "It was a blur, a glorious, happy
blur."

The next day Diana moved back to Clarence House
whence she would go to her wedding in the famous Glass
Coach. Charles sent her a package containing a gold ring
engraved with the Prince of Wales feathers and a note that
read: "I'm so proud of you and when you come up I'll be

there at the altar for you tomorrow. Just look 'em in the eye and knock 'em dead."

Jane was to spend the night with her at Clarence House. Supper was served to them on trays in Diana's sitting room. Diana stuffed herself, then forced herself to vomit. Jane helped her through it, but viewed the incident lightly. It was just Diana being Diana.

there at the altar for you tomorrow. And look 'em in the
eye and kneel," she said. "..."

[...] said the night [...] it [...] more [...]
[...] opened to [...] by [...] it [...]
Doris [...] her [...] then conversation [...] took time
[...] tell her about it [...] know of her [...] wouldn't. If
they met Doris along those [...]

PART TWO

ROYAL WEDDING

THE NEXT MORNING, her wedding day, 29 July, Diana awoke at about five to a rush of noise. People were shouting, policemen's whistles were blowing and there was the *clop, clop, clop* of horses' hoofs. Her bedroom overlooked the Mall, which was already a solid mass of people with mounted police riding up and down on their splendid horses, trying to keep the main road clear. Many had camped for over twenty-four hours on the streets, and the scent of bacon frying and coffee being brewed on portable stoves pervaded the early-morning air. It was still too early to tell what the day was going to be like, but outside Clarence House an air of optimism prevailed.

Jane joined Diana in her room at about half past five. Neither of them had had much rest: at nine the previous evening, Prince Charles, to whooping cheers from the multitudes gathered in Hyde Park, had lit the first in a chain of 102 bonfires strung across London's parks and squares. Moments later, the night sky had been ablaze with a huge firework display to celebrate the wedding. The strident sound of patriotic music played by five military bands and two choirs, the steady barrage of exploding rockets, timed to match the musical crescendos, had assaulted Diana's bedroom windows.

Twelve hundred fireworks had been incorporated into a vast pyrotechnic palace: it was a reconstruction of a display created for George II 250 years earlier to celebrate the signing of the treaty of Aix-la-Chapelle, which recognized the Protestant succession in England. The crowds—an estimated 500,000 in Hyde Park alone and an equal number lining the streets—screamed and shouted as each new stream of light shot across the sky. As a climax, a sun in the form of gigantic catherine wheel rose high above London.

Diana had tea and toast when breakfast was brought in to them. She was, however, suddenly "very, very calm, deathly calm," feeling like "a lamb being led to slaughter." But now it was the panoply of the day before her that she feared, for as the early-morning sunlight streamed through the windows of her room, it brought with it a reassurance of her love for Charles. Never, she believed, could she have come this far if her love was not solid and true; neither could he have put up with her jealousy and nerves if he did not love her.

At six thirty Kevin Shanley and his wife, Claire, arrived to do her hair. Diana had been emphatic that she wanted to keep the simple style that she normally wore and with which she felt comfortable. She was to wear the magnificent Spencer tiara with its crestlike waves of diamonds, worn by Grandmother Spencer and her mother at their weddings. It was heavy and would have to be tightly secured, her veil attached to it. This had to be done early so that she could get used to the weight of it. While Shanley was drying her hair, the Emanuels and Nina Missetzes arrived with her gown.

When she was dressed she stood looking at herself in the full-length mirror with some disapproval. She felt now as if the dress overpowered her. She was trembling as she turned to Missetzes and asked, more to herself, "Do I really have to go out in front of all those people?" The fitter just smiled and patted her hand. It was ice cold.

The gown's design was chosen by Diana to help her maintain her Spencer identity. She had asked the Emanuels to copy it from a 200-year-old John Downman watercolour of Georgiana, Duchess of Devonshire unaware that the Duchess had entered into a marriage crossed by infidelity, illness and emotional breakdown.

The gown did not flatter Diana's figure although it did capture a romantic air. Made of rich ivory silk from the only silk farm in England, the pie-frill neckline framed Di-

ana's shapely *décolletage* as it had Georgiana's. The balloon sleeves were decorated with lace, and the voluminous
skirt glittered with pearls and sequins. Diana had lost several more pounds in the last few days, and the Emanuels
had to adjust the waist once again as she waited to put it
on.

The amount of fabric on the bodice, as she had feared,
overwhelmed her. The gown seemed to be wearing Diana
and not the other way around. The Emanuels had obviously
given less thought to the wearer than to the setting in which
their creation would be worn. Christopher Wren's great
masterpiece of English Baroque architecture, St. Paul's Cathedral (completed in 1711 after his death), is one of England's largest and finest buildings. A simpler dress might
have been more flattering to Diana, but it would have been
eclipsed, the bride dwarfed, by the awesome height of the
domed canopy over the high altar and the majestic, long
sweep of St. Paul's centre aisle down which she would
walk. The most spectacular feature of the Emanuels' creation was its magnificent twenty-five-foot, lace-trimmed
train, difficult for Diana to manoeuvre, but a striking image
for high-positioned television cameras.

Diana had had a blue bow (something blue) and a gold
horseshoe encrusted with diamonds (a gift from her father
and something new), sewn inside the skirt. A piece of lace
that had edged one of Georgiana's underskirts now edged
hers (something old), and to complement the Spencer tiara,
the only other jewellery she wore were her mother's diamond drop earrings (something borrowed).

By eight thirty, Barbara Daly, the makeup artist, arrived
carrying "a little shiny black bag from Asprey's," which
contained all the makeup she would be using to ensure that
Diana looked natural yet had enough colour to survive under the hot lights and glare from the forty television cameras inside the cathedral. In the basement of Clarence
House, florist Doris Wellham, who had helped create the
bridal bouquet carried by the Queen thirty-four years earlier, was assembling Diana's, using only British flowers—

gardenias, freesias, orchids, lilies-of-the-valley, sprigs of
yellow myrtle and veronica from the gardens at Osborne
House, and yellow roses, named in memory of Lord Mountbatten.

Diana remained cool, her only complaint that the tiara
hurt her head. Shanley rearranged some of the pins that held
it in place. Wearing a heavily jewelled tiara with a sturdy
platinum frame does not come naturally to any woman: the
first time the young Princess Elizabeth wore one to a ball
at Buckingham Palace she was found late in the evening
sitting on the stairs leading to the ballroom, holding her
head in pain, the tiara beside her.

When she was finally ready, Diana looked very young
and defenceless and incandescently beautiful. Jane, who
had been with her for most of the morning, was so overcome that she cried, "Oh, Duch, it's really, really true!"

Before she departed for St. Paul's the Queen Mother,
dressed in seafoam green, with a hat of matching flowers
and osprey feathers, seeming to be preened for flight,
popped in. "My dear," she said, "you look simply enchant-
ing," smiled encouragingly, then disappeared as quickly as
she had come.

At nine fifteen Doris Wellham and her assistant brought
up the fragrant white and yellow bouquet and showed Diana how to hold and carry it for the most graceful and
comfortable effect. Diana walked with it several times
across the room. "One hand, Lady Diana," Doris instructed.
"You will need the other to hold your father's arm." Moments later Diana was informed that Johnnie, who would
escort her to the cathedral, was waiting downstairs.

When he greeted his daughter Earl Spencer was all
smiles. This was, after all, his dream as well as hers that
she had brought to fruition: his grandchildren would be
royal and, God willing, one would ascend the throne. He
looked at her with immense pride and approval. It was what
she had craved for years and, at last, been given. "Diana
had finally got something right."

Johnnie was very frail and unsteady on his feet. Usually

he used a cane but refused to do so to escort her down the aisle. This was his great moment almost as much as it was Diana's, and he was determined to play his part well. He would be seated with Frances in the front row of the cathedral while Raine sat towards the back, not far from Peter Shand Kydd.

While her father watched, Diana's train was attached to her gown and, with the help of the Emanuels, folded so that she and it could get into the Glass Coach, now waiting for her in the courtyard of Clarence House. As she was being helped inside it the sun shone brightly, creating an aura around Diana in her diamonds and shiny silks that was startlingly otherworldly.

Once the bride was safely seated, her father was assisted inside. At ten thirty-five, the Glass Coach pulled out of the cobbled courtyard and into the Mall. A great roar of delight went up from the crowds who had waited so long for this moment. Diana, her face hidden beneath her veil, waved to them.

"Father was so thrilled he waved himself stupid," Diana recalled of that momentous ride up the Mall, the Strand, Fleet Street and Ludgate Hill to St. Paul's. "We went past St. Martin's-in-the-Fields and he thought we were at St. Paul's. He was ready to get out. It was wonderful, that."

Until she viewed the wedding later on their honeymoon, Diana was not aware of the full grandeur of the parade of horse-drawn open landaus carrying a galaxy of European royalty. There had not been such a gathering of crowned heads in London since the Queen's coronation. It was an impressive sight: the Household Cavalry, in their burnished breastplates and helmets with red plumes, the Yeomen of the Guard resplendent in scarlet, the royal horses, caparisoned in silver, coaches polished and gleaming with a blinding sheen as they moved through the brilliant summer morning.

The female members of the Royal Family were dressed to look like an English summer garden—each wearing a different colour that, in archaic custom, other female guests had been informed they could not wear. They sat in their open-topped vehicles, raising a hand every minute or so along the route as their scarlet-uniformed coachmen controlled some of the finest horses in the royal mews. The Queen, in a turquoise ensemble, with Prince Philip in full naval regalia, led the parade of British royalty in an open semi-state postillion landau. Then came the Queen Mother and Prince Edward followed by Princess Margaret in "Princess Margaret Rose," Princess Anne, in white and yellow, Captain Mark Phillips and Viscount Linley close behind.

By 10:46 A.M. the 2,650 guests were seated in the cathedral. A special chair had been built to accommodate the King of Tonga's 350-pound bulk. Outside, Prince Charles, dressed impressively in his heavily bemedalled Admiral's uniform with jaunty cap, arrived with Prince Andrew, also in naval uniform, who was his brother's best man. The bridegroom acknowledged the crowd and then disappeared inside the grand front arches of the cathedral. Moments later, everything timed to the split second, the Glass Coach was seen approaching St. Paul's from Ludgate Hill. People shouted, "Diana! Diana!"

The door of the coach was opened by a footman clad in scarlet and gold livery. Earl Spencer navigated the high steps with the help of his chauffeur, John Harmon. Then Diana was assisted from the coach. Attendants set her train straight and smoothed it as she followed her father, her train an ivory stream of silk behind her, as she went past a line of guardsmen at attention on either side of the steps. There was a nervous moment when her father faltered on a step. Diana paused while Harmon help him recover his balance, then the bride continued her ascent.

Once inside, the five bridesmaids and two pages* sur-

*The bridesmaids were seventeen-year-old Lady Sarah Armstrong-Jones; India Hicks, thirteen, Lord Mountbatten's granddaughter; Sarah-Jane Gaselee, eleven, daughter of Prince Charles's racehorse trainer; Catherine Cameron, six, the daughter of another of Prince Charles's friends, Donald Cameron; and five-year-old Clementine

rounded her excitedly. "Hush! . . . Hush!" they were told. As they formed a line behind her, Diana leaned down and touched the cheek of the youngest, little Clementine Hambro, the great-granddaughter of Sir Winston Churchill. Then she asked her father if he had seen Charles. "Yes," he answered. "He looks very handsome indeed."

The doors to St. Paul's were closed as Big Ben struck the last count of eleven. A trumpet fanfare sounded and everyone stood as the Queen led the Royal Family to their seats on the right side of the altar. Then came the procession of foreign sovereigns who occupied a block of front seats. There followed a second trumpet fanfare and, as the stirring music for his march to the altar began, Charles, with Andrew and Edward on either side of him, took measured steps down the aisle. Three and a half minutes passed before another trumpet fanfare signalled Diana's entrance. She held her father's arm firmly, lest he slip and fall. Earl Spencer said later, "Diana . . . was so determined that she wanted me to do it, she was quite insistent. Most fathers support their daughters on their wedding day—but it was Diana who supported me . . . She believed in me and that gave me the strength to get through it all. It's funny because everyone remembers me taking her up the aisle, when it really wasn't that way at all, it was the other way round."

Diana kept her gaze steady as she moved towards the altar. She was worrying about curtsying to the Queen, as protocol demanded, when she reached the altar—her gown and bouquet were so heavy that it would be difficult to keep her balance.

Half-way down the aisle she caught sight of Camilla in a pale grey, veiled pillbox hat. Her small son Tom, Charles's godson, was standing on his chair beside her so that he could see the bridal procession as it passed. That remained one of Diana's most vivid memories of the day.

Hambro. The two young pages were Nicholas Windsor, the Duke of Kent's son, who was seven and Edward van Cutsem, eight, dressed in midshipman's uniform of 1863.

When she arrived at the altar Charles said, "You look wonderful." She glanced sideways at him, smiled and whispered
back, "Wonderful for you."

When they took their vows both bride and groom made
nervous gaffes. Diana confused the order of Charles's
Christian names, calling him Philip Charles Arthur George
in error ("She's married my father," Prince Andrew later
quipped) and Charles said, "And all *thy* worldly goods with
thee I share." He slipped the simple wedding band, made
from a gold nugget found sixty years before in a Welsh
mine, on the third finger of her left hand and Dr. Robert
Runcie, the Archbishop of Canterbury, pronounced them
man and wife. The new Princess of Wales lifted her veil
as her Prince kissed her respectfully. The royal couple then
walked over to sign the marriage register, and boldly, her
lessons from Oliver Everett well practised, the bride signed
only her Christian name—DIANA—as was the right of a
British princess. "This is the stuff of fairytales," Dr. Runcie
had said during the service, and it certainly was.

"She looked so young, so terribly, terribly vulnerable,"
a guest recalled. "She was barely twenty and seemed—
well—like a teenager. It was exquisitely moving. And all
those children as bridesmaids. And the Queen grim-faced
through it all, the whole Royal Family wearing a unified,
solemn façade. I wondered if she [Diana] realized what was
before her. I had a curious attack of fear. I remember turning to my husband and saying, 'Oh, God, they'll eat her
alive.' "

For Diana the splendour of her wedding was to be the
beginning of the happiness she had always sought. For the
British people it symbolized the continuity of the monarchy
and thus of the nation itself. Sir Winston Churchill had
described the marriage of the Queen when she was the
young and very-much-in-love Princess Elizabeth as "a flash
of colour on the hard road we have to travel." Times were
different. There were few signs of the war that had so devastated London just a short few years before Elizabeth's
wedding. Yet, the road was still hard and this joyous day

afforded surcease from a year of steadily climbing jobless-ness, urban unrest, intractable problems in Ireland, and crip-pling strikes by civil employees and seamen and no one yet was entirely sure that Prime Minister Margaret Thatcher's government could lift the country out of its pres-ent depression.

But no other nation could put together a show of glo-rious panoply like Great Britain, and the Queen with un-erring instinct had known that the pomp and spectacle of a royal wedding would do much to lift the spirits of her sub-jects. The polls being taken only days before proved she was right. It had been a long while since the monarchy had enjoyed such popularity.

The parade back to Buckingham Palace, where the wed-ding breakfast was to be held, started at twelve twenty as a peal of twelve bells from the north-west tower of St. Paul's was answered by bells ringing out from almost every church in London. People thronged the way, waving flags and banners. Diana and Charles led the carriage procession in an open state landau escorted by mounted police. Earl Spencer, in what must have been the second most glorious moment in his life (the first being walking with his daughter to the alter of St. Paul's), rode with the Queen while Fr-ances Shand Kydd was escorted by Prince Philip.

Before lunch could be served, the wedding photographs were taken by Patrick Lichfield. There were portraits of the wedding couple, Diana almost lost in ivory silk taffeta, Charles in theatrical pose, one hand on his hip, his other resting on his gold sword, and looking directly at the cam-era. "I was basically wandering around trying to find where I should be," Diana recalled, "clutching my long train with my bridesmaids and pages." Charles never came over to her during this time to take her hand, "nothing tactile, noth-ing," she remembered. Then they went out on to the Buck-ingham Palace balcony and she was overwhelmed by the thousands of cheering people—"so humble-making." Shouts of "Kiss her!" wafted up, and it was then that

Charles put his arm loosely about her waist and they kissed. The cheers grew more intense.

"Neither of us spoke to each other," Diana said, "we were so shattered." The crowds, the shouting, the people's enthusiasm had overwhelmed them. But it had been a long day, a difficult week, and Diana was exhausted. She mustered up her spirit when Charles cut the five-foot-tall, five-tiered, 255-pound wedding cake with his ceremonial sword, laughing as she fork-fed her groom a small taste from her own piece. She disappeared moments later to change into her coral pink going-away outfit with its bolero jacket, frilly white organdie collar and cuffs, and matching, Edwardian-style tricorn hat with plumes. At four o'clock, in a hail of rice (the Queen joining in as a "tossing" participant), the newlyweds got into an open landau for Waterloo station to take the royal train to Broadlands, where they were to spend the first two days of their honeymoon before joining *Britannia* in Gibraltar. On the back of the landau, Andrew had pasted a handwritten sign reading "Just Married," and tied above it a big bunch of heart-shaped silver and blue balloons.

Once again the royal couple rode through throngs of cheering people until they reached Waterloo, Diana with her anticipation sky-high and Charles smiling wanly through his own exhaustion and troubled thoughts. When they arrived at Romsey station, they were met by a limousine with a canopy of flowers on its roof. Photographers raced alongside the car as it moved slowly through the narrow old streets lined with more cheering people. When the car pulled into the Broadlands driveway, Diana turned her head slightly as black iron gates closed behind them.

Diana's dream was now reality. She was the Princess of Wales. However, the fantasy had been passed on to the millions who had watched her and Charles take their vows. For the multitudes it had been the stuff of fairytales. For Diana it had only been a prelude to the real life she now faced.

PART THREE

A Ship on Troubled Water

DIANA WAS IN love with love. She had believed that once they were married and she had given herself to Charles, he would become the adoring husband and lover of her dreams. Yet she awoke on the first morning of their life together anxious and depressed. The fine linen pillow beside hers was empty and Diana feared that somehow she had displeased her husband.

Except for the servants (who included Charles's butler, Stephen Barry) they were alone in this great house set amid six thousand acres of rolling countryside with a stretch of the River Nest that locals boasted had the finest trout fishing in England. Charles had risen early to try his luck, and would return for lunch. Diana remained in her room, resting, working on a piece of needlepoint, a gaily flowered cushion cover that would eventually decorate a sofa in the garden room at Highgrove. She had always enjoyed doing tapestry: it calmed her nerves and gave her time to think.

She was now married and her royal life begun, but she was unsure as to what her role was to be. From her marriage she wanted children, of course, and a loving, bonding relationship with her husband. She needed to know that she was not alone and that, with her beside him, Charles would never be alone again either. There was so much about Charles that puzzled her. He seemed at times to be almost besotted with her, but at others he would stiffen, pull back, and there would be an invisible wall that she could not penetrate. He was in constant battle with his father, in awe of his mother, and could not communicate with either on a purely personal level. Diana wanted to bridge that gap, to be there as his physical mate and confidante. She was struggling for a way to make that happen.

However, it seems that, during their honeymoon, Charles

had intended to transform his fun-loving young bride of just twenty into a serious and intellectual woman, forgetting that at her age, in his first years at Trinity College, Cambridge, his academic abilities were publicly acknowledged to be less than brilliant. Diana was unable to make such an immediate change. She had brought with her a copy of the recently published first novel of Barbara Taylor Bradford—*A Woman of Substance*—which she quickly packed away when Charles seemed disdainful of it and offered her instead a book by Sir Laurens van der Post.

Since Mountbatten's death, Charles had grown ever closer to Sir Laurens, the then seventy-five-year-old South African writer and philosopher. During the Second World War, he had been Lord Mountbatten's military political officer, and had been taken prisoner by the Germans during the African campaign. At the war's end he undertook several missions for the British government in Africa and made many films and had written numerous books about his experiences. His life had been one of high adventure, and dedication to wildlife. Charles had brought seven of his books on honeymoon and was deeply immersed in their philosophy, influenced by Jung. He had intended that he and Diana would read the books and discuss them while they were away. Diana read a few pages, but was woefully unprepared for the first lunchtime quiz.

The first two days of the honeymoon at Broadlands, whose beautiful décor and magnificent gardens she had so admired, were "grim," she later confessed. She was elated when they left early on Saturday morning, 1 August, for Eastleigh airport where Stephen Barry waited with their luggage. With Charles's bodyguard, John Maclean, and Paul Officer, the newlyweds flew to Gibraltar where they would join *Britannia* for the cruise. On the flight they stayed at the back of the plane in their own compartment, the door closed for privacy.

Neither Charles nor Diana was prepared for the reception they received in Gibraltar. Hundreds of cheering people lined both sides of the road of this small but strategically important British colony, as they drove in a converted, open-topped Triumph Stag through the town to the enclosed harbour where the yacht was anchored. The sixteen-day Mediterranean and Aegean cruise would pause at Tunisia, Sicily, Santorini, Crete, and traverse the Red Sea through the Suez Canal. On the penultimate evening of their sea journey, they would stop off in Port Said where President Anwar Sadat and his wife Jehan were to dine with them aboard *Britannia*. On the morning of 16 August, they would fly from Hurghada to Scotland, where they would spend the next six weeks, first at Balmoral and then at nearby Craigowan Lodge which backed on to the excellent fishing waters of the River Dee.

In the royal suite of *Britannia* the twin beds had been lashed together and made up as one bed: Princess Anne's suggestion, as she and her then husband Mark Phillips had also honeymooned on *Britannia* and spent a rather crowded first night in one twin bed. Everything on *Britannia*'s royal deck was pristine white with deep red upholstery and dove grey carpets, which, though elegant, lent an austere ambience to the apartments. The royal suite consisted of two large bedrooms, a dressing room, and a sitting room that led to a comfortable veranda. The corridor joining the rooms was lined with drawings of previous royal yachts. A hushed feeling pervaded their apartments as all the hustle and bustle of shipboard activity was kept out of their hearing on lower decks.

On the first morning Charles and Diana slept late, had a cold breakfast of fruit, cereal and yogurt in the sitting room, then went out on deck to sun themselves. The sky was cerulean blue, the ocean a vast expanse of softly rippling waves, the sun shining, and as the royal deck was completely private, they seemed to be sailing alone, a bit reminiscent, Diana said later, "of 'The Owl and the Pussycat.' " It was the ultimate dream of any two people in love. To the crew and the Prince's staff, who had seen them the previous night and that morning, they appeared to be just that as they held hands and Diana smiled and looked at her husband with adoring eyes. They called each other "darling." Even Stephen Barry, who had been privy to Charles's long relationship with Camilla, and who had harboured serious doubts about the marriage, believed the two were in love.

Mid-morning the Admiral (there was always an admiral, not a captain, aboard the royal yacht) brought them the charts of where they were, pointing out beaches along the coast that might be good picnic spots. After he left they each fell to making their daily entry in their diaries. Two photographs slipped out of Charles's and fluttered on to the deck near Diana. She picked them up and found, to her horror, that they were of Camilla. Recriminations and tears followed. Diana insisted that he tell her the truth: what did Camilla really mean in his life? had he seen her before the wedding? was he planning to see her again? Charles would not reply and there was a cold look in his eye. Perhaps she did not want to hear the truth, but his implacable silence only confirmed her fear that from the beginning there were three people in her marriage.

From that moment on the cruise was a nightmare for both of them. Diana's bulimia grew worse each day and the one other woman aboard, her dresser Evelyn, often found her red-eyed. There was always food in the royal suite, fruit, biscuits, sweets, and Diana would devour great quantities of it then purge herself. This occurred four or five times a day, exhausting her and disgusting Charles, who did not know how to handle the situation. As the ship travelled through the night, she would wake, gobble up whatever food she could find, make herself sick then return to bed feeling wretched. Charles was at a complete loss as to how to help her, but they kept up a loving façade before the staff and crew.

They ate lunch alone in their quarters, with Charles still insisting on discussions of van der Post's books. It seems he was attempting to occupy her mind with something other than Camilla and the bulimia. Although Diana has said that almost every evening they were doomed to entertain the top staff in the main dining room for dinner, Stephen Barry claimed, "They rarely used the main dining room [which also functioned as a cinema]. They preferred intimate dinners in their sitting room where they could serve themselves."

Diana was most content when they engaged in some form of exercise. They swam, snorkelled, windsurfed and, indeed, had picnics and barbecues on the beaches along the North African coastline they were following, mountains rising in the distance, the sea calm. A small boat would be sent out first to make sure that the chosen spot was deserted. Once assured, it would return to bring the royal couple with John Maclean and Paul Officer for the outing. Charles would usually sunbathe while Diana swam close to shore. A seaman would start the fire for a barbecue, or lay out the picnic, then retreat to the boat to wait for their signal (a police whistle) to pilot the royal couple back to *Britannia*.

An escort vessel kept a short distance behind *Britannia* and came abreast from time to time to deliver mail and business papers to Charles. His assistant private secretary Francis Cornish also came and went. "His role," Barry said, "was to make sure that there would be no problems in the host countries we were passing, and he observed the formalities and courtesies to the other heads of state on behalf of the Prince. The odd helicopter, completely ignored by the Prince, flew over trying to get pictures but no one succeeded." No crew member was allowed to have a camera on board, but Diana had brought hers and took pictures wherever they went. Charles remained pretty much in the royal apartment or on the veranda, but, as the first week drew to a close, Diana began to roam the ship, going unannounced into the galley to talk to Mervyn Wycherly, the chef, and his assistants, and take some "goodies" away with her. They commented on her enormous appetite and were puzzled that despite it she seemed to have lost a lot of weight since stepping aboard. "By the end of the voyage I would venture the Princess had lost a stone," one staff member said. Diana was brought the menu choices in the morning to make her selection for the meals to be served that day. When they dined in their apartments they ate from trolleys and served themselves. Ice cream was always included for dessert. "They both loved it," Barry said. "The royal deep-freeze looked like the freezer of an ice cream shop."

In the evenings, after dinner, movies were shown, and videotapes of the wedding. Charles seemed thrilled to see "the bits he had missed," and they both had a good laugh over the moment she got his Christian names wrong. During the second week, Diana's spirits had risen and she attended some of the parties being given by crew and staff, often without Charles. They had both brought along some of their favourite tapes and music wafted in the breeze from their deck as she played Elton John and the Beach Boys and Charles put on Barbra Streisand. Together they listened to Tchaikovsky, Rachmaninov and Elgar. A staff member reported that by the end of the second week they did not "seem to be able to keep their hands off each other."

Diana had managed to block out the incident of the photographs. Love notes were exchanged, and she believed that Charles now truly loved her. Then came the only official engagement scheduled for the cruise—the dinner on board *Britannia* with President and Mrs. Sadat. *Britannia* docked in Port Said. The evening was warm with soft breezes and Diana wore a pretty floral gown. When Charles met her in the sitting room to go down to the main dining room together, he was still trying to put in his cufflinks. Diana went to help him but Charles drew away, and she noticed that they were designed in the shape of intertwining Cs. Diana caught the meaning immediately and was shocked but not at a loss for words. When had he received them and exactly what did such a gift imply? Only friendship, Charles replied, and tried to drop the subject. Diana would not let it go. She suspected that Camilla had sent the cufflinks to the ship. She saw it as a bold act by Camilla to show Diana that she was still in Charles's life, and a gross betrayal by

Charles to accept and wear the gift, especially on their honeymoon. She felt humiliated and unloved.

There followed an unpleasant scene. Diana insisted he choose another pair of cufflinks. Charles refused. She wanted to remain in their suite. But she knew she could not offend the Sadats. She went back into her room, repaired her makeup and pulled herself together. When they greeted the Sadats on their arrival, she was still agitated, her usual radiance dimmed.

The four dined in the huge dining salon always used with visiting heads of state, and if the much older Sadats had not been such warm, interested people the evening might have been a fiasco due partly to the size and formality of the room and the number of staff hovering nearby. Also, Diana was clearly upset and withdrawn. Mrs. Sadat sensed her insecurity and made a special effort to bring her into the conversation. It was Diana's first official engagement and she was woefully ill-prepared. She had not been briefed on any matter that might be of interest to either of the Sadats, nor had she been able to obliterate the shadow of Camilla.

After the Sadats' departure, Diana once again broached the subject of the cufflinks. Charles was cool, unsympathetic, but he agreed not to wear them again.

The final night on board, the staff and crew presented a theatrical on the forecastle. Diana seemed to regain her good humour as she, Charles and the ship's officers watched the entertainment, which included one lanky sailor, dressed in women's clothes, impersonating Diana and telling salty jokes. Diana giggled and blushed. Stephen Barry and four other members of the household staff did a song-and-dance routine dressed in swimming trunks and flippers. "How long were you rehearsing?" Charles asked Barry later. "I noticed you were out of step."

Early Sunday morning, 16 August, the crew "lined the decks, saluted, and gave three cheers" as Charles and Diana left *Britannia* to be driven to Hurghada where they boarded a plane to Scotland and Balmoral. "The place was incredibly worn inside," one house guest recalls, "full of ghastly tartan antimacassars. I'm not convinced it had been redecorated since Victoria's occupancy. It had an antiquated heating system and without the fires being kept burning I am sure everyone would have froze."

Shortly after they arrived rumours began to circulate within the family that their marriage had not got off to a good start. Diana's weight loss and unhappiness were evident as she often seemed on the edge of tears. However, her in-laws never discussed anything personal or troubling. "Certainly not in front of the staff," she was told—and, of course, there was seldom a time when staff were not present. Every night the routine was the same. Two bagpipers in full Scottish regalia would march around the dinner table as soon as everyone was seated. Afterwards a film was shown. Except for Princess Margaret, the others said little to her.

Diana felt very much the outsider. She gorged herself and vomited more often with each passing day and was continuing to lose weight. She was isolated from anyone she could talk to. After three weeks she and Charles moved to Craigowan Lodge and while he fished, she did her tapestry in the comfort of a small sitting room that overlooked the wooded grounds. With October's approach came relentless rain. Diana admitted later that she had been "about ready to cut my wrists." Charles told her that she must not discuss their problems with anyone, including her family, that they would have to be sorted out in a private, dignified manner.

Of all the royal residences, Charles was most relaxed at Balmoral. The vastness of the grounds allowed him a chance to walk great distances alone—although John Maclean was never far behind him—without fear of someone jumping out of the bushes. It seemed he knew almost every foot of the estate and when stalking enjoyed plunging deeper and deeper into the moorland, never losing his way. He fished every morning and later would sit for hours on a heather-covered hill in the mist, reading or sketching if the light was good, or just deep in thought. Most evenings he and Diana dined at the castle. Charles liked being surrounded by his tightly knit family and sharing "in" jokes and small gossip. A contemplative man, not really a social creature, he was happiest in the country away from the prying public eye.

That might have been one reason why his affair with Camilla continued so long. Due to the clandestine nature of the relationship they were almost always alone, and his immediate staff were responsible for seeing that they enjoyed complete privacy. Camilla had not been born into the aristocracy but she had been exposed since childhood to the world of courtiers who served the Royal Family. She knew all the "in" stories, shared a frame of reference with Charles. They were the same age, had many mutual friends, and Camilla made certain she was available whenever Charles called. Even her marriage had not interfered with their liaison, to the extent that Andrew Parker Bowles had joked about being "a man willing to lay down his wife for his country." In fact, the Parker Bowles marriage had not been happy for many years, and Andrew was known to be an obsessive womanizer, once dubbed "Old Roaming Hands" by a dinner partner.

Though older and more experienced than Diana, Camilla was not intellectual: she knew a lot about horses, but little about ecology, economics, international current events, politics or religion. But she was "good fun, comfortable, very adaptable and *earthy*," a former schoolmate said. "Men liked her. I guess you would say she was sexy. But not because of her figure or beauty. Nor was she particularly feminine. That is coy, coquettish. But she let it be known when she was interested in someone and it didn't take long for them to get the message."

Charles had often given her literary novels to read, but in fact she leaned towards the same romantic fiction Diana enjoyed. She was as desperate to make Charles proud of her as was Diana. She looked up to him as an intellectual. "Andrew Parker Bowles was not only outrageously unfaithful," one of her friends of this period recalls, "he was always telling her she was useless . . . She would constantly be saying things like, 'I wouldn't understand that, I'm too thick' [strangely echoing Diana's "I'm as thick as a plank."]" She appeared, as she approached her mid-thirties and middle age, to be a "modest, good-egg Englishwoman but actually her self-esteem was dangerously depleted." She joked that she looked like "an old witch of Wiltshire."

Charles liked her lack of glamour, her geisha-girl attentions to him that were in direct conflict with her raucous humour and love of the outdoors. Her friends said she was "a scream, with her fag and her drink, cracking jokes and telling very funny stories . . . in fruity language."

Giving up Camilla had been, perhaps, the worst wrench in Charles's life. But he had vowed to his father that he would do so, at least in the physical sense, and he had not yet gone back on his word. But he telephoned Camilla from Scotland—more than once, according to Stephen Barry. Diana suspected that he discussed her bulimia with Camilla. By 1 October she was so thin that her bones protruded.

Charles sought professional help. He accompanied Diana to London and over a fortnight doctors and psychiatrists made secret night-time visits to Buckingham Palace, where the Waleses were living until their apartment at Kensington Palace was ready for them. Diana was fed enormous doses of Valium to calm her nerves. Neither consultation nor medication worked. Then she found she was pregnant. She was sure that now everything would change: the Royal Family would open their arms to her, and Charles would became a loving husband and father.

13

ONCE SHE WAS married to Charles, Diana had expected media interest in her to abate and that she would go about her life with some modicum of privacy. This did not occur. The press hounded her every move. A day seldom passed without new pictures of her in the newspapers. Magazine covers with her image lined newsagents' shelves. She was the most photographed woman in England and was quickly becoming the darling of the American media too, her face more familiar than those of established move stars. Her image raised the circulation of any newspaper or magazine. She had become a product eagerly sought after by media consumers.

Part of this was the romantic aura that clung to her history, part that she was extraordinarily photogenic. Like many film personalities, she was not actually beautiful, but the camera loved her face, the bone structure, the dazzling smile, the expressive eyes that gazed out with warm compassion and a lively twinkle. Her image spoke to people. She needed no words.

In effect she was selling the monarchy in the same way that a movie star sold their current film, or a rock singer their latest record. At no recent time had it been so popular, yet no help was forthcoming from the Palace on how Diana should handle her lack of privacy or the media attention.

Before the world knew of her coming motherhood (and, indeed, before her own suspicions had yet been confirmed), she and Charles went on a three-day official visit to Wales. Charles helped her through this public appearance, for which she had learned a little Welsh to use in the short speech she was to give at Caernarfon Castle.

The short tour, made in the royal train, was fraught with danger and difficulty. Nausea combined with the bulimia overtook her. There had been terrorist warnings, and at some stops she saw placards that read "Go Home, English Prince" by the Welsh Nationalist. At Bangor paint was sprayed on their limousine. Fire bombs were discovered at Pontypridd and Cardiff. A threatening letter was sent to the BBC, warning, "We will not forget 1969—Beware of Caernarfon."* Wherever the royal couple appeared, marksmen lined the rooftops. Squads of uniformed police stood guard. Diana had been shaken by the recent news of the assassination of President Anwar Sadat by Muslim extremists opposed to his peace initiative with Israel. Suddenly she realized that her life and Charles's might be at risk.

Everywhere they went, crowds pressed forward to get a glimpse of her, "holding out their hands and calling her name as if for a blessing," Jonathan Dimbleby reported. Diana smiled resolutely. The press was ever-present: pictures of her surrounded by masses of well-wishers bombarded British and foreign newspapers daily. The schedule was gruelling and there was little time for either Diana or Charles to relax. They returned to the train exhausted each evening and with only a night's respite before they had to start out again early the next morning.

When they reached the last stop of the tour, Gwynedd, in north-west Wales, Diana was sick, grey and gaunt. It was pouring with rain as their limousine drew up to the fortress-like entrance of Caernarfon Castle. Seeing the vast crowds waiting for them, the hovering police, and still suffering surging waves of nausea, Diana began to tremble and sob, "I can't do it." Both Charles and Anne Beckwith-Smith, Diana's new lady-in-waiting, attempted to calm her. Then Charles said, "You've got to pull yourself together and do it." And she did, his hand beneath her elbow for support as she took her first steps out of the car, security

---

*Two members of the extremist group Meibion had blown themselves up the morning of 1 July 1969, when Charles had been invested as Prince of Wales at Caernarfon Castle.

men rushing towards her with open umbrellas, Beckwith-Smith close behind her.

Once on the podium she gave her speech, and her Welsh words, correctly pronounced and carefully spoken, were greeted with enthusiastic applause. Then she and Charles went "walkabout." This was the first time that Diana had been exposed to this royal way of meeting more humble people. "I saw something almost miraculous overtake her," one of the staff who accompanied her said. "It was pouring. But this didn't seem to bother her. She stood to her full height and walked right over to an elderly man, removed her gloves and took his hand in hers. I'd never seen a royal do that before. 'Your hands are freezing,' she said. 'So are mine. But yours are much worse. You must be soaked to the bone. Thank you so much for coming to see us.' Then she leaned down, fully exposed to the rain as a little girl reached out to hand her a bouquet. 'What lovely flowers.' She smiled. 'Now you must get under some cover or you'll ruin your pretty dress.'

"The Prince seemed to be taken by surprise and stood rather at an awkward distance as the Princess, so sick only moments before, 'worked the crowd', as we say, heedless of her own cover until, with her husband's mandate, Security ushered her gracefully back to the car. Her hat was dripping, her face wet and she was shivering. But she was not the same terrified, crying woman she had been when she arrived at Caernarfon. It was simply amazing."

Others report that she "stooped to talk gently with children, touched the blind, embraced the elderly . . ." It was clear that it was Diana, not Charles, that the crowds wanted most to see. Charles took it with humour when he was given flowers for his wife. "Diana, love," he would say, with a self-deprecating smile, "over here," when someone he greeted asked if they could shake hands with her. Neither knew that this was the harbinger of things to come. The spotlight was shifting from Charles to Diana. For now Charles was amused by it, and also proud of her.

The Welsh tour made a great impact on Diana. She had

seen the warm look in people's eyes when she touched someone's hand or shoulder, how a simple remark could make a stranger smile.

The official announcement in early November of her pregnancy was met with joy by the country. The Queen hoped that the imminence of a child would help to settle Diana. Diana herself had greeted her pregnancy with fresh hope, but she had not anticipated the nausea she endured. Every time she stood up she was sick. She could not sleep or eat. She grew so weak that she fainted several times. Never having had morning sickness, the Queen attributed Diana's illness principally to her bulimia, which she did not understand and for which she blamed her daughter-in-law. Instead of gathering her to them and helping her, Diana's in-laws were cool and without understanding. She was made to feel she was a nuisance, very un-royal to get sick or to faint in public (which Diana did one day at an official gathering, to the displeasure and censure of the Palace).

In late November, the family gathered at Sandringham. Diana's sickness and her anxiety had reached a peak. Protocol demanded that despite her ill-health she eat with the Royal Family and leave the table only after the Queen's departure. At dinner one evening nausea overcame her and she ran from the room. Later, she and Charles—who had not come after her—had a terrible row over this and she said something to the effect that she might as well kill herself for all he or his family cared. Charles bristled. Dressed to go riding, he brushed past her and into the corridor, Diana right behind him sobbing, threatening to throw herself down the stairs. Charles told her that she was being ridiculous and that she would do no such thing. He started to descend. Diana rushed to stop him and catapulted down several steps.

The Queen appeared from a room below, horrified to see Diana sprawled on the stairs (the Queen was "shaking," Diana said later), fearful that she might have injured herself and her baby. Family members and staff filled the corridor.

No one seemed to know what to do. Charles muttered that she was "crying wolf," and went out. Princess Margaret came quickly to Diana's aid and helped her up, the doctor was called and confirmed that Diana and the baby were unhurt. A sedative was administered and she spent the rest of the day in bed.

Such a melodramatic scene had never been played out at Sandringham before, and the only way the family knew how to deal with it was to ignore it. The incident was simply not discussed. For weeks, Charles hardly spoke to Diana. "Things had degenerated so that he never wanted to be in the same room as her, unless someone was there with him," one courtier has been quoted as saying. Apart from her domestic staff, her bodyguard, Anne Beckwith-Smith, Oliver Everett, who was now Diana's private secretary and comptroller, and Princess Margaret, Diana was more or less isolated from the court, who had allied themselves to those who held the power over their jobs—Prince Charles, the Queen or Prince Philip, who openly expressed his disgust at Diana's "charade."

Diana, still at Buckingham Palace as she waited for work to be completed on their home in Kensington Palace, felt the full force of this icy wind of rejection and it chilled her to the core.

Kensington Palace is a complex of many apartments, some grand, some not so grand, others surprisingly humble. It is owned by the Crown and all the accommodation is grace-and-favour. Over the years it has been home to well over a hundred members of the Royal Family. Queen Victoria was born there in 1819; Prince Philip's mother, Princess Andrew, and his grandmother, the Dowager Marchioness of Milford Haven, were long-time occupants; the Queen's aunt, Marina, Duchess of Kent, and her three children, Edward, Michael and Alexandra, moved in shortly after the death of the Duke in an air crash. Prince and Princess Michael of Kent lived there, as did Princess Margaret and her two children, the elderly Princess Alice, Dowager Duchess of Gloucester, and her son, Richard, Duke of Gloucester and his family.

In the 1930s through to the 1960s, insiders referred to Kensington Palace as the "aunt-heap," a bit of a royal rest home; and there was much backbiting among the residents (who also included current and retired members of the Royal Household who lived in staff quarters and cottages in the grounds). In general, the occupants were much younger than in previous years and as there were numerous children of various ages, the courtyard of Kensington Palace rang with the sound of their voices and their music.

Kensington Palace was originally the country home of the then Earl of Nottingham, who sold it to William III in 1689 as a country retreat for the monarch. Christopher Wren designed the Orangery for Queen Anne. Later Grinling Gibbons decorated the interior with carved panels, fluted columns and flower-bedecked archways. It was only in the early years of the nineteenth century, when its 274 acres of parkland were opened to the public, that it was divided into apartments. Since then the large brick building with its eye-catching green slate roof had undergone many additions and improvements, but ti still showed its age. The plumbing was often sluggish, hot water unreliable, and the heating inadequate, unless augmented by electric fires.

Despite these last drawbacks, KP—as Diana soon called it—was grand and she was thrilled to be moving there. Highgrove had two drawbacks where she was concerned: its proximity to Camilla and the horsy set, and its distance from London and the urban life she preferred.

The Queen had given Charles and Diana two apartments (numbers 8 and 9) to combine into a large one. This gave them an L-shaped, three-storey home (kitchens and domestic staff quarters on the lower ground floor, reception rooms at ground level, and bedrooms and family space on the first floor), with twenty-five principal rooms and numerous subsidiary ones. Their nearest neighbours were Prince and Princess Michael of Kent and their children. Best of all, Diana's sister Jane and her husband had been given a grace-

and-favour cottage, the Old Barracks, in the grounds.

Diana said later that decorating her London home during her pregnancy saved her sanity. She had found she had an eye for colour, design and the use of space when she assisted Charles at Highgrove, and she hired interior designer Dudley Poplak, a South African who had helped her mother and her sister Jane with their homes. Poplak had also overseen the final decoration of Highgrove. For the country, Diana had chosen bright floral chintzes for the sofas and chairs, and pastels for the walls, giving a cheery but elegant look. The rooms at Kensington Palace were far grander in size and detail than at Highgrove and called for a somewhat different approach.

One problem she encountered was using the many expensive, but not always co-ordinated, wedding gifts that she and Charles had received, and the antiques and paintings the Queen had allocated them from her private collection. Charles allowed Diana a fairly free hand but insisted that grey carpet with the Prince of Wales feathers was laid in the expansive hall. Diana claimed it was too intimidating, announcing the occupant's royal title, as might well be done in his Buckingham Palace office, but which she believed set the wrong tone for their home.

The largest reception room could comfortably accommodate seventy-five guests and up to ten footmen to serve champagne and hors d'oeuvres. It contained a Broadwood grand piano, salmon pink sofas, and yellow silk wall coverings, with a magnificent Aubusson rug. There was a smaller drawing room for gatherings of up to twelve, a "family room" with television and a fine music system, and a well-shelved library, as well as Diana's office suite, staff rooms, and two dining rooms—one for the family, the other for dinner parties. The main dining room boasted a handsome round eighteenth-century mahogany table that comfortably sat sixteen.

A beautiful Georgian staircase curved up to the first floor where the master bedroom held a magnificent oversized mahogany four-poster bed (originally made for the massive

bulk of King Edward VII). Off this bedroom were two bathrooms and two dressing rooms, each equipped with a single
bed—Charles often slept in his. Then there was Diana's
sitting room, the cosiest room in the house. A large circular
mirror over the handsome fireplace reflected the soft floral
designs on the sofas. Several circular tables covered in
floor-length silk of robin's egg blue, held a multitude of
silver frames in assorted sizes containing pictures of all her
loved ones. There were cabinets for her favourite collections; a colourful display of Herend glass animals, her
stuffed animals, and children's books, including Grandmother Spencer's copy of *Grimms' Fairy Tales*. A small
lady's desk was stocked with her personal stationary embossed with a crown and her name *Diana* beneath it. She
had developed the habit from youth of writing a thank-you
note to her host as soon she arrived home from a small
dinner or meeting with a friend.

Her wardrobes were state-of-the-art, designed for the
meticulous person she was, every item of clothing co-
ordinated and hung or shelved impeccably, never put away
unless freshly cleaned, pressed or in the case of her dozens
of pairs of shoes, buffed or just returned from repair if they
were in any way worn. However confused Diana was at
times about her life, there was incredible order to the material side of her existence. This was one place where order
would reign, and there would be no unwanted surprises.

Israel Zohar, later commissioned to paint a portrait of
Diana for the Russian Hussars, recalled his vivid impression of the Waleses' home in Kensington Palace, its comfortable elegance and the way Diana had integrated the
historic antiques and paintings. It was "like seeing the chain
of what makes the culture of a nation, of humanity grow
and develop through art, through furniture."

What is amazing is that Diana was only twenty-one at
the time. True, she had Poplak to guide her, but every final
decision was hers. It was a job extremely well done, one
of which Charles and her in-laws could have well been
proud. "No one gave me any credit," she later complained

to a close older friend. "No one. Not Charles. Not the Queen."

Charles preferred Highgrove, and he spent many weekends there alone. Diana, who suffered with nausea almost to the end of her pregnancy, remained in London working on the decoration of their home, especially the nursery wing. Five weeks before she was due to give birth, she and Charles moved into Kensington Palace. It did not keep him in London at weekends, so Diana spent her time with Jane, and prepared for the baby's arrival.

From the day the pregnancy had been announced, newsmen waited daily for a photo-opportunity wherever they thought she might turn up, at the back gates of Buckingham Palace, her hairdresser's salon and outside her favourite shops. The country was seized with Diana fever. The press commented on how thin she was. On the one hand there was concern for her health, on the other a complete disregard for any right to privacy she might want or need.

In February, she and Charles had flown to the Bahamas for a much-needed holiday. They found themselves seldom out of the view of the press, who used long-range lenses to take pictures of them sunbathing and swimming—Diana in a bikini at five months pregnant. Charles was furious, Diana was in a terrible state. In her private apartments she was watched constantly by staff and security, who were never more than a few feet away from her at all times. Someone was even stationed outside her bedroom door at night. ("They're even checking me in the loo," she complained, to a close member of her staff.) The claustrophobic nature of her life, the loss of her freedom, was almost more than she could bear. She turned to Anne Beckwith-Smith for understanding, for even Jane was too close to the court for Diana to trust with her deepest feelings. Her parents were insensitive to her plight: they wanted her to make no waves with Charles or her in-laws.

In fact, Diana's husband and her mother-in-law had more serious matters on their minds than Diana's problems, however difficult they were for her. Great Britain was at war. On 2 April 1982, Leopoldo Galtieri, President of Argentina and commander of its army, landed thousands of troops on the Falkland Islands and reclaimed them as national territory. The Falklands are bleak, rocky moorlands, windswept, rain-drenched, and home to just over two thousand people. Located about 350 miles off the coast of Argentina, the Falkland Islands were seen by that country as important to their strategic defence. English residents, however, considerably far out-number Argentinian. Great Britain moved swiftly: on 21 May five thousand British Marines and paratroops landed, Prince Andrew among them. Charles, as colonel-in-chief of six regiments and the Army Air Corps "felt extremely guilty and frustrated" that he could not be with the troops. His schedule remained filled with the usual work for the Prince of Wales Trust and the obligatory appearances, but he made time for letters to be written to the families of men who were reported injured or lost and fastidiously read the communiques on the progress of the campaign sent to him by the Palace.

It was a short—just ten weeks—but brutal war. Great Britain had lost 257 men by the time Galtieri surrendered the island garrison on 14 June. Scores of others were brought home on stretchers, seriously injured, and Charles was patron of the South Atlantic Fund, which gave its support to the bereaved and injured. Nor was Diana, as Jonathan Dimbleby suggests in his biography of Prince Charles, oblivious to the solemnity of what was occurring in the country and within her husband's family. According to members of her staff, she wrote to many who had met with tragedy caused by the war and was genuinely grieved by their misfortune.

In the final weeks of her pregnancy her obstetrician considered a Caesarean birth: 21 June was the date they settled on as it "would not interfere with Charles's polo schedule," but when she arrived on the previous evening at St. Mary's Hospital, Paddington, and had settled into the Lindo wing, security thick in the corridors, the decision was to induce labour instead. Diana spent sixteen hours in labour before she had an epidural spinal injection which eased her pain. At 9:03 p.m., with Charles at her side, she gave birth to a seven-and-a-half-pound baby boy.

Charles was euphoric. He grasped her hand, kissed her brow and held his son. When he left the hospital an hour later, the massive crowds outside went "berserk with excitement," and greeted him with a rousing chorus of "For He's A Jolly Good Fellow." He grinned, waved and walked with a spring in his step to his car.

Diana had been aware of his close presence during her labour and filled her with renewed hope for their marriage. Their son, who was named William Arthur Philip Louis, was healthy and strong of lung. Diana was happier than she could ever remember being. She was a mother, a role she had always wanted to play. When a member of her close family came to see her the next morning she cried. "Happy tears," she told them, "the first ones I can remember."

She was so excited by having a healthy son, that it was some time before she grasped that she was the mother of a future King of England.

"I'LL NEVER BE QUEEN," Diana told close friends repeatedly. "No, it's so," she insisted. "I'll never be queen." She would not explain why she felt this. Divorce was never a consideration. "I'll never divorce Charles," she maintained. "I've experienced what divorce can do to children."

She was in a grim mood. There had been terrible rows with Charles about Camilla, who had been hunting with him five times that season. However, there was no clear evidence of an adulterous union, and Charles protested that he was honouring his vow to Diana and to his father, that the Parker Bowleses were friends of his sister, well established in the Gloucestershire hunts to which he felt committed, and that there was no one-to-one contact between Camilla and himself at these events. These explanations did not appease Diana. Charles was secretive about calls that came in on his cellphone: his voice would drop to an inaudible mumble as he continued his conversation, often in his dressing room or the bath.

Even if Charles was not actually sleeping with Camilla during the early years of his marriage to Diana, his continuing attachment to and frequent contact with his former mistress was cause for his wife to feel betrayed. Under the circumstances, it would be difficult for any woman to believe her husband had not returned to his lover's arms, or that he was about to do so. But the insecure Diana was certain to suspect infidelity and to feel threatened by it, and considering her youth and state of mind during this time, Charles showed an unforgiving lack of sensitivity.

After her return from hospital with William, Diana suffered intense post-natal depression. There was talk of suicide attempts after rows with Charles. She later admitted to four incidents: she had cut her chest and thighs with a penknife, and her wrists with the serrated edge of a lemon slicer, drawing blood. As Charles, a staff member or a security guard was always close at hand, she knew that she would be saved from any serious consequence, but when she slashed her wrists with a razor she required medical attention. Another time she threw herself against the glass of the cabinet in her sitting room. Luckily, the shattered glass caused only minor cuts.

The strain on Charles must have been immense. The Prince and Princess of Wales were not an ordinary couple who could walk away from their vows. Charles was not accustomed to a woman who did not accept and worship him as he was. Diana was too young, too modern in her thinking, too feminist in her outlook to subjugate her own emotions, and what Charles hated most was ugly feelings expressed openly that he thought best kept hidden. He began to feel increasingly justified in his withdrawal from Diana, while her feelings of unworthiness intensified as did the bouts of bulimia.

According to Peggy Claude-Pierre, a well-known specialist in the causes of anorexia and bulimia, and the author of *The Secret Language of Eating Disorders*, some sufferers "mutilate themselves, scraping, scratching, or cutting their skin. This is an attempt to escape from the relentless hounding of the negative . . . 'I am a bad person and deserve to die.' The physical pain of the mutilation temporarily blots out the internal voices." She continues, "Society had inadvertently created the perfect puzzle—a person so distorted in self-image, so much in the grasp of the Negative Mind, so undeserving of help, that she must suffer psychological purgatory until we—the outsiders—understand her secret language and deliver her from her plight."

Bulimia is a mainly female illness and for substantive reasons. The goal for too many women is "You can never be too rich or too thin." In the last quarter of the twentieth century, a wraith-like figure became the major component in the idealized Western vision of seductive womanhood, styles geared to small-breasted woman with narrow hips.

Diana was taller than average and had a fairly large frame. She continued her destructive cycle of bingeing and vomiting and was not getting the nutrients she needed, especially after childbirth.

Nothing in Diana's experience had prepared her for life in the gilded royal cage. "She was in an alien environment with little freedom of action or privacy even in her new home at Kensington Palace, where telephone lines were tapped and a policeman was on duty day and night, as well as her personal detective. She was reminded of the kidnapping attempt on Princess Anne while she and her husband were driving down the Mall.* A potential kidnapper or assassin could appear in the most ordinary setting. She was put through a "terrifying" driving course, in which she learned how to dodge bombs and bullets in case of a terrorist attack while she was in a car. Fear of danger to William, Charles and herself added to her confusion. On the one hand she resented having to get Palace approval for anything she wished to do that was not prescheduled—she could not lunch with a friend in a restaurant without detectives seated at a table next to them—but, on the other hand, she was always looking over her shoulder when she did have some private time. Unlike Charles, Diana had not lived with possible danger or security restrictions and she did not know how to handle the depression it triggered.

*This outrageous attack on Princess Anne and Captain Mark Phillips occurred in March 1974. The would-be kidnapper blocked their car with his own, jumped out and then, two pistols pointing directly at them, demanded they open the door. He then grabbed Princess Anne's arm and tried to drag her out while her husband hung on from the other side. Their bodyguard drew his pistol. Before pulling the trigger he shouted for the Princess to duck, which she did. The attacker dodged the shot. Then the chauffeur tried to tackle him, along with a policeman patrolling the Mall and a passing taxi passenger. All four were shot and critically injured by the gunman before he fled into St. James's Park. Reinforcements were called and the man was captured. Both Princess Anne and Captain Mark Phillips were shaken but unharmed.

"Charles did try to understand. He called in several specialists in chronic depression† and had his close friend and adviser Laurens van der Post talk to her," a member of Charles's staff said. "But there is a limit to where understanding can go before it develops into disgust and the need to fight for one's own survival prevails."

During all this private angst, Diana had little support. Some of that was her own fault. She did not tell her parents how bad things were and Sarah and Jane had their own agendas. Her in-laws remained cool. She had been devastated at William's christening on the morning of 4 August 1982, officiated by the Archbishop of Canterbury. Royal photographers took dozens of pictures of the Queen, the Queen Mother, Charles and William, but Diana was almost entirely excluded because she appeared frail (having lost the thirty pounds she had gained during the last months of her pregnancy, and ten pounds more, in a record six weeks after the baby's birth) and the Palace did not want the public to see her looking in such poor health.

"She told me," one of her closest friends said of this period, "that this was the only time that she truly tried to commit suicide. She said Charles introduced Scotch to her and she took too much. Then he gave her some pills [antidepressants] and she took too many and had her tummy washed out and said, 'I'll never do that again. I kept thinking about Wills and how awful it would have been and I will never do that again.' And she said that she flushed the pills down the loo as soon as she was able.

"She also told me that the fall down the stairs at Sandringham was due to her having had an argument with

†Dr. Allan McGlashan, a Jungian psychotherapist, analysed her dreams, while Dr. David Mitchell saw her every evening over a period of several weeks to hear her recount her daily reactions to, and conversations with, her husband. This produced great sobbing and deeper depression. Her personal physician, Dr. Michael Linnett, suggested various means for her to gain weight, all containing high nutritional and calorie count, but she continued to induce vomiting. No one appears to have dealt directly with the eating disorder.

Charles. It started in the bedroom and she ran out of the
room and slipped and came tumbling down the stairs, but
that everyone thought she had done it intentionally." She
claimed that the only person she trusted on her staff was
Anne Beckwith-Smith, that she was sure all others reported
everything she did and said back to Charles or the Palace.

Diana felt, rightly or not, that some members of
Charles's staff were hostile to her, suspicious that her influence could change their relationship with the Prince of
Wales. A great turnover in staff at this time occurred for
which the press blamed Diana. She denied the allegations,
especially where Stephen Barry was concerned. Because of
Barry's complicity in shielding Charles's relationship with
Camilla and his influence on Charles during his twelve-year
stint as valet, keeper of secrets, adviser on clothes, food
and restaurants Diana felt he should leave when she and
Charles were married. She was openly critical of Oliver
Everett, who was not sympathetic to her need for spontaneity. He insisted she clear all engagements with him beforehand and when she sometimes made a date for the same
day with her hairdresser or to go shopping he would be "in
his finger-wagging mode," because a security check had to
be made on anywhere she was to visit.

The person to whom Diana was now closest was her
lady-in-waiting, Anne Beckwith-Smith, eight years older,
sturdily built with "a jolly-hockey-sticks, upper-crust, head-
girl look." She was the daughter of Major Peter Beckwith-
Smith, Clerk of the Course at Epsom and a friend of the
Queen Mother. She had also attended West Heath, but it
was her knowledge and experience that most intrigued Diana. Beckwith-Smith had studied art in Florence and Paris.
She spoke excellent French and Italian, and she had had an
interesting career, first working as an authors' researcher,
then organizing exhibitions for the Arts Council of Great
Britain, and for four years in the painting department of
Sotheby's.

It had been Beckwith-Smith who had been so helpful to
Diana during her tour of Wales. Through the years she

proved herself a loyal friend and companion. She was a good listener and Diana grew to rely upon her judgment when she ventured an opinion, although she did not always follow her advice. Eventually Beckwith-Smith took on Everett's job along with her own.

There were two other ladies-in-waiting: the Hon. Mrs. Lavinia Baring and Mrs. Hazel West, both older than Diana by nearly a decade but attractive and with sharp minds. The most important new member of staff was William's nanny, Barbara Barnes, who for fifteen years had taken full charge of the children of Colin Tennant and his wife, the former Lady Anne Coke, who were close friends of Princess Margaret. Nanny Barnes never wore a uniform and believed that children should express themselves freely. She had two helpers: her assistant, Olga Powell, and the night nurse, Ann Wallace. As heir to the throne, William was never left alone. Diana would have preferred to have more day-to-day responsibility for her child, but she was informed that this was how child-rearing had always been done in royal circles and that she must respect tradition. But mothering was something that Diana was certain she would do well and she was resentful at having to turn over so much of her baby's maternal care to Nanny Barnes and her helpers.

Everything had happened so quickly for Diana. Not only did she have to put up with her every move being monitored by press photographers and security men, but at twenty-one she was Princess of Wales, mother of a future king, châtelaine of two homes, with a combined staff of close to fifty people. Only two years earlier she had been a giggly teenager from a privileged background who had yet to sample life's more sophisticated pleasures. She had had too little preparation for the instant fame, too many expectations and too little understanding of what she had taken on, and no real insight into the man and the institution she had married, for the two were inseparable.

Stephen Barry called Diana "a spoiled, wilful child," and Charles "a sad, lonely Prince." But Diana was also frightened and unsure, and Charles was arrogant and self-centered. It would have been a miracle if he had been otherwise: Charles's every wish was pandered to, his orders instantly carried out by fawning staff. He demanded deference and received it.

At heart, though, Charles was a sensitive man and not without feelings for Diana. It was his expectations of her behaviour that were askew. He had based them on the only measure he knew: his own insular royal background. True, Diana was twelve years his junior, but when he had been her age, duty had come before any other consideration: he had kept personal problems private, illness had been sublimated, and respect for the monarchy always upheld. He believed that Diana could overcome the bulimia and depression if she put her mind to it. He grew impatient with her and cool. And Camilla was always so sympathetic to the difficulties in his marriage and his life.

Her own marriage was in disarray. Parker Bowles was living a separate life, although in the same house. Camilla had her horses, hunting, her children, a circle of close women friends and her position as confidante to the Prince of Wales.

"But Camilla was never that sure Charles would, in the end, pick up the pieces where they were before his marriage," an intimate of Camilla has said. "She was obsessive about keeping absolutely *au courant* of his everyday affairs, reading up on those things that he was championing, his polo games, the horses he rode, the hunts she did not attend and the people who were at them. It was obvious that Diana was too consumed with her baby and her illness to do the same. This gave Camilla the upper hand. It disturbed me and caused a break in my friendship with her when I, ill-advisedly I suppose, deigned to tell her what I thought. I got the 'chill' treatment for a long time, which is what both Charles and Camilla do when someone has displeased them. They freeze them out. Frigid response when you meet at some event. No more invitations to small gatherings. Telephone messages replied to by a secretary. There's never a confrontation. You are just *out*."

Surprisingly, Charles was a hand-on father. He was proud of William, bragging about his every new achievement, amused by his first word ("Yuk," which Diana used whenever she didn't like anything), ease with dogs (they had a golden retriever named Harvey whom William played with). Charles picked William up, held him, changed his nappy on occasion. Diana had instilled in him an acceptance of the need for close parenting and Charles had happily accepted it.

With the start of a full schedule of royal engagements Diana's depression and bulimia began to ease. Clothes became more important to her, and selecting, fitting and coordinating accessories took a great deal of time. In Beckwith-Smith she found an able assistant. Diana set fashion trends each time she wore a new gown or had her hair coiffed differently for a public appearance. She would have preferred to be known for her work, but for now the Palace did not want her to compete in this area with Charles.

What the Palace did not yet comprehend was her tremendous power to endear herself to the public. If the Queen Mother was everyone's favourite grandmother, Diana was their beloved daughter, evolving from naïve teenager to gracious lady. People wanted to touch her, give her flowers, talk to her.

The Royal Family did not recognize that Diana was the first real bridge between the people and the Palace. In public she reached out to people, singling out the elderly or the children. She was approachable and natural when talking to people. When she and Charles appeared together, it was always she who drew the most interest, and as her popularity increased with each day, he privately fumed. After all, he was the man who would be king.

Being Britain's sovereign was not what it once had been, but the Queen has the right to see state papers and to discuss their contents weekly with the prime minister. Unlike Queen Victoria, who kept her heir away from anything of significance, the Queen allows Prince Charles regular access to secret cabinet papers, and to discuss matters of state with government leaders. He may also act in the Queen's place as senior councillor of state when she is abroad, and give the royal assent to bills.

Since Queen Victoria's reign, the monarchy's influence has become more a matter of public relations than of political power, and by allowing themselves to be seen in public and on television, the Windsors had become a national treasure. Diana had played an important part in this and the Palace believed she had to be seen as a modern young woman who respected her husband and his mission. Her problems must be kept away from the scrutiny of the press.

The Palace knew that just as the monarchy might be damaged by events such as Edward VIII's abdication and Victoria's prolonged period of seclusion following Prince Albert's death, it would be enhanced by a good public image. British author and journalist Anthony Sampson wrote aptly: "Between this fairyland palace and the practical world, there is a drawbridge which is only let down on special occasions. There is not so much secrecy that the public eventually loses interest, but there is enough hidden to stimulate intense public curiosity." The Palace wanted the public interest in the lovely young Princess of Wales to continue, but they did not want its passion for pictures of Diana in a new outfit to divert attention away from Charles, or his charitable interests and work for his Prince's Trust, a foundation he designed to assist deprived and disadvantaged youth. The Palace decided that Charles and Diana should be seen as a couple and that they should tour Australia and New Zealand. William would be left with Nanny Barnes and her staff. Then Charles and Diana received a letter from Australian Prime Minister Malcolm Fraser suggesting that they bring William and present themselves as a young family. Charles agreed, and Diana was ecstatic, recalling Charles's sad stories of his parents' absence on such trips when he did not see them for months on end. William was only an infant, but Diana hoped that this would set a precedent for the future.

   There was much heated discussion at the Palace before it was agreed that this could be arranged and might, indeed, present a view of modern royal attitudes towards the raising of children. The one condition was that William must follow on a separate flight to ensure that an air accident would not take the lives of both the first and second heir to the throne. The six-week tour was planned for March—April 1983. William would be eight months old at the time of departure. His mother's schedule in Australia and New Zealand would be so full that it was doubtful she would see much of him but at least she would be near him. Nanny Barnes would come too. Diana was determined to regain her strength and control her bulimia and her depression before they left. She saw the tour as a chance to win Charles's total devotion.

   Her personal physician, Dr. Linnett, convinced Charles that she needed some rest before such a strenuous journey. He also advised them to spend some time together so they went to Highgrove to accomplish just that.

Highgrove was where Charles felt most at home. It is a square Georgian house, standing in 348 well-frosted, cultivated acres just off the A33 from Tetbury to Bath, situated in the rural heart of the picturesque Cotswolds. The Prince's original attraction to Highgrove was twofold. First, it was close to Camilla's home, Bolehyde Manor, to Badminton, where the Duke of Beaufort's Hunt and Horse Trials was held, and ten miles from the polo grounds at Cirencester. Princess Anne and her husband Captain Mark Phillips lived at Gatcombe Park, six miles away. Second, the Prince knew that this part of England is where "the horse is the name of the game and the object of the exercise." Badminton, the Duke of Beaufort's great Palladian mansion, where Queen Mary, Charles's great-grandmother, had spent a good part of the war years, its kennels, the huge hunt stables and the estate of 20,000 acres in superior hunting country, were the essence of foxhunting in England. Charles had been introduced to hunting in 1975 by Princess Anne who helped

him to conquer his initial fear of jumping fences so that
within a few years he "became a bold cross-country rider,
capable of tackling the toughest obstacles in the hunting
field."

Camilla was an avid huntswoman and the two of them
looked quite splendid on the mounted field whenever they
did ride together. The sturdily built Camilla seemed constructed for hunting clothes, the broad bones of her face
complimented by her cap, her mousey colouring suddenly
coming alive with the excitement of the hunt. Few partic-
ipants in the hunts in which she and the Prince rode were
unaware of the close relationship she still had with him.
She was treated with a certain deference. "Well, let's be
honest," one hunt follower commented, "there is a great
deal of oiling about when it comes to the Prince of Wales.
If one wants to remain part of his set, one has to swallow
a certain amount of pride and keep one's opinions to oneself. Whether the Prince of Wales and Camilla were lovers
in the biblical sense at that time meant very little to those
who were a part of the Highgrove set. It was obvious that
Camilla was his closest confidante. He treated her with the
deference one would give to a wife or lover. They looked
a pair on the field. Hard to imagine that they were not a
pair sexually."

For hunting, Charles wore "the Windsor coat," designed
for him from a model of one originally worn by George
III: a dark blue coat with scarlet collar and cuffs, the brass
buttons bearing the Prince of Wales feathers. With this he
wore white cord breeches, black boots with tan tops, and a
navy blue cap with a high crown. Style in clothes and riding
are important when hunting but there would be no hunting
on this visit, for Charles was committed to helping Diana
improve her health so that she could sustain the ordeal of
the coming tour.

Highgrove is in the tiny hamlet of Doughton (pronounced Duffton) which has neither church, pub, nor post
office. The nearest town is Tetbury, which has the lovely
eighteenth-century church of St. Mary the Virgin, a pub,

several antiques shops, saddlers, greengrocers, a newsagent, and the Tetbury Furniture Company, which then did "a roaring trade in practical joke kits": cushions, foaming lighters and leaking glasses, all much favoured by Mark Phillips and Princess Anne's set to get a party going. Diana never properly fitted into the social set that surrounded Highgrove, who were her husband's friends, older, horse-mad and who treated Charles in a sycophantic manner which she abhorred. But she did enjoy the chance it gave her to spend private time with Charles, and perhaps even more to the point—that her presence at Highgrove would discourage any contact with Camilla.

Charles had brought Diana to Highgrove a number of times between their engagement and their marriage. At that time the house had little furniture and the four reception rooms and nine bedrooms were painted white. At Charles's invitation, she chose soft, pastel tones for the walls and gay chintz for the furniture. Charles supervised the gardens, for which he selected plants and the materials for the walls and pathways.

Highgrove, which was previously owned by Prime Minister Harold Macmillan's son, Maurice, was built in the late eighteenth century. The Duchy of Cornwall had bought the house for the Prince of Wales at a cost of £800,000 which, with the going rate of £2,000 an acre for land, meant the house itself was valued at approximately £100,000. Diana, with Poplak's guidance, had spent triple that in refurbishing it. Modernization of plumbing, heating and lighting along with security costs had driven that figure up to more than double the purchase cost of house, outbuildings and property. Closed-circuit television cameras were strategically placed inside and outside. For security purposes, there was an impregnable, windowless room, twenty feet square, in the centre of the ground floor, set down like a house within a house and kept locked like the fictional Secret Garden, and loathed by Diana who considered it intrusive, and never quite believed that such a means of protection was necessary.

The fortified room was lined with steel, well armed, had its own air purifier and plumbing system and was kept fully equipped with enough food and medication for the family to last for months in case of a terrorist attack. The family and staff had to submit to practice alarms on a regular basis. Computerized monitors were installed in the attic of the main house that transmitted from cameras set strategically on the property. Police officers were on duty day and night at the cottage as well as at the house. Diana had a second back staircase built that led from the attic to the rear of the house so that the detectives could be kept out of view.

Charles flourished at Highgrove—"Absolute bliss," was the way he described his country home, his housekeeper reported—but Diana did not share his love of it. However, the time she spent there with Charles before their tour of Australia and New Zealand was the happiest since their marriage. But there were grim times: "The trouble is one day I think some steps are being made uphill only to find we've slid back one and a half steps the following day," Charles is reported to have written to a friend.

She was trying hard to overcome her illness, but small things sometimes set it off: Charles would retreat to his study with a cellphone; a letter would arrive by private messenger and he would stuff it in his pocket to read later in privacy; she might see something on television or read a passage in a book that would cause her to go into the kitchen, eat everything in sight then force herself to vomit it. However, Charles's attitude was generally caring and they would play happily in the walled garden with William, or walk hand in hand through the fields of wild flowers Charles had planted and of which he was justly proud.

DURING A SMALL dinner party at Althorp early in 1983, a guest suggested to his host that, with William's birth, the monarchy might one day be known as the House of Spencer-Windsor. Lord Spencer started visibly. Then he said, "Yes, yes. It does seem about time."

Johnnie Spencer might have seemed to lack ambition and let Raine run the show, but he was never ambivalent about the past, present or future of his family name and ancestral home. He saw himself now as the forebear of future kings of the United Kingdom, and Althorp as an historic estate where a future queen had spent her youth. But William's birth had a still more profound bearing on Johnnie: it placed his father Jack's accomplishments in the shade.

"Outdoing his father meant more than one can imagine to Johnnie," a family member said. "Jack Spencer had been the cause of his greatest unhappiness as a child, an adolescent and all the years until the old gent's death. Johnnie never won his father's approbation. Now his daughter would one day be queen, his grandson king, and the name Spencer would be entwined with the monarchy. It was a delicious comeuppance. His future and that of the Spencers seemed for ever secure. The one uncertain element in this equation was Diana. Johnnie never stopped worrying that she would throw a wrench into the works, perhaps bolt like her mother. He never saw the other similarities. The unhappiness and cruelty in their marriage that Frances endured for so many years before she left him. I always believed that had he lived to see the marriage of Charles and Diana in jeopardy, he would have backed Charles in the same fashion that Lady Fermoy had supported him . . . Yes, I do believe he would have betrayed Diana if it ever came to that. His own future and that of his family name meant more than one person, even if that person was his daughter."

Johnnie Spencer refused to recognize that Diana was suffering great unhappiness or that she was ill. Her cries for help to him were answered with platitudes such as "None of this will seem so important in years to come," or "I'm sure Charles loves you deeply. This is all part of your over-active imagination. Having a baby does that to some women. They can push their husbands away instead of bringing them closer to them." Diana repeated his comments to close friends later, explaining that "Daddy just wanted me to be happy."

Like her father, almost everyone with whom she came into contact had their own agenda where she was concerned. Jane's loyalty was torn between Diana and her husband, Robert, a rising member of the Palace élite. Lady Fermoy remained steely in her iron-clad dedication to the Royal Family. Frances, in her new-found devotion to Catholicism, advised her daughter to honour her vows and her husband. Diana's in-laws were unapproachable, and her staff were employed by the Palace. Their careers depended not on pleasing Diana or supporting her—although they certainly attempted to do this—but in maintaining a good relationship with the Prince of Wales and the Palace.

Princess Margaret, at fifty still pretty, bright, filled with the nervous energy that led her to chain smoke, tried to give Diana the benefit of her knowledge of how the court worked and she extended a warm hand to her. But even her friendship could not be relied upon. Sometimes "Margo," as Diana called her, would be gay, amusing, friendly, "then suddenly you [could] feel her psychologically draw herself up with the unspoken, 'I am the sister of the Queen,' " and an invisible glass wall would separate them. Diana adored Princess Margaret, and looked upon her as a mentor, but began to fear rejection and saw less of her she might have wished, especially since they were close neighbours.

Diana had stayed friends with Carolyn Pride who knew

nothing of court machinations and was a concerned ally. A newer confidante was Janet Filderman, to whom Diana had gone before William's birth when she had developed minor skin problems. Filderman produced her own skin and beauty products, and both Jane and Diana's mother had been her clients for a number of years.

Filderman was a handsome blonde woman with glowing skin, a warm smile and a nurturing manner. Diana had come into her small salon for the first time "looking stunning—no makeup—hair wet. Our friendship came very fast," Filderman recalled. "Being a beautician is such a private, personal thing. You are revealing your naked self. We shared problems. She seemed more comfortable with older women. She had no friends within her husband's circle and that made it difficult for her at the beginning. I, unfortunately, had the pain of never having children so I mothered my clients instead. Our friendship quickly spread from the salon to one of a more personal nature. She called me often at night when she was alone. Sometimes I'd serve us a simple meal in my office. Or we would have dinner on trays in her sitting room. It wasn't palatially furnished. It was very cosy, with cushions and table mats and trays for the drinks and photographs covering the tables. Diana was at ease in plain surroundings."

Filderman claims that she and Diana discussed the bulimia, but "I never believed it was quite as bad as she asserted. Now I do have clients who have bulimia and anorexia and they are totally, totally different in appearance. Their skin is dull, their hair is brittle because you are putting no nutrients in it. I'm not saying she did not have bulimia. But there is the possibility that she magnified the extent of it in order to get sympathy. When she talked about doing it [vomiting], I told her, 'Do you realize that you can make your teeth drop out?' I tried to frighten her into thinking about her health and her looks."

"Diana's appearance was of prime importance," Anthony Holden, Charles's biographer, recalls of the time he spent in the company of Charles and Diana during that

period. "They [the Palace, Charles's staff] would never let
her open her mouth. Everyone had underestimated how
bright she really was and were now afraid that the competition for Charles would be too much. Anyone who understood music as she did, who picked up languages as quickly
as she did, could not be a dumb-head. And when she gave
a public speech she was no slouch either."

The press was fed material that gave the impression of
a flighty, naïve young woman, interested in clothes and
purely feminine things, and stories were printed about her
choice of designers and shops. She lacked the ability or
power to countermand the image being drawn of her. With
no support group to turn to the pressures were tremendous.

"Charles, in fact, felt threatened by Diana," Holden
added. "He had read her all wrong, been blind to her charismatic appeal. Camilla was never a threat to him—she was
all about horses and being there when he needed her. She
is perfectly happy to stay in the background to get what
she wants—Charles and power within his close circle as
well as the financial security and extravagant gifts that being the Prince of Wales's mistress engendered. You
wouldn't hear Camilla saying, 'Gosh, I can't wait to hear
the draft of your new speech,' or comment on it behind the
scenes as Diana often did—and not always in a complacent
or flattering manner. Camilla is not, and never has been,
involved in that part of his life. She is wise in the ways of
womanliness and he came to her for escape from his royal
prison and to be accepted on any terms he chose."

Charles, like a traditional royal, expected his wife to bear
him children and to turn a blind eye to his mistress. But
Diana was a more modern sort of woman than he had bar-
gained for—even Camilla had got it wrong, as had Prince
Philip and the Queen. Born into a different generation, in
which women were no longer expected to merge their identity with their husband's or tolerate infidelity, Diana could
not be expected to accept such demands with quiescence.

The press were well aware of Camilla's position in
Charles's life. "The official line at that time," Holden ac-

knowledged, "was that he foreswore Camilla, but he did not sound or seem to me like a man who was going to give up his mistress. [And] Diana was too hungry for his love to ever accept being second best, or worse, just a breeding machine for the monarchy. It killed something inside of her and many of us [in the press] could see this taking place."

"She had a lot of time to herself during the early years," Janet Filderman added thoughtfully, "because Charles definitely wasn't there. She spent many evenings alone. The thing was, he had to have his schedule and she had to have hers. They led separate lives in a way, which she had not been prepared for and which was something she hated and I think that brought her unhappiness and loneliness. She was truly in love with him and wanted to be with him. But in that situation it was not easy.

"She would take me and my husband to the ballet or a concert where we would sit behind her in the royal box. She never forgot a birthday or any special occasion. She was a very special person. She wasn't all sweetness and light, but she had this unique gift of making people think they were the only ones in her life. And despite her great personal problems she still had a joy of life. She could be, and often was, joyous and funny, truly funny. She had a quick tongue, did amazing and hilarious good-natured imitations [of celebrities, friends and members of the Royal Family]. There could be a devilish gleam in her eye, and she had an infectious laugh—more a giggle, girlish, most winning.

"She adored her father and felt deep, *deep* concern over the effect of his strokes. He had much difficulty with his speech and had to shamble walk. I thought he seemed like a great big teddy bear and I felt sorry for him from his illness point of view. Of course, she had done what he wanted her to do. There was a deep, *deep* need in the Spencer family to connect with the Royal Family. Once she was in the position of being able to give to someone who was needy—physically and emotionally—that empowered her. So that once her father was a weakened man, the relationship upended. But it had a vicious backlash. She seemed to be in control, though she wasn't. In fact Lord Spencer, because of his infirmity and her sensitivity to it, now had more influence on her than in the past. She had achieved what no other Spencer had managed to achieve and there was no way he was going to be a party to her losing any of the power that she had achieved by becoming, first, Princess of Wales and then the mother of a future King of England.

"I saw her when she was in London two or three times a week," Filderman continued, "and spoke to her on the telephone, I believe, most of the evenings when she was alone, which during her pregnancy and the year following it, was quite frequently, at odd hours, late at night, eleven or twelve o'clock sometimes. Never in the middle of the night. She knew that I had a sick husband and that I had to be up early the next day. You could hear music in the background, often Mozart. She would say, 'I'm on my bed and I have lots of my stuffed animals around me.' "

Charles was often away overnight, even when Diana was at Highgrove. Still, she wore her most dazzling smile when she went into Tetbury to do a little shopping, pick up the latest magazines at the newsagent's, or something at the chemist. Anne Beckwith-Smith was always with her and, to Diana's annoyance, so were the pack of photographers who continued to dog her path. None the less, the short errands that took her away from Highgrove were welcomed. She felt as though she were under house arrest. Therefore she looked forward eagerly to her trip with Charles and William to Australia.

It appeared that Diana was leaving the dark days of her despair behind her as she mounted the steps to the Royal Australian Boeing 707 aircraft on Sunday, 20 March 1983. Aboard were Charles, Diana, William and twenty members of their personal staff,* eight with Diana and William and

---

*Diana had a personal staff of eight with her which included: Anne Beckwith-Smith, Oliver Everett (who scheduled and briefed her on

twelve with Charles, on the first leg of their tour. The bar on Charles and William flying together had been lifted by the Queen so that Diana would not have to be separated from the baby during the long flight, which played havoc with his normal routine.

They arrived at Alice Springs early in the morning, twenty hours later, everyone exhausted and unprepared for their tumultuous reception. Hundreds of press from all over the world were waiting, cameras poised to catch them as they disembarked. Nanny Barnes handed William to his mother and there were good-natured shouts of "Here's Billy the Kid!" which brought a bright smile to Diana's face just before she handed him back to Nanny Barnes and Anna Wallace and threw him a kiss. Wills and his minders were then briskly escorted by security to a waiting car that whisked them across the field to another plane which would transport them to the location that would be the family's "home away from home" while they were in Australia.

Alice Springs had just emerged from a month of storms that had left three people dead, caused a hundred families to be evacuated from their homes, ripped out trees and bridges, cutting off the central part of town, and severely damaged the luxurious hotel where Charles and Diana were to have stayed. Instead they were given the best suite of rooms at the comfortable, but more humble, Gap Motor Lodge. While their accommodation was being readied Diana and Charles freshened up at the home of a local car dealer, Dino Diano. Then they both were taken to see the flood damage.

Despite the severe storms the town had endured, the day was almost unbearably hot. Diana was suffering from jet lag, yet she went on her own to tour a local school, talked

---

all her engagements and wrote her speeches), her dresser, Evelyn Dagley, Detectives Graham Smith and Sergeant Allan Peters, Nanny Barbara Barnes, Anna Wallace, and press secretary Victor Chapman. Her hairdressers Kevin Shanley and Richard Dalton made individual trips during the time of the tour to tend to her hair.

to the children one-to-one and joined them for a few minutes in a group game. She then asked if she could visit the shelter where those made homeless by the flood waters were being housed. When she returned to the motel, she had only an hour to prepare for the dinner that was being given in their honour and at which Charles gave a speech that was enthusiastically received. She was asked to say a few words, and told the gathering how courageous she thought the people of the town were. Her audience cheered. There would be no turning back for Diana now: she had emerged in Australia as a star and Charles appeared as a supporting player.

For both of them the tour of Australia was a gruelling round of forty flights from one state capital to another for a succession of walkabouts, meetings, receptions, banquets, photo-sessions, press interviews, tours of schools, factories, hospitals, government buildings and historic monuments, and always there were the endless crowds to face, the cameras flashing, microphones thrust at them and security men pushing people out of the way.

There is one unforgettable image taken by royal photographer Jayne Fincher, in Maroochydore, Queensland: children in the vast crowd had grabbed the fabric of Diana's yellow dress and were tugging so hard at her skirt that she could not move forward. Fincher recalls how Charles guided her through their ceremonial duties. "I saw him whispering instructions as they laid a wreath at Canberra's Cenotaph, and he held her hand and gave her reassurance."

Charles was aware of how taxing their schedule would be for someone as frail as Diana and as unaccustomed to the unique pressures of a royal tour. They travelled 45,000 miles, and fulfilled up to eight official daily engagements. This would have been unendurable except for the prearranged use of a house at Woomergama, an isolated 4,000-acre sheep station in New South Wales near Albury, where they were reunited with William. It was a seventy-year-old, six-bedroomed farmhouse with a vine-covered veranda and a shaded swimming-pool. William and his nannies were in nursery quarters that had once housed the owners' children. Whenever they had a few days off, they went to Woomargama. On these too rare occasions, they had private time together and it seemed that the rigours of the trip had bridged some of the difficulties in their relationship. "The great joy was that we were totally alone [at Woomargama] together," Charles wrote to his friends the van Cutsems.

There were times when Diana told Anne Beckwith-Smith that she could not take another walkabout, speech or dinner. Wherever she went there were the hordes of photographers all clamouring for a picture of her. Charles was practically ignored. People would rush the car as they drove up and shouts of disappointment were heard from the press if they were on *his* side and might not get a shot of Diana as she stepped out of the vehicle showing a very shapely bit of royal leg. She was having the kind of mad reception that only the most popular movie or rock star might receive. Only the hard work of the security team kept her from having bits of her clothes torn from her. It was "the excess of idolatry."

At times Diana was terrified "by the surge of collective emotions she had aroused by her mere presence." She did not understand it, but she smiled, shook hands until hers were raw, posed endlessly, looking vital, natural, fashionably dressed and impeccably groomed. She gave some speeches that others had written for her, but when she spoke one-to-one or ad-libbed the press and public found she had a quick mind and a good sense of humour. Her greatest quality was her artlessness. The camera revealed the depth of feeling in her eyes, the invitation to love her in her smile, and the people responded.

The Palace and Charles's advisers were not pleased that Diana was getting the lion's share of attention, and she was asked, in no uncertain terms, to stick to the script when she spoke, which she did—although at times she would forget and make some highly quotable unrehearsed remark. ("When a Maori Chief charged at them with a spear in the traditional challenge to strangers," Fincher remembered,

"Diana at first backed away, saying, 'Goodness, I thought he was going to stab me!' Then she collapsed with laughter.")

The Palace and Charles had indeed underrated Diana's intelligence, and would continue to do so for years to come. She may not have done well at school, but she possessed the two key elements of intelligence: curiosity and the need to satisfy it. She read up on all the places they visited, asked interested questions, was quick to catch the Australian lingo and to appreciate the Australian humour. For Diana, this first foreign tour was an exhausting experience, but it was also the beginning of her adult education and she resented that the world's interest had fastened on what she was wearing. She wrote home to a close friend that she felt ashamed to be judged just on her appearance and her status.

They reached Canberra just days after bushfires in South Australia had killed forty-six people and destroyed the homes of more than two thousand families. Charles and Diana visited the worst-hit areas and Diana would ask the survivors, "Do you mind talking about it?" and if they said, "No," she would listen keenly and ask questions. She took the badly scarred hand of an eighteen-year-old Cudlee Creek fireman, who had been trapped by a ninety-foot wall of flames. "My heart goes out to you," she said, her eyes blurred with tears. "I so admire your bravery." She added, "I'm older than you, but I don't think I would have had your courage."

"There was more depth and warmth in her concern for us than any words can describe," district fire chief Mike Kemp said after she left.

They continued to Sydney, where Diana was mobbed again by wild crowds. That evening she whirled with Charles around the dance-floor of the Wentworth Hotel at a ball in their honour, looking amazingly bright, happy and in love. They went on to Newcastle on the Pacific Coast, from there to Maitland and Hobart in Tasmania; then Adelaide, Renmark, Port Pirie, Freemantle, Ballerat, Bendingo and Melbourne. Diana had seen extreme suffering, touched and been touched by many people, been subjected to severe weather changes, constant moving about, and criticism from the Palace for doing what came naturally to her in reaching out to people. With the pressure of the tour, her bulimia returned with a vengeance. Charles was resentful of the attention she was getting and the lack of it he was receiving, but he was deeply worried about her. "I do feel *desperate* for Diana," he wrote to a friend, explaining that she could not move without "these ghastly . . . mindless people" clicking away at her with their cameras. He wondered how anyone, "let alone a twenty-one-year-old, could be expected to come out of all this obsessed and crazed attention unscathed?"

This was the first glimmer of understanding that Charles had of how young and inexperienced Diana was to have been thrown into a media "circus" without any preparation. He had made dozens of tours, and knew how arduous they could be, but he had never experienced anything like this. "It really has been a terrible baptism by fire for her," he wrote to the van Cutsems. And he told them and others how marvellous Diana had been, how she had helped keep him going, despite her fear of the crowds who constantly surrounded her.

What balanced it for Diana was Charles's empathy with her while they were in Australia, and that they were a family unit. True, they did not see much of William, but at least they were on the same continent, "under the same sky," and in those brief periods when they were reunited as a family they made it as private as possible.

After four weeks in Australia they flew to New Zealand where they were sequestered at Government House in Wellington, the capital. Security was thicker than at the most rigid of prisons, but they were with William, who crawled for the first time as they watched him "knocking everything off the tables and causing unbelievable destruction."

They returned home in triumph, every day of their tour having been front-page news with a steady flow of photographs of Diana, smiling and beautifully turned out. Ac-

cording to the polls, she was now the favourite member of
the Royal Family next to the Queen, and was taken to task
by her brother-in-law, Robert Fellowes, who advised her to
talk less and to present the image of a good, supportive
wife.

The next tour came fast on the heels of the first. Three
weeks after their return Charles and Diana flew to Canada.
Outwardly they were still the same glamorous couple, but
Diana was nearly a stone thinner than when she had left
for Australia and her bones showed prominently. Charles's
impatience with the return of her bulimia was evident in
his private attitude to her, although his public demeanour
was much at odds with this. On 1 July Diana celebrated
her twenty-second birthday, and at a dinner that evening he
prefaced his obligatory speech with a tribute to her. "Ladies
and gentlemen and competitors . . . Today is a very special
day for three reasons. It is the birthday of my dear wife,
not only that but she had the good taste and the good sense
to be born on Canada's national day."

Privately he made little of her birthday. There was no
time in their schedule for a celebratory dinner, and her present, he told her, would have to wait until they were home.
His concern for her in Australia had dissolved. In the in-
terim period between the two tours, Charles had seen Camilla and rekindled their affair.

Diana called the next year of their life together "total
darkness"—because it was filled with such pain that she
could remember little of it. But a journalist who covered
the Prince of Wales for one of the leading papers said, "I
do think Charles was trying to make a go of it during 1984.
He realized Diana had not had an easy time of it and was
doing a good job of being Princess of Wales. For about
eighteen months following the Australia, New Zealand,
Canada tours, Diana did not travel with him. Charles went
to Brunei, to East Africa. Then he was in Papua New
Guinea to open the new parliament building. Other times
to France, Monaco, Italy. All in one year. His wife was
alone quite a bit, and perhaps, more importantly for their

relationship, he was not subjected to daily reminders of her sickness and their differences. But he did seem happier and very proud of his son. He always carried new photos of Wills with him and showed them around to the press on these flights. He liked fatherhood."

In February Diana found herself once again pregnant. Charles was ecstatic. He called this "the breeding period." He wanted a second child and so did Diana. Their second son was born on 12 September weighing six pounds fourteen ounces and named Harry. Charles was present at the birth and it is recorded that at his first glimpse of his son, he said, "Oh, God, it's a boy." This reminded Diana of her father's original disappointment at her sex, and she reacted strongly to it. Then, she claimed, he added, "And he's even got red hair [which is common in the Spencer family]." He emerged from the hospital to face the tangle of waiting press. It had been a much easier birth than the last, he informed them. The baby had pale blue eyes and both mother and child were doing well. Then he hurried away, saying he was going to have a stiff drink.

With Charles beside her and cradling her new baby, Diana left hospital less than twenty-four hours after Harry's birth. It dawned on her quite soon after they had introduced William to his new brother and settled Harry in his cradle in the nursery that now that she had delivered the obligatory "heir and a spare," Charles's "duty" to her as a husband was over and that he would turn fully to Camilla. Her instinct was right. From then on, Charles was away from home even more frequently. "He's seldom here to notice me," Diana confessed to a friend.

Until Harry's birth, Charles's affair with Camilla had been a fairly close-kept arrangement. Diana, of course, had been aware of it, as were Charles's numerous confidantes who lent the lovers their homes for trysts. By now, they were blatant in their behaviour. "It was too much for any wife to bear," insisted Lord Beaverbrook, Andrew Parker Bowles's first cousin. "He has a lot to answer for. It was Charles who ran to Camilla when things began to go wrong with Diana. And once Camilla was ensconced, she started throwing her weight around. When she saw the romance was a runner, she simply took a proactive role. Of course, Diana was upset. She had every right to be.

"The first I knew was when Charlie Shelburne was getting married for the second time and his fiancée had to move out for the night from Bowood and went next door to Camilla's. Andrew wasn't there—but Prince Charles was. And after dinner Camilla made it pretty clear that the fiancée had to go up to bed pretty quickly, straight away."

The affair was still kept out of the press, but "it was a scandal being discussed as openly in London as the state of the Princess of Wales's obvious unhappiness." Then Andrew Parker Bowles became open in his wooing of the attractive Charlotte Hambro, daughter of Lord Soames and granddaughter of Sir Winston Churchill, which resulted in a shocking confrontation in early 1987 between Parker Bowles and Soames. Both men were members of White's, the oldest gentlemen's club in London and called by historian Percy Colson "an oasis of civilisation in a desert of democracy." Parker Bowles was going up the grand staircase on his way to lunch when Lord Soames was coming down. The two men halted before the floor-to-ceiling mirror mid-way. Soames glared furiously at the younger man and accused him loudly of turning his daughter into "a common mistress." Parker Bowles stood still for a moment. Then, without a word, turned on his heel and left the premises.

Diana was visiting Althorp with the children when she heard of the incident. Lord Spencer was well aware of the scandal surrounding his daughter's husband and threatening her marriage. What she must not become, he warned her, was "another beautiful, vacuous, spirit-broken Queen Alexandra to Charles's Edward VII," infamous for his affairs with married women. She must remember that one day she would be queen and that William would be king, the first of the Spencer-Windsor line. He advised her to make the most of her popularity with the public, to play a more important role in the royal show, and to use the media as they

Above left The man whose love Diana always sought—her father, Edward John Spencer—in uniform during the Second World War.

Above His marriage to Frances Fermoy in 1954 was called "the wedding of the year" and was attended by many members of the Royal Family.

Left Diana's maternal grandparents, Lord and Lady Fermoy. He was the only son of an American heiress and an impoverished Irish fortune hunter; she gave up a promising career as a concert pianist for marriage.

Althorp, in Northamptonshire, circa 1840. Royal guests were frequent.

Inset The enormously rich and powerful Sarah Churchill, First Dutchess of Marlborough (1660–1744), Queen Anne's close friend. She passed on her wealth to her favourite grandson, John Spencer, who also inherited Althorp.

The Honourable Diana Spencer on her first birthday. Her parents had been anxious for a son and heir.

Right At age three on a visit to Althorp, she was frightened by her austere grandfather, the Seventh Earl Spencer, but adored her grandmother, Cynthia, Countess Spencer.

Below left Diana and her young brother, Charles, at Park House in 1967 shortly after their parents separated. She felt responsible for him and guilty that she could not go to him when he cried at nights.

Below right On holiday summer, 1970, just days before her ninth birthday. At her school, Riddlesworth Hall, she won a cup for diving, hated the dark and surrounded herself with a menagerie of stuffed animals.

A Spencer family portrait circa 1972. Her father is seated between Charles and Jane. Diana kneels (end right), as does Sarah, (end left).

In 1975 Diana's father became the Eighth Earl Spencer and inherited Althorp. Soon after he remarried. His children did not get on with their step-mother Raine, Countess Spencer. Here, the Spencers are photographed on the grand staircase of Althorp.

Right At her next school, West Health, Diana would sneak downstairs at night to practice her ballet. Over her bed was a portrait of the Prince of Wales, who was dating her oldest sister, Sarah.

Middle Once her education was completed, Diana bought a London flat with money inherited from her American great-grandmother and went to work as a kindergarten teacher.

Bottom The Prince of Wales, pressed by the Palace and the media to marry, asked his two married favourites, Camilla Parker Bowles and Kanga, Lady Tyron, for suggestions. They drew up a list of five young women. Diana topped the list. Their first date was to a concert.

Above Charles claimed the Australian, Kanga was the only woman who ever understood him.

Above right But it was Camilla who he truly loved. She believed that shy, naïve Diana would not interfere with their royal liaison.

Middle Diana's grandmother, Lady Fermoy, (pictured in her London flat), welcomed the possibility of strengthening her ties with the Royal Family through her granddaughter.

Below "Wait until you see this!" Prince Charles told the press before Diana appeared shortly after their engagement in the startling strapless gown which she had refused to change before their departure.

Diana supported her frail father as she made her way up the aisle of St. Paul's Cathedral.

Inset "You look wonderful," Prince Charles whispered at the altar. "For you," she replied.

The new Princess of Wales with her royal groom on their way from St. Paul's to Buckingham Palace.

A father's proudest moment as Earl Spencer shares a carriage with the Queen knowing that at last the Spencers are linked by matrimony to the monarchy.

Above Bulimia plagued Diana but she was sustained by her love for her sons.

Left Diana, with Princes William and Harry in Majorca on holiday. Her marriage was greatly troubled and Charles returned early to Camilla's arms.

Below September, 1987, Harry's first day at school. Unnoticed by his father and brother he tries to shake hands with his distracted head-mistress, Jane Mynors, while Diana smiles down encouragingly at him.

Rejected by her husband, Diana entered into an affair with her riding instructor, James Hewitt who would later betray her confidence and spill-all in a book.

On tour in the Middle East, 1989. By now Diana and Charles are living separate lives.

She danced on stage with Wayne Sleep at a charity benefit performance and drew criticism from Prince Charles and the Palace, but the appearance gave Diana great personal satisfaction.

Above left and right She dedicated herself to work on behalf of children's charities, and she was rewarded by their immediate response to her whatever their race, religion or nationality.

Middle Right Her divorce from Prince Charles final, she became a symbol of mercy and love to the disabled and disenfranchised. In July, 1993, she visited a refugee camp in Zimbabwe.

Dr. Hasnat Khan, the dedicated surgeon who became the object of her love and admiration.

In Pakistan Diana visited Hasnat Khan's parents. She then met with Dr. Christiaan Bernard in South Africa to seek a post for Khan there.

Below In July, 1997, Diana and the Princes joined millionaire Mohammed al Fayed at his estate at St. Tropez where his luxurious yacht the *Jonikal* was moored and where she would be protected by his staff of 45 guards. (Here with Trevor Reese-Jones.)

Above Diana and friend Rose Monckton planned a private cruise of the Aegean for August, 1997. Diana was in love with Dodi Fayed and talked to him daily when that time came.

Dodi Fayed was also a guest on the *Jonikal*. Within 24 hours staff and crew saw that he and Diana were drawn to each other. She did not know that Dodi's current flame waited for him on a nearby yacht.

16 July, 1997. The al Fayeds, father and son with Diana aboard the *Jonikal*. Diana and Dodi would spend their last idyllic cruise on this yacht, called the "Love Boat" by the media.

Days of happiness for Diana off the shore of the Emerald coast with Dodi. They ended this carefree cruise a day early to spend a night in Paris before Diana returned to England.

The men in Diana's family life—Earl Spencer, her sons, and Prince Charles mourn together.

Far left, left
Prince William and Prince Harry march with their father, Prince Philip and Earl Spencer behind their mother's flag-covered coffin, a floral tribute of white roses from Harry with the handwritten word *Mummy* on top.

Below Diana's funeral in Westminster Abbey—fit for the title she was never to bear.

Right Earl Spencer, the brother she mothered as a child, delivered a moving and controversial eulogy that blamed the media for Diana's death and took the Royal family to task.

Below Diana's last ride to Althorp where she would be buried.

used her. She should never forget that she was a Spencer, and that she was the Princess of Wales, future Queen of the United Kingdom. Diana returned to London with renewed confidence that she could and would demolish Camilla's interference in her marriage.

IN THE AUTUMN of 1985, Diana welcomed with particular joy the plan that she and Charles embark on a second tour of Australia that would end in her first official visit to the United States of America. This was a chance to share an experience with Charles, far removed from Camilla's shadow, and to visit the country of her maternal great-grandmother. Charles had little enthusiasm for the tour and in Australia was withdrawn and cool to her overtures. Diana led a double life: their private time was fraught with hostility, but in public her smile glowed and she was radiant. Once again the problem was that Diana eclipsed her husband. She looked more glamorous than she had in years, the new designer clothes she bought for the tour were sophisticated and flattering, as was her smartly styled short hair.

However, she was deeply disturbed over Charles's reception in Australia, but there was little she could do about that or her own popularity. It was difficult to understand why placards and cartoons that exaggerated the protuberance of his ears should be so in evidence, "gestures made, plastic masks waved about, woundingly unnecessary things written in the papers." His anguish and resentment were twisted into further hostility towards Diana, who was treated like a goddess. On the morning that they were to visit his old school in Melbourne, he started a terrible row. Later, when they had arrived at the school his former music teacher produced a cello and he was forced to play it, which he did—badly. No sooner had he put down his bow than Diana, still festering from their earlier battle, walked to a piano on the far side of the stage and began to play a lyrical theme from Rachmaninov's second piano concerto with surprising command. It was an act she would regret.

"She was genuinely musical and loved music," a musician friend recalled. "She knew all the Tchaikovsky symphonies. You could discuss any one of them with her in some detail knowledgeably, which is very striking because even quite serious musical buffs only know four, five, and six, one, two, and three being regarded as much lesser works." Robert Pritchett, who was to teach voice and piano to William and Harry and often heard Diana play, contends that her playing was "competent but not outstanding," consistent with that of an above-average advanced pupil. She also loved to sing and had a sweet soprano voice.

However limited her technique might have been, though, Diana appeared almost a virtuoso at the keyboard next to Charles's rusty cello performance. But in upstaging him she had committed, in Charles's eyes, an unforgivable crime. He hardly spoke to her for the rest of the tour, and sat anywhere but beside her on the long flight from Australia to Washington D.C.

It seemed that the United States had gone temporarily crazy over the Waleses' impending arrival. Lady Wright, the wife of the British Ambassador Sir Oliver Wright, with whom the Prince and Princess would be staying, had seen her recent status of "hostess *par excellence*" soar to queen bee of American society. She was deluged with requests for invitations to the dinner in honour of the royal couple on 10 November 1985. But the most sought-after invitation was for the ball President and Mrs. Reagan were hosting on the ninth at the White House. The rich, the powerful and the famous were vying for seats at Nancy's gala. "An invitation is the equivalent to the conferring of a social sainthood," reported a Washington society columnist. Pamela Harriman, who claimed she was the "token Democrat on the list," also said, "If you haven't got an invitation the best idea is to leave town and pretend your mother is ill."

Mrs. Reagan's guest list included few politicians. The party was to be more for fun than diplomacy. A number of film stars were included: Clint Eastwood, Tom Selleck, and—at Diana's personal request—John Travolta, whose two films, *Grease* and *Saturday Night Fever* had made him one of the top stars of the moment and put him in a class of his own as a dancer.

Diana stepped off the Royal Australian Air Force plane at Andrews Air Force Base just a few steps behind Charles on 9 November. The early-morning winter sun made her stunning red ensemble glow and lit her golden halo of hair. Over a thousand people, including members of the British community and the families of American airmen, had come to welcome them to America. Before boarding a helicopter for the short flight to Washington, the royal couple met a group of elderly people and children. Diana lingered, touching their hands, kneeling beside the children, some in wheelchairs and seriously disabled.

Two hours later they were met by the President and the First Lady at the North Portico of the White House overlooking the lawns leading to the Washington Monument, the giant obelisk glittering against the unseasonal sun-streaked sky. The two couples exchanged pleasantries over morning coffee until Diana and Charles were scheduled to return to the embassy, ostensibly to rest before their activities began with the Reagans' ball that evening.

Diana was revitalized by Washington. Unlike Charles, who complained that they had been "going the wrong way around the world," she seemed impervious to the jet lag that would have been normal after such a long flight and the disparate time difference from take-off to landing. (Charles had added, "I'll survive. It's all in the breeding.") She insisted on meeting terminally ill patients at the Washington Home Hospice before she went off to the ball.

"She came into my room," a woman dying of lung cancer told a reporter later, "took my hand and said, 'Hello, Edith Pittman.' It was a sweet voice, soft, intimate. It was as though she was an old friend. She looked so beautiful, glorious blonde hair, such blue eyes and wearing a scarlet suit that cheered my room. 'May I sit with you a few moments?' she asked. She sat down, and the first thing she did was brush a stray piece of hair back from my forehead.

It brought tears to my eyes and she said, 'Oh, no! I don't want to make you cry.' It was a very great moment for me."

Thousands of people lined the way that evening, hoping to catch a glimpse of Charles and Diana as they drove back to the White House. Diana had never looked more lovely. She exhibited no sign of fatigue as she entered the anteroom, her hand lightly on Charles's arm, and was greeted once again by the Reagans. The President complimented her, and Mrs. Reagan commented, with a broad, pleased smile, "My husband has a sharp eye for a beautiful woman."

Indeed, Diana did look dazzling in a sumptuous, low-cut, off-the-shoulder gown of midnight-blue velvet, a multi-strand pearl choker with a circular diamond clasp around her long neck, and diamond and sapphire earrings that dropped gracefully below her short hair. She was seated at the President's right at dinner in the magnificent state dining room, which was heady with the scent of massive flower displays. (Each time Mrs. Reagan had inspected the room as it was being readied that day she would say, "More flowers!") While dinner was served, a Marine orchestra played music from Broadway shows, including *My Fair Lady* and *Camelot*. Diana laughed at Reagan's jokes, chatted earnestly to opera diva Leontine Price seated opposite her, and appeared to enjoy her dinner—lobster, crab, glazed chicken, brown rice, asparagus, fresh peach sorbet and *petit fours*.

This was the height of the Reagan presidency. Having survived the bullets of a would-be assassin ("Honey, I forgot to duck," he later told Nancy), colon cancer, battled against terrorist attacks in Beirut, the old "Gipper," still a handsome, charismatic figure, easily won a second term, and was accomplishing with his Reaganomics the beginning of the longest peacetime economics in US history. He loved the ceremonies of office from signing autographs to entertaining foreign dignitaries and Britain was a country he most admired. Although one critic has said, "You could

walk through Ronald Reagan's deepest thoughts and not
get your ankles wet," Reagan was considerably sharper than
his perception. An astute and wily politician, he used his
affable front to great advantage. At this point his memory
was still sharp and his instinct for the publicity that would
maintain and raise his stature (bred in his studio, film-star
past) was keener, except for Nancy's, than any one of his
personal staff. He knew that this gala for the Prince and
Princess of Wales would make headlines around the world
and he played his role to the hilt. "Charm to his hair roots,"
Diana would comment.

For Diana, the evening's greatest moment came after
dinner when the guests were ushered into the grand, mar-
bled entrance hall, to where the orchestra had been relo-
cated. After Miss Price had sung arias from Puccini and
Gershwin, there was dancing. Diana was in the President's
arms when John Travolta approached, apologized to Reagan for intruding and asked Diana to dance. What followed
was a scene "more sensational than any in Travolta's disco
movie."

To the beat of his current hit single, "You're The One
That I Want," the tall, darkly handsome Travolta spun Diana around the room as everyone else cleared the floor. "It
was really sensational—very wild, very swinging, very
sparkling," one bystander noted. "She was charming, ador-
able and down-to-earth," Travolta said later. "She's good.
She's got style and good rhythm. She knew how to follow
me and we did quite a few spins and turns. I'd give her ten
out of ten." They did an encore and afterwards there was
a round of applause. Travolta returned her to Charles, with
whom she next danced. "Compared to dancing with Travolta, it was very stiff and formal," another guest commented.

The next morning, at a press conference, Charles was
asked how the Princess had enjoyed her whirl around the
floor with Travolta. "I am not a glove puppet," he replied
sharply, "so I can't answer for my wife, but she would be
an idiot if she didn't enjoy dancing with John Travolta."

When asked for Princess Diana's impressions of America, he smiled wryly and answered, "We have both been overwhelmed and amazed by the warmth of our reception. I think it has something to do with my wife."

But once again her success had not pleased Charles, for she had stolen the show. On Sunday morning, when they attended a service at St. Paul's Cathedral, more than six thousand people were waiting outside and sent up a cheer, "Diana! Diana!" the moment she stepped out of the limousine. She received the same tumultuous greeting on their arrival at the National Gallery of Art to see The Treasure House of Britain Exhibit.

That evening they were guests of honour at the dinner given by the British Ambassador. This was a somewhat stiffer affair than the White House gala had been. Vice-President and Mrs. Bush represented the Reagans (who did not attend embassy functions to disavow any accusations of country favouritism). They had mostly high-powered figures from the international community who were all taken by the grace and elegance of the Princess. The people she met in the United States gave Diana a new awareness of herself as a woman who had more to offer than her status and designer clothes. They asked intelligent questions of her and listened and responded to her replies.

After just three whirlwind days, they flew into Palm Beach, Florida, where Charles went to play polo. That evening they were to attend a $50,000-per-couple star-studded ball in support of the United World Colleges, a privately funded organization of which Charles was president. He gave an impassioned, well-received speech on the need to promote peace and understanding through international education. Diana looked her glamorous best in a raspberry velvet evening gown, cut low at the back and draped sinuously across the front. With all eyes on her she waltzed with movie star Gregory Peck (still ruggedly handsome at sixty-nine) and foxtrotted with comedian Bob Hope, who had recently celebrated his eighty-second birthday.

Diana's only competition for attention at the affair was

a befrilled, flounced and garishly diamond-bedecked Joan
Collins, "the soap queen" as she was called, due to her
notoriety on the television show *Dynasty*, as a nasty,
scheming but seductive charmer. In the end, the Princess
outflanked the "queen," who left in a blaze of flashbulbs
but received very bad notices in the press the following
morning for her "vulgar display."

After four days in America, Charles and Diana left Palm
Beach for home on an RAF jet, arriving on Thursday, 14
November, Charles's thirty-seventh birthday. Her popularity abroad now gave Diana the idea that she could be useful
as a kind of goodwill ambassador, perhaps going on tours
on her own. As soon as it was made, this suggestion was
rejected by the Palace, who felt that the tour had not been
as advantageous to Charles's public image, dwarfed as it
had been by Diana's all-too-popular presence.

To the public, Diana's life remained "the stuff of fairytales," their interest in her more avid than ever. What was
published in the press and in books, however, only perpet-
uated the myths, for the Palace's long arm of censorship
extended into every area of the media. Stephen Barry's
memoir as a valet for twelve years to Prince Charles was
not published in Britain, and it was not the first book on
the Royal Family to have been banned. Nor would it be the
last. *The Housekeeper's Diary* by an erstwhile Highgrove
employee suffered the same fate.

The British press knew that Diana was suffering from
bulimia, yet it remained a taboo subject, as did the signs
of stress in her marriage. Camilla's name was not to be
linked with Charles, although from mid-1985 onwards,
when Charles was not on tour, they saw each other at least
three times a week, spoke on the telephone daily, and Camilla was hostess at Highgrove when Diana was in London.
Charles and Camilla had a circle of close, trusted friends
and Charles looked forward to these dinner parties. He sat
at the head of the table, Camilla opposite him. Camilla
oversaw the menus and served food as Charles liked it:

organically grown vegetables, poached fish, no artificial ingredients, measured servings—one guest insists that when peas were served there were always *exactly* thirty-two on his plate.

Camilla knew where to find anything she wanted—linens, dishes, silver. She supervised the flower arrangements. It was *déjà vu* of Edward VIII and Wallis Simpson at Fort Belvedere at the height of their affair. The similarities between the two couples did not end there: just as with Charles and Camilla the British people had known little of Mrs. Simpson until the abdication crisis because the British press did not reveal their knowledge of the intimate relationship. In the United States, there appeared a rash of magazine articles that hinted at problems in Diana's marriage, suggested she had anorexia (bulimia was not mentioned), and that Charles was having an affair long before the story broke in Britain. Camilla's name was never revealed, but in an article I published in *McCalls Magazine* in February 1987, I identified her with the letter C.

When Diana went to Highgrove, she would notice that things had been moved from where she kept them, and see Camilla's hand in it. Since Harry's birth, she and Charles had spent less and less time together. When not on tour, or at Highgrove "living the life of a dairy farmer," as the press had it, he was in Africa with Laurens van der Post, studying the primitive ways of the Kalahari Bushmen, and nicknamed "the Loony Prince" by a disdainful press. By the mid-eighties he had emerged as a committed environmentalist, banning aerosol sprays from royal residences and persuading the Queen to convert the fleet of royal cars to lead-free fuel. Soon his concerns spread to the ozone layer, global warming, the destruction of tropical rainforests. These were all important planet-saving considerations, but on occasion he was thought to be touching issues beyond the domain of a Prince of Wales, especially in his condemnation of Britain's move towards a consumer-oriented society, a state of spiritual decay encouraged by the Thatcher government's apparent credo of "every-man-for-himself" rush for wealth. The more attention Diana received from the press over her latest outfit or hospital visit, the further he plunged himself into his study of philosophy and spirituality. Diana was making about 170 public appearances a year and submitting, at the Palace's request, to dozens of at-home photo sessions with her sons. She was seen as the most glamorous yet nurturing woman in Britain, perhaps in the world, while Charles was viewed as eccentric, his "half-hatched metaphysics . . . and Jungian concepts," his confession that he talked to his plants, making him look somewhat ridiculous.

His failure to outshine his wife only increased his hostility towards her. Diana's former nanny, Mary Clarke, who had remained a friend, has said, "There is no doubt of the tremendous pain and hurt she must have endured when she realized that her husband had never loved her. How betrayed and used she must have felt. No wonder she came to hate him." However, another friend contradicted this assessment. "I don't believe Diana ever hated Charles. She suffered so because she was as obsessed with love for him as she was with hatred for Camilla, who she saw as the evil force that was destroying her marriage and her life."* She substituted the love of which she had been deprived with two other means of proving her worth—her dedication to her children, and the tremendous outpouring she received from the public. But she could not take that love home with her at night; nor would it be there for her if she woke at three o'clock in the morning, lonely and unable to sleep or find comfort.

She renewed a friendship from her Coleherne Court days with James Gilbey, a relative of the gin makers and a representative of a car dealership. She confided in him all her unhappiness. With him, she was able to become once again

---

*Still another friend commented: "Because of Camilla's avid passion for the hunt, Diana would refer privately to her as *Cruella De Vil*. "[evil Disney character who tried to catch and skin 101 Dalmatians to make a coat for herself]."

the carefree girl she had been before her marriage. His friendship boosted her ego so that she could deal with the real issue.

"Diana and Charles had separate bedrooms, but [by 1986], they were seldom even in the same home at the same time." A similar situation had existed between the Queen and Prince Philip during the decade that separated the births of Princess Anne and Prince Andrew. They had been reconciled, so in royal circles it was hoped that Charles and Diana would one day settle their differences. However, Diana had not been born royal with the credo instilled in her that duty came before all else, and she was of a new generation of women.

She was twenty-five and her sex life with her husband was over unless somehow she could lure him back to her bed. She was unable to control her bulimia, but it occurred to her that if she could conquer her fear of horses, which dated from a childhood fall, she might be able to accompany him out hunting. That, after all, was what Camilla had feared when they had had lunch together before Diana's marriage. Diana knew she needed help to surmount her phobia of horses. Enter Captain James Hewitt.

Diana had singled out Hewitt, at a cocktail party in Mayfair, shortly after she and Charles had returned in May from an official tour to Vancouver for the opening of Expo '86. Her experiences on that trip had fired her desperation to put an end to the mockery of her marriage. The worst moment had been when they visited an exhibit in the American section. Diana had been walking behind Charles, trailed by staff, press and crowds. She had vomited before coming and had not held down any food for several days. She was feeling weak and looked frail. Finally, the heat, the crowds and her illness overcame her. She put her hand on Charles's shoulder and whispered, "Darling, I think I'm going to disappear," at which point she collapsed. Anne Beckwith-Smith and Charles's aide David Roycroft immediately lifted her up and led her to a private room.

When Charles joined them, he was furious. A Princess

of Wales did not faint in public. She should have managed
to control it until she was somewhere that she would not
be seen. Diana was stunned. She perceived a loathing of
her in his tone, his cold glance. She did not doubt that her
mood swings and her "disgusting illness" had placed a
strain on their marriage, and for this she suffered guilt and
intense pain. Of their marriage, Charles wrote to a friend,
"It is like being trapped in a rather desperate cul-de-sac
with no apparent means of escape." Diana felt much the
same. The difference was that she had always wanted
Charles's love while he had needed a wife for, as Diana
had told a friend, "child-bearing and ceremonial purposes."
Hence her decision to try to win his love in any way she
could and her choice of a course that she hoped would
lessen Camilla's influence. She did not anticipate finding
love outside her marriage.

Hewitt was a good-looking man in his late twenties with
the assured carriage of someone with a rigid Army background. He had wide, bright eyes, an easy smile and a popular bachelor's polished way with women. He was staff
captain for the Household Division in charge of the stables.
This was not the first time he had met Diana: he had been
an avid polo player for the Army when he had been in the
Life Guards, and had played against Charles, who represented the Navy, at Tidford, a match that Diana had attended. Their paths had crossed since then: for a time he
had been attached to security at Buckingham Palace and
had come upon Diana, before her marriage, sitting barefoot
on the stairs leading to her apartments and talking animat-
edly to members of her staff. He was transfixed by her
sensuality as "her fingers danced across her bare toes." The
image stuck with him, and he developed a bit of a crush
on the lovely Princess, about whom he could only fantasize.

Through sporting ties, Hewitt knew Prince Charles and
Princess Anne rather better, so when Diana approached him
he was not in awe of her.

Diana told him about her childhood accident, how she
had lost the nerve to ride, and that she would greatly ap-

preciate any assistance to regain her confidence. Hewitt said he would be pleased to give her instruction at Knightsbridge barracks, where he was stationed, and which was conveniently located less than a five-minute drive from Kensington Palace. Diana discussed her decision with Charles, who did not discourage her.

Hewitt consulted his commanding officer, Lieutenant Colonel Morrisey Paine, who agreed that he might conduct the lessons early in the morning if the Princess would consent to that. She did, and within a few days arrived with her lady-in-waiting Hazel West and her detective Graham Smith at the indoor riding school. She was given a quiet, grey horse accustomed to beginners. The first lesson was successful, and Diana went once or twice a week for nearly three months before she ventured into Hyde Park, flanked by Hewitt, Hazel West, her detective and several other officers. After a few weeks, she had regained a lot of confidence—and had become aware of Hewitt's charms.

Their relationship moved on to a new plane: Hewitt became a mentor-teacher, someone she could trust. He was always encouraging, never pressing her to go further than she wanted to, never ridiculing her fear. She was comfortable with him. He made her laugh, and although he treated her with deference, she knew he was attracted to her. Soon they had made a habit of having coffee after the morning lessons seated side-by-side on one of the lumpy chintz couches in the Officers' Mess with its wall cabinets filled with gleaming silver military trophies and decorations. Although the detectives and Hazel West were close by, and other officers came and went, they were able to talk in relative privacy.

Diana asked Hewitt a great many questions, which he answered frankly. He had been raised in a family of women—two sisters, one his twin, and his mother. His father had been a Royal Marine and at sea much of the time. When John Hewitt was at home in Kent he liked to hunt, and horses were an important element in the Hewitts' lifestyle. From an early age James had been expected to ride well. He was also an able sportsman: he played polo, fenced, and was a keen shot.

By the end of four months, Diana and Hewitt had confided more intimate things to each other. Yes, there had been a number of women in his life, but he had not yet met anyone he wished to marry. He wanted more from marriage than what he had seen in his parents' home and which had ended in separation only a few years earlier. His mother, Shirley Hewitt, was now living in Devon and the proprietor of horse stables.

Diana told him of her unhappiness in her marriage, of Camilla's presence in it, and of Charles's withdrawal. They had not made love since before Harry's birth. She was terrified that her life from now on would be loveless and that she would be expected to stay in a sham marriage, left to fulfil herself in duty and through her sons.

This was a point when both these mature people should have, and perhaps still could have, ended their growing intimacy, for the signs of a fast escalating and mutual attraction were obvious. Instead, Diana began to telephone Hewitt daily and discussed with him the most intimate details of her unhappiness with Charles and the joy she felt when she was with Hewitt, who told her he loved her. Both knew that they were playing a dangerous game.

DIANA WAS GUARDED at all times by armed detectives from the SAS-trained Royal Protection Squad. Wherever she went, there had to be at least one detective with her and a back-up car carrying two more. These men were considered to be the best there was in the Metropolitan Police. They had to be crack shots, intelligent, fit, and fast on their feet. More than that, they had to be well-mannered, attractive and well-spoken so that they would blend in wherever they were, as a Palace equerry might.

Before she had confided in either Gilbey or Hewitt, Diana had turned to her protection officer, the personable Sergeant Barry Mannakee, who was married with two children. Diana was never alone; even in her own home, a bodyguard was always present, and it was only natural that a closeness evolved between her and the one person she saw more frequently than her husband, her friends or her sisters. She had to put her life in the hands of her protection officer, and this man had pledged to give his life for hers if put to the test. ("The one thing about guarding a woman," another of Diana's detectives, Allan Peters, once said, "is that if the worst happens you can pick her up and run for it.")

Mannakee was keenly aware of Diana's marriage problems, of how much an outsider she felt in the cold confines of the royal world, and he became her friend and confidant. Diana respected his opinions and the honest advice he offered. He was intelligent, with a calming demeanour, and a genuine fondness for children that made outings with the boys and Diana especially pleasant. William became quite attached to him.

Within about six months, Mannakee's friendship had become indispensable to Diana. A decade later she told Anthony Holden, during a private meeting at Kensington

Palace, that Mannakee had been "the love of my life." Still, it is doubtful that they were ever lovers. Mannakee was fifteen years older than Diana, and his attitude towards her bordered on the paternal. "I never saw any giveaway glances between them," one of William's detectives said. "No touching, or sign of body familiarity. They were on the same wavelength, shared similar views on some things and the Princess did seem better humoured in Mannakee's company, able to laugh more easily rather than giggle— which she did usually out of nervousness. I think she might have had a breakdown if it wasn't for his solid presence. She was a very unhappy young woman and I only saw her lighten up when she was with her children. You could see by the way she gathered them up to her how much she loved them, and she could become a bit of a child herself when she was playing with them."

Another royal detective confided, "The Princess of Wales was so tragic during Barry's time of duty with her, and he was a very caring man. All of us felt great empathy for her. We knew the truth and she was so young and lost. Until Barry came along, she really had no insider to turn to. I would swear it never went beyond that. Barry was a very sharp person, very dedicated to his work. He appeared to be happily married, loved his kids. It was simply not in his character to jeopardize everything he had worked hard for."

Later, gossip suggested that there had been an affair and that Charles and Camilla had restrained their passions until this time. However, by 1985, Camilla and Charles had been meeting at close friends' houses whenever they could not be at Highgrove together. From 1984 the Queen no longer received Camilla at her homes, and referred to her as "that woman who has seduced Charles into an adulterous relationship." But the gossip about Mannakee and Diana also reached her ears.

"This created a new aspect that could prove dangerous," a courtier has offered. "If such a story got out about the Princess of Wales, the public might immediately guess that the marriage was crumbling and cast their sceptical glance towards Charles as also being to blame. It was an extremely touchy situation." Mannakee was transferred from the Royal Protection Service.

Diana was upset: she felt responsible for his demotion and bereft of a trusted friend. More isolated now than ever before, she contacted him to convey her feelings. Mannakee warned her that her calls were monitored and not to call him unless she did so on her cellphone. Soon afterwards, he was killed in a motorcycle accident that Diana always believed had sinister undertones. Now she became frightened; if Mannakee could be killed in an "accident," why not herself? She did not believe she was paranoid: there had been something ominous in the way Mannakee had cautioned her to be careful.

This fear never left her. She recalled stories of the suspicious death of Baron, the personable royal photographer, who had been Prince Philip's friend and whose Mayfair flat had been used as a love nest by the Prince. (The story was that Baron would invite a suitably attractive, and hopefully discreet, young lady for tea in his lounge, which was situated beneath a balcony. The Prince would eye the prospect from above and if she appealed to him would join them for tea, after which Baron would take his leave.)

Diana was still afraid of the dark. A lamp was always kept lit outside her bedroom and the door left ajar. Sometimes she would scoop up William and Harry from their beds, bring them into her room and let them watch television until they fell asleep. Then there were frequent late-night calls to friends. "She'd call and tell me what she was watching," Janet Filderman recalls, "and she would add that William and Harry were sound asleep on her bed. Some time later she would ring back and say she had taken them back to their room. She was alone many more evenings than you would suppose."

She missed the kind of warm, masculine friendship that Mannakee had offered her. About this time, Sarah Ferguson became an important influence on her life. Diana had first

become aware of her shortly after her engagement to Prince
Charles. "She kept rearing her head for some reason and
seemed to know all about the royal set-up, things like that,"
Diana told Andrew Morton. Sarah's father, Major Ronald
Ferguson, was Charles's polo manager, and the two young
women met at various games in which Charles played.
When Diana was staying at Buckingham Palace, in the
weeks before the wedding, Sarah came to have lunch with
her and, according to Diana, was more comfortable there
than she was. Despite this overture, Diana was surprised to
see her name on the Palace guest list for the wedding.

Diana was fascinated by Sarah. She was "a woman with
a past." Although only two years older than Diana, she had
been the lover of widowed businessman Paddy McNally,
twenty-two years older and the father of two children. He
owned a large chalet in Verbier, Switzerland, and during
1980 and 1981, she had lived with him there. McNally was
smitten with the fun redhead, and was known to carry with
him a cutting of her pubic hair—which he called "the burning bush"—in a locket on his key-ring. But he had no intention of marrying her and Sarah had an eye open for a
husband who would raise her status. Diana was someone
who might help her.

By 1985 Sarah was a frequent caller at Kensington Palace and soon an invited luncheon guest. She was full of
high spirits, which was just what Diana needed given her
depressed state after Mannakee's death. That summer, in
answer to Sarah's cries of desperation that the years were
going by too fast and would soon overtake her biological
clock, Diana put forward her name as a guest at a Windsor
Castle house-party during Royal Ascot week. The hope was
that she would catch Prince Andrew's eye. He was known
for his attraction to lusty women and Sarah was certainly
that. She was also a cousin of Robert Fellowes, which put
her on the periphery of royal circles, she came from a
horse-oriented family and—like Andrew—rode well and
enjoyed challenging sports.

Sarah's parents were divorced; her mother, Susan

Wright Ferguson, had left her husband for Hector Barrantes, a wealthy South American polo-playing chum of her husband and of Prince Philip, with whom she had had a warm and intimate relationship only a few months before her affair with Barrantes. In July 1975, when Sarah was fifteen, her mother married Barrantes and moved with him to a horse ranch south-west of Buenos Aires. Sarah and her sister, Jane, were left in the care of their father. The parallels of their early years sealed the bond between Sarah and Diana.

Andrew and Sarah hit it off immediately. They had a similar raucous sense of humour, a strong sexual appetite, the same try-anything nature. As a seaman, Andrew was frequently away and the time they spent together, mostly in his rooms at Buckingham Palace where they often dined alone, was intense. At New Year in 1986, Sarah was a guest of the Queen at Sandringham. The Queen took to her second son's red-headed girlfriend straight away. As he was unlikely now with the birth of William and Harry to succeed to the throne, Sarah's romantic past was not a problem. The Queen enjoyed the company of this robust young woman, who "loved horses, rode well, liked dogs and even enjoyed playing charades." More important, Sarah was always good-natured, easy to be with, and devoid of the complicated neurosis that afflicted Diana. By mid-March 1986, Andrew had secured his mother's permission to marry her.

The press made a good deal of Fergie's "fast past." "Any girl who has reached the age of twenty-six without at least one boyfriend has something wrong with her," her father said in an interview at the time. Once the engagement was announced, Sarah moved into Buckingham Palace, as Diana had, to wait for her wedding day. She continued to go to work daily at a publishing house, where she was editing *The Palace of Westminster*. She claimed she would continue to work after her marriage, which endeared her to masses of British working women.

Diana did not feel competitive with Sarah until Charles started to make comparisons, complaining that she was not

"jolly" like Sarah. Diana wasn't sure how to achieve
Sarah's easy-going attitude. She had hoped that with Sarah
married to Andrew, she would have a close friend, an ally.
(She told a member of the press, "You won't need me any
more, now that you have Fergie.") However, as the wedding day, 23 July 1986, approached, she was no longer
sure. But it was on that day, and at the festivities, that she
realized how deep her feelings had grown for Hewitt who,
as a captain of the Life Guards, was responsible for the
deployment of troops during the day's ceremonial. She had
recently celebrated her fifth wedding anniversary and her
twenty-fifth birthday, which had both ended in tearful con-
frontations with Charles. As Sarah and Andrew exchanged
vows, their passion for each other obvious to all, Diana was
overcome with an overwhelming feeling of emptiness and
abandonment, the two emotions that had plagued her since
childhood. She turned to Hewitt, increasing the number of
her calls to him.

Despite the warmth and companionship Camilla gave
him, Charles was not much happier than Diana. He wrote
to a close friend: "Frequently I feel nowadays that I'm in
a kind of cage, pacing up and down in it and longing to be
free. How awful incompatibility is, and how dreadfully destructive it can be for the players in this extraordinary
drama. It has all the ingredients of a Greek tragedy."

Not long after Sarah and Andrew's wedding at Westminster Abbey, Charles, Diana and their sons were guests
of King Juan Carlos and Queen Sophia of Spain at Mari-
vent Palace near Palma on Majorca. Juan Carlos was a man
of great charm and Diana immediately warmed to him.
Queen Sophia, a former princess of Greece and a cousin to
Prince Philip, was most welcoming, the palace comfortable,
while the reliable Spanish sun, warm waters and smooth
sand beach gave promise of a perfect family holiday.

On the trip to the island aboard the King's luxurious
yacht *Fortuna*, Charles and Diana hardly spoke, and
Charles seemed to avoid her when he could. Once they
reached their destination, Diana spent her days with the

children swimming and building sandcastles, while Charles remained inside, reading. He was withdrawn, restless, not a happy or easy guest. Finally, to the Spanish Royal Family's surprise and annoyance, he left two days early for Scotland where he was joined secretly by Camilla. Diana remained until the end of the scheduled visit, then returned to London. On the Saturday night of her homecoming, Charles was still in Scotland so she invited Hewitt to Kensington Palace for dinner. He stayed the night. And thus began the affair that, for Diana, was the reality of her image of what love should be.

With Hewitt she felt protected, comforted and loved. She saw him as an Arthurian knight, come to rescue her, although she could never leave the castle where she was imprisoned. And then, of course, there was the gnawing question: did she truly want to be rescued? She might have felt loved by Hewitt, but that was not enough. What she truly wanted was to feel loved by Charles.

With a queen on the throne, a Princess of Wales more famous and admired world-wide than her husband (presumably the next monarch), and Margaret Thatcher having been elected on 11 June 1987 to a rare third term as prime minister, the country seemed to have become a matriarchal society. Queen Victoria, Britain's last female monarch, had created the title Prince Consort for her husband, had given him access to government boxes, and had listened to and acted upon his advice. The twelve prime ministers during Victoria's sixty-four-year reign all had been men of strong personality, and Alexandra, the wife of Victoria's son, Edward, Prince of Wales (later Edward VII), although much loved and a determined woman, remained in the shadow of her imposing husband. Elizabeth had followed the example of neither of her forebears.

She had not created Philip a prince of the British Empire until five years after she succeeded to the throne. When she did bestow on him this honour, she did not add his surname to hers. This meant that their children would be of the

House of Windsor, the name that George V had adopted at the time of the First World War in place of Saxe-Coburg & Gotha, which was thought to be too much of a reminder that the British Royal Family were of German heritage. This was difficult for Philip, with his strong male persona, and there was no doubt that even as he entered his seventh decade, "his skin flecked with liver spots, his hands swollen and twisted by arthritis," his age slowing him down a bit, it still rankled.

While the Queen's style was more domestic—dogs trailing her about the Palace, yipping at the occasional stranger, a scarf tied about her head as she strode around the grounds of her homes in sturdy boots or shoes—Mrs. Thatcher was alarmingly regal, dressed and coiffed impeccably at all times, it seemed, an aristocratic lift to her chin. One close political observer comments that "the weekly meetings between the Queen and Mrs. Thatcher were dreaded by at least one of them," and that Mrs. Thatcher would return to 10 Downing Street "badly in need of a drink." He added: "Without a Queen she would have been terrifying."

There is a story that was widely circulated about Mrs. Thatcher's first weekly meeting with the Queen in the spring of 1979. She had chosen a blue dress to wear for the occasion and to her horror found, on being presented, that the Queen was also wearing blue. Upon her return to Number Ten, the new prime minister sent a letter to the Queen's secretary requesting that she be notified in advance of what colour Her Royal Highness was wearing so that the incident would not happen again. An immediate reply was sent by the Palace assuring her that there was no need for such an arrangement as "Her Majesty never notices what other people are wearing." However, surprised at this first meeting to see that the Queen, who appeared taller in her photographs and at occasions with tiara or crown in place, was actually a good two inches shorter than herself, Mrs. Thatcher never again wore the high heels she preferred to her meetings with the Queen.

The truly powerful men in Britain at this time were two

newspaper moguls: Robert Maxwell and the Australian Rupert Murdoch.*

Both Murdoch and Maxwell were keenly aware of the huge profits to be made from the current popularity of both Diana and Sarah, and a day seldom went by without at least one of their papers featuring an irreverent front-page story about them. Freelance photographers were offered high sums for pictures of either woman, around which a story could be moulded. If Diana was caught hurrying from her car to an appointment, she might have been only late and wanting to avoid the cameras, but the caption would hint at how "troubled" she looked. The public regarded Murdoch and Maxwell as "heavies," but avidly read their papers for any news of Diana or Sarah, positive or negative.

Sarah's spiralling popularity increased Diana's sense of insecurity in her marriage. It was not just the press coverage she attracted. Her husband and in-laws were now making comparisons. Sarah was such fun, "a breath of fresh air," whereas Diana seemed unstable and depressing. In fact they saw her infrequently during this period: Charles was living a separate life; the Queen and Prince Philip saw the boys about once a month; and all the Windsors gathered for Christmas at Windsor (which Diana hated) and Easter at

---

*Rupert Murdoch's communication empire at this time included three of Britain's most powerful papers: the *News of the World,* the *Sun,* and the prestigious *Times.* In the United States he owned the tabloid *Star,* the New York *Post,* the *Village Voice* and *New York* and *New West* magazines. He had recently purchased Twentieth Century Fox film studios, as well as six television stations. Robert Maxwell's career was not this stable. A Czechoslovakian by birth, he became a British citizen after fleeing the Nazis in 1939. Elected to Parliament in 1964 as a Labour member, a financial scandal cost him his political career. Heavily in debt, he still managed to raise money to repurchase his former publishing company Pergamon Press as well as the Mirror Newspaper Group, Macmillan Books, and the New York *Daily News.* He drowned mysteriously in 1991 while on a Mediterranean cruise on his lavish yacht (suicide was suspected). After his death it was found that he had misappropriated hundreds of millions of dollars from his companies and their employee pension plans.

Sandringham (not her favourite either). There were no small family dinners or Sunday lunches. Charles saw his mother and grandmother on his own, and spoke to the Queen several times a week, wherever he was.

Sarah was also alone quite a lot, with Andrew at sea. She, too, felt an outsider despite her early acceptance by her in-laws. The jovial redhead had become a little too raucous, and Diana's mistake was to go along with her pranks and her unroyal behaviour. They had attended a David Bowie concert at which Diana—wanting to be "with it" and her age for once—wore mod leather trousers, and was castigated in the dailies for her unseemly attire. That summer, she and Sarah were at Ascot when they poked someone's behind with their umbrellas. That photograph circled the globe and was reprinted time and time again.

Viscount Althorp, Diana's beloved younger brother, Charlie, was now based in London where he had a £35,000-a-year job as a television reporter for the American morning show, *Today*, for which he had covered Andrew and Sarah's wedding. He was high-spirited and cut a rather dashing figure. He had a penchant for beautiful models and a thirst that helped earn him the soubriquet "Champagne Charlie." He was a concerned and loving uncle, saw his sister regularly, spoke to her often, and they were confidants. "I could make a fortune writing a book about Diana," he admitted, "but of course I never would."

Both Diana and Charlie still found Raine difficult, and neither visited Althorp very often. Their father came up to Kensington Palace once or twice a month to see Diana and his grandsons. He had had a tree-house built at Althorp six feet above the ground, "with steps up to the front door and inside a sink with running water and miniature utensils," for the boys' rare visits. "I love it when they're here," he confessed, "because they fill the place with their noise and energy. The moment they arrive they are everywhere, up and down the stairs, in and out of all the rooms, climbing over everything. It's always William [who, he was proud to note, was left-handed as he, himself, was] who's the ringleader."

Diana's relationship with Raine was strained: Raine's recent money-making schemes had shown an extraordinary lack of judgment and taste. Paying visitors to Althorp did not bring in the revenues she had expected and Johnnie had put an end to the sale of any more Spencer art, antiques and rare book collections after she had sold a mid-eighteenth-century Capodimonte ewer and basin to the Getty Museum in California. To ensure that the treasure did not go out of the country, early in 1986 the British Museum bought it back for £100,000. However, while she and Johnnie were in Japan in March, to promote *Japan and the East*, a book containing photographs by Johnnie with text by Raine, which they published themselves incurring losses of tens of thousands of pounds, Raine decided to raise funds by selling the rights to the Spencer name, crest and motto for a hefty fee to a Japanese promoter to build a golf club to be called the Royal Spencer Golf Club.

The Spencers, of course, were not royal, and the plan soon collapsed when the would-be developer, Matasaka Takahashi, was arrested on suspicion of illegally obtaining £500 million in loans. Then Raine decided to market copies of Diana's wedding dress in Japan and engineered a deal whereby a replica would be available to hire for display at department stores at £1,100 a day (orders were taken for the actual gown so that it was made to the bride's measurements, as Japanese women were generally much smaller in build than Diana). Several hundred facsimiles of the ivory gown were sold ("Japanese ladies dream of being Princess Di," one store manager averred), for over £9,000 each, 30 per cent of which was paid to the Spencers. This was the last straw for the Queen, who from then on never invited Johnnie and Raine to her homes.

Diana's love for her father did not waver despite her stepmother's ill-chosen schemes, which he had apparently approved, and that Raine had not asked permission to copy and sell Diana's wedding gown. It was about this time that

Johnnie got to know Mohamed al Fayed, who had recently
bought Harrods and had considered marketing Raine's replica wedding dresses but had quickly abandoned the idea.
Al Fayed advised the Spencers on investments and in return
Raine invited him and his wife to the lavish balls she loved
to throw with important and influential families as guests,
contacts al Fayed hoped would gain him entry into the British establishment.

Her father and stepmother's crass behaviour was another
source of unhappiness for Diana, who increasingly found
herself living a double life. A recent poll had revealed that
she and the Pope were the two most popular people in the
world. This seemed absurd to her and she could not understand it. Although she was not religious, Diana revered
the Pope and the goodwill he symbolized. In 1985, she
made an official visit with Charles to the Vatican. The pon-
tiff met them in an enormous, high-ceilinged room. During
their forty-minute private audience Diana held her hand to
her stomach when asking if he had recovered from the gun-
shot wound he had sustained in an assassination attempt
two years earlier. He misunderstood what she had said and
thought she had told him she was pregnant. He replied that
she was "the creator of life," and when the audience was
over, he rose, blessed their marriage and then, his hand
gently touching her stomach, the child she would soon bear.

Neither Diana nor Charles corrected his false impression. Diana was especially moved by their audience with
the Pope and it had a great impact on her.

No matter how foolish the media made her appear, the
public adored Diana. Yet she remained plagued by insecurity. Although apparently it was never discussed between
them, Charles was aware of her close friendship with Hewitt. Diana had the impression that he was glad she was
occupied and less likely to make things difficult for him.

In November 1986, Charles and Diana made an official
ten-day tour of the Gulf States. The desert rulers in this
region had enjoyed a special affinity with the British Royal
Family for generations, and Charles was warmly welcomed

"by the ritual audiences in their air-conditioned palaces." But it was Diana who visited the hospitals, schools and orphanages, and won the hearts of the people. When they returned, Charles's staff tried to sharpen his image—a task, Jonathan Dimbleby wrote, that "was doomed to failure. The Prince was a man for all seasons and for none, a man for his time but not of his time. Any attempt to hone his image or to strait-jacket his role to the vagaries of a shifting market would be . . . impossible in practice."

However, for the next twelve months Charles made a concerted effort to change the government's and the media's perception of him. He had private meetings with government ministers. He wrote more than a thousand personal letters to ministers, to charities and organizations: a schizophrenia helpline, a centre for Islamic studies, an architectural summer school in Italy. No gift, however small, was received without a personal note of thanks, and he smiled more in public. Still he was perceived as an oddball. This was curious because, privately, Charles has tremendous charisma. He could also be sharp-tongued and slow to praise, but he would reveal deep compassion for his close friends at times of illness, loss or hard times. Charles was perhaps as desperate for love and acceptance as Diana. Their tragedy was that they could neither give it to nor receive it from each other.

During 1987 they spent a total of thirty-eight days together. Diana made appearances for charities, schools, hospitals and a boat christening, mostly in or around London, and infrequently abroad. Charles spent time with Laurens van der Post viewing "the intangible wonder of the Kalahari Desert." He made an official visit to Swaziland, Malawi and Kenya. He launched the publication of his *Visions of Britain*, the book that accompanied his television assault on modern British architecture. He went to Hungary and lectured at Budapest University on the evils of Communism, and made other official visits to Indonesia, Hong Kong, Nigeria and Cameroon. He skied in Switzerland, went shooting at Sandringham, stalked deer at Balmoral, hunted in the Midlands, painted in Italy and played polo in June and July at home. Whenever it was possible, Camilla joined him. And when he was free of outside commitments, he was to be found at Highgrove, while Diana remained in London. It was no way to conduct a marriage, but by this time only the boys and duty held them together.

With Charles away so much, Diana's affair with Hewitt intensified. They spoke once or twice a day, saw each other on one or two nights a week, and the riding lessons continued close to Windsor, where Hewitt had been transferred to Combermere Barracks.

Diana had told Hewitt about her struggle with bulimia. The disease revolted him, but once he had accepted it, he supported her efforts to overcome it. He confessed later that he had always felt she was still in love with Charles and that in her heart she wanted Charles to see how attractive she could be to a man. In other words, he sensed he was being used.

The risks that Diana and Hewitt took were enormous. The affair might have cost Hewitt his career, but Diana stood to lose much more. For her there was always the fear that Barry Mannakee had been right in warning her of certain dangers. Charles would survive the revealing of his affair with Camilla, but if her liaison was discovered there would be a terrible scandal, which might lead to her disgrace, separation from her children, and perhaps the threat of mortal danger. But Hewitt's passion for her and his tender regard were impossible for her to sacrifice. And so many good things had come out of it. Although she was overtaken with panic when they were apart for more than a few days, her bulimia was less frequent. And when she and Charles were together, their hostility towards each other had diminished.

Diana and Hewitt's affair carried on into 1988, when on several weekends she joined him at his mother's small, comfortable home in Devon. She drove there with either of her current detectives, Ken Wharf or Allan Peters, and four policemen in a back-up car. The security team kept a low profile while the lovers relaxed with the gregarious Shirley Hewitt, who was probably less than ecstatic about her son's liaison with the future queen. He was playing a dangerous game. Diana's security team were well aware of the reason for these bucolic visits to the English countryside where Diana and Hewitt took long walks along the rocky coast, the detectives a few paces behind. They remained at a discreet distance when the pair picnicked. Two men took posts at the front and rear doors at night. The claustrophobic nature of all this finally got to Hewitt, and towards the end of one of these weekends he became silent and aloof.

Diana began to doubt the depth of his love, but she was incapable of breaking off the relationship. On Charles's fortieth birthday a ball took place in his honour at Buckingham Palace. Diana was given a dozen or so invitations for her friends, and she sent one to Hewitt. In May 1989, she invited him to a gala evening at Althorp to celebrate Raine's sixtieth birthday, at which they danced in the long picture gallery beneath the portraits of her Spencer ancestors. Hewitt got on well with Charles Spencer and his new bride, the lovely but too-thin Victoria Lockwood, whom Diana sensed instantly was also suffering from an eating disorder. Johnnie was gracious, but Raine was withdrawn. She sensed Hewitt's role in her stepdaughter's life and strongly disapproved, although she too, had been an adulteress. The difference was that Raine had not been married to the future King of England. The royal connection through her husband's daughter meant a great deal to Raine, and she was now seriously concerned that Hewitt, a virtual nobody, was placing the entire family, and especially her own social standing, in jeopardy.

PART FOUR

A Struggle to Survive

18

BY 1989 DIANA'S affair with Hewitt had begun to wane, although the following year the flame would flare up briefly again when he went off to join the British forces in Kuwait for the Gulf War. Shortly after he returned, the affair ended: he had fallen in love with another married woman "whose husband did not understand her." Diana refused to speak ill of him and, to a large extent, blamed herself for the parting; their meetings had always been cloaked in secrecy, in the presence of her security staff, at her convenience not his, and their relationship had been a threat to his career. All this was true, but Diana had matured in the years of their affair. She no longer needed to prove to herself that she was a desirable woman. Rather, she had to prove that she was a worthwhile person.

The young woman who, when cautioned by Charles to mind her head as she went under a low archway and had replied, "Why? there's nothing in it," now found it packed with opinions and ideas on how she, as a member of the Royal Family, could make a difference to the lives of ordinary people.

Her visits to the sick, disabled and elderly became more frequent. When she was unable to sleep at night, she would alert the detective on duty and make a late-night unofficial visit to the wards of the seriously sick who no longer knew night from day. She wrote hundreds of letters to patients she had talked to at their bedsides. She went to see some when they were able to return to their homes. She always came with small, thoughtful presents—nail polish for a youngster who had commented on how pretty the colour on her nails was, a box of pastels for a talented boy who had shown her his drawings. Above all, she tried to make patients laugh. "Being a princess is not all it's cracked up to be," she confided to one awestruck, bedridden teenager. "The trouble is it's so hard to have a pee."

Despite advice to the contrary from the Palace, Diana centred her energy on Aids patients, addiction, abused and battered women. And always children. She retained her patronage of such organizations as the Royal Ballet, but she made it clear that there were more important things than dance: "People are dying on the streets," she replied, when asked to give more time to her patronage of the company. Hostels for the homeless took her attention, and she spent hours, sometimes accompanied by Cardinal Basil Hume, the head of the Roman Catholic Church in England, talking to the destitute, listening intently to their stories, shedding tears when she was moved. She did not hesitate to put her arms round someone, whether they were suffering from Aids or living and sleeping rough.

"She seemed not to smell the decay and the dirt," one hospital attendant noted. "She did not pull back or turn aside when faced with a horrific injury or the results of a ravaging disease. There was something noble about her in the truest sense. I just could not put it together with the image drawn of her in the press, the glamour that her life entailed, all those gala affairs and the clothes. *My God*— the health care that could have been bought with the cost of her wardrobe."

Diana was torn by a great duality of purpose. She wanted to serve mankind and to represent the monarchy properly, and she was convinced that she could achieve both. Her life had taken a major turn: her bulimia was now infrequent, and this—and the knowledge that she could win a man's love—had empowered her. The emotional rows with Charles had tempered but there were times when her depression returned and she made fairly hysterical, late-night calls to Highgrove.

Charles was not in an enviable position. His over-wrought wife threatened his one sanctuary: his relationship with Camilla. His mistress, however, used this to her advantage. Camilla remained collected, no matter what the onslaught. If it was at all possible, Diana's outbursts brought the lovers closer together. Sides had been taken: it was Charles and Camilla with Charles's dedicated, well-trained militia of courtiers and camp followers, against a fearful Diana and her few close friends.

The boys were not unaware of the War of the Waleses, although Harry was now at Wetherby, a day school in London which William had previously attended, and since September 1990, William had been at Ludgrove, a boarding-school near Wokingham, Berkshire. Wills was viewed by his peers with a mixture of jealousy, resentment and discomfort. His personal bodyguard came with him and he had to wear a device to alert his detective if anything was wrong. Diana had argued against this, but there had been no alternative.

Will's first term at Ludgrove was traumatic. Before then, although he had often been separated from his parents for days and weeks at a time, he had been left in the care of the nursery staff who had spoiled him—to Charles's displeasure. At Ludgrove, he was subjected to the same discipline as the other boys. Also, he was self-conscious and his classmates regarded him as untouchable. He was unhappy at the school and could not wait for the holidays. "I know how he feels," Charles told a close staff member, when the family reunited at Highgrove for Christmas 1990. "I felt the same way as a child. It's difficult for him." But even more stressful for William and Harry was the drama being played out by their parents. With Hewitt gone from her life several months now a terrible loneliness took hold. She dissolved into floods of tears if Charles became confrontational, and equally if he ignored her. William had always been close to his mother, and seeing her cry upset him. "William had elected himself his mother's protector," a staff member says. "It was very touching to see them together. They were openly affectionate. Much hugging and kissing. The Princess was in a wretched state at about the time he went off to school. You couldn't help but feel sorry for her, or for the Prince [of Wales]. It was a tough call. It must have been absolute hell for both of them. I've seen tears in Prince Charles's eyes on more than one occasion. He is only human and he truly loves his children."

One day, over Christmas, William found his mother crying on the stairs at Highgrove. He ran up to sit in front of her, put his hands on her shoulders and asked her what was wrong. Diana tried to compose herself but could not control her tears and told him she would explain when he was older. Suddenly Charles appeared. William was close to tears himself. He turned to his father and shouted, "I hate you, Papa! I hate you so much! Why do you make Mummy cry all the time?" Then, according to embarrassed staff who were witnessing this family crisis, the little boy ran down the stairs and into the garden, followed by Charles, then Diana shouting, "Now look what you've done, Charles!"

"[From that point] when they were at Highgrove together, Prince Charles spent the days in the garden and his evenings going over his papers, and the Princess remained mostly sequestered in her room or with the boys in the nursery. The night before William was to return to school, she called down to the kitchen to order their dinners to be sent up with hers on trays. When Prince Charles came down at seven he was shocked to hear this. He had planned for the family to dine together on this particular evening. He immediately rang the Princess, but was unable to reverse her orders and so he ate alone, also on a tray, in his study, but went upstairs to say goodnight to the boys later, before going out. The next morning, a Sunday, there was a repeat of this wilful attempt to keep the boys separated from their father. Breakfast was served to them and their mother on trays in her room. Lunch was ghastly. No one interacting really. The boys talked to their mother or to their father, but there was no real conversation between them. When William was leaving a short time later everyone trooped out to the car. He clung to both his parents and by the time he was seated and the car was ready to leave, he had lost control and was crying quite bitterly.

"Without the children," the staff member said of Prince

Charles, "he seemed to prefer to be anywhere but with her—and who could blame him?"

Her deep self-disgust, her terror that she might be injuring her children by her emotional behaviour, set off an alarm inside Diana. She knew she was drowning and dragging others down with her and that she had to fight her way to the surface, face her fears.

The spiritual side of her had been reawakened by consultations with the respected astrologer Penny Thornton, who with her husband, Simon Best, was a friend of the Duke and Duchess of York, whose marriage was also at breaking-point. Diana saw Thornton several times a week. The sessions pressed Diana into a process of self-empowerment.

One of her first positive acts was to confront Camilla face to face. Charles and Diana were at Highgrove during a school exeat when a party was being given for Camilla's sister's fortieth birthday. Charles had assumed that he would attend alone but at the last moment Diana insisted on joining him. He was uneasy all the way to the party and kept asking her to change her mind. She stood fast on her decision. She walked into the house ahead of him as Camilla loomed into view in the hallway. She looked shocked at seeing Diana, who held out her hand. Camilla took it haltingly, her glance moving instantly to Charles.

Most of the other guests were a decade or more older than Diana and at a loss as to what to make of the situation. Conversation was strained—Diana might have been from another planet. (They even seemed to be speaking a foreign language. Charles and his friends spoke an upper-crust English practised mainly by the Royal Family and their courtiers in which the letters *er* or *re* are substituted with a broad *ah* like *pah* for power, *Empah* for Empire; a *w* is inserted before *th*, like *mawth* for mouth. Diana, on the other hand, had never acquired "aristospeak." Her speech had a distinct preppie touch to it, no drawl or emphasis on the vowels. The letter *t* at the end of a word was often completely swallowed, bringing in a reminder of Cockney. This is the way her Sloane Ranger friends spoke and she had found that it had a way of cutting through class differences.)

After dinner she was hustled upstairs to the sitting room with a group of other guests. Within moments she realized that neither Charles nor Camilla had come with them. An hour and a half later, she rose and headed for the staircase. Someone stopped her and suggested she had better not go. To everyone's horror, she went downstairs. She found Charles, Camilla and another man in close conversation, which stopped when they saw her.

All three stood up.

"Boys," Diana claimed she said, to her husband and his friend, "go upstairs. I am just going to have a quick word with Camilla."

Camilla appeared surprised, but Charles withdrew and his friend followed. Diana asked Camilla to sit down and then, a surface calm belying her inward angst, she told Camilla that she was not an idiot and that she did not want to be treated like one. "I'm obviously in the way and it must be hell for both of you but I do know what is going on." It was a bid to get things out in the open. "I just want you to know that I still love my husband despite his unfaithfulness with you." Camilla, like the well-disciplined royal mistress she was, said nothing. Diana went upstairs where Charles was waiting and the two left almost immediately.

On the way home, Charles ranted and she cried, all the anger and pain of the past eight years spilling out in a wash of tears. As always they slept in separate rooms. The next morning she came down to have breakfast with him and told him what she had said to Camilla. It was obvious that he had spoken to Camilla after they had got home, but the confrontation had served its purpose. Diana, by facing the enemy, had regained her own strength. All along she had mistakenly believed that becoming Princess of Wales was the end-all. Now she realized that it had been just the beginning.

Her first priority was to her sons. She would see to it that they were not distanced from real life as their father had been. She wanted them to be as normal as possible despite their royal birth. Away from school, she dressed them in baseball caps and jeans, had picnics, went to fun-fairs, bought them the music that other youngsters of their age listened to. Also, she had taken her father's advice and was working on her public persona. Her style had grown more mature, sophisticated, and she had learned how to use the media to her advantage. There had been hours of speech training, in which she learned to control her voice and be more relaxed before an audience or a television camera. She became an advocate for causes she deemed important, and in conversation with diplomats, politicians or intellectuals she held her own: 1990 and 1991 were the years of the true education of the Princess of Wales.

"I don't know why there continues to be such interest in me," she told one American reporter. "These are such important times," and she pointed out that since her marriage there had been the Gulf War, East and West Germany had reunited, Soviet Communists had relinquished power, Nelson Mandela had been freed after twenty-seven years' imprisonment and the South African government had repealed its apartheid laws. Margaret Thatcher had resigned and John Major was the new prime minister, deaths from Aids were terrifyingly high, and more and more homeless were sleeping rough on the streets.

Despite the difficulties in her marriage, she was looking better than ever and she was perceived as a woman of character. Then came the unexpected. In June 1991, William suffered a depressed fracture of the skull in a school accident when he and another boy were practising their golf swing. William had been standing too close to his friend, whose club had struck him in the head.

Diana was lunching with a friend at her favourite restaurant San Lorenzo, in Beauchamp Place, Knightsbridge, when her detective received a call on his cellphone informing him that William was on his way by ambulance to the Royal Berkshire Hospital. Charles had been at Highgrove and was already *en route* and the Queen had been informed. "The Princess turned dead white and raced from the restaurant in front of her detective," a waiter recalled. "No one knew what had happened, of course. But it was clear that it was something serious."

When Diana reached the hospital, Charles was already there and had agreed to William having a CAT scan. Both parents waited by his bed to hear the results. He was conscious and talking sensibly. The decision was that he needed surgery and that he would be transferred to the Great Ormond Street Hospital for Sick Children in London. Diana rode with him in the ambulance while Charles followed in his Aston Martin sports car. They were met on arrival by the Queen's physician, Dr. Anthony Dawson, and several other doctors, including the well-known neurosurgeon, Richard Hayward. The prognosis for William with surgery was extremely good, they were told. Still, they must understand that there was a risk, however small, that the surgery could damage the brain, or that the brain could have already been affected in the initial trauma.

The operation was scheduled within the hour. Diana remained by William's bedside, holding his hand as he was prepared for surgery. At one point she asked where Charles had gone and was told that he had decided to attend a performance of *Tosca* at Covent Garden at which he was to host a large party of foreign environmentalists, several of whom had flown to London expressly for the occasion. The decision had been taken with the advice of his staff and the Palace, who did not want the public to think that William was in serious danger. Diana was aghast: she understood the royal viewpoint, but in her mind nothing was more important than for his father to be with William at this crucial time. It was the ultimate divergence between the royal mindset and that of the rest of the world.

Diana waited with a detective in a private room while William underwent brain surgery nearby. The operation was delicate, and Diana had been advised of all the problems that might arise during the procedure. After an agonizing wait of seventy-five minutes, Dr. Hayward, still in his operating-theatre clothes, came to tell her that her son had responded well and was being taken to intensive care, where she could join him. Charles was reached by cell-phone. "Thank God," he said, on hearing this news. But he did not return to the hospital after the opera. Instead he boarded the royal train for the overnight journey to North Yorkshire, where he was scheduled to speak early the next morning at an environment symposium.

Diana remained with William, holding his hand. There remained the danger of his blood pressure escalating, which might cause irreversible brain damage or death. At about 3 a.m. he opened his eyes, appeared to recognize her, then went back to sleep. The immediate crisis was now over. She asked the detective to call Charles then broke down in convulsive sobs of relief.

The morning papers headlined William's narrow escape. Two tabloids hinted that the injury had been caused by a fall during an attack of epilepsy, from which he did not suffer. Diana was furious at this, but her greater wrath was directed towards Charles, who had continued with his visit to the Yorkshire Dales, ill-advised, it turned out, by the same pundits who had insisted he attend the opera the previous night. Bystanders, nearby, as he progressed on his mission, shouted their indignation in rude, bold terms. The banner on the front page of the *Sun* read, "WHAT KIND OF DAD ARE YOU?"

The next day he was at the hospital. Diana could barely acknowledge his presence. He accused her of blowing up William's condition out of proportion and of allowing members of the press to see her looking distressed rather than registering controlled concern. Charles later claimed that the doctors had told him the operation was a routine procedure involving negligible risk, that there had been no need for both him and Diana to remain at the hospital, and that he had not left for North Yorkshire until he received word that the operation had been a success and William was sleeping peacefully with his mother still by his side.*

*In his authorized biography *The Prince of Wales*, Jonathan Dimbleby spends three pages in defence of Prince Charles during this episode.

Diana was with William when he was released from the hospital to home care five days later. He had suffered no debilitating effects from either the accident or the operation, but such was not the case with his parents' marriage, which was now virtually over. Still, the pressure remained for them to appear to be a closely bound family. To some degree Diana went along with this, but she was beginning to investigate means of bolstering her defence if Charles and the Palace decided to destroy her reputation in order to secure his.

Six months after William's surgery, Charles insisted that the family go together to the Austrian ski resort of Lech. Diana was not easily convinced that William should be skiing. Finally the doctors convinced her that he was completely recovered and could now return to normalcy. A week before their scheduled departure Johnnie Spencer was taken ill with pneumonia and driven by ambulance from Althorp to the Humana Hospital in St. John's Wood, London. However, medical staff were more concerned about his heart. Diana was at the hospital every day and was cheered to see how well her father was responding to treatment. On 26 March 1992, just two days before she and her family were to leave on their skiing holiday, the doctors agreed that Lord Spencer could expect to return to Althorp on 30 March. Diana visited him on the twenty-seventh, a Friday. He was sitting up and complaining loudly about how bored he was and how anxious to be back at Althorp where the gardeners were busy with the spring planting.

"The theme had become a refrain, the gist of which was that the Prince was a neglectful parent, indifferent to the well-being of his children . . . The lies about his feelings for his children were a source of persistent torment to him. Yet he thought it was impossible for him to allow the truth to be known [that Diana sometimes denied him access to the boys and that she revelled in the media seeing her hugging and kissing them while he found public display of this sort unroyal], which he believed would wreak even more havoc on his marriage and, in the process, open the institution into which he had been born to a form of ridicule that he feared might prove fatal."

The Waleses arrived on 28 March *en famille* at Lech, a charming mountain village in West Austria. The next afternoon, a Sunday, Diana had just returned from the slopes when she received word that her father had died after a heart-attack. She wanted to return to London immediately, but suggested that Charles remain in Lech with the boys. There was a heated discussion. Charles's staff were fearful that if Diana returned alone the press would jump to the conclusion that there was a rift between them and that she "could not bear to be with her husband during such a crisis." Diana relented. The boys remained in Lech with staff, but Charles flew back with her to London.

By the time they arrived, they were no longer speaking. A dour Charles and a grief-stricken Diana were photographed as they left the plane and got into the car for Kensington Palace. Lord Spencer's body had been taken to Althorp for burial. On the morning of the private funeral service to be held in Great Brington, Diana left Kensington Palace by herself after another row with Charles. He had wanted to accompany her but Diana believed—rightly or wrongly—that his motive had been to counteract any press comments and had little to do with comforting her or respect for her father. She refused to be party to such a sham. Charles chartered a plane—she was driven from London to Northamptonshire—so that he could arrive at the service, if not with her then at least simultaneously.

TWENTY-FOUR HOURS AFTER the funeral, Diana was still at Althorp and Raine had returned to the town-house she and Johnnie had bought in Farm Street, in Mayfair, London. Charles Spencer—now the 9th Earl Spencer with an inherited fortune worth approximately £89 million, and owner of the estate, its land and treasures—called together Raine's staff. "We were told that her ladyship could take only what belonged to her and not one thing more," a senior member of staff recalled. All portraits and photographs of his stepmother were to be removed immediately, as were Barbara Cartland's books, which were presently being sold along with signed postcards in the gift shop.

A short while later, Sue Ingram, Raine's personal assistant and hairdresser, arrived to collect some of her clothes. Charles told her she was no longer on the Althorp payroll, then he refused to allow her to touch or remove anything. Diana intervened and eventually Charles agreed that Ingram could collect Raine's personal belongings from her wardrobe but that she would have to be supervised and the contents of the cases examined before they left the premises. After all these years, he was getting his revenge on his stepmother for selling the treasures he felt should have been left at Althorp. He did not trust Raine, or her staff and they were all given immediate notice.

The following day Raine presented herself unannounced at the locked blue gates of Althorp. The gate-keeper allowed her Land-Rover to pass. An unpleasant scene ensued, in which Charles barred her entry to the house. This was unreasonable behaviour towards the woman who had been devoted to his father for years, and had made him happy. Raine had brought with her a book of red stickers and wanted to place them on items that she believed were hers and wished to have moved to London. She could not help but notice that her portrait had already been taken down and replaced with one of the 3rd Earl, Charles Spencer, Duke of Sunderland, who in 1700 had married Anne Churchill, daughter of the Duke of Marlborough and his wife, the fiery Sarah, Queen Anne's close friend, thus merging two great families. Charles would have done well to do a bit of research on his ancestor, for he was known to be "bad-mannered, rude to everyone [including Queen Anne]" and was "touchy, assertive, one of the most unpopular of men, his own worst enemy."

Neither Diana nor Victoria, the new Countess Spencer, could influence Charles in his attitude towards Raine, which embarrassed both women. Trailing Raine through the house, the new Earl Spencer allowed her to sticker only her portraits and personal memorabilia. Raine left, head high, outraged but in control. The following day her maid, Pauline Shaw, appeared. She had come, she said, to collect the rest of her ladyship's clothes. Charles was not there and she was allowed upstairs. About two hours later she rang for help.

Lined up in the doorway of Raine's former sitting room were four large Louis Vuitton suitcases, which she wanted staff to take to the car. Charles reappeared with Diana, who noted that the cases bore her father's initials, not Raine's. Charles insisted that the cases were opened and the contents searched. If they were Raine's possessions, they were to be transferred to boxes or bins. In the end, large, black plastic dustbin bags were used. The cases were thoroughly searched, found to be justifiably Raine's property and stuffed into their ugly containers like last week's newspapers. One staff member recalled that Charles kicked "the bags down the stairs . . . I think it made him feel better."

In contrast to his brother-in-law's brutish behaviour, Prince Charles wrote Raine a warm letter of condolence. Diana struggled with her mixed emotions, her grief at the loss of her father, her desire to honour him in death, which should have meant respect for his widow, her own antipa-

thy towards Raine, and her wish not to create a schism
within the close circle of her siblings. Within three days of
their father's death, Charles had ordered an inventory to be
taken of the contents of Althorp to ascertain what had been
sold since his father's marriage to Raine. The final account-
ing filled him with even greater venom towards his stepmother. It was what he would call "the rape of Althorp's
treasures": paintings, furniture, silver, gold, rare books,
archives, manuscripts and drawings, china and porcelain,
land and cottages had been sold, worth millions of pounds,
which appeared not to have been reinvested in the upkeep
of the estate. Of course, at this time, Charles had no idea
of what it actually cost to maintain Althorp.*

Immediately he learned of his father's death Charles had
closed the house and the gift shop. Three weeks later he
reopened them to paying visitors, and raised the entry fee
by 20 per cent. "The atmosphere at Althorp was not what
it had been with the former Earl Spencer," an employee
recalled. "The new Countess Spencer was a scared rabbit
of a young woman. She never seemed happy there, or in
her husband's presence. And his lordship was an arrogant,
inconsiderate man. After her father's death, the Princess of
Wales seldom came to Althorp. She had not been there too
often when he was alive, but her visits, especially with the
young princes, had been happy occasions."

A memorial service for Johnnie Spencer, organized by
his son, was held on 19 May 1992, at St. Margaret's
Church, Westminster. Charles had made sure that the Spencer family, Frances, and Raine's family, including a sub-

---

*Raine, Countess Spencer, had received a fortune in jewels from her
husband during their seventeen-year marriage. She was left an estimated £4 million, as well as her husband's cash and investments and
an annuity of £10,000, their two houses in Bognor Regis and the
contents, and the house in London with all its contents. Diana, Sarah
and Jane were left only a memento each to be chosen by Johnnie's
trustees, and each of his grandchildren £1,000. However, trust funds
had been made for his daughters at an earlier time, although the
amounts are unknown.

dued Barbara Cartland in black, were kept separate, entering from different sides of the church and seated with a centre aisle between them. Diana sat with Prince Charles, William and Harry in the front pew with the Queen, the Duke of Edinburgh, the Queen Mother, the Duke and Duchess of York, Prince Edward, Princess Anne and Princess Margaret. Johnnie Spencer would have been pleased at such a royal send-off. Raine was photographed, controlled and smiling, as she left the service. She was not going to let the Spencers or the Royal Family see her crumble under what she considered her ill-treatment.

With her father's death even the façade of Diana's marriage disintegrated. She knew she was now in a vulnerable position. In August 1992, the famous "Squidgy tape" of telephone conversations between Diana and James Gilbey was published in the *Sun*. It had been recorded, Diana was certain, by Palace detectives and leaked to the newspaper to make her look like a wayward wife, and place her in the same category as the Duchess of York, who had recently separated from Prince Andrew after photographs had been published of her with her then lover nibbling her toes by a swimming-pool in the South of France.

The possessor of the thirty-minute tape had held it for three years, waiting for the moment when it would prove most valuable. This appeared to be the time: not only was the public fully aware that something was very wrong within the marriage of the Prince and Princess of Wales, they were opening their eyes to his intimate friendship with Camilla Parker Bowles. But another reason was given by Diana's close friends for the timing of the release of the Squidgy tape. "There was sufficient evidence that still another tape existed," one of Diana's staff has said, "not one between the Princess and Gilbey, but a shocking taped conversation between Prince Charles and Mrs. Parker Bowles. This one was made by an outside party, however, and the Palace only had knowledge of it, but had not heard or been able to acquire it. The chances were that it would surface sooner or later. Therefore the rush to leak the Gilbey tape,

which would point the finger first at the Princess of Wales
having engaged in adultery and thus mitigating to some
degree the Prince's unfaithfulness."

In fact, the Squidgy tape, which the *Sun* edited, cutting
out any direct reference to sexual contact between them,
does not make clear that Diana and Gilbey had been to bed
together and it is couched in tiptoeing language. Diana refers to the House of Windsor as "that fucking family" as
she complains about their cold treatment of her "after all
I've done." Later, Gilbey admitted that they had an affair,
but the sexual references in the tape are neither blatant nor
explicit. And Diana ends the conversation by telling Gilbey
about a recent visit she had made to Sandringham, when
she had wandered off with her detective to see Park House,
now converted into a home for the disabled.

DIANA: There was something really strange. I was leaning
over the fence yesterday, looking into Park House, and
I thought: Oh, what shall I do? And I thought, Well,
my friend [Gilbey] would say go in and do it. I
thought, No,'cos I'm a bit shy, and there were hundreds of people in there. So, I thought, Bugger that.
So I went round to the front door and walked straight
in . . . It was just so exciting."

GILBEY: How long were you there for?

DIANA: An hour and a half . . . And they were so sweet. They
wanted their photographs taken with me and they kept
hugging me. They were very ill, some of them. Some
no legs and all sorts of things.

Diana's relationship with Gilbey was never as deep as
the one she had had with James Hewitt. But the pattern was
much the same. These were men who she could talk to
about her feelings for the bruised and sick, her need for
love and compassion, the poor treatment she received at the
hands of her in-laws and how empty her marriage had been
for years. There was a driving desperation in her need to

communicate and to have a man express warmth towards her.

The publication of the Squidgy tape humiliated Diana, and frightened her. She sensed that only one shoe had dropped and feared when the next one would follow. She realized that she had to get her side of the story to the public. "She felt," a friend said, "the lid was closing down on her. Unlike other women, she did not have the freedom to leave with her children." Her greatest terror was that Charles and the Palace would discredit her, claim she was an unfit mother, remove her sons from her care, and prove that their father was the injured party. Having seen the same warped justice applied against her mother, she had every reason to be concerned.

She set in motion her counter-attack. What followed was a plot as secretive and suspenseful as the best John le Carré spy story. She could not give a revealing interview to the press, neither could she write a book telling her side of the marriage. But she could find a willing, sympathetic, respected and talented author, gather together her few trustworthy friends and communicate through them to the writer.

In July 1991, Andrew Morton, a journalist who had published several informative royal books,* wrote a series of articles for the *Sunday Times* that coincided with her thirtieth birthday. It was known that he was currently working on a biography of Diana, as were several other writers. But Morton had more credibility, a higher profile and, most important, had been sympathetic to her in his writings. He was contacted surreptitiously by one of Diana's intermediaries who proposed that, if total secrecy was observed, the Princess of Wales might be willing to co-operate with him in his present project. Morton agreed at once. It was a decision that entirely altered both their lives.

*At that time, Andrew Morton's credits included *Inside Kensington Palace, Duchess, The Wealth of the Windsors, Diana's Diary* and *Inside Buckingham Palace.*

At no time during the interviewing process, which took place at Kensington Palace over the next six months, did Morton come into personal contact with Diana. He composed questionnaires, which were delivered to her at her home. Morton, who had the code-name Noah, began with questions about her childhood, then the wedding, and the years since she had become Princess of Wales. Diana sat in her private sitting room with the door locked, answering the questions by "speaking into a rather ancient tape-recorder." When Morton played back these tapes, he was amazed at Diana's candour, rush of words and her confessions of attempted suicide.

Could she have been twisting or embellishing the truth to her benefit? "No. At no time did I or anyone involved in the project ever feel manipulated," Morton insists. "Far from it. What we all [the go-betweens and the editorial staff of the publisher Michael O'Mara Books] felt we were trying to do was give Diana a voice, for the truth to be told and to give her the chance to make a life for herself on her own terms. Was she manipulative? Yes, she was, but in a rather guileless way. The whole point about manipulation of the media is that it should not be seen to be done, rather like marionettes. [Later] Diana, unlike Charles, the Queen or, for that matter, Hillary Clinton, was found out, talking to journalists in their cars or phoning editors direct. Her manipulation, such as it was, was more a demonstration of her own poor sense of self and begs the question, Why should the world's most famous woman worry about her public image? Answer: Her constant insecurity."

However, there was more at stake for Diana now than her ego. She made it clear to her confidants that she feared for her life and for her ability to retain custody of her sons if Charles and she were to separate, which she now believed inevitable. Confessing to her attempts on her own life was taking a tremendous risk, for such an acknowledgment might backfire. But there was no other way to show how desperate she had been, how far Charles had driven her to the edge, how blatantly and cruelly he had deceived her, and that their marriage was a sham. She had been the sacrificial lamb to his image and his duty, the perfect cover for his affair with his mistress. During the course of her cooperation with Morton, she proved the validity of her claims by making available to him passionate letters and postcards written by Camilla.*

In 1995, she told interviewer Martin Bashir, in her appearance on *Panorama*, "I was at the end of my tether. I was desperate. I think I was so fed up with being seen as someone who was a basket case because I am a very strong person and I know what that causes in the system that I live in."

While Diana was surreptitiously feeding Morton the gritty truth of her marriage, she cunningly set the stage. In February 1992, with the book about to be delivered to the publisher, she set off with Charles on a tour of India, no longer the enchanted land of the British Raj, which Queen Mary, Prince Charles's great-grandmother, had visited as Princess of Wales at about the same age. Diana was not blind to the mystery and adventure of this exotic country, but she was aware too of the great poverty and suffering within it. Like Queen Mary, she had read several relevant books before her departure, learning what she could of the Hindu, Muslim and Buddhist religions, as well as words of greeting in several dialects. Unlike Queen Mary, she was immediately approachable.

When Charles was photographed playing polo, or addressing business groups, Diana took advantage of solo photo sessions. The most lasting image of the tour is of her sitting alone on a bench before the magnificent Taj Mahal, built by the Moghul emperor Shah Jehan as a tribute to his

*Morton was not allowed by British libel and copyright laws to use these letters in his text. In fact, in the original book (there was to be a second book, and a new edition with added material to the first book), he never comes out and says that the Prince of Wales and Mrs. Parker Bowles were lovers, but refers to them as having a "secret friendship."

great love for his favourite wife, the beautiful Mumtaz Mahal, who died in 1632. There is Diana, the intense brightness of the Indian sun lighting her hair like a halo, the garden tomb in the distance, the four shimmering water channels behind her that echo the four rivers of Islamic paradise as blue as her eyes. This poignant image made its way around the world, and the contrast between a princess deceived by love and one who gained love eternal, aroused great sympathy. Its irony was not lost on the public.

She was photographed alone again in Calcutta with the Sisters of Mercy; Mother Teresa was not there as she was ill in Rome. Diana ladled out bowls of food for the hungry, placed her bare hands on the heads and faces of lepers, and sat on the beds of the incurably sick. Four days after her return to London, she flew to Rome, where she was photographed leaning humbly over the diminutive nun, who told her, "To heal other people you have to suffer yourself."

"My life is torture," Diana confessed.

Mother Teresa grasped her hand. Diana smiled shyly, tears visible in the corners of her eyes. *Click* went the cameras. Pious nun and bruised supplicant prayed together. Diana looked almost transfixed. "I'm not saying it was all a sham," a photographer says, "but Diana knew the advantage of such images. I was told that she herself chose the place and time for the photo sessions. She was not being led by anyone. She was her own woman and she knew exactly what she was doing. These photos appeared before there was any knowledge of Morton's book, which she was co-operating on at that very time. Her public-relations instincts were brilliant."

This was the year, 1992, that the Queen called her *annus horribilis*. After a two-and-a-half-year separation Princess Anne and her husband, Captain Mark Phillips, had divorced (they had been living separate lives with new partners for a number of years);* the Yorks had parted after the front-

*"In a way, the Phillipses" marriage is sadder than the Waleses'," a Highgrove friend of both couples said in 1989. "The Phillipses are

page stories of her infidelity (his own indiscretions were never revealed in the press), and a story appeared in the *Daily Mail* in March, written by Andrew Morton and supposedly leaked by Diana, that the Prince and Princess of Wales were separating. In a matter of months the Queen had been assailed with the disturbing news that all three of her married children were on the verge of divorce, and in each case adultery was a factor. Then came the notorious publication of Morton's book, followed by a costly and destructive fire at Windsor Castle. In December, just a few days before the Princess Royal was to marry her lover of five years, Commander Timothy Laurence, RN, the text of the revealing, and often lurid, three-year-old taped conversation between Charles and Camilla (forever after to be known as Camillagate) was published in a London tabloid.

Morton's book was published on 16 June 1992. Diana distanced herself from it, claiming that she had not cooperated. Morton was under hostile fire. "The animosity, scepticism, and sheer vitriol," he wrote, in the foreword of his revised edition five years later, "with which the Establishment and their media acolytes first greeted the publication of my book graphically demonstrated the difficulties of presenting the truth to the British public." But the barrage of criticism he attracted was a small price to pay for the instant fame and tremendous financial rewards he gained from its publication. For Diana, her calculated risk had turned out to be a hand grenade locked in her grasp with the pin out. However vehement her denials, Charles and the Palace were certain of her co-operation, for there were too many things in the text that only she could have known. Doors were closed to her; telephone calls were not returned. Courtiers did not want to be found guilty by as-

---

friendly to each other, but emotionally indifferent, whereas at least the Waleses still quarrel spectacularly. He can still make her rush upstairs in tears; the nitrogen is very much there. On the other hand they have *nothing* in common, and the Phillipses do have the great shared interest of the horse world."

sociation. Charles no longer made a pretence of sharing their home in Kensington Palace. The publication of the book had accomplished two things, however: the public now knew how callously she had been betrayed by Charles, and he would be forced to end the pretence that was their marriage. But Diana worried that she had placed herself in even greater danger.

It has been said that Diana knew about her husband's taped conversation with Camilla and was an instigator in the leak to the press because she wanted to force Charles into a public declaration of his infidelity. Certainly, the publication of the tape corroborated the facts in Morton's book, instantly transformed her into the injured party and propelled Charles to acknowledge publicly that they were no longer living as man and wife. But, to the threat of all she held dear, there was every sign that events now forced Charles and Camilla into an adversarial conspiracy.

Despite her condemnation of "that woman," as she referred to her son's adulterous mistress, the Queen held Diana responsible for her husband's unfaithfulness, blaming it on the eating disorder and her emotional instability. However, public sympathy turned to Diana, for no wife in the late twentieth century could be expected to remain with a man who said the lurid things that Charles, in those pilfered tapes, had professed to his married mistress:

CHARLES: I want to feel my way along you, all over you . . .

CAMILLA: Oh, that's just what I need at the moment.

CHARLES: Is it?

CAMILLA: I know it would revive me. I can't bear a Sunday night without you.

CHARLES: Oh, God.

CAMILLA: It's like that programme *Start the Week*. I can't start the week without you.

CHARLES: I fill your tank!

CAMILLA: Yes, you do!

CHARLES: What about me? The trouble is I need you several times a week.

CAMILLA: Mmmm. So do I. I need you all the week, all the time.

CHARLES: Oh, God, I'll just live inside your trousers or something. It would be much easier!

CAMILLA: [Laughing.] What are you going to turn into? A pair of knickers? [They both laugh.] Oh, you're going to come back as a pair of knickers.

CHARLES: Oh, God forbid, a Tampax, just my luck! [Laughs.]

CAMILLA: You are a complete idiot! [Laughs.] Oh, what a wonderful idea!

CHARLES: My luck to be chucked down the lavatory and go on and on forever swirling round on the top, never going down!

CAMILLA: Oh, darling!

CHARLES: Until the next one comes through.

CAMILLA: Or perhaps you could just come back as a box.

CHARLES: What sort of box?

CAMILLA: A box of Tampax, so you could just keep going.

CHARLES: That's true.

Later in the tape the lovers attempt to work out a rendezvous at the home of a mutual friend, away from her "rampaging kids" and at a time when her husband will be in London. This is the most damaging segment of the conversation, for Charles proves that he places love over duty to his country. When the lovers were hoping that Camilla's husband's business would detain him in London, the nation was caught in a crippling ambulance strike that had lasted six months, cost more than £35 million, and had created life-and-death situations while the police and the Army tried to take the place of true medical assistance. Andrew Parker Bowles was on duty in London helping with the crisis. On the tape Charles seems almost exultant that the emergency will keep him away. "Just our luck," he moans, at the suggestion by Camilla that the strike might end sooner than expected.

The international press went wild with the release of the tapes. Charles came under severe criticism and Camilla, who received threats to her life, was too terrified to step out of her house. She had become the most loathed woman in Great Britain and possibly the world. She had turned a fairytale into a story of lust and deception. Sympathy was all with Diana, now being viewed as "Diana the Good" and "Diana, the Abused and Sinned Against." The fairytale marriage was over.

Prime Minister John Major addressed the packed House of Commons in December to say that "With regret the Prince and Princess of Wales have decided to separate," and that "The Queen and the Duke of Edinburgh, though saddened, understand and sympathize with the difficulties that have led to this decision."

Despite the evidence on the tapes of adultery by the Prince of Wales, the announcement was met with staggering political and public disappointment. The popularity of the Queen and Prince Charles dropped almost overnight, while Diana's ratings in the polls were on a meteoric rise, for Morton's book had been validated.

Diana spent Christmas 1992 alone. William and Harry were with Charles and his family at Sandringham. Her victory had been Pyrrhic, for she still feared the possibility of losing her beloved sons. The most recent events had caused her much pain. Despite her control of her bulimia she was losing weight and could not sleep. Great black circles appeared beneath her eyes. She looked haunted. She thought it might help if she could spend some time in the country with the boys, but Charles now had Highgrove. She called her brother and asked if she could have the Garden House, a four-bedroomed cottage at Althorp that was currently vacant along with a small house nearby where her armed bodyguards could be housed so that she and the boys would have some real privacy together. He agreed and Diana made plans to have her future "cosy nest" decorated to suit her needs.

She had already picked out fabrics with Dudley Poplak when in mid-April Charlie called to tell her that he had had to reverse his decision. The problem, he asserted, was security, hers and his nephews'. An intrusive police and surveillance presence would be required as Althorp was open to the public on certain days and it would be costly to close it.

Diana took her brother's refusal as a stinging rejection. The boy she had mothered and protected when she had been no more than a girl had left her to struggle on her own. She was deeply hurt and the incident caused a breach between them. However, it had one positive effect. Diana now shared with the stepmother she had so disliked a sisterhood based on rejection, for Charlie had been cruel to Raine, too. In May Diana contacted her and the two women had lunch together. They would never become fast friends, but at long last the bitterness had gone.

Diana was at a crossroads in her life. She hated who she was, but wasn't sure who she wanted to be. She wanted to put her fame and her ability to capture the attention of others to some good. Her meeting with Mother Teresa had had a powerful impact on her because she had seen how one person could make a difference in the world. She was sure her Spencer genes would not fail her, so she pulled herself together and prepared to fight for her freedom, the well-being of her sons, and a purpose.

ONCE THE SEPARATION had been announced, a plot was hatched by the Palace to derail Diana's popularity. At its centre was Jane's husband, Sir Robert Fellowes. Diana was in danger of being trapped in a web of duplicitous, disloyal and destructive forces. The Palace was determined to enhance the Prince of Wales's image. Diana was accused of denying Charles access to his children, of being "irrational, unreasonable and hysterical." A story was leaked to the press stating that "Her behavior is endangering the future of her marriage, the country and the monarchy itself."

Charles's circle had shut her out. Diana's few friends in the press informed her that daily calls were being made to newspapers by the Prince's friends and staff accusing her of everything from megalomania to near madness. Diana rang Charles and "scathingly asked, 'Why don't you save yourself a phone call and ring the papers direct?' " Charles denied any knowledge of the source of such rumours, but Diana did not believe him.

All members of the Royal Family stood solidly behind Charles and closed the avenues of communication with Diana. The Queen even overcame her own moral indignation and invited both Camilla and Andrew Parker Bowles to the royal box at Ascot. Prince Philip wrote a vitriolic letter to Diana, then refused to acknowledge her when they met at William's eleventh birthday party. The Queen and Prince Philip viewed Diana's popularity as the cause of the monarchy's problems.

Even Princess Margaret snubbed Diana. And, to rub salt into a raw wound, Lady Fermoy, age not mellowing her duplicitous character, visited Charles just three days after the separation was announced to extend her sympathy to him and to agonize with him over her granddaughter's in-

gratitude. She did not see Diana. It was clear that her loyalties remained, as ever, with the Royal Family and not with
her own.

Diana also knew that members of her staff were passing
on information to "the other side," and to the media. She
began to include unscheduled stops in her day, not notify-
ing staff until moments before her departure. By the time
she reached her destination—her local Marks and Spencer
food hall, her favourite boutique, or a friend's house for
lunch—squads of press would be waiting for her. She fired
one chauffeur whom she suspected of selling information
of her about-to-be visits, but the leaks continued. Diana
knew she must work out a plan to gain more freedom.

At present, she was a patron of over a hundred charities
and made more than two hundred appearances annually as
a representative of the Royal Family. The venues were selected for her by the Palace, her words were closely monitored, and her actions restricted. Clearly she had to divest
herself of this huge workload. On 3 December 1993, at a
charity luncheon, she made the following announcement:
"Over the next few months I will be seeking a more suitable
way of combining a more meaningful public role with,
hopefully, a more private life. I hope you can find it in your
hearts to understand and give me the time and space that
has been lacking in recent years . . . I could not stand here
and make this sort of statement without acknowledging the
heartfelt support I have been given by the public in general.
Your kindness and affection have carried me through some
of the most difficult periods, and always your love and care
have eased the journey."

Diana was acting as her own person, as she had since
the publication of Morton's book. She no longer trusted
anyone's advice, fearing the loss of her sons, or of her own
life. She did not view either of these possibilities as paranoid delusion. Her high profile and the Prince's acknowledged adultery had caused a steep dive in the popularity of
the monarchy and in the public's belief in Charles's fitness
for kingship. The history of the British monarchy was

strewn with the bodies of wives who had been replaced in the affections of their royal husbands or who had displeased them.

However, Diana was more concerned with the possibility of losing her sons than her life. The memory was ever-present of her own mother's lost battle to retain custody of her children and was a central reason in Diana not pressing for a divorce. She also knew that shortly after publication of the Morton book, Charles had agreed to full co-operation with Jonathan Dimbleby on both a biography and a lengthy television interview. Dimbleby was an insider in Charles's court, and Diana now felt she had made a mistake in co-operating with Morton, for it appeared that she had given Charles the opportunity to have the last word.

Out of the myriad charities with which she had been affiliated before her announcement that she was devoting herself to a more private life, she retained active participation in five areas that were the most meaningful to her: Aids, leprosy, the homeless, the Great Ormond Street Children's Hospital, and the elderly. The Palace had never approved of her dedicated involvement with Aids and HIV patients. When her friend Adrian Ward Jackson, a governor of the Royal Ballet, had been in the last stages of Aids she had driven six hundred miles to be at his bedside and had kept vigil for three days and nights, leaving his room just long enough to catch a few hours' sleep, then returning to hold his hand and tell him stories. When the end came, she remained at the hospice for several hours comforting family and friends of other terminally ill patients. "God has taken our mother," said one, "but put an angel in her place." Diana's long vigil and her appearance at Jackson's funeral impelled Lord Wyatt of Weeford, a friend of the Queen, to avow that the "Princess of Wales's work for Aids patients elevates them to heroes to be copied by the young. It's well known that Aids stems mainly from sodomy." This unconscionable statement had been meant to discredit Diana but had the reverse effect: it was considered by some to be the view of the Palace. The liberal press made much of it. Next a plethora of editorials broached the issue of there not being one person of colour among the Queen's 300-plus personal staff. This was followed by articles questioning whether or not there would or should be a monarch at all once the Queen was no longer on the throne.

Diana became increasingly isolated from Charles and his world. She removed all trace of his presence from Kensington Palace, and her social life centred around a few close friends—Rosa Monckton, Kate Menzies, Carolyn Bartholomew, Elizabeth Tilberis and Lucia Flecha da Lima among them. Her butler, Paul Burrell, became her right hand—her "rock," as she called him. She no longer spoke about anything personal on a telephone as she thought that Kensington Palace, her office at St. James's Palace and her cars were bugged.

A terrifying game was being played, but Diana seemed to be making the most incisive moves. On 4 December 1993, *The Times* headline posed the question, "Did Diana Go or Was She Pushed?" The press and the public now considered her to have been the victim of a cold, unfaithful husband and a system too strong for her to fight. Three days later, the Archdeacon of York, speaking on BBC Radio 4's popular *Today* programme, shocked listeners and the Palace by saying that the Prince of Wales was not fit to be king. "He has broken the vows [of marriage] and broken vows to God . . . How can he then go into Westminster Abbey and take the coronation vows?" This was followed by unfounded reports that the Queen had considered passing over Charles to declare William her heir. "The monarchy is self-evidently in crisis," the *Evening Standard* proclaimed.

The Palace, with Nicholas Soames as spokesman, immediately countered: "Being heir to the throne is not an ambition but a duty and one which will befall him at a sad moment later in his life. [Prince Charles] will inherit the throne and that is the end of the matter." But as far as the press and the public were concerned, that was not so. Diana had paved the way for doubts to be raised as to Charles's suitability to be king. She was derided for having lied about her participation in the Morton book—yet, to the further fury and frustration of the Palace, her popularity continued to rise. Peaceful demonstrations had taken place outside Kensington Palace where banners were carried by the faithful stating, "Diana, we love you" and "God Bless the Princess." But to Charles's horror, they also carried banners with the words "Camilla the Godzilla."

By now, Diana's anger towards Camilla had abated. She discovered that it was both nonproductive and misplaced. She had been used and abused by her husband, not by Camilla. She filled her week with the life-and-death causes she felt her presence could most benefit, twice-weekly sessions with her psychotherapist, Susie Orbach, and with Dr. Mary Lovejoy who specialized in allergy and clinical ecology (Diana took vitamins and Prozac to counter her bulimia), lunches with friends, letter-writing, gym workouts, the occasional shopping trip, and in the evening a private dinner, a good book (P. D. James, Daphne du Maurier and Danielle Steele were her current favourites), magazines (*Vanity Fair, Vogue, Harper's Bazaar, Cosmopolitan* and *Hello!*), television (*EastEnders*, Oprah Winfrey and old movies) or a video. She gave a casual dinner-party for six or eight friends every other Saturday night.

When the boys were on holiday she cancelled almost all social engagements and devoted as much time as she could to them, having their friends on sleepovers ("I want them to know that Kensington Palace is their home, not a public building," she was fond of saying), going on excursions with them to amusement parks, museums, team games and shopping.

She was an early riser and had a daily early-morning meeting with her secretary, Patrick Jephson, her press liaison officer, the Australian Geoff Crawford, and Anne Beckwith-Smith, who was, however, no longer on her regular staff. This would be followed by a conference with her dresser if she was making a public appearance so that her clothes would be ready. She had dispensed with the services of an equerry, but she still had a bodyguard with her twenty-four hours a day.

The press became increasingly oppressive. A dramatic photo of her was worth tens of thousands. If a photographer snapped her with a man, the price escalated wildly. Misleading captions would top a picture of her slipping into her car with "a secret lover," who was, in fact, her bodyguard. The man who ran the gym she went to, and whom she trusted, took unflattering pictures of her without her knowledge and sold them for £100,000. She could not walk from her car to a building without being mobbed by the press, who were determined not to allow her any form of private life. They stalked her from cars and motorcycles. They used long-range lenses to catch her sunbathing on a private terrace or beach, and jumped out from behind bushes and doorways to capture an image. Photographing Diana put money in their pockets, paid school fees, mortgages and placatory presents for their wives. Their constant presence so unnerved Diana that she would break down and shout at them to leave her alone. Whenever possible, she would place her handbag in front of her face—which earned her the nickname, within their circle, of "the bag lady."

She had thought the separation from Charles might give her greater freedom, more privacy, but she was wrong. Instead she was stalked more intensely by the media. When she travelled abroad the foreign press dogged her on revved-up motorbikes, shouted at her, disguised themselves as waiters, clerks, even, on one occasion, as a dental assistant, to get a picture of her. Life outside Kensington Palace was harrowing. She remained the most photographed woman in the world, her popularity topping the Queen's by 25 per cent.

Desperately Diana struggled to find a niche for herself. She remained happiest with her sons, and in her visits to the sick and dying. "Anywhere I see suffering is where I want to be, doing what I can," she insisted. But her mature good looks were even more striking than her youthful beauty. Her smile dazzled, the startling blue eyes captured everyone's attention. Magazines continued to clamour for pictures of her on their covers. Her face meant money, her message love: "The biggest disease this world suffers from is the disease of people feeling unloved. I know that I can give love, for a minute, for a day, for a week," she maintained. The hounding paparazzi did not doubt this, but photographs of Diana holding the hand of a child with cancer or a black Aids patient did not command the same price as one that featured her with a suspected new suitor.

She was still searching for a formal role and wondered if she could become a roving "ambassador," a job she was sure she could do well, especially after all her experience on royal tours. She appealed to the Queen to create such a job for her, but the Palace refused.

In October 1994, Diana was crushed when the tell-all book *Princess in Love*, by Anna Pasternak with James Hewitt's full co-operation, appeared. In it Hewitt revealed details of their love affair that Diana had believed belonged only to them. Besides its tawdriness, it was a terrible betrayal, and sent Diana into an emotional spin. Pasternak claimed that "*Princess in Love* was born out of a desire that the truth should be told in the most sympathetic terms to everyone involved." However, at the time of its publication, Diana's affair with Hewitt was over and had not been public knowledge. Now that she had separated from Charles, it could only harm her in negotiations with him and the Palace and perhaps give him cause to seek full custody of the boys.

Suspicions began to fester in Diana that the Palace might have had something to do with Hewitt's impassioned confession. She saw herself as the potential victim of a plot to destroy her credibility, which might sound like paranoia but there was enough evidence, however circumstantial, to convince close associates that she was in danger and to propel her into action.

Her power rested with the public. They were her army and, although some in her camp attempted to dissuade her, she was determined to rally them behind her by once again using the media, television this time. But before she could set the plan in motion Charles's long-awaited BBC interview with Jonathan Dimbleby was aired on 29 June 1994, to commemorate his twenty-five years as Prince of Wales. Meant to re-establish Charles as an industrious, caring man focused on his work with the Prince's Trust, the Prince's Youth Business Trust, the Prince of Wales's Institute of Architecture, his work for the Duchy of Cornwall and his position as chairman of the Royal Collection Trust to make the Royal Art Collection (which is larger than the combined collections of the Tate Gallery, the Victoria and Albert Museum and the National Gallery) more accessible to the public. The programme stuck to this script until Dimbleby asked suddenly: "Did you try to be faithful and honourable to your wife when you took on the vow of marriage?"

"Yes, absolutely," Charles replied.

"And were you?"

"Yes," Charles said, then added, "until it became irretrievably broken down, us both having tried."

What followed was not part of the text approved by the Palace, who had tried, along with the Queen and Prince Philip, to persuade Charles to abandon the interview and failed. Dimbleby asked him about his relationship with Mrs. Camilla Parker Bowles. Charles admitted to having committed adultery with her, that she had been "the mainstay" of his life for many years, and would continue to be a part of his life in the future. He admitted to three separate periods during which she had been his mistress: before her marriage in 1973; after the birth of her children and before his marriage to Diana (1979–81); and since 1986. The following day, Dimbleby released a statement claiming that the Prince of Wales had told him off-camera that the marriage had broken down immediately upon his resumption in 1986 of his relationship with Mrs. Parker Bowles.

Charles had believed that truth would be his best defence. Instead, it shifted sympathy into Diana's court, infuriated his parents, the Palace, Andrew Parker Bowles and

Camilla's parents, and made the "mainstay" of his life a focus of mass loathing.

Dimbleby's biography, written with his subject's full approval, was published the following October. It proved the long and intimate relationship between Charles and his mistress, relating intimate details only Charles could have supplied, and it painted Diana as an obsessed, neurotic woman. Just reading the index under her name reveals the position of the text: "volatile behavior . . . jealousy of Camilla Parker Bowles . . . alleged suicide attempts . . . photographed in a bikini while pregnant . . . resentment of the Prince's interests . . . attempts to control the Prince's life . . . self-absorption . . . outshines the Prince in public . . . persuades the Prince to drop some of his friends . . ." It was made clear by Dimbleby that Charles had never loved Diana, that she was nothing more than "a hired womb," and that her behaviour was "hysterical, obsessive and prone to violent mood swings."

But Charles's criticism of his parents, his admission of adultery with Camilla over so many years, his harsh treatment of Diana and her emotional and physical problems served him poorly. The Queen and Prince Philip were angry, Andrew Parker Bowles sued for divorce, the public and the press flew to Diana's defence, and Diana seized the moment to make her next move.

Shortly after publication of Dimbleby's biography, Diana entered into secret negotiations with two of the producers of the country's most popular news documentary programme, *Panorama*. There were many months of clandestine meetings at Kensington Palace to work out a programme format, and everyone involved was aware that if the Palace knew what they were planning, the project would either be axed or severely censured. Royal interviews were always subject to Palace approval.

At 11 A.M. on 5 November 1995, a Sunday, a camera crew and television reporter Martin Bashir entered the service wing of Diana's Kensington Palace apartment, opened for them by one of Diana's most trusted staff members.

The others, except her bodyguard, had been dismissed for the day.

Bashir and his crew made their way to Diana's first-floor study, where she was waiting for them. Her initial appearance jarred them. She was already made up to appear before the cameras. Her eyes were rimmed with black, giving her a haunted, gaunt look. She wore a conservative dark suit and a tailored white blouse which completed the sombre impression she made. It was an entirely different Diana from the woman known for her vibrant use of colour. Bashir is a low-key personality, an interviewer who never competes for attention with his subject, and it was no accident that Diana chose him. The programme would have an aura of dignified discussion. She had approved the questions, and it had been agreed that Bashir would not digress from these. If he did, she would not reply.

Diana sat in a straight-backed chair looking somewhat isolated from her surroundings. In response to Bashir's straightforward yet probing questions she related, in a controlled, modulated voice, her struggle with bulimia, the shattering realization that her marriage was a sham, her awareness of Camilla Parker Bowles's affair with her husband, her depression, and her own affair with James Hewitt, "Yes, I adored him, yes, I was in love with him." She added that his betrayal had "devastated" her. But a reference to Parker Bowles defined her appearance was when she said, "There were three of us in this marriage, so it was a bit crowded." She confessed concern about the Prince of Wales's fitness to be king, but affirmed her belief in the monarchy and her hopes for Prince William. She finished by saying that she would "like to be a queen in people's hearts. . . . Someone's got to go out there and love people and show it."

The interview was shot during five tedious hours in which Diana took many breaks so that she could prepare her answer to Bashir's next question. During all that time she never lost control or said anything she had not thought through carefully. She appeared greatly sincere, intelligent and mature. Her hurt and disappointment were over-shadowed by her love for her sons, and those who suffered more than she. Her demeanour, coupled with her dramatic appearance, made a stunning visual impact.

She waited until Tuesday, 14 November, Charles's forty-seventh birthday, which was less than a week before the programme was to be broadcast, to call her brother-in-law Robert Fellowes to inform him that she had done the interview. Fellowes was in a state of shock. "Does Her Majesty know of this?" he asked. Diana replied that she did not. Had the Prince of Wales been informed? No. He panicked. He informed her that he had to tell the Queen immediately and that he must speak to Diana after that. Fellowes was in a tight spot: Diana had "pulled one off." For any member of the Royal Family to give a personal interview and for the BBC to sanction it without Palace approval or knowledge was unheard of. The Prince of Wales was on a five-day official tour to Germany, and when Fellowes tried to contact Diana later that day, he was told she had gone to Broadmoor, a top-security jail for the crim-inally insane. He could not contact her. Diana avoided him for the entire week, and the BBC did not bend under pres-sure from the Palace.

Diana's bravura performance attracted the largest tele-vision audience to date for any interview-format pro-gramme, and was an unqualified success in terms of public relations and as a counter to the Palace's campaign to dis-credit her. But it had two immediate repercussions. Diana had planned that she would increase her public service workload again and was to appear at a large event for the Red Cross. Notification that this had been cancelled by the Palace reached her within a few days of *Panorama*. Three weeks later she was summoned to an audience with the Queen and Charles.

They met on a rainy Wednesday afternoon, 28 February 1996, the date Diana referred to as the saddest in her life. It was a private meeting, held in the Queen's study. Prince Philip was not present. The Queen sat behind her large eighteenth-century desk, the top neatly organized, with pictures of her grandchildren displayed in silver frames. She beckoned Diana and Charles to sit down in two facing chairs. Her expression was serious. Diana confessed later that she had felt like a schoolgirl before the headmistress for some peccadillo.

Elizabeth was now an aging woman approaching her seventh decade. She looked curiously *démodé*, her hairstyle popular with elderly women in her mother's day, her expensive ensemble matronly. Where once she had sparkled with youth and given the country a renewed sense of vitality after the grim tenure of the Second World War, she now seemed older than her years, a woman who had never developed the *joie de vivre* her youth had promised, nor her mother's lovable façade. The blue eyes had remained bright, but now there was more ice than fire in them. Charles had always cowered somewhat in her presence and left it in a disorienting mood. He seemed to Diana equally uneasy as the Queen requested that they file for divorce as soon as possible. This was an amazing order coming from a monarch who had always shunned divorce within the Royal Family to the extend that she had refused to allow her sister Margaret to marry the man she truly loved because he was divorced. The wrecked marriages of her three older children, along with Princess Margaret's to Lord Snowdon, seemed a revenge of biblical proportion.

The audience lasted forty-five minutes, and by the end Diana had agreed with Charles to a divorce. She determined that she would try to make their sons' lives as normal as possible under these terrible, disruptive circumstances. She was conscious of the hurt they must already be suffering from the public airing of their parents' problems. This was the last thing Diana had wanted, and the thing she most regretted. She returned to Kensington Palace that afternoon, inconsolable. She spent the evening alone, but was on the telephone to her closest friends until early in the morning. By noon she had issued a statement that "The Princess of Wales has agreed to Prince Charles's request for a divorce.

The Princess will continue to be involved in all decisions relating to the children, and will remain at Kensington Palace, with offices at St. James's Palace. The Princess of Wales will retain the title and be known as Diana, Princess of Wales."

To have made such a statement without the Queen's knowledge was, by royal standards, shocking and insolent. Diana appeared to have acted without advice and in fact she was on her own: Patrick Jephson, her private secretary, had left her employ some weeks earlier. Diana's ill-conceived reasoning seemed to have been that pre-empting the Palace would increase her bargaining powers.

The Queen met this presumption with icy disdain, immediately issuing a public rebuke countermanding Diana's statement and adding that "The Princess's future role and her title remained to be addressed."

Diana was well aware that the war between herself and the Windsors had been stepped up and that she had to be expertly prepared for any mines that would be laid in her path. She hired as her lawyer Anthony Julius of the firm Mishcon de Reya. Julius was known as a bulldog in his negotiations, and not likely to be intimidated by the Palace. But it would be the Queen, rather than Charles, Diana or their representatives, who would make the final decision as to Diana's position after divorce. The sticking point was going to be her title.

Diana believed, as the mother of a future king, that the honorific HRH was her due. The Queen was adamant (especially after Diana's unauthorized public statement) that she would lose it. It was a royal put-down, forged of resentment, and it was not the first time that a Windsor monarch as a means of retaliation had denied the title, which negated any royal privilege she now possessed. King George VI had been obdurate in refusing his brother, the ex-King Edward VIII, the right for his wife to be known as Her Royal Highness, an edict that Edward fought unsuccessfully for many years.

"They might think I'm a fool," Diana was quoted as

saying, "but I know their game. It's as plain as a pikestaff. Well, if they want me out of the way that much, they might have to pay for it."

Through Julius she demanded a lump payment (the original figure was somewhere in the neighbourhood of £50 million). Charles wanted to give her approximately £1 million a year, to come from the Duchy of Cornwall, his private estate. He would have to turn to the Queen for any substantial sum, which he did not want. The matter of Diana maintaining her office in St. James's was an especially contentious point. St. James's was now Charles's London home, and he did not want Diana to intrude upon his privacy there.

Negotiations dragged on for four months. Finally it was agreed that Diana would receive a lump sum of £17 million, advanced by the Queen, and that Charles would be responsible for the children's education, holidays, clothes and medical needs. Custody was to be shared equally between Charles and Diana. She would no longer be styled Her Royal Highness, and would henceforth be known as Diana, Princess of Wales. Prince Philip had fought hard for her to be demoted to Duchess of Cornwall, but the Queen's lawyers were certain that public reaction would prove devastating to the Royal Family and that Diana would only raise her financial demands.

Diana was permitted to remain in her Kensington Palace apartment, where she and the two princes would be under the efficiently managed security of the Royal Protection Squad. The IRA had renewed their bombing campaign and there was well-grounded fear that members of the Royal Family were targeted. For this reason, Palace lawyers argued successfully, Diana would not be given a home in the country which would create additional security problems. To Prince Charles's chagrin, she was granted the continuing use of her offices in St. James's Palace and £400,000 yearly for her expenses. Finally a clause was put into the deed of settlement that Diana must agree never "to write, speak or communicate any further information concerning the mon-

archy, the House of Windsor, Prince Charles, her marriage
or her divorce settlement."

Diana signed the document. She had been stripped of
her HRH and formally expelled from the Royal Family. "I
don't care what you're called," William told Diana.
"You're Mummy." On 15 July the couple were granted a
decree nisi. Six weeks later, on 28 August 1996, fifteen
years after "the marriage of the century," the divorce became absolute. Diana was free at last—or was she?

PART FIVE

A NEW LIFE

21

DR. HASNAT KHAN was an imposing figure, broad-shouldered, handsome, with intense eyes. Diana had met the Pakistani heart surgeon through mutual friends in 1995 while he was in Britain studying new operating techniques. A thirty-eight-year-old bachelor, Dr. Khan was dedicated to his work and to his wish to bring to his poorest compatriots the best modern medicine. Diana was in awe of him yet his company gave her a sense of inner peace. They became friends, and Diana soon realized she was in love. Dr. Khan, however, had higher priorities than satisfying his own romantic emotions and would not abandon them easily.

When Dr. Khan, whom Diana called Natty, managed some free time, they had quiet dinners together at Kensington Palace. "At first, I wasn't sure this was a romance," one of her friends says. "Diana was searching madly for psychological help at the time, attempting to define what her role, with the divorce pending, would be. Dr. Khan had a tremendous impact on her. She had never known another man so dedicated to helping people and able to do so. She told me that he had the gift of touch—something she always believed she had as well."

She was certainly acting like a woman in love. At the invitation of her young, newly married friend Jemima Goldsmith, daughter of multi-millionaire Sir James Goldsmith, and her husband, the Pakistani cricketer turned politician and humanitarian Imran Khan—no relation to the doctor—she travelled to their home on the Ravi River in Lahore, capital of the Punjab province, where Dr. Khan's family also lived. Lahore is one of the most romantic yet tragic cities in Pakistan. The great palace and mausoleum of the Moghul Emperor Jahangir and the Shalimar Gardens are just outside the city, which according to legend was founded by Lava, son of Rama, the hero of the Sanskrit epic *Ramayana*.

Imran and Jemima Khan lived in comparable splendour as a large segment of Lahore's population suffered unimaginable poverty and, as Hasnat Khan had told Diana, a shocking shortage of physicians and medical equipment. Echoes remained of the pomp and luxury of the lost land of the Raj, the panoply of imperial power once wielded by the British Empire. The great palaces and government buildings of that era remained, but they often seemed like a luminous mirage that disappeared into crumbling disarray upon close inspection.

One afternoon Diana sought out Dr. Khan's parents, who lived in a middle-class area reasonably near her friends. It was a pleasant enough visit but his family were strict Muslims and Diana sensed that they would put up great resistance to their son becoming seriously involved with a divorced Christian woman.

Still, she was happy in Pakistan. Hasnat Khan had given her reason to hope that they could somehow find a way to be together. In view of this she sent a letter to Dr. Christiaan Barnard, the famous South African heart surgeon who had performed the first heart transplant in 1963, asking if they could meet when she reached Cape Town, the next stop on her journey. Dr. Barnard agreed. Diana planned to ask him to sponsor Dr. Khan in a hospital in South Africa.

Hasnat Khan had not yet committed himself to Diana. Her attempt to find a place where they could live useful lives, yet be distanced from their cultural baggage, was made on a strictly private basis. She had wanted to have something concrete to offer him before she made the suggestion to him. This proved a serious miscalculation.

However, her desire to help Imran Khan raise funds for a cancer centre he had established had been her main purpose in coming to Pakistan, and she set to work almost upon her arrival in Lahore. Wherever Diana went the paparazzi followed, and this trip to Pakistan was no exception. As she often did when she wanted a cause to gain public

exposure, she encouraged press coverage and often manipulated the photo shoots. The images the photographers
caught of Diana in Pakistan were heart-wrenching, but she
found most rewarding the private time she shared with the
cancer patients.

"There was a young boy," recalled the hospital's medical
director, Dr. G. M. Shah, "who had a tumour on his face.
That tumour was festering. It smelled, it really smelled. I
was sitting four feet away, and I could smell it. And she
picked him up. She held him, completely oblivious to
everything. The boy could not open his mouth; one eye
was closed. It was not a happy scene. But she held that
child on her lap throughout a party we had. She was happy
to keep that child with her through the whole function."

There was no doubting that Diana had a talent for love.
"She felt she could inspire it, transmit it, increase its general
sum," British author Martin Amis recalled. "There is no
question that she made a difference in the homosexual community in England, and perhaps elsewhere. Her support
came at a crucial time, in defiance of tabloid opinion as
well as royal prudence."

Having seen the impact of her association with Aids patients, Diana now saw herself carrying the torch for others
who suffered. She believed she could heal—perhaps this
was delusionary, but her touch, her calming presence had
a strong effect on the sick—and she felt that with Natty
she could achieve even more. Shortly after her divorce,
Diana had told *New Yorker* editor Tina Brown, "[Charles
and I] could have been a great team, he giving his speeches
and me shaking hands and helping where I could." Now,
though, her vision was to raise the world's consciousness
of the plight of the afflicted.

After six days in Pakistan she flew to Cape Town where
Charles Spencer, his wife Victoria and their children had
established a second home. It was to be a reparative visit
to mend the schism in their relationship caused when her
brother refused to give her the cottage at Althorp. While
she was there, she had her meeting with Christiaan Barnard,

who has said that she thought she might be able to start a
new life in South Africa with Dr. Khan.

Besides her brother's presence, Cape Town offered other
inducements. Because of its historic ties to Great Britain it
seemed unlikely that the Queen would veto any plan for
the princes to spend school holidays there with their
mother. The city enjoyed a good climate, contained many
educational and cultural opportunities, and had a large Muslim community, which might have appealed to Dr. Khan.
Dr. Barnard could promise nothing, but he agreed to be
helpful if her friend should approach him.

By the time Diana returned to London, the tabloids had
wind of her new romance. She was quoted as saying, "I
want to marry [Dr. Khan] and have his babies," but Diana
disavowed having made such a statement. The doctor did
not welcome the publicity and refused to comment to the
press. With Diana he was gentle, caring and apologetic, but
they began to see less of each other.

"Diana was greatly disturbed," a friend said. "She realized she had jumped the gun and been too forward. She
had the glums for weeks after her return from Pakistan. I
think she had this whole fantasy going and now it had burst
and she thought she had been responsible. I don't believe
she saw Dr. Khan's decision to distance himself from her
as a rejection, rather as an admission that she meant too
much to him and would therefore stand in the way of what
he considered—and in the end, she did, too—his main objective: to help his people." Soon after, Dr. Khan returned
to Pakistan. His influence, however, was a key turning point
in Diana's life and in her deepening dedication to her favoured causes and in her philosophical views.

Dr. Khan was Muslim. Diana had close friends of that
faith and had become familiar with it during the years of
her marriage, for Charles, a regular communicant of the
Church of England, felt it important to understand Islam.
He and Diana had often discussed the religion's guiding
tenets. Diana had never been as strongly religious as
Charles. It was faith coupled with dedication to helping

others that appealed to her. She had found those qualities in Mother Teresa, a Catholic, and in Hasnat Khan, a Muslim. Caring for people crossed the boundaries of race and religion, and she was growing more certain that this was where her future lay.

She plunged deeper into introspective study. Staff noticed that her bedside table now contained biographies of the great, Tchaikovsky ("He killed himself because of his homosexuality," she told a friend. "He was only fifty-three. All that glorious music he could have written lost because of the intolerance of the world"), Gandhi and Dr. Barnard among them, although she still took the latest Danielle Steele or Jeffrey Archer novel with her when she travelled.

Diana was a great contradiction. She loved the glitz her position engendered, the exciting power-people she met, and the glamorous clothes that were designed for her. Yet she was a needy woman who hungered for love and was often happiest in simple clothes and with the dispossessed and the afflicted whom others have found repugnant. This duality of personality was the most fascinating aspect of this woman who had caught the attention of the world and held it with awesome regard.

Long ago she had shed the persona of the dim Sloane Ranger, whom Camilla and Kanga had thought they could manipulate, and whom Charles believed was "rather absent upstairs in the brain department." Diana had her full wits about her now and she was proving cleverer than anyone could have supposed. She was fond of saying, "I got it all wrong." But it was Charles and his acolytes who had been misled.

"They have a class uneasiness about everything that smacks of intensity," a close observer comments. "What few people understood is that Diana's love for Charles, like everything else about her [was] embarrassingly intense. If she had been a chilly opportunist, she might have accommodated the marital arrangement favoured by so many of her former husband's friends. But her love was tenacious, desperate, uncompromising. Her temperament was not the

sort to take a husband's infidelity in her stride. Charles
thought he had married a demure deb, but Diana harboured
a cache of emotions straight out of Emily Brontë."

Now, severed from the bonds of her restrictive marriage,
Diana was able to follow the inner logic of her heart. Her
overwhelming need to love and be loved made friends feel
she was hell-bent on finding the right man with whom to
achieve this. Both William and Harry were rugby mad, and
Diana developed a friendship with rugby star Will Carling,
who arranged for the boys to spend time with the England
team during a training session. Within a short time, Diana
and Carling, who was married, began meeting for breakfast.
Rumours flew and although Diana denied there had been a
romance, Julia Carling threatened a divorce suit naming
Diana as co-respondent. The couple did divorce, but without implicating Diana.

Certainly there were men in Diana's life. Her beauty and
fame drew them to her. Also she was not timid in making
it known to a particular man that she found him attractive.
In any other recently divorced woman, none of this would
have seemed unusual or scandalous. But Diana was the
mother of a future king, and still the Princess of Wales,
which changed the equation considerably. The media ex-
ploited her supposed "affairs," which distressed her, but she
remained determined to have a life of her own.

In August 1996, she had received a telephone call from
Hollywood film star Kevin Costner. Diana had always
loved socializing with the stars and suspected that he might
be asking her to appear at a gala benefit of some sort. Instead, Costner told her that he was in the process of developing a script as a sequel to his recently successful
movie, *The Bodyguard*, in which he had co-starred with
Whitney Houston. The story was to be about a princess
who has to be rescued by her bodyguard from kidnappers.
He was planning to reprise his role and he hoped she might
consider the possibility of playing the princess. Diana told
Costner that she didn't know if she could act and wouldn't
want to make a fool of herself. She spoke with him "about

the level of sophistication and dignity that the part would have to have."

Costner says she told him, "Look, my life is maybe going to become my own at some point. Go ahead and do this script and when it's ready I'll be in a really good spot." She joked about the call to her staff. It seemed an unlikely project to come to fruition and she did not expect to hear from Costner again. But he called her a second time to tell her that the script was being written. Still she pushed the whole idea out of her head.*

In early October 1996, Diana was a privileged spectator at a life-saving heart-transplant operation on a seven-year-old child from Cameroon, the medical team led by Sir Magdi Yacoub, a well-known surgeon and a friend of Dr. Khan. "All that blood. I'm sure I would keel over. How can you stand watching those things?" Anthony Holden asked her a week later, when he interviewed her at Kensington Palace.

"If I am to care for people in hospital," Diana replied, "I need to know every aspect of the long treatment they have been through." This was after the affair with Dr. Khan had ended, but her prerogatives had not changed. When Holden enquired if she was considering marrying again she was pensive for a moment. Then she said, "I'm in no hurry to get married. I'm looking for a man who knows what I'm about."

"And what is that?"

"Caring. I'm about caring. I thought I'd married a man that understood that first time around, but I got it wrong. I'm not going to make the same mistake twice." She still retained remnants of bitterness. "They can't get me now,"

---

*Kevin Costner received the finished script of *The Bodyguard II* on 3 September 1997, three days after her death. "I picked it up and the first thirty pages were totally her," he said. "It was dignified, sexy, smart, funny . . . and I couldn't finish it. I stopped. It broke my heart." He had not spoken to Diana during the intervening year, and she is not known to have mentioned the idea to any member of her staff.

she said, referring to the Royal Family. "In fact, I think they're frightened of what I can do to them."

The Palace, if not yet "frightened" of her, was alert to the danger she represented to its well-being. "It wasn't just the divorce, the tell-all boyfriend, the married rugby star," British author Martin Amis reflected. "She introduced an informality, a candid modernity, into a system that could offer no resistance to it; she had a beauty in her life that made [the Royals] seem ugly." She could easily be seen as a potential saboteur of the monarchy. For she was *real*. People could and *did* touch her. She combined youth, caring and beauty, where the Royal Family were cold, distant and, on the whole, rather graceless.

A fortnight after her return from Pakistan and South Africa, she had arrived at Harrods for a charity book launch honouring Sir Magdi on the arm of her father's old friend, Mohamed al Fayed. Although he was controversial Diana liked him: he had treated her with kindly warmth and he respected her need to work. He shared with her the experience of having been turned away by the Royal Family, in al Fayed's case at great financial expense.

He had sponsored the Royal Windsor Horse Show to prove his loyalty to the Queen and to support her interests. He had bought Harrods department store, and placed Raine Spencer on the board, when it was in serious difficulties, believing he was saving a British landmark. Then he acquired the quintessential British magazine *Punch*, Fulham Football Club and the historic Balnagown Castle in Scotland, all in a failed effort to break into the establishment. His brother Ali became the owner of the prestigious Turnbull & Asser gentlemen's outfitters and was similarly ignored. The Fayeds never understood that no matter how rich one was, the British aristocracy did not welcome merchants easily into their ranks. Many among them called al Fayed an "Arab" in a most pejorative manner. He countered that he was Egyptian. Accusations were made that his entire background as told by him was a lie, and that the huge sum (£656 million) he had paid for Harrods and its affiliated stores in the House of Fraser, had been given him by his former brother-in-law, the arms dealer Adnan Khashoggi. Al Fayed's friendship with Diana, however casual, was interpreted as social climbing, and the Queen considered his lavish presents to the boys ostentatious.

Harry, "the impish one," had one more year at Ludgrove before joining William at Eton. William now towered over his father. "Finding jeans to fit him is a problem," Diana confessed, with an edge of pride. To Tina Brown on a trip to New York, she said, "I would like him to grow up as press savvy as John F. Kennedy, Jr. I try to din into him all the time about the media, the danger, and how he must understand and handle it." She was grooming Harry to be "a huge support to his brother. The boys will be properly prepared. I am making sure of this," she added. "I don't want them to suffer the way I did."

William was already being groomed elsewhere for his future role. On most Sunday afternoons he had tea with the Queen and she had begun her tutelage of his royal heritage and duties. "Relationships with grandchildren are always easier than those with your own children," says one of the Queen's courtiers. "She may have stressed duty over spontaneity with her son, but she may have learned her lesson. Her Majesty has mellowed quite a bit."

"Not to any noticeable degree," said another courtier. "The Queen is playing her hand carefully. Her objective is to win Prince William over to the Windsors from the Spencers' influence, to make him aware of his duty and his future. Her Majesty is applying a different spin to this message than she did to Prince Charles. However, with her grandsons, she does not feel committed to answer to Prince Philip. Her relationship to her grandsons, and especially to Prince William, is entirely of her own making. But the Queen still finds it difficult to touch or be touched. A normal show of affection, like a hug or an arm about a child's shoulder, is hard, if not impossible, for her. She is always aware of her oneness. Except perhaps when she is out walking with her beloved corgis. I've seen her take them up in her arms and hold them to her. In the very expansive way in which she makes this gesture you can see the shocking need she has to be able to grasp life to her. When one of her dogs dies she grieves for months and visits their graves for years."

Diana understood this in the Queen for she had been subject to the rule that members of the Royal Family must not be touched. One of her ladies-in-waiting confessed to a moment of torment when "the Princess was crying most poignantly. It was when she had just learned of her father's death and I was alone with her. I wanted desperately to put my arms around her. It was what any decent person would have done in ordinary circumstances. But it would have been unpardonable to have done so with the Princess of Wales. An important code would have been broken. No, no, I couldn't bring myself to do it. So I slipped quietly out of the room. I've never forgiven myself for that. I think it will haunt me to my grave."

On the other hand, Diana was quick to hug and kiss her children. She called William "the deep thinker," and she worried more about Harry, because as the younger brother to the heir to the throne, he would not receive the same attention as William. But it was William with whom she shared a greater affinity. Since his parents' divorce he had taken on the role of his mother's protector. Shy by nature, he was attuned to her moods. Once, when he heard her crying in her room, he had slipped an affectionate note beneath the door. Diana encouraged his sensitivity. During school breaks when he was at Kensington Palace, they spent as much time as possible together. He had inherited her height, good looks and crusading spirit.

It was William who, on seeing her go through her vast wardrobe to store some of it away, suggested that she auction her old gowns to raise money for charity. "Yes! Why not?" she replied and set this into action immediately. A sale of seventy-nine gowns would be held in New York six months hence, in late June 1997. One evening, in the spring of that year, Diana and William were watching television together in her sitting room, as they often did. Tears formed in his eyes as haunting images, from Angola, Somalia, Cambodia and Afghanistan, flashed on the screen of landmine amputees. Many of the victims were children. "Maybe you could do something to help," he said.

She spoke to her friend Lord Attenborough, a dedicated anti-landmine activist, who encouraged her to become involved in Red Cross efforts to rid the world of the more than 100 million landmines planted in over sixty countries, and where up to one in 350 people had been injured by them. Two months later, Diana was in Angola with a camera crew shooting a segment for the popular BBC programme *Heart of the Matter*, this edition directed by Attenborough. Dressed simply in a cotton shirt and capri pants, her hair brushed back from her face, she seemed impervious to the heat as she took child amputees on her lap and hugged them to her. Then she was seen in protective clothing walking behind an expert bomb-disposal team as they worked cautiously to remove the mines.

To the world she was the humanitarian princess, but in conservative circles in Britain she was chastised for being what Tory MPs called "a loose cannon, whose landmine campaign had drawn her into the political arena in the run-up to a general election." In 1996 Labour took power with Tony Blair as prime minister. Diana concentrated on establishing a rapport with him.

Blair was young and handsome, with boundless vitality. Labour pledged to work for a world-wide ban on landmines and Diana continued her efforts. In June, as scheduled, she went to New York for a preview of the sale of her gowns. She had begun her eight-day visit to the States in Washington where she had breakfast with First Lady Hillary Rodham Clinton and attended the venerable *Washington Post* publisher Katharine Graham's eightieth birthday celebration. In New York she had already appeared at a Red Cross benefit in Manhattan and visited an Aids hospice with Mother Teresa in the Bronx. Pictures of the tall Princess and the diminutive nun in her grey and white habit circled the globe. Though no two women ever seemed so disparate, there was a firm bond between them. Before they parted, Mother Teresa placed a rosary in Diana's hand as a gift. Diana was moved and when she returned to England she hung it over the silver frame of a signed photograph of the Pope, which had a prominent place on her desk.

In New York she lunched at the Four Seasons with Tina Brown and Anna Wintour of *Vogue*. They discussed the auction, and Diana's new friendship with Tony Blair. "I think at last I have someone who will know how to use me," she confided. "He's told me he wants me to go on some missions."

Tina Brown queried what she meant.

"I'd really like to go to China," she replied.

And where would she like eventually to live? She was drawn to America, she confessed, the options, the openness. She thought she would be happy there. After all, she had American blood. To her knowledge no one from the Work side remained in Chìllicothe, Ohio, but she had distant cousins in Florida, whom she had met and liked. However, it seemed impossible that she could move to the USA. Neither the Queen nor Charles would ever allow the boys to leave Britain for the United States.

She returned to England glowing. The tension between Charles and her had eased. They had travelled together to and from William's confirmation in the spring, and for the first time ever, it seemed, they had not had to be told to be pleasant to each other before the cameras. Diana would never forgive Camilla or Charles for their deception, but she now felt less animosity. Her sons and her mission meant everything to her. She had told friends in New York that she imagined one day she might fall in love and get married again and hoped that it would happen sooner rather than later as her biological clock was ticking away and she wanted a daughter. Right now, though, she was thinking only about the near future. Her plans for the summer were already set: she would spend time with the boys in the

South of France aboard Mohamed al Fayed's super-
luxurious yacht, then she would take a cruise with her
friend Rosa Monckton around the Greek islands. There
would be a short interruption when she visited Bosnia for
the landmine campaign.

At the end of June she was in London. The park beyond
Kensington Palace was filled with people sunning themselves, couples walking hand in hand, children running
along the edge of the Serpentine feeding bread to the ducks.
Such normal, everyday joys were for ever out of her grasp,
at least in public places. But in a few hours she would be
in the South of France where, on Mohamed al Fayed's estate and on his yacht she could soak up the sun in privacy
and swim in the warm waters of the Mediterranean. Best
of all, William and Harry would be with her.

PART SIX

THE STUFF OF DREAMS

22

TUESDAY, 1 JULY 1997 was Diana's thirty-sixth birthday. Rosa Monckton called and asked if she would like to have lunch. Diana declined. That evening she was to be guest of honour at a gala hosted by Chanel for the centennial of the Tate Gallery, and there was much she had to do during the day. Both boys had called her early in the morning and she had opened their gifts. Her staff had not forgotten, and giant bouquets of flowers had arrived during the day (one from the Queen and another from Charles among them). There were dozens of packages from close friends and family, many hundreds from admirers, and thousands of cards. She felt she must forgo lunch to write as many personal thank-you notes as she could.

She arrived at the Tate, the museum's pillared entrance hall hung with its striking collection of Andy Warhol silk-screen prints of Chanel perfume bottles, in a party of five, which included a bodyguard and staff. All eyes, and cameras, were on her as she entered the main reception room wearing a form-fitting, low-cut, backless, glittery black Jacques Azagury gown. Around her bare neck was the magnificent emerald and diamond choker that the Queen had given her as a wedding gift, and she wore matching earrings and bracelet, a gift from Charles after William's birth. She carried a small bouquet of white camellias and pink roses. Never had she looked more glowingly beautiful.

She was exhilarated from the success of the auction of her gowns, which had raised $3.26 million for Aids and cancer charities. The Queen, she had been told, was appalled at the idea of her selling her clothing, and Tory critics had said that some of the dresses had been worn on official state occasions, thus were paid for by taxpayers and were not hers to sell. Others called it "a vulgar affection."

Whatever she did would be controversial, but Diana was at a stage in her life when she followed her best instincts. Selling the gowns to help her causes had felt right to her, and William had been equally pleased with the results.

William and Harry joined her at Kensington Palace on Friday, 11 July, the day they were to leave for the South of France. Diana had everything ready for their departure in one large suitcase and three small ones. Royal tours usually included piles of baggage, but gowns, hats, wraps, accessories and jewels were not needed for this trip. She was wearing a comfortable beige three-piece trouser suit and was in high spirits as the three, with their bodyguards and two members of Diana's staff, were driven to a private airstrip to board the Harrods Executive Gulfstream jet, with its pink plush seats and green carpets patterned with pharaohs' heads. With them were Mohamed and Heini al Fayed with their four children, aged between ten and sixteen. Diana was immediately drawn to Karim, who had been born unhearing. Diana knew sign language so they could communicate.

The flight was joyous—so many young people aboard and all looking forward to a vacation by and on the sea. There was nothing more that Diana and the boys enjoyed than sun and water sports. In addition, they would be in al Fayed's safe compound, able to relax. Al Fayed had assured her that his forty-eight armed security guards would guarantee their safety as there were six on duty at all times.

On the party's arrival in Nice, they were driven the short distance to the harbour at St. Laurent du Var where they boarded al Fayed's 190-foot, $32-million yacht, *Jonikal*, for the leisurely five-hour sea journey to St. Tropez. The *Jonikal* surpassed any of Diana's expectations. Of course, it was not *Britannia*, but it had been equipped with two pools, a gym with a sauna, and suites with marble bathrooms and gold fixtures, and a sixteen-strong crew that included a French chef, an Italian chef and two masseurs. There was a playroom for the teenagers with a soda fountain for nonalcoholic drinks. Huge bowls of exotic fresh flowers stood in every room as well as a television and a large selection of CDs. Dinner was served on deck as they followed the coastline.

Harry said he had never seen so much food before: caviar, great platters of lobsters and prawns, sweet delicacies of infinite variety. The yacht's staff for security reasons had not been told in advance who the guests were to be. The bounty aboard the *Jonikal* was neither more nor less than it would have been for anyone else. Al Fayed lived a life that the Royal Family might once have lived, but certainly not during Elizabeth II's reign.

About ten o'clock that evening, the *Jonikal* docked in St. Tropez next to al Fayed's two-masted schooner *Sakhara* in his private harbour at Castle Sainte Hélène, his vast estate with indoor and outdoor swimming-pools, roof gardens, tennis courts, miles of private beach, a forty-six-room main house and eleven-room guest "cottage," which Diana and the boys occupied. There were also comfortable staff quarters.

In July the sun rises in a spectacular blaze on the Mediterranean and Diana, William and Harry rose early. By nine they were on the beach racing to see who would be in the water first. It was Diana, crashing into the waves head high as though it was her life. Soon the paparazzi were to be seen bobbing about in their small boats a distance away as Diana sunned herself on the deck of the *Sakhara* before lunch. In England, the papers were printing critical articles about her exposing the two princes to Mohamed al Fayed, but her host could not have been more generous or warm-hearted, or the atmosphere at the castle more convivial. William and Harry had immediately made friends with the younger al Fayeds. Heini's brother and sister-in-law had now arrived with their children and it was a real family gathering, in contrast to the chilly visits Diana had endured at Sandringham or Balmoral for so long.

Two days after she arrived in St. Tropez, al Fayed's son

by his first wife arrived. Emad "Dodi" Fayed's* mother,
Samira, was dead. She had been the sister of billionaire
arms dealer Adnan Khashoggi. Dodi's parents had divorced
when he was only two and al Fayed, like Johnnie Spencer,
had won custody, and like Diana, Dodi had grown up without his mother. Unlike her, though, he had seldom seen
Samira until he was an adult. His father claimed that this
had brought him and his son closer than most fathers and
sons, and the bond between them was evident when they
were in each other's company—although it evoked speculation. Was there too much dependence of the son on the
father? Was Dodi always dancing for al Fayed's attention?
An aura of sadness clung to Dodi despite his apparent free
spirit, undeniable charm, and ability to laugh easily—often
at himself. It was evident in his searching dark eyes and
the way a smile at times would play wistfully at the corners
of his mouth.

Diana and Dodi had met eleven years earlier when he
had played polo with Prince Charles. Since then, they had
met at galas and premières, and had exchanged casual conversation. In the last six months their paths had crossed
more frequently and they had flirted openly with each other.
But then Diana often enjoyed playing the flirt with an attractive man without serious interest. Dodi was involved in
the film industry and had co-produced and financed several
films, including the Academy Award-winning *Chariots of
Fire*. The press had never been kind to him: he was al
Fayed's son, he was too rich, he was the nephew of an
arms dealer, a good-looking guy who had dated film stars
like Brooke Shields and Bridget Fonda, a playboy caught
on his daddy's money-belt. Most of it was true, but Dodi
Fayed was also sensitive, brighter and more talented than
given credit for, and he was emotionally bruised.

Diana became attuned to this quickly. They spent that
first afternoon on the *Jonikal* with the rest of the house

*Dodi did not use the prefix "al" before his surname. It designated
an honorary title, to which he said he was not entitled.

party, although after lunch they found a quiet corner in which to talk. They remained apart from the others for several hours. He reminded her a little of Hasnat Khan. They were of the same faith, both exotic with good looks who spoke with a hint of an accent in a mellow, intimate voice. Dodi's eyes were a deep liquid brown, like richly brewed coffee. His manners were impeccable. The scent he wore was tinged with a light spicy aroma, and he had remarkable hands. Much of her tension dissolved with his touch. Unlike Hasnat Khan, though, Dodi Fayed was used to celebrity. He understood how it could be used to further his own agenda.

Both Diana and Dodi have said that they discovered quickly how much they had in common, that their histories were so similar. "One immediately sensed the chemistry between them," a crew member noted. For Diana, this was certainly true: within an hour of their first private conversation, she had felt she could confide in him. She shared her painful childhood memories, the fear of abandonment she had known as a small child when her mother left home; her father's seeming indifference to her unhappiness.

"Like me, like me," he had echoed, and told her how he had cried at nights for his mother, how his father had sent him away to school at seven and how, at seventeen, he had been given his own apartment at 60 Park Lane in London, which he still occupied, a Mini Cooper, a twenty-four-hour chauffeur, bodyguards, and a warning that he was always to be cautious because an enemy of his father might try to kidnap or murder him. Born in Egypt, he had spent his life between England, Egypt, France and the United States, and never thought of himself as an Arab, although he was often described as such by the press. Yes, he was rich. And yes, there was an ex-wife, and there had been many more women than the tabloid press had reported. But there had never been that one great love. Diana was immensely drawn to him.

The following day, 14 July, was Bastille Day and there was a party on the *Jonikal* and the boat dropped anchor offshore near Nice where everyone could see the splendid firework display. Diana and Dodi, his arm about her waist, stood at the rail of the upper deck and shouted as each rocket exploded in the night sky, the flash brilliantly reflected in the dark blue of the sea. Later Diana called her friends in London on her mobile phone—the much older Lady Elsa Bowker, who had become a close confidante, and Rosa Monckton. Her voice vibrated with happiness.

She did not know, though, that Kelly Fisher, the tall, beautiful, willowy Calvin Klein model, was close at hand. Kelly had been Dodi's girlfriend for over a year and was in St. Tropez also on a yacht belonging to al Fayed. She had come to the South of France with Dodi, wearing a $200,000 diamond and emerald engagement ring, with which he had recently presented her, and she had told her parents that they would be married on 9 August. Dodi had refused to introduce Kelly to his family, who knew nothing of this liaison. He had told her that she could not join him on his father's yacht "because the Princess wants privacy." Kelly was an intelligent woman who had made a success in a highly competitive field and she was not unaware of Dodi's womanizing history. But she was in love, too, and wanted to believe that Dodi was telling her the truth.

But Dodi was dazzled by Diana. On 15 July Diana rang Rosa Monckton to tell her that "there was a karma that was drawing them closer." Diana strongly believed in mystic signs and it had occurred to her that Dodi's appearance in her life at this time was such. She further remarked to Rosa that she felt "suddenly uplifted. We've each suffered a great deal of personal pain and somehow it makes us feel not so all alone."

That afternoon Diana, accompanied by the boys, Dodi, his bodyguard, the imposing Welshman Trevor Rees-Jones, and two of al Fayed's security men, went to see an ancient Romanesque church. Having made her way from the car through the gathered media—there had been a leak by staff to the press—she removed her sunglasses and her amazing blue eyes fixed on the church's famous bust of the saint for whom the town is named.

She knew something of the history of the area, for it was her habit whenever she visited somewhere new to read about it. The legend ran that St. Tropez had been martyred under Nero. His body was set adrift in a boat with a dog and a cock that were to feed upon it. But they left it untouched, and an angel steered the boat to the shore of what was now the Gulf of St. Tropez. Diana was greatly moved by the idea of an angelic presence hovering over the water to protect the corpse. The sea gave her a keen sense of freedom, and she had always felt that her much loved Grandmother Spencer was looking down on her, guiding her away from danger and into safe, if uncharted waters and so the myth, with its vague similarities, had intrigued her.

With one of al Fayed's men leading, she entered the church flanked by Dodi, William and Harry. The boys were dressed casually in sneakers and jeans, looking relaxed, tanned and healthy. Each member of the small party lit a candle and said a short, silent prayer. Then, English guidebook in hand, Diana led the others around the interior of the centuries-old church. She was in no hurry to go out into the blazing sunlight where a pack of hustling paparazzi impatiently awaited her. Here, she could be the private Diana.

When Diana and her party were ready to leave, two bodyguards stood by the doors ready to intercept the crush of photographers waiting for them to emerge. Sunglasses in place, shoulders squared, Diana started forward. William and Harry were in front of her, a bodyguard on each side, Dodi and Trevor Rees-Jones behind them. She stepped out into the glare of the stifling hot day. *Click, click, click* went the cameras as newsmen shouted to get her attention. Instead, she glanced over her shoulder at Dodi. "That's tomorrow's front page," she said, but a smile eased across her face.

The photographers paid little attention to Dodi. "He was just another guy," a member of the French press corps said.

This was a reasonable reaction, even for members of the media. Dodi was not an outsider. His father was Diana's host. His presence during Diana's visit did not seem in any way unusual, as all the other members of his family were there.

On her divorce, Diana had insisted on forfeiting the twenty-four-hour security she had previously received from the Royal Protection Squad, although she still used official bodyguards at public events, or when her sons were with her. She wanted a semblance of normality in her life, to be able to get around more on her own. It was not long before she realized that this had been a grave error of judgment. It was not that she feared danger from a potential assassin or lunatic. It was the frenzied pursuit of the press that terrified her.

The al Fayeds and their guests spent the next few days sunning themselves and being pampered. Every morning, at about eleven, Diana either went for a swim or jet-skied, often with the boys, off the beach that fronted the al Fayeds' pink-stuccoed villa. They usually boarded the yacht for lunch and for an afternoon excursion. With each passing day her relationship with Dodi intensified as they spent more and more private time together. The paparazzi had still not realized that Diana was embarking on a new romance, but they were an invasive presence. They even used their long-range lenses to photograph her hundreds of yards away, sunning on the roof terrace of al Fayed's house. One morning when she and the boys were swimming near the villa, a boatload of photographers drew as close as they could and began to shout at them.

"Hey, Diana! Hey, Wills!" they called.

"I can send my son to a good public school next year if you just look this way!" an English photographer yelled. William was very upset and went back to the villa. Diana got into a small boat docked at al Fayed's pier. Still wearing her wet, *faux*-leopardskin bathing suit, she drove it out to the surprised tabloid hacks, who were mostly British. "Could you please leave my boys in peace?" she demanded, her voice clarion clear. "William really gets freaked out." She recognized one of the men and addressed him personally. "And you've been particularly unfair to my host and cruel to me. Mr. al Fayed was my father's best friend." She was referring to an article in an English tabloid that week that rather blatantly accused al Fayed of attempting to use Diana to break into the British establishment.

"What can I do to say I'm sorry?" he replied. "Fifty roses? A hundred roses?" At that moment a photographer leaned forward precariously to get a shot of her in this feisty mood and lost his balance. As soon as she saw that he could swim, she laughed. "I wish I had a camera so that I could have had that shot!" Then she started the boat and as it began to move through the water she called, "Expect a big surprise with the next thing I do!"

The men looked at each other. Everyone was puzzled. "Always the tease," one said.

Her affair with Dodi Fayed had begun, and after four days she confessed to Rosa Monckton, "I am in love with him and I know he is with me." The couple sat up talking every night until two or three A.M. They walked along the beach, went for midnight swims. They exchanged confidences. They trusted each other. She believed that the man the world thought of as a suave playboy, "a man whose idea of work was showing up for the Harrods polo team—store and team both owned by his father," and whose idea of home was a jet plane or a yacht, was more than that. The close proximity of Kelly Fisher remained unknown to her, as did the fact that over the first few days Dodi had returned to his "fiancée's" side. Dodi gave Kelly Fisher a cheque to cover her expenses and suggested she return to California where he would join her. Kelly was still not convinced that she should leave. "Is it the Princess?" she insisted. He denied any romantic attachment: he was escorting Diana on a request from his father. Kelly did as he asked.

Relieved, he continued his romance with Diana. Her effect on him was both nurturing and seductive. They laughed together over simple things. Diana loved a good joke, could tell a dirty one as well as any man, and was an excellent mimic. "She was lively, fun and in excellent spirits," a close member of al Fayed's party commented, "and we were not blind to the fact that the two had fallen in love."

No one could have been outwardly happier than al Fayed himself. Dodi had caused him great anxiety, always living beyond his generous allowance. Time and again al Fayed had covered Dodi's debts. He had little regard for his son's career as a film producer: he felt that Dodi's contribution had been on a financial level and that he had not been an active participant even in *Chariots of Fire*, one of the few investments made by Dodi that had reaped financial rewards. At the age of nearly forty-two, Dodi was unmarried and childless. His reputation as an international playboy suggested to al Fayed that his son was not ready to help him manage his empire. But if Dodi could win Diana's hand . . . Al Fayed was something of a romantic, but he had strong personal reasons—his hope that through Diana he might finally achieve his desire for a British passport—for encouraging his son in his wooing of the Princess. And in this area he had faith in his son's abilities.

The courting had begun, and not just of Diana but of William and Harry too. Dodi rented a discothèque where the young princes ate pizza and showed considerable skill on the dance-floor. William, who was self-conscious about his height, loosened up while learning disco steps from Diana. Neither he nor Harry had ever been to a disco before and it was a heady experience, although Diana was heard to comment that she wished security concerns had not made it obligatory for the public to be excluded. She was ecstatic, though, that her sons were comfortable with Dodi, who took them with her to an amusement park—in public, this time, but with al Fayed's security men in attendance. There, they crashed around on bumper cars and later had a picnic in a secluded spot on the beach outside the al Fayed villa.

They parted at midday on 20 July, after hearing about the shocking murder in Miami Beach of Diana's friend the fashion designer Gianni Versace, who was gunned down by a lone assailant on the front steps of his magnificent home. Diana was distraught as she boarded the Harrods jet with the boys to return to London, where William and Harry were to join the Queen, the Princess Royal and her husband, Prince Edward and his girlfriend Sophie Rhys-Jones, and their cousins Peter and Zara Phillips aboard the *Britannia*. Prince Charles would meet them in Scotland, where they would spend time at Balmoral. Meanwhile, Diana departed for Milan to attend Versace's funeral.

Dodi offered to go with her, but they decided that that would alert the press to the depth of their relationship. Instead, they planned a reunion ten days later, with a private cruise on the Mediterranean, again on the *Jonikal*.

Diana believed that she had found love, but she wanted to be sure that on Dodi's part it was more than infatuation. They planned to meet in Paris, then cruise for five days off the coast of Sardinia and determine whether or not a deeper relationship was viable. Diana knew she could not keep the press at bay once she joined Dodi on the *Jonikal*, but she was ready for that. She had learned how to use the press to her advantage, and now she wanted them to know how happy she was, how desirable as a woman, and, with someone who loved her, how little Charles and his family could hurt her.

Not everyone close to her approved of her decision to holiday alone with Dodi. Friends felt she should have insisted on having her own bodyguard in attendance. Then there was the obvious backlash of bad publicity. Al Fayed was not a popular figure. Dodi was not a man of any consequence, and he was a Muslim. The Palace would pounce on that if ever the relationship were to become serious. But Diana was a long way from making any commitment. She just knew that Dodi made her feel loved and cared for.

Shortly before they began their cruise Kelly Fisher, now back in Los Angeles, hired the American lawyer Gloria Allerd, known for her strident advocacy of women's rights, to represent her in a breach-of-promise suit against Dodi.

As yet this had not been leaked to the press, but Dodi had been notified of Kelly's intention. He and Diana spoke twice daily and he told her of the possibility that Kelly would sue. He claimed vehemently that he had never promised to marry her, and although she had come with him to the South of France, she had done so of her own volition. Two days after he had joined Diana on the *Jonikal*, he had told Kelly she should return home. When he had given her the cheque to cover her expenses and she had departed, he had believed that was the end of it. Diana accepted this and went on with her plans.

On the morning of 31 July, she prepared to leave London to meet Dodi in Paris. In the hallway outside her sitting room were two suitcases with the pink Princess of Wales identification tags (each member of the Royal Family had their own colour code—the Queen's was gold), waiting to be collected. She was in exceptionally high spirits. And for once, she was looking forward to the future.

DIANA ARRIVED IN Paris in the late afternoon of 31 July, and was met by a chauffeured limousine furnished by the Ritz Hotel, owned by Mohamed al Fayed, who had sent along a security guard. Trevor Rees-Jones was also on hand. Dodi was in the back seat, hidden from the press by tinted windows. Everything possible had been done to protect Diana's person and privacy. They went first to the Ritz on the Place Vendôme. Originally it had been a magnificent town-house but in 1898 the Swiss-born César Ritz had converted it to "the luxury hotel of luxury hotels offering all the refinements that a prince could ask for in his own home." Nearly a full century later it retained its regal claims.

Diana was given the hotel's grandest suite of seven high-ceilinged, elegant rooms, decorated with French antiques and crystal chandeliers. It had been occupied previously by monarchs from many countries and was once Winston Churchill's favourite Paris lodging. It now rented for $10,000 a night. Diana, however, was a guest of Mohamed al Fayed. That afternoon, Diana and Dodi, driven by his Paris chauffeur, Philippe Dourneau, had been to see the Duke of Windsor's villa at 4 Route du Champ d'Entrainement on the edge of the Bois de Boulogne near Neuilly. Dourneau cleverly out-foxed the paparazzi by using the hotel's private rear entrance and switching cars. For a short while, anyway, they would have some private time together. The Windsor villa also belonged to al Fayed. Until this summer, the ground floor had been open for viewing while he occupied the luxurious second floor. Arrangements had been made for the sale of the furnishings with Sotheby's, New York, the proceeds to be distributed among

various charities. The house, therefore, was presently unoccupied.

This was no ordinary sightseeing visit: the al Fayeds,
father and son, had discussed the possibility of Diana using
the villa as a second home outside England. The idea had
appealed to her, but she had not taken it too seriously. Dodi
led her enthusiastically on a room-by-room tour. The walls
were bare and huge packing-cases stood in many rooms,
labelled and ready for their voyage to Sotheby's auction
rooms in New York. Diana was aware that the villa was
being offered to her as an enticement either to cement her
relationship with Dodi or for some reason that she didn't
yet know, and was wary of expressing more than interest
in its history and appreciation of the beauty of the Windsors' *petit palais*. Twenty minutes later, the couple returned
to the Ritz where she telephoned the boys and Rosa Monckton. She had decided to spend the night with Dodi at his
ten-room apartment on the rue Arsène Haussaye near the
Arc de Triomphe, just a few doors down from the Champs
Élysées.

Dodi's apartment was furnished in an expensive, modern
adaptation of art-deco design, but the colours and designs
were somewhat garish. Nevertheless, it exuded comfort,
with thick rugs, deep sofas and chairs. There was a control
board for the lighting, which faded down to a soft, romantic
glow. From the sitting-room windows there was a full view
of the Arc de Triomphe and beyond that the glittering lights
of the city.

Dodi spent about eight months a year in London, the
remaining four in Paris, Los Angeles and New York. He
had a home or an office in each city and had placed objects
and memorabilia in them that would make them feel lived-
in. Several photographs of his dead mother positioned to
catch his eye in passing from one room to another. As a
lonely child who had been shifted around so often that rel-
atives did not know where he actually lived (nor did he),
he had occupied his time by assembling model cars from
kits. Examples of his expertise at this were displayed along

with a collection of worn teddy bears. The building was a grand Paris landmark, with twenty-four-hour service. No one got further than the striated marble front lobby without being announced. Triple locks secured the front and back doors of Dodi's apartment, and when he was there, a bodyguard was on duty at all times, as well as his long-term butler, René Delorm.

"Dodi was very cautious, you know," his friend Johnny Gold, owner of Tramp nightclub in London, recalled, "even paranoic in his caution. I mean, I could talk to him while he was having a drink in the club. If he got up to go away from the table, he'd order a fresh drink. And I'd say, 'Why do you do that?' He'd say, 'Well, you can never tell, in case someone puts something in your drink.'

"And he would always have his security around. Sometimes one, sometimes two . . . one upstairs with a walkie-talkie and one downstairs with a walkie-talkie." Welshman Trevor Rees-Jones had worked for him for several years and was almost always by his side. Dodi trusted and liked him. Rees-Jones dressed well, was attractive and well-mannered, and looked more like a colleague than a guard. Diana had taken to him in St. Tropez.

At about nine o'clock, they were driven to the elegant, four-star restaurant Lucas-Carton on the Place de la Madeleine. They went in at the side entrance and up to the second floor, which contains several small dining rooms, popular with politicians and others who wanted a more private environment than the main floor provided. These rooms were named Le Cercle and were in Louis XVI décor, while downstairs the theme was *art-nouveau*. As Diana's appearance caused people to wander curiously near their banquette, they did not linger over coffee, departing at about ten thirty and returning to Dodi's apartment.

The following morning, with Dodi's arm about Diana's waist and Rees-Jones in attendance, they boarded the Harrods jet and flew to Nice. The *Jonikal* was anchored close by and, as twilight approached, it set sail for Porto Cervo in Sardinia. This was the evening of 1 August, a humid night, a mist veiling the stars in the night sky. The crew had been pared down to ten, but Rees-Jones had come aboard, with Alexander (Kes) Wingfield, two more of Mohamed al Fayed's security men, René Delorm and Diana's personal maid. There were no other passengers.

En route to their destination Diana and Dodi dined on caviar and lobster Thermidor. The mist lifted and they went up on deck, the soundtrack from the recent film *The English Patient* playing over the yacht's sound system. "Have you seen the film?" Diana asked stewardess Debbie Gribble, who was serving them coffee and drinks. Gribble said she hadn't. "Well, you'll cry when you do. I howled." The sea was calm and they danced when the music segued into a series of Frank Sinatra songs. Later Gribble saw them kiss passionately, "But they still went back to their separate cabins."

Although Sardinia is the second largest island after Sicily in the Mediterranean, thirty years earlier it was home only to fishermen in the villages along its coastline and bandits in the craggy mountains that constitute the greater part of the island. Since then, Karim Aga Khan and a syndicate had developed the north-east corner of the island into one of the most luxurious resorts in the world. It was called the Costa Smeralda (Emerald Coast) because it was edged by the sparkling green waters of the Tyrrhenian Sea. Porto Cervo, its sophisticated new harbour, was filled with some of the handsomest yachts that sailed the Mediterranean.

The *Jonikal* remained a little further out at sea than the other vessels. Diana was completely relaxed. She and Dodi swam and sunbathed the next day. That night they shared Dodi's cabin, breakfasted in his suite and made calls from their mobile telephones, Diana to the boys and Rosa Monckton. By now she was confident of her feelings and wanting to let the world know. On their last day, photographers appeared in small craft in the waters around Porto Cervo and shot pictures of the couple as they drove one of the *Jonikal*'s speedboats to the beach on Corsica where they were photographed strolling hand in hand.

The famous, grainy picture of Diana and Dodi embracing in swim-wear was taken on the *Jonikal*, on 4 August, by a photographer with a long-range lens. Licensed for more than $1 million, its publication guaranteed that the lovers would be followed everywhere they went from now on by the voracious paparazzi. The image that was labelled "The Kiss" was an obvious personal statement. Certainly both Diana and Dodi knew that the paparazzi were within range and they could have had their passionate embrace in a more concealed spot on the boat. Neither did they seem surprised the next day to see the front page of the *Sun* emblazoned with five frames under the banner headline "Di and Dodi: The Love Album."

"They were two people very much in love," a member of staff explains, "and they seemed proud of it."

To Max Clifford, the public-relations supremo, Dodi had confided via his mobile phone, "The fact that she loves me as much as I love her is just incredible."

On the return voyage to Nice, the *Jonikal* anchored for several hours in Monte Carlo. Dodi and Diana ended up in an exclusive jeweller's where Dodi bought her a diamond bracelet. Then they looked at ring designs. Dodi ordered a $205,400 diamond-encrusted one with a large, square-cut centre stone framed by four triangular ones mounted on a wide diamond and platinum, dome-shaped band. Its catalogue name was "Tell Me Yes."

"As far as I could tell," Alberto Repossi, the jeweller, recalled, "this was not an engagement ring that Mr. Fayed was buying for the Princess. The Princess had a rather large ring size and it had to be adjusted to fit her properly." In fact, the ring was being made to fit the finger on her right hand, not her left.

By the time they returned to London on 6 August, the media was almost impossible to escape. "I can't walk out of my apartment any more," Dodi told his long-time friend Julian Senior, a Warner Brothers executive. "I was very moved by the whole nightmare [of the press deluge]," Senior recalled. "Somehow this gentle, polite man—it's like comets colliding—touched the aura of this lady, and his life went upside down. [I told him] 'But, Dodi, you love her.' He said, 'Yes, of course I love her.' I told him that was the kind of life he was going to have to live with. He said, 'I can't do this. It's just extraordinary. I can't move without somebody taking pictures." ' Senior added, "In many ways Dodi was a man-child."

That was easy enough to say, but even a man like Dodi, who loved being in the aura of famous women and was used to the media, had no conception of the bizarre public life Diana led. On their first tour, Prince Charles had been overwhelmed by the media's fanatical attention to Diana. She was the most famous, most photographed woman in the world. Her image brought huge profits to photographers and their media outlets. She was being bought and sold on a scale unheard of previously. Diana never quite got used to it even when they worked on her behalf. "Why me? Why me?" she often cried. Dodi could not help but be over-whelmed by their mob tactics, but despite his protests to close friends, he remained controlled and protective with Diana.

On the morning of 8 August Diana prepared to leave for a three-day visit to Bosnia as part of her anti-landmine crusade. She planned to be with Dodi in London for a few days before she and Rosa Monckton embarked on their Greek cruise. Following that, Diana and Dodi would board the *Jonikal* again for a second cruise in the Mediterranean, this time for nine days.

Diana was certain that their feelings for each other were the real thing. Prince Charles surprisingly made the statement that "If she is happy, then I am happy." Al Fayed commented: "I understand they had a wonderful time together and enjoyed themselves immensely [on their cruise]. I don't know exactly what their plans are for the future but as long as they both remain happy, that warms my heart." Diana did not conceal her joy, but she told Rosa and others close to her that she was *not* considering re-marriage.

On Thursday evening, 7 August, shortly before eight o'clock, she arrived at Dodi's Park Lane apartment with a small parcel in her hand, rushed past the crush of reporters at the gates of the building, and took the private lift to Dodi's penthouse. As a gift for Dodi, Diana had brought with her a pair of her father's gold and ruby cufflinks, a sign of her trust and love. They dined alone, and she departed at about midnight, Trevor Rees-Jones escorting her through the maze of waiting photographers who flung unanswered questions at her and exploded flashbulbs in her face.

The next morning she flew to the Bosnian capital of Sarajevo in a privately hired Gulfstream jet, the guest of the Washington-based Land Mine Service Network founded by American Ken Rutherford, who had lost his right leg while working in the minefields in Somalia. Wearing a blue shirt, navy blazer and matching leggings, Diana looked calmly radiant as she descended the plane's metal stairs. There was great anxiety about her safety during this trip, which followed, by only a fortnight, the shooting of a Bosnian Serb war criminal. Her first glimpse of Bosnia was of armed French legionnaires, Army troops and Bosnian police who circled the landing field. Once settled in a Land-Rover, she was shown the destruction in Sarajevo and the desperate conditions in which the population lived.

She went to work immediately visiting the poorly equipped hospitals, talking to victims as she sat by their beds, listening to their tragic stories of loss—children, husbands, wives, limbs. She never rushed these conversations, and always there was some form of personal contact, hand on hand, on shoulder where there were no hands. No patient ever saw her give way to tears or pull back in revulsion. But at night, in Red Cross headquarters where she stayed, she would appear shaken by the events and scenes of the day.

The next morning under heavy escort she was driven to the northern town of Tuzla, the scene of one of the worst Bosnian Serb mortar attacks. *En route*, her convoy stopped at the small town of Olovo, where there were a huge number of landmine victims. Bosnia was said to have over a million landmines scattered throughout it, the majority planted without maps so that their removal was hazardous. In Olovo she visited the modest apartment of Franjo Kresic, a forty-seven-year-old father of two daughters, who had been blinded in one eye and lost both legs from stepping on a hidden landmine not far from his home. "I could not believe it when the Princess walked in. She was so natural, so comforting. She wore a simple blouse and jeans. She asked my wife how she was able to manage, was there enough food. She sat down next to my wheelchair and placed her hand on my arm. I could hardly speak. There was something that transferred itself through her touch, like a warm wave. She stayed nearly half an hour. She didn't seem to be in a rush. I felt like someone I had known for years was visiting us. 'You *are* going to walk again,' she said, when she left. And I believe one day I will, with the help of artificial limbs."

She put in three fifteen-hour days in grinding heat and choking dust. Wearing protective gear she trudged behind a mine-detecting team as they inched their way through suspect fields. In Tuzla, she hugged legless children and lovingly touched the stumps of those who entreated her to do so. She sat down to talk with a paraplegic volleyball team. "They are all so brave, so brave," she told members of her party. She had a cold and was fast reaching the point of exhaustion, but she refused to quit before she had seen and accomplished all that had been planned for her. At night she called Dodi on her mobile telephone. "She laughed and laughed with him," said Sandra Mott, a Red Cross worker stationed in Bosnia, who hosted her on the tour.

When she returned to London Dodi was waiting for her. She was elated to see him. They remained sequestered in his penthouse in the evenings rather than "keep running from the paparazzi" who were now desperate for a photo or a quote. Neither was forthcoming. Although Diana, by

telephone, told Taki Theodoracopoulos, Britain's well-
known society columnist, "I haven't taken such a long time
to get out of one poor marriage to get into another." That
statement had a curious tone: she seemed unconvinced of
Dodi's suitability as a husband.

They knew that Kelly Fisher had been infuriated by the
loving photographs taken of them on the cruise and that
she was not going to fade easily into the night. On 14
August, the day before Diana was to leave with Rosa
Monckton for their Greek cruise, Fisher held an emotional
press conference in Los Angeles. Holding up her left hand
with Dodi's $200,000 "engagement" ring, and with an ear-
lier gift from him of a diamond and sapphire ring, worth
$45,000, on her right hand, she revealed that she had filed
a $1 million lawsuit against him. She also displayed a
$200,000 cheque signed by Dodi and stamped "Account
Closed." She alleged that Dodi had agreed to pay her
$500,000 in two instalments before their planned 9 August
wedding, the first in January 1997, at the time of his proposal, the second six months later. This cash award was to
compensate her for loss of work since he had insisted she
give up her modelling career. By June she had not received
the initial payment. At the time he was in Europe, and when
she pressed him for the money he wired her $60,000, say-
ing, "This was the largest amount he could sent at the time,
but that he would give her the rest when they next met."
After she had joined him in Paris in early July, they had
gone together to St. Tropez, planning to take a Mediterranean cruise. Instead, she alleged, he had left her alone on
one of his father's yachts while he entertained the Princess
of Wales. He had rejoined her after the Princess left and
then, a few days later, gave her the $200,000 and told her
to return to Los Angeles. As far as she knew, the wedding
was still on, although no formal plans had been made, no
invitations sent and, except for her parents, no one else
appeared to have been informed of the date of their intended union. Dodi had not joined her, as she believed he
would, but had gone off on a cruise with the Princess of

Wales. When Fisher deposited Dodi's cheque, it bounced. She was therefore seeking payment in full of $440,000 plus the additional amount of $560,000 for damages, humiliation, a broken agreement (although there was nothing in writing to substantiate this), and the interruption to her career.

This performance, with her lawyer Gloria Allerd standing supportively at her side, was followed by her appearance on American television, in which she declared, "Dodi is just really in love with the media attention of being with Princess Diana. He loves it, his family loves it."

Her brother, Brian Fisher, warned the press, "Kelly worked damned hard to get where she is today. If I know Kelly, this man Dodi will wish he never crossed her. She is a tough lady. She feels she has been wronged, and she won't let him get away with this without a good fight."

Dodi repeated his denials to Diana that he had never proposed to Kelly or promised her money to give up her career. The cheques he had given her were because she had claimed her relationship with him had taken her away from her modelling and had cost her bookings. He had felt that this was probably true. He also insisted he had not known that the account on which the $200,000 cheque had been written had been closed by his accountants just weeks before his trip to St. Tropez.

They spent an entire afternoon in his penthouse discussing the situation. Diana was shaken, but she believed him. She was also convinced he had cared for Kelly, but not in the way he felt now about her. She knew how generous with jewellery and gifts Dodi was, and that the ring he had ordered for her had not been to celebrate an engagement. It seemed logical that Kelly's ring, too, had been just a generous gift. Also Diana was well aware of Dodi's disregard for money, his habit of letting his father pay his outstanding bills. His own money was tied up in such a fashion that he could not have free use of it.

Other debts were now humiliatingly exposed by the press: back taxes, an angry ex-landlord who claimed Dodi had left without paying several months' rent, the 21 Club in New York where he had run up a considerable, and long overdue, tab.

The lovers parted on Saturday, 15 August, Dodi for Los Angeles to see a friend in hospital with cancer and to try to settle some of his financial problems there, while Diana, again travelling on the Harrods Gulfstream jet, departed for Athens where she and Rosa would board the small boat they had hired for their Greek cruise. As Dodi left his lawyers' offices in Los Angeles, he was mobbed by a pack of paparazzi. "Why are you hiding?" one shouted at him.

"I'm not hiding! I'm not hiding!" he yelled, and broke into a frenzied run chased by photographers.

The cruise with Rosa Monckton was decidedly downscale from the ones Diana had taken on the *Jonikal*. The *Della Grazzia* was a small motor-cruiser with three crew: Captain Manolis, Vassilis the deckhand, and a young Greek woman as cook and maid. As soon as they boarded at Piraeus, Diana disappeared down to her unpretentious cabin. She reappeared ten minutes later. "I've nested, Rosa. Have you?" she asked. Monckton wrote that this meant "the photos of the boys would be stuck in the mirror, her clothes put away. She had brought very few clothes—some swimsuits, pants, shirts, a sweater in case the evening grew cool and a halter-top dress. She let her hair dry naturally."

The two women stood on deck watching "the bare, shaven skulls of the surrounding hills slowly absorbing themselves into the night." The water was smooth and a mild breeze beginning to ease the airless heat of the late summer day.

Rosa (real name Rosamond) was managing director of Tiffany's, London, and her husband, Dominic Lawson, a respected editor on the *Sunday Telegraph*. She and Diana were long-time friends; their relationship had grown strong through the tragedies and problems they had both surmounted. Rosa had miscarried a much-wanted pregnancy at six months, and Diana had "instinctively found the words to ease the pain, and at the same time knew I should name my daughter and bury her. She always remembered her anniversary and talked about her often. I will never, ever forget her face, her touch, her warmth and compassion on the day we buried Natalya," Monckton recalled. "Similarly when my daughter Domenica was born and we learned that she had Down's syndrome, she was at my bedside immediately with emotional support and practical help. She offered herself as her godmother, told me which doctors had experience in this field, and gave me the names of people to contact who had gone through the same thing."

Some years older than Diana, Rosa had been there for her when her father had died, in her battle against bulimia, as a confidante during her most difficult times with Charles. In her present situation, Diana needed to talk to someone she could trust so the timing of their cruise could not have been better. Diana knew that these five days with Rosa would be important for her to work out, and talk out, some of the things that were worrying her. She spoke often of the boys, the effect the divorce might have had on them, how difficult it would be for her ever to leave England, however much she might want to, and her relationship with Dodi. She told Rosa she had not made any decisions about her future. "She was happy enjoying herself, and liked the feeling of having someone who not only so obviously cared for her, but was not afraid to be seen doing so."

She also talked a lot about Bosnia. "She cried one night," Rosa remembered, "while we were motoring along for three hours under the full moon, and told me what she had witnessed. She needed to digest the horrors she had seen, to make some sense of the ghastly stories she had been told."

They left at night from Piraeus and cruised in the Gulf of Athens. Captain Manolis would ring his friends around Greece to find out where the paparazzi were, and would steer them in the opposite direction. The news over the boat's radio reported that they had been on the island of Khios, near Mykonos, where they had taken a plane for Naxos. This was on the other side of Greece in the Aegean

Sea. Then it had been said that they were moving in a fleet of five boats and four helicopters and were going to fly to Turkey. None of it even resembled the truth. The captain remarkably managed for the most part to evade the massive numbers of journalists who were searching for them—the count said to be as high as 250 in the press corps and 10 press helicopters.

Almost immediately upon embarking, Diana tried to reach William and Harry on her mobile telephone. She got the switchboard at Balmoral but the boys were out. With arched eyebrow and a perfect Scottish accent she imitated what she thought the operator would now be saying: "Och, there goes the Princess of Wales on yet another sunshine cruise." She tried again, unsuccessfully, the following day. "Out killing things," she said to Rosa. She did not condemn hunting. She was, after all, a country girl, and knew it was part of the culture and heritage.

On 17 August, they docked in the harbour of the small village of Kipazissi and went into a Greek Orthodox church and lit candles for their children. When they left Diana turned to Rosa and said, quite emotionally, "Oh, Rosa, I do so love my boys." No one had seemed to recognize Diana. The townspeople apparently took them for ordinary tourists. "The rich people, they don't come to Kipazissi in August," one villager said. "Too hot."

Hydra, which they reached two days later, was the only other stop they made before returning to Piraeus. In August Hydra was much hotter than the other islands in the Gulf of Athens. It was a popular tourist spot but the brutal heat discouraged tourists so late in the summer. A volcanic island, carved from barren rock, and waterless, Lawrence Durrell wrote of it, "It crouches there in the austere splendour of its nudity, glowering at you . . . as silent and watchful as a Mycenaean lion."

The *Della Grazzia* had docked in Hydra's little funnel of a harbour on the night of 18 August. Diana and Rosa were woken at dawn by the first arrival of fish and vegetables, "turning the whole waterfront into a coloured flower-bed." The distant mountains were already burned white by the sun. By mid-morning, Diana had urged Rosa to go with her for a stroll in the town. Dressed in a sleeveless blue shift and wearing a red baseball cap, Diana, with Rosa in white T-shirt and shorts, left the boat, still reasonably sure that the paparazzi were a good distance away. There weren't many people on the streets as the women followed the convolutions and curves of the town's labyrinthine walls and coiling stone staircases. To get out of the fierce heat they stepped into the cool interior of a shop.

The shopkeeper recognized Diana and insisted the two women sit down. "Do you realize the whole country is looking for you?" he warned, and suggested they return to the safety of their boat.

As they passed a café on their way back to the *Della Grazzia*, a man recognized Diana, leaped out of his chair and took a picture. Diana grabbed Rosa's arm and quickened her pace to a near run. She was furious. "That's it," she said. "All over the front pages tomorrow." Rosa tried to reassure her that the man had been an ordinary tourist and that she was wrong.

That evening on the news they heard one newspaper had made an offer of 280 million drachmas (about $700,000) for any picture of Diana taken on this holiday. Neither could believe what they were hearing. It was as though a bounty had been put on her head.

For the majority of the cruise Diana had gone without makeup, but two hours before they were due to arrive in Piraeus she went into her cabin to put on her public face, blow-dry her hair, and iron the dress she had brought along, a chore she seemed content to do herself. Dodi was not in Piraeus to meet her, but one of the al Fayed limousines and several solid-looking bodyguards were. She needed them: her arrival in the harbour had sparked off a mob scene. The picture of the two women strolling through the streets of Hydra had already appeared in the morning editions of the press.

"It's unbelievable," Rosa cried.

"I'm being hunted, Rosa," Diana replied. "When you get back to London I want you to write about it for Dominic." Rosa promised she would. They flew on the Harrods jet to Nice where she was to meet Dodi, and Rosa would continue to London. When the stewardess brought each of them a tin of caviar, Diana gave hers to Rosa. "You see, I know I'll be having some for dinner." She smiled.

She was pleased to be reunited with Dodi. The two were to board the *Jonikal* the following day, 21 August, for their nine-day cruise. Since they had been apart they had spoken several times a day, their conversations filled with laughter. Once, when he had left a message on her mobile answering-machine, she had played it for Rosa to hear "his wonderful voice." But when he left his next message, a list of expensive presents he had for her, she was angry. "That's not what I want, Rosa. It makes me uneasy," she confided. "I don't want to be bought. I have everything I want. I just want someone to be there for me, to make me feel safe and secure." She was confident in her plans to go on with her work, "which will be more important than ever because the world that Dodi inhabits is so far removed from reality."

She might have added that hers was, too.

FOR THE THIRD time that summer, Diana and Dodi returned briefly to St. Tropez. Their reunion on Wednesday
evening 20 August, was joyous. He had been at Nice airport
to meet her with several security personnel. They contained
themselves until they were in the back seat of their car,
concealed by the tinted windows. Then they kissed. And
then they both started talking non-stop. It hardly seemed
possible that they had been lovers for just over a month.
Diana had missed him on the cruise with Rosa more than
she had wanted to admit. With Dodi she felt as she had
always wanted to feel with Charles, that they were a team.
Paparazzi besieged them from the moment of her arrival in
Nice but she refused to allow their presence to interfere
with her happiness.

While they were apart Dodi had been dealing with Kelly
Fisher's lawsuit. They more or less laughed it off, convinced that his former girlfriend had no grounds for her
case. He repeated his oath to Diana that he had never set a
date for them to wed. For the year that they had been seeing
each other, he knew he had treated her well: he had given
her large sums of money, expensive gifts, and his affection.
And from the mercenary tone of her press interviews and
the size of the "compensation" she was seeking, it was clear
that Kelly was more interested in his money than she was
in him. In fact, nothing in Kelly's actions or her public
statements indicated that she had ever loved him. Her anger
seemed to spring from losing a large source of income. He
told Diana, as he had his father and a few close friends,
that he felt betrayed. Diana certainly knew about betrayal.

That night they stayed at the cottage on his father's
beachfront estate that Diana had occupied with William and
Harry. They had a private dinner—with, as she had pre-

dicted to Rosa, "gobs of caviar and champagne." The next morning they walked across the beach looking for a perfect spot to enjoy the sun. Paparazzi circled the waters and buzzed the villa and beach in helicopters. Earlier, there had been a nasty scuffle between photographers and the crew of the *Jonikal*, which was docked nearby and being readied for their embarkation. The press intrusion was unsettling: it presaged their continuing presence during the next few days. They tried to make light of it and ignore the telescopic lenses trained on their every move. After a picnic lunch they went jet-skiing; both of them were good at it, and they larked about, Diana "swinging her leg over Dodi's shoulder" in a daring mood.

"Her attitude, joined by Dodi, I assume, was 'What the hell! Give them what they want, maybe they'll go away.' " one photographer said. "But I don't think any one of us planned to do so."

They boarded the yacht late in the afternoon and were off within moments, the paparazzi still lurking. By the time the *Jonikal* reached the calm waters off the coast of Sardinia, Diana and Dodi had settled into a warm, all-enveloping haze of affection. Diana called one of her friends from her mobile telephone and told her, "I think this is it." Al Fayed claims that Dodi rang him to say that he was going to propose to Diana. "I urged him, 'Slowly, slowly.' "

With each passing day on the *Jonikal* their relationship strengthened. They were two people sailing the seas alone. Yes, the eyes of the paparazzi were always upon them, and there were the crew and staff, but they were each other's only companion twenty-four hours of each day. Such exclusive proximity can destroy romance as easily as it can deepen it, and Diana could not forget the anguish she had suffered sixteen years earlier on her honeymoon cruise with Charles, the tears she had shed, the pain they had brought each other because neither had understood what the other was about. This time everything was different. There seemed to be nothing separating Dodi and herself, nothing too awful, or silly, or shocking that either of them could not say. They were, above all else, extremely natural with each other. Their physical union was almost tangible. A *Jonikal* crew member called it, "a visible oneness that was ripe with loving."

Still, Diana did not want to be rushed, and conveyed this in her calls to friends. There was much to be considered, and above all, how a serious liaison with, or marriage to, Dodi would affect her sons.

A crew member went daily by launch into Porto Cervo to fetch the papers. The front-page insinuations about the couple were not only fictional they were ugly. Dodi had been promised £1 million by his father if they became engaged, £20 million if they were married. He was being used to a tool by al Fayed to win acceptance in Great Britain, or to spite the Royal Family and the Conservative Party—to "cock a snook" at the British establishment, as the *Independent* saw it.

Without question, al Fayed was bitter about the prejudice he had experienced in Britain. He had recently told the *New York Times*: "They [the Conservative Party] say, 'You own Harrods, you bloody Egyptian coming from Africa. How can you dare buy Harrods?' " They had nothing but contempt for him, he declared, although he had invested millions in the British economy and given a fortune to British charities. Admittedly, he had helped bring down John Major's Conservative government by disclosing that Tory MPs had taken "money from him in paper bags or accepted his hospitality at the Ritz Hotel in Paris in exchange for political influence." This revelation did nothing to increase his popularity. Nor did it help when he boasted to *The Times*: "I was proud because I showed the masses and I showed the voters that they were ruled by a bunch of crooks, and my message got through."

Then Dodi's uncle, Adnan Khashoggi, had told a Saudi Arabian newspaper, "We welcome Diana into our family." The large Muslim community in Great Britain made their approval known. "The relationship [between the Princess of Wales and Dodi Fayed] has led to an inflated sense of pride for England's Middle Eastern and Asian communities," Fuad Nahdi wrote, in rebuttal of the *Independent*'s negative articles. "You might hate and abuse us on the high streets and in alleyways, but our boys are cruising off with your biggest catches on the high seas."

By simply falling in love, Diana had stirred up anger between races. This was the last thing she had ever wanted to cause. She was, she believed, free from such prejudice. A significant liaison with Dodi would bring much of this wrath on her, and she had no one to advise her. Dodi assured her that such statements need not affect them. There was, after all, a large world outside Britain.

It seemed to Diana that the world no longer felt she had the right to her own life. That was something for which she was willing to fight and Dodi gave every impression of supporting her in the battle. By their fifth day at sea, the crew noticed that they had been drawn together in a deeper way. Dodi asked that the daily papers were not brought aboard. They hugged a lot and laughed a lot. "There was a great harmony between them," one crew member recalled. "They treated each other with great caring. They were what I would call—on the same wavelength. In the entire length of the cruise, nine days, neither of them ever appeared out of sorts or bored with the other. They seemed even to come to terms with the paparazzi who were always within view. We all thought that this was surely a great love."

At some time during the last days of the cruise, they decided to cut it short by a day and go into Paris for a romantic evening before Diana returned to London for a reunion with her sons. They planned their departure carefully from the *Jonikal* to avoid, if possible, the notice of the paparazzi. This involved giving the appearance that they were taking the launch into Porto Cervo for a shopping expedition.

Early on the morning of Saturday, 30 August, before the photographers arrived, the yacht's crew loaded the launch with their luggage. Diana, travelling light as she preferred, had only two suitcases, Dodi the same. They appeared on deck mid-morning and had breakfast. At about eleven thirty they went inside. A short time later, Diana now in a beige trouser suit and Dodi in all-black casual attire, got into the launch along with René Delorm, Trevor Rees-Jones, Kes Wingfield, Dodi's masseur and Diana's maid.

The launch headed straight for the harbour at Porto Cervo. As it drew close, it veered suddenly, and steered instead into the private jetty behind the exclusive Calla di Volpe hotel. There was always the fear, no matter how trustworthy they considered their staff, that someone might have sold information to the paparazzi. But no one lay in wait.

The party transferred into two cars: Diana, Dodi, Rees-Jones and Wingfield rode in a white Mercedes, the rest of the group in a black one, both driven by employees of al Fayed. It was general procedure for there to be a backup car. The small convoy made its way slowly around the sharply curving coastline to Sardinia's Olbia airport, where the Harrods Gulfstream IV jet was waiting to take them to Le Bourget airport in Paris. It was now one fifteen. They were met by several dozen paparazzi, who had, after all, been advised of their plans beforehand, and decided that their final departure from the airport would present better photo opportunities than the transfer to the cars on the jetty of the Calla di Volpe hotel.

The two Mercedes pulled on to the tarmac. Rees-Jones, Wingfield and al Fayed's security men surrounded them as they got out of their car and hurried across the field towards the plane. The paparazzi could not be kept back. Cameras flashed and questions were shouted: "Hey, Dodi! What about Kelly Fisher?" And to Diana: "Do your sons approve?" Diana kept her head down. She reached the metal steps of the plane first and was rushed up them, ducking as she disappeared inside. Dodi paused for a moment to talk to the security force, then followed her.

They now knew for certain that the paparazzi would be waiting for them in Paris. Dodi was trying to work out some arrangement that would give them the best protection. Of all the paparazzi, Diana feared the Paris pack the most. They were a ruthless, wild bunch, who in chase sat astride their motorcycles with fearsome tenacity as they cut in and out of traffic, often blinding her driver with their electronic flashes and terrifying her. Now she realized how lucky they had been in their last visit to Paris to have been free of them even for a short time.

Their plane took off at one forty-five. The sky was a brilliant blue, soft clouds drifting across it. There was no point in fretting over how the paparazzi had found out about their departure. The immediate concern was to protect Diana from over-zealous Paris pressmen. Rees-Jones and Wingfield suggested that they reroute the plane to London, a manoeuvre that would not be expected by the British press and should guarantee at least some respite from photographers and reporters. But Diana and Dodi were determined that they would not allow their lives to be run, or their plans ruined, by the press.

Unknown to Diana, Dodi had made special arrangements in Paris. There was the diamond ring that would be ready at Repossi's, and at his apartment there was a silver plaque engraved with a special poem. René Delorm would have chilled champagne waiting for them and it would be there, when they were finally alone, that he would give her the ring (resized to fit her third finger on her left hand), and, despite his father's warning, propose. Arrangements had also been made for them to revisit the Duke of Windsor's villa, where they would meet an Italian interior designer.

Diana had not been averse to the idea of their living together. Occupancy of the Windsor villa had been discussed and Dodi was aware of the inherent problems in this: comparisons would inevitably be made with Windsor's exile from Britain. And the connection between the mansion and this sad chapter in the history of the monarchy might prevent Diana being happy there. However, there were good reasons why they should consider it. Dodi's father had offered it as a gift. It was private and had protec-

tive walls. His current apartment would not be suitable to
the needs of William, Harry and their bodyguards when
they visited. The Windsor villa had numerous private suites,
and well-protected, vast and beautiful gardens where a
swimming-pool and a tennis court could be installed. Diana
was open to the possibility of it as a second home, but she
would not consider giving up her apartments in Kensington
Palace.

The plane touched down at Le Bourget at ten past three.
From the windows of the jet they could see the paparazzi,
telephoto lenses poised. Dodi placed his arm around Diana's waist as they stood up, and Diana giggled—she often
did when she was nervous. It was a habit she had had since
childhood. Rees-Jones was the first to disembark with Diana directly behind him and airport security staff on each
side of her. Kes Wingfield followed with Dodi and more
airport security staff.

Diana followed Rees-Jones down the stairs. A breeze
blew wisps of her blonde hair across her face as she stepped
out into the bright sunshine. She brushed them back and
took a deep breath. At the bottom of the steps, amid shouts
of "Are you going to marry him?" Diana was rushed across
the tarmac towards a Mercedes Benz 600 with tinted windows. The rear door was held open by Philippe Dourneau,
Dodi's chauffeur.

The paparazzi were still crowding them as Dodi slipped
into the back seat beside Diana. Rees-Jones sat in the front
with Dourneau. Directly behind them were Kes Wingfield
and the rest of their party in Dodi's Range-Rover, being
driven by Henri Paul, acting security chief of the Ritz, who
often drove VIPs when extra security was required. He was
armed, as were Rees-Jones and Wingfield. The two cars
were escorted by the French police to the A1 *autoroute* then
left to continue alone. In just a few minutes paparazzi on
motorcycles and in cars were following. At one point,
Dourneau was almost blinded by the flashes of cameras
held close to the window of the car as several photographers whipped up beside him at a furious speed.

Diana let out a small cry of mingled disappointment and fear. Dourneau did not attempt to out-distance them, but kept the speed of the car at the legal limit. Henri Paul, in the Range-Rover, followed his lead. Having got their photographs, the motorcycle jockeys fell back behind both cars and were finally lost when Dourneau made a sudden turn into the Porte Maillot exit, Paul continuing in accordance with the prearranged plan. The Mercedes was headed for the Windsor villa, the Range-Rover for Dodi's apartment.

The Mercedes pulled into the driveway of the villa, the gates closing after it. With the fullness of the summer foliage, it could not be seen from the road. Dourneau had outwitted the paparazzi.

They were met inside by the interior designer who had worked on numerous projects for al Fayed. The crates now were gone, the rooms almost entirely empty, the floors—some in beautiful parquet, others of stone or marble—were bare. Despite the heat of the August afternoon the villa was cool. Many of the ground-floor rooms had French windows that led to the rear and side gardens, shaded by magnificent wide-branched trees. To convert the place into the kind of home where Diana and the boys could feel comfortable would take considerable work, but it could be done with enough money, time, and the right furniture and fabrics. Dodi was enthusiastic, pointing out all the advantages, the large, pleasant quarters the boys could share, the privacy that the house and gardens offered. They visited the Duke's former suite, lingering there for a while as Diana talked to the designer. Then they went out into the gardens.

Flowers had always been Diana's weakness. Wherever she was, her rooms were always filled with them. Although she did not have private gardens at Kensington Palace, she had installed a greenhouse on the roof and her apartments overlooked the adjoining park and its lush environs. She had felt "locked out" of the gardens at Highgrove, which Charles had appropriated as his own domain. The villa's grounds and gardens, with their lovely pathways and colourful displays, appealed to Diana. The property must have been a welcomed sanctuary for the Windsors, yet sad and lonely for the Duchess after the Duke's death. It was not a house that lent itself to a solitary life. Everything was on too grand a scale, and if she was without the boys, or if things did not work out with Dodi, the place would be overwhelming. There had been numerous published pictures of the Windsors with their four pugs ridiculously dressed in wing collars and bow-ties scooting about in the gardens. As the keeshonds had been her mother's dogs when she was a child, and the Jack Russells during their marriage Charles's, Diana had never had a dog of her own and had once mentioned that to Dodi, who was an animal lover.

Dodi had three dogs. Due to British quarantine laws he kept them at his Paris apartment. They were Bear, a German shepherd, Shoe, a miniature schnauzer, and Romeo, a standard schnauzer. Diana had fallen in love with Romeo, the most affectionate of the three. She did not know it but when Dodi had been in California to try to settle the Kelly Fisher problem, he had contacted the kennel Romeo had come from and ordered a female. He had been told that it would be several months before a puppy could be delivered. Dodi was happy with that: it seemed an ideal Christmas gift for Diana, and he had decided to call the dog Juliet.

Diana and Dodi wandered around the gardens of the Windsor villa, then sat down on a stone bench to talk. It was after four o'clock. Shadows were beginning to creep across the garden. Dodi put his arm around Diana's shoulder as Rees-Jones came out to tell them that the Range-Rover had arrived with Henri Paul and Kes Wingfield. The lovers lingered a few more minutes and left forty minutes after they had arrived. A decision on their occupancy of the house appears not to have been final, and as the lease belonged to al Fayed, his would be the last word, although there seemed to be little doubt but that she could have stayed at the villa if she chose.

When Diana stepped out of the car at the Ritz, a photographer jumped into her path. A security guard quickly intervened. There were shouts, which ended in a broken camera and punches between the photographer and a security guard. Claude Roulet, the manager of the Ritz, greeted her party as they came in, and they were led up the grand front staircase to the first floor to the Imperial Suite, the one she had occupied before. Diana was looking particularly lovely, her smooth, bronzed skin a striking contrast with her blonde hair. She and Dodi were about the same height, but her long legs and marvellous posture made her seem taller.

One of the true queens of Paris hotels, the Ritz was set like a jewel in the Place Vendôme, which had been originally planned by the controller of buildings under King Louis XIV as a huge octagonal area to surround a statue of the Sun King. The enterprise had proved too costly and was relinquished to rich bankers and merchants with élite salesrooms for jewels, furs, perfumes and extravagant fancies. The Place, and the Cour Vendôme that led off it, still had some of the most elegant shopping in Paris, and Diana had hoped she might have a chance to purchase gifts for Harry's thirteenth birthday on 15 September, and additional presents for William and close friends. The suite overlooked the front of the hotel where she could see the crowds of onlookers and paparazzi. A shopping trip was impossible. Instead, she made out a detailed list of what she wanted and for whom it was to be bought, and a Ritz employee was sent out to do the shopping for her, with instructions to have each package labelled and gift-wrapped.

Once they were settled, Diana went down to the beauty salon on the lower level for a manicure and pedicure and to have her hairwashed and blow-dried. Dodi made a number of telephone calls, one to a cousin, Hussein Yassin, to whom he confided that he was going to propose to Diana that night. A short while later, he left with Rees-Jones to go to the jeweller's. The ring was ready, the centre stone brilliant. Dodi asked to look at others. He chose one, a large emerald-cut diamond with sapphires. "He told me he was very much in love with the Princess," Alberto Repossi recalled. "He said he wanted to spend the rest of his life with her."

Dodi left both rings at the shop so that the jeweller could arrange to invoice him for whichever one he chose. His father had already agreed to underwrite the cost, roughly $205,400 for whichever ring was selected. Both men's love of giving lavish gifts of jewellery was well known, and Repossi hoped Dodi might decide to take both. However, when they were later brought to the Ritz, Dodi went with his and Diana's first choice, the "Tell Me Yes" ring, mainly because he had realized that the other might be too close in design to her engagement ring from Charles—and the one Dodi had given Kelly Fisher.

He kept the ring in its box inside the small leather case he carried with him to hold his spectacles, money and credit cards. He was going to wait until they were back at his apartment for the night before giving it to Diana. When Diana returned to the suite she also made phone calls, first to the boys, who were still fishing with their father in Scotland, and then to Richard Kay of Britain's *Daily Mail*, one of her few press confidants. She often called Kay when she was about to break a story. This time she told him, "I've decided to radically change my life," adding that "she was going to complete her obligations to her charities and to the anti-landmines cause and then, around November, would completely withdraw from public life." She sounded to Kay happier than he had ever heard her before. "I cannot say for certain that they would have married, but in my view it was likely."

Dodi wanted to go back to his apartment to change for dinner. They left the hotel by the rear door at seven o'clock in the black Mercedes 600, with Philippe Dourneau behind the wheel. Henri Paul had gone home for the day, and a second driver, Jean-François Musa, followed in the Range-Rover with Wingfield and Rees-Jones.

A gaggle of paparazzi waited for them in front of the apartment block. Rees-Jones, Wingfield and two security

men flanked the couple to get them safely to the door and
into the lobby. The photographers, who had been fighting
for pictures all day, were in no mood to be pushed aside.
One narrowly missed hitting Diana as he thrust his camera
into her face. A security guard knocked it out of his hand.
"It will be too bad for the Fayeds," the man shouted. "If
you don't let us work we'll tell everybody they're scum!"

Diana was shaken and Dodi furious when they were finally safe inside his apartment.

They were greeted effusively by the dogs and after a
few minutes Dodi went into his bedroom to change while
Diana unpacked some carrier bags that had been delivered
earlier. They contained the presents the personal shopper
from the hotel had bought. They were gift-wrapped, their
contents marked in pencil on the outside. She spread them
out on the marble cocktail table in the sitting room and
carefully wrote the initials of the recipient-to-be on each
gift. Then she put the packages back into the bags and went
into one of the marble bathrooms to freshen her makeup.
Dodi had placed a large bottle of Diorissimo, her favourite
perfume, on the vanity unit, along with a vase of pink roses.

René Delorm recalled that while Diana was in another
part of the apartment Dodi slipped into the kitchen.
" 'René,' he said, 'make sure we have champagne on ice.'
A few minutes later, he returned. 'I'm going to propose to
her tonight,' he whispered, a big smile on his face."

They had a nine thirty reservation at Benoît, a bistro on
the rue Saint-Martin, chosen because the food was good,
the atmosphere casual, and neither would have to dress.
Diana wore a black linen blazer over a black shell top and
white jeans, with pearl stud earrings, while Dodi was in a
tobacco-coloured shirt, open at the neck, blue jeans and
cowboy boots.

At Benoît a table had been set apart for them to ensure
privacy. Kes Wingfield, Trevor Rees-Jones and Claude
Roulet would be seated nearby. There was a frightening
moment when they were rushed by photographers as they
were about to get into their car, driven as usual by Dour-

neau, but the numbers had thinned out and the most threatening had left. However, as they approached Benoît they could see paparazzi waiting for their arrival. Someone, either in the restaurant or on the hotel switchboard, had revealed their plans. Dodi suggested that they turn back and eat at the hotel and Diana agreed.

They returned to the Ritz at 9:47 P.M. Paparazzi were lined up on the kerb, along with a number of tourists and the plain curious. Diana often worried that one day one of these innocent bystanders would get injured if they got in the way of the paparazzi.

It was several minutes after they arrived at the Ritz before Diana and Dodi could even get out of the car. Security finally forced back the photographers and the couple, looking glum, made their way through the revolving doors and into the lobby. Arrangements had been made for them to dine at a quiet table at L'Espadon, the elegant two-star Michelin restaurant on the ground floor of the hotel. Diana looked as though she were about to cry. Kes Wingfield suggested she sit down. They lingered for a few minutes in the famous bar behind the restaurant where, in the twenties, expatriate Americans like Cole Porter, Scott Fitzgerald, Ernest Hemingway and Louis Bromfield would meet their friends and hang out until late into the night. During the war the Germans had occupied the Ritz, but it was at this bar that General Leclerc had raised a toast in celebration of their departure.

Arrangements were now being made for another driver to take them later to Dodi's apartment. Dourneau would drive the Range-Rover as a decoy, leaving from the front of the hotel. When they were ready, Dodi and Diana would depart from the rear in a leased Mercedes driven by Henri Paul, who had been called back on duty but had not yet arrived. Neither Rees-Jones nor Wingfield thought it was a good idea to separate the vehicles, but Dodi was insistent and the two men, as employees, had to agree.

It was after ten o'clock when Diana and Dodi entered the dining room and were shown to a deep-rose-coloured leather banquette. The room is decorated in neo-Louis XVI Baroque style, and was warm and inviting. There were pink rosebuds on the table. The far wall of the large room was glass and looked on to a garden, romantically lit. Palm fronds divided the banquettes.

Dodi ordered a bottle of Taittinger champagne, his favourite, and grilled turbot; Diana an asparagus and mushroom omelette, to be followed by Dover sole and vegetable tempura. Since the divorce her bulimia had disappeared. She no longer had a problem with eating. The sommelier was opening the champagne when Dodi glanced at a table in their direct line of vision. A man was reaching for something from a plastic bag at his feet. Dodi rose immediately, turning his back to the man and shielding Diana. "I think he has a camera," he told her, then requested that their dinner be served to them in the Imperial Suite. Diana rose and, eyes straight ahead, walked with him back through the dining room, across the lobby and up the grand staircase to their suite.

Two waiters brought up trays with their dinner. A fresh bottle of chilled champagne was opened, then Dodi asked them to leave. They were alone for most of the next two hours. Dodi was getting up his courage to propose, but he still preferred to wait until they were back at his apartment where the silver plaque with its loving message had already been placed beneath her pillows on the king-sized bed. Diana was upset because this evening wasn't the romantic one they had wanted, but she suspected Dodi would propose to her before it had ended. Although she had told others during the early days of their cruise that she had no intention of marrying anyone at the present time, her actions on this particular day indicate she was at least considering the possibility.

Mohamed al Fayed claims that Dodi called him around midnight and did not say anything about having proposed. He did tell his father that he and Diana were about to leave the Ritz for his apartment. About thirty paparazzi were still out front, he explained, along with a large crowd of a hundred or more sightseers, and he told his father of the plan he had devised to bypass them.

Its success rested on the premise that if the Range-Rover departed with a bodyguard, the paparazzi would believe that he and Diana had decided to spend the night at the Ritz. His father disliked the idea. "Don't go. Why not stay the night at the hotel?" he asked.

"We can't, Moomoo [his pet name for his father]. We leave in the morning and all our things are at the apartment," Dodi countered.

"Why split up the bodyguards?" al Fayed questioned.

"The car is not that big," Dodi replied. The second bodyguard could easily have sat in the back of the Mercedes with them, but Dodi wanted to be alone with Diana.

"Just be careful," his father warned him. "Don't step on it. There's no hurry. Wait until you see the atmosphere is perfect, get in your car and go away. Don't hide, it's unnecessary. You have security with you. Let them shoot [their pictures]."

About fifteen minutes later, Dodi called security to alert them that they were on their way downstairs to the rear exit. He had his arm around Diana's waist, while Rees-Jones and Wingfield walked one in front and one behind them as they made their way down the first-floor hallway with its regal French blue carpet embossed with the Ritz seal, to the back service stairway. Wingfield recalled that Diana was fearful for the safety of the paparazzi on their motorcycles but Dodi told her not to worry. She was smiling by the time they reached the rear entrance. They stood together in the service vestibule with its black and white tiled floor and windows looking out on a grimy alley.

It was only a few moments before Henri Paul pulled the leased Mercedes near to the rear service door, emerged from the car and came inside to report that the paparazzi had not been outwitted: about thirty stood across the alley. However, he was certain that he would lose them quickly: there was not much traffic at this time of night and they could probably make good time by heading down the

Champs Élysées. But if they took that route the paparazzi could pull their motorcycles alongside the car and shoot through the windows. He suggested that instead they go via the Express and through the Alma tunnel, as they had earlier in the day. That way they would not take the chance of being stopped in traffic, surrounded by paparazzi. Dodi agreed. It was already nineteen minutes past midnight and he was anxious that they reach the apartment soon: Diana was exhausted from the day's experiences.

Neither Wingfield nor Rees-Jones saw anything unusual about Henri Paul's appearance. He was a volatile man, moved quickly, was very confident. He stepped out of the door first, followed by Rees-Jones then Diana. Instantly cameras whirred and flashed. "Where to? Where to?" shouted a paparazzo. There was a small construction barrier next to the rear entrance and Diana walked round it to the parked Mercedes. Dodi was right behind her. Rees-Jones hurried to open the rear door of the vehicle. Diana ducked inside and slid over as Dodi joined her. He was sitting behind the driver and she behind Rees-Jones in the right front passenger seat. Wingfield and Dourneau had gone round to where the Range-Rover was still parked. They would take the alternative route.

Henri Paul revved the engine of the Mercedes as he shouted to the paparazzi through an open window. No one seems sure what he said, but his voice was taunting. Then he closed the window and headed forward towards the Place de la Concorde, the Express and the Alma tunnel.

DIANA AND DODI leaned back in the rear seat. The ring in its box was still in Dodi's leather case which, with Diana's handbag, had been placed on the floor. At this point none of the occupants had buckled their safety-belts. The Mercedes drove along normally with its entourage of paparazzi on motorcycles and in cars until it reached a red traffic light at the Place de la Concorde. Rees-Jones could see the couple in the back seat through the rear-view mirror. It was at this stage that he realized that none of them had fastened their belts. Usually bodyguards do not buckle up as the strap might inhibit action in case of an attack, but Rees-Jones now did so. Perhaps he felt that something was not right: perhaps Henri Paul was not in full control of the wheel, that he acted oddly. It is not clear if he called back for Diana and Dodi to fasten their seat-belts. He had asked them to do this before the car left the Ritz, but Dodi never liked to use the device and Diana had ignored Rees-Jones too. Considering Dodi's fear for Diana's safety and the lengths to which he and his father had gone to ensure it, his lapse of this precaution seems out of character and is contrary to his past behaviour: others recall that he helped Diana secure her belt as soon as they got into a car. But, then, Dodi was lulled by champagne, the night was warm, the sky covered with stars. Traffic was sparse due to the hour and because many Parisians were on holiday. And Dodi was in love, his mind on what he intended to say later, his passion aroused by the nearness of the woman he so desired.

Mohamed al Fayed reportedly claimed that Dodi had told him in one of their last conversations that he and Diana planned to be married in October or November and thus now wanted to be certain they could have the Windsor villa by then. That fits with the date from which Diana told Richard Kay she planned to live a more normal life and withdraw from public duties. Still, Dodi had not yet given her the ring, although she knew it was in his possession, and she never corroborated this to Kay or Rosa Monckton. It seems likely that she had agreed to live with Dodi that autumn, but wanted to discuss the marriage proposal, which she was expecting, with her sons when she returned to London, as it so directly concerned them. She might also have wished to seek legal advice.

Diana had much to occupy her mind in the short span of time before reaching Dodi's apartment, usually a twelve- to fifteen-minute drive when taking this route. Given the lateness of the hour, her exhaustion, and intake of champagne, she could well have been distracted. But, also, she was sitting snug-close to Dodi and had she buckled up, the position of the safety strap would have separated them by a good twelve inches.

Suddenly, before the light turned green, Henri Paul took off with a roar, racing towards the embankment road. The paparazzi shot off after him. Rees-Jones remembered later that a Jeep, two motorbikes and "a little three-door car," which he identified as belonging to paparazzi, had also turned off and were tailgating the Mercedes. Paul headed straight for the Alma tunnel. Dodi and Diana voiced their concern at this juncture that the paparazzi were too close.

Paul pressed harder on the accelerator. The car was now travelling at about sixty-five miles an hour, well over the speed limit for this stretch of road.

Henri Paul, a forty-one-year-old bachelor, was a conscientious man, well regarded by friends and co-workers at the Ritz and people from his home town of Lorient, Brittany. "He liked to drink, but no more than the next man," his close friend Jean-Jacques Guillou has said. His lifelong passion was flying. He had been a licensed pilot from the age of nineteen and worked for a time as a flying instructor. He also loved fast cars and motorbikes, and owned a powerful Honda VMAX with a top speed of 130 m.p.h. "He liked to pose with it, but that was all," Guillou insists. "He was a good driver and a safe one." Then he added, "He was a serious man. He liked a laugh but was very committed to the job. He was a friend to Dodi. He used to tell me how they sometimes went out for dinner together [when Paul was assigned to Dodi as security]." One of Paul's hobbies was playing jazz on the piano, and Dodi was also a jazz enthusiast.

A military-security specialist, Paul had taken two courses in high-security driving at Mercedes-Benz in Stuttgart, Germany, before coming to work for the Ritz in 1986. He had been promoted quickly and now answered only to the Ritz Hotel President Frank Klein and hotel manager Claude Roulet. He supervised a twenty-man force and was about to receive a sizeable pay increase. Known to be an excellent driver, he had no previous record for speeding or for drunk driving. Co-workers and friends, although not necessarily the Fayeds and his immediate superiors, knew he drank, but never when he was working. He was also taking two powerful anti-depressants, Prozac and Tiapridel, which he had been on since he had separated from his girlfriend.

"He was calm and collected and always very serious," a co-worker at the Ritz concurred. "But that place [the Ritz] is very hierarchical. If someone gives an order you follow it. No questions asked."

He kept his motorbike at his parents' home in Brittany and his poky black Austin Mini near his fifth-floor apartment in a rundown building on the rue des Petits-Champs, about half a mile from the Ritz. He earned about $45,000 a year, and had accrued over $200,000 in savings, perhaps because his tastes were simple. As a driver for rich guests at the Ritz he is likely to have received large tips. He spoke fluent English and German, had a pleasant demeanour, a ready smile and an amusing, somewhat cocky, swaggering walk—"a little like a Western gunslinger in a Hollywood movie," one friend commented. Wealthy Arabs were known to give their drivers thousands of dollars if they were pleased with their services, and Paul was proud of his work, seemingly tireless on duty. But there were also rumours, not confirmed, that he moonlighted as an informant for a French government agency.

An energetic man with a receding hairline, shortish but robust, Paul was in good physical condition from his early-morning tennis games and the barbells with which he liked to work out. He was short-sighted and always wore glasses when he drove, and he was making every effort to overcome his depression. Essentially a private man, few knew that he was battling this disease, certainly no one at the Ritz.

On 30 August, Paul had played tennis in the morning before coming to work. At midday he was informed that Dodi had requested that he meet the Harrods jet at Le Bourget. He returned to the Ritz at approximately 4:30 P.M., and left at 7 P.M. in his own car believing his workday was complete. His diary listed no evening engagements. An unwashed glass with traces of Martini, and a bottle of the aperitif, a third of its contents consumed, that were later found in his apartment, indicate that he had had at least one drink, possibly two or three, when, shortly after 9:30 P.M. Claude Roulet called to tell him that Dodi wished him to drive the Princess and himself later that evening. Paul left almost immediately, wearing the same clothes he had worn earlier: dark grey suit, blue patterned tie and shirt. A neighbour saw him walk out to his car. "He was perfectly steady on his feet," she said. He waved to the owner of a lesbian bar across from where he had parked his car. They were friends and he often stopped to chat with her.

He drove back to the Ritz, parked his car in a side-street, walked through the crowd now gathered there, and into the front lobby of the Ritz, where he was met by Rees-Jones and Wingfield. The three went into the bar where the two burly Britons had a light snack. Paul said he wasn't hungry, but ordered a drink. When it was served, he told them it was pineapple juice. In fact, the yellow liquid was *pastis*, a strong liquor. Then he ordered a second. Neither Rees-

Jones nor Wingfield noticed any hint of intoxication in Paul as they left the bar.* "He usually ordered a Coke when he was on duty," one of the barmen said later. "I knew he had worked a full day and thought he was just arranging the schedule for the morning shift. He often did that in his own time."

No one at the Ritz was aware that Henri Paul had an alcohol problem that had required medical help in the past. The French drink wine from an early age and many can tolerate a high level of alcohol without showing it. Henri Paul was one of these people. Dodi had always been strict with his drivers. He knew Paul well, and apparently—like Rees-Jones and Wingfield—observed no deviation from his usual demeanour. He was with him for several moments before they left the service area of the hotel and did not question his ability to drive.

Dodi was known to be a nervous car passenger, and although it was rumoured that he liked to drive fast he seldom drove his own cars, certainly not in London or Paris. It is inconceivable that he would have knowingly allowed a man who was drunk to drive when he could easily have asked for another driver. The truth was, he felt safest with Paul, of all the other Ritz drivers, at the wheel.

No one was aware that the leased Mercedes in which they were travelling had had mechanical problems earlier in the day. A persistent warning light on the dashboard indicated a problem with the brakes. Henri Paul was told that the car had been checked and "found to be in perfect working order . . . The steering and anti-lock braking system seemed perfectly normal." Also, the car had been stolen in April and discovered in a Paris suburb two weeks

----

*It is not known if Rees-Jones had anything to drink that night. Several years earlier, he had been arrested for drunk driving in Great Britain and had his licence revoked for one year. His job as bodyguard would have precluded his taking over as driver of the Mercedes. Under any circumstances his position required he be alcohol-free when on duty.

later, stripped and requiring $20,000 worth of repairs.

When Paul accelerated, the paparazzi were galvanized into action. The one among them whom Diana had found so fearsome, Romuald Rat, was the only photographer with a two-seater Honda motorbike. Riding pillion with Sté-phane Darmon, who was driving, Rat was able to shoot pictures on the move. But when Paul jumped the light at the Place de la Concorde, Rat temporarily lost sight of the Mercedes. When the light turned green Darmon increased their speed to 60 m.p.h.

"We continued for two to three hundred metres because there is a slight rise and we wanted to see if [the Mercedes] was on the other side," Rat said later. "The Mercedes" tail-lights had disappeared. I decided there was no point in try-ing to catch up. It had to be so far ahead." But he and Darmon continued in their pursuit.

The Mercedes was now doing over 80 m.p.h. Paul over-took a taxi that was also approaching the Alma tunnel. The passenger, Brian Anderson, a businessman from California, claimed on CBS News that the Mercedes was being tailed by two motorcycles, one mounted by two people, being driven "aggressively and dangerously," the taxi driver Michel Lemmonier recalled. "The [Mercedes] was flying as it passed me. It was like the hounds of hell. There could be only one ending. The poor [passengers] must have been in terror."

The chase seemed now to take a more personal turn. The Mercedes was travelling so fast that it would have been pointless for the photographers to pull alongside it to take pictures. "A moving photo of a car with tinted windows would have no value at all," Goksin Sipahiouglu, head of the Sipa photo agency says, and those who were racing with Paul were experienced professionals. They were also fairly certain that the Mercedes was headed for Dodi's apartment and that competitive photographers who had followed the green Range-Rover would be on their way there. Given the speed of their chase, though, they had a chance to beat the others to photos of Diana and Dodi getting out of the Mercedes and going into the apartment block. Paul might have suspected this and increased his pressure on the accelerator.

The Mercedes was now less than thirty seconds from the Alma tunnel. Directly in its path was a small white car travelling much slower.* At the entrance to the tunnel there is a curve, then a sharp dip, and experienced Parisian drivers know that it should not be taken at high speed. Paul had already come this way earlier in the day, at which time he had worn his seat-belt and slowed before entering the tunnel. At the current speed of the Mercedes, and without seat-belts, Diana and Dodi must have been flung about in the back, and Paul distracted as he entered the tunnel now dangerously close to the white car.

The Alma tunnel is marked by reinforced steel pillars fifteen feet tall, supporting the roof. They are set a few feet apart and separate the two lanes of eastbound and westbound traffic. With the white car directly in his path, Paul had no option but to pass on the right. He swerved to overtake the car, misjudged the distance and clipped it on the side. The driver of the white car kept going, his car not seriously damaged, but the Mercedes veered out of control, hit the right cement wall on Diana's and Rees-Jones's side of the vehicle, then ricocheted diagonally across the carriageway, colliding head-on with the thirteenth pillar, which was unprotected by a safety barrier. The crippled Mercedes spun round and skidded to a halt, facing the wrong way. It was now 12:24 A.M. The trip from the rear of the Ritz to the moment of impact had been less than seven minutes.

François Lévy and his wife were just leaving the tunnel when, Lévy later told the police, they heard "a huge bang

*This vehicle was believed to have been a white Fiat Uno. Police questioned three thousand owners of cars matching that description without being able to place any of them in the Alma tunnel after midnight on 31 August. Al Fayed had offered $1.65 million as a reward for information on this car, which created numerous false leads for the French police. Finally, on 15 February 1999, someone came forward to say that the car he had been driving, a white Citroen AX, had been the "mystery car," and his story seemed to check out.

like an explosion. It really shook me, so I pulled over to the side of the road." They sat there for a few moments, frightened, certain there had been an terrible accident. While travelling through the tunnel, Lévy claimed to have seen flashing lights and, through his rear-view window, a motorcycle cut in front of a black Mercedes. From this interview, the first flames of conspiracy were ignited. Lévy turned out to be a convicted criminal who, in 1989, had served a prison sentence for theft, housebreaking and forging cheques. He had claimed previously on French television to have sold a baby he had fathered to a German couple. But although he had lied in the past it did not mean that he was not telling the truth this time. It was the first bizarre twist in the horror that later created a crisis for all concerned.

The tunnel was mayhem. Smoke clouded around the mangled car. Henri Paul's body, thrust half-way through the windscreen, was pressed against the horn. He had died on impact, when the Mercedes had hit the cement wall. Traffic had halted and car occupants leaped out to see what had happened. A couple with a cellphone called the *sapeurs-pompiers*, the civilian rescue unit.

"The guy in the front passenger seat [Rees-Jones] was badly injured but conscious," one of the first witnesses on the scene reported. The front passenger door had been ripped off and Rees-Jones, his white shirt covered in blood, was leaning sideways, held back by his seat-belt: "The lower half of his face was ripped off and hanging loose," the witness recalled. "It was hard to look at. I told him not to panic, help was on the way. He looked at me and struggled but could say nothing. The driver didn't move. The man in the back seat was also lying still, his legs [twisted grotesquely] obviously broken."

In fact, Dodi, too, had died on impact and was lying prone across the rear seat. Diana had not been visible as she had fallen on to the floor, slumped so that she was facing the rear of the car with her shoulder touching the right side door. When two people tried to open it, someone shouted, "Don't do that! If you move them you can kill them!"

Rat and Darmon had ridden their two-seater Honda to a halt about twenty yards from the scene of the accident. Rat jumped off and ran to the Mercedes, "the bonnet caved in, the engine rammed back through the car with such force that the radiator ended up in the driver's foot well. Virtually the full force was taken head-on. The back of the car remained remarkably unscathed. On the shelf under the tinted rear window a box of tissues had slid off-centre but was otherwise undisturbed. The boot was undented, with just two scratches on the top." He knew Diana was in the back seat, where there appeared to be less damage. Still, he doubted that anyone could have survived the power of the impact.

"At that time I thought they were all dead," he said, in his police deposition. "I was shocked. For several seconds I stayed back from the car. After a moment, I got a hold of myself and went to the car to open the door, because I wanted to see what I could do to try to help them . . . I saw that, for the chauffeur and Monsieur Fayed, they were obviously dead, and I could do nothing. So I leaned over the Princess to see if she was alive."

Diana he said was trapped in the foot well, "half kneeling, her legs buckled under her. Her head was resting in the gap between the two front seats, with her chin pressed tightly against her chest." One arm was extended across Dodi's twisted leg. Blood trickled from her ear, nose and mouth, but except for a gash on her forehead she seemed to have no external injury to her head. "I tried to take her pulse," Rat continued, "and when I touched her, she moved and breathed. So I spoke to her in English, saying, 'I'm here, be cool, a doctor will arrive.' "

Rat had heard from the first man on the scene that a call had been placed to the *sapeurs-pompiers*. In fact, medical help was closer. A doctor was making his way towards the crash site. His name was Frédéric Mailliez, he worked for an emergency service but was off-duty and driving home from a party when he approached the Alma tunnel from the opposite direction. "The horn was blaring. People loitering," he said, when interviewed. "I looked inside. The doors were open. I saw that two of the passengers were almost certainly dead, but the man in the front passenger seat and the young blonde woman in the back of the car were still alive." He had no idea at this time that the woman was Diana. "I remember thinking it was strange that there were so many photographers around but when you have a serious accident like that you focus on the victims."

Mailliez raced back to his car for oxygen masks and to telephone the emergency services. It was now 12:26 A.M.

When he returned to the Mercedes, two police officers had arrived. One had immediately checked the victims. In his official report he stated that he believed he heard "the woman in the back mumble something like 'My God . . .' But then she appeared to lose consciousness. The second officer had his hands full, trying to keep back the paparazzi. "The camera flashes were going off like machine-gun fire around the back right-hand side of the vehicle where the door was open," he said, in his official report. When he tried to push the photographers back, one shouted at him, "You're pissing me off. Let me do my work." Another joined in, "Yeah, go to Bosnia, then you'll see how we do our work."

Mailliez, accustomed to the chaos of accident scenes, concentrated on his patient. He recalled someone shouting to him, "Speak to her in English!" He later said she was "unconscious . . . agitated and moaning." He received no audible response when he first spoke to her. But when he cradled her head and administered the oxygen, she muttered something that he did not understand. A police officer was trying to comfort Rees-Jones until a doctor could attend to his injuries. Assistance came at 12:33 A.M. when three *sapeurs-pompiers*" ambulances, each staffed with a doctor and nurse, arrived on the scene.

By now Paris police chief Philippe Massoni had been notified of the identity of the crash victims. He informed the interior minister Jean-Pierre Chevènement. Next he placed a call to President Jacques Chirac, but the duty officer decided not to wake the President in the middle of the night as it did not seem to be a serious government matter. However, the man rang the British embassy to tell them that the Princess of Wales had been in a major car crash. This was also conveyed to the British Ambassador, Michael Jay. He was told that Diana, unconscious, injured and bleeding internally, was being taken to the Pitié-Salpêtrière, the nearest hospital equipped for such serious trauma patients on a twenty-four-hour basis. However, it would not be until 2:05 A.M., an hour and forty minutes after the crash, that Diana finally reached the hospital, which was less than five minutes away.

In Britain and the United States accident victims are treated with what is called the "scoop and run" approach. This means that as soon as an ambulance reaches the accident site and the victim has been extricated from the wreckage, they are rushed by ambulance or helicopter to the nearest hospital, receiving what life-saving care can be given *en route*. Ambulances are not equipped to perform major surgical work and are staffed by paramedics. A team of doctors would have been alerted and be waiting in emergency for the victim to arrive, when they would be prepared for surgery if necessary. In France, ambulances are better equipped, the medical staff sent out with them are fully qualified, the theory being that the victim will receive more immediate sophisticated care this way.

"The philosophy [in France]," Dr. Mailliez explained, "is to try to stabilize the patient as much as you can, because travelling . . . can be very dangerous for a patient. So we try to restore a little bit of blood pressure and some other things before we start to drive." Similarly, it is not uncommon for emergency doctors to tell ambulancemen to drive slowly. "If you are braking or accelerating it can be very bad for the blood pressure."

The ambulances were at the Alma tunnel at 12:33 A.M. Rees-Jones was removed from the wreckage within ten minutes. But it was a slow, delicate operation to get Diana out of the car, even though the door was open. One of her legs was pinned under the seat and emergency workers had to cut through metal to free her. It was about one o'clock before she was placed on a stretcher inside the ambulance. She was connected to an IV drip of liquids and dextrose, attached to a respirator and given external cardiac stimulation. She was unconscious and barely responded.

"You couldn't try to repair [such serious injury] at the scene," Dr. John Ochsner, one of America's pre-eminent cardiovascular surgeons asserts, further stressing that external chest massage would probably be "the worst thing that could happen. Once you start beating on the chest, you increase pressure in all the chambers at one time. If anything it could hurt the patient." But the extent of Diana's injuries had not been ascertained and the French emergency staff were using a regular medical procedure applied to a victim in her condition and with her visible injuries.

Another American specialist, Dr. David Wasserman, adds, "You could never diagnose that kind of injury [the extent of a tear to the main artery to the heart] in the field. Never. . . . Spending all that time on on-site treatment was absolutely the wrong approach for this patient, who would have had a far greater chance if they had gotten her to the operating room sooner."

Diana's ambulance did not leave the Alma tunnel until 1:45 A.M. The driver had instructions from the on-board medical team to avoid shocks and bumps and a drive that normally takes five minutes (the hospital was only 3.9 miles away) took fifteen. Every minute that passed before the surgery was undertaken to close the tear from the puncture in her pulmonary vein lessened her chance of survival. Shortly after 2 A.M., Diana was wheeled into La Pitié-Salpêtrière hospital through the side entrance of the emergency wing where staff rushed her to the operating theatre. She was still breathing but had gone into cardiac arrest when the medical team first saw her.

The surgeons were well prepared. They had been alerted

an hour earlier of her imminent arrival. The team was headed by Professor Bruno Riou who was joined by Professor Jean Pierre Bénazet, an associate, and Professor Pierre Coriat, head of anaesthetics. There were four senior nurses and four other surgical staff. It was not until Diana was on her way to the basement operating theatre for open-heart surgery that they learned her identity.

"She looked like a china doll, so beautiful,"* one nurse said. "Here was the most famous woman in all the world, everything to live for, and we knew her chances were slim. I could not contain my tears." Two of the nurses "momentarily lost their professionalism," and became physically sick when they saw who it was. They were immediately replaced.

The medical team worked for two hours, trying to repair the damage to Diana's torn vein and to stop the massive internal haemorrhaging. Blood had flooded the cavity surrounding her left lung; the extensive blood loss had damaged her heart and starved her internal organs of fluids. The surgeons worked against time to seal off the blood flow and repair what damage they could. at 3:55 A.M. Diana had no pulse or heartbeat. They tried manual heart massage, which had no effect. Electric shock was administered but Diana's heart would not beat on its own. The medical team had done everything they could. It was 4 A.M. on 31 August. Diana, Princess of Wales, was pronounced dead.

Professor Riou closed the chest wound. Grim faces, some with unabashed tears, looked down at the lovely young woman they had not been able to save. Riou noticed that Diana wore only one delicate pearl earring: the other

---

*Apart from a wound on her forehead and a small cut over her lip, Diana's face was not disfigured. Her clothes had been cut off her and she was covered from foot to neck by a white sheet and surgical blankets. Aside from the injury to her chest, several ribs had been crushed, her right arm was fractured, and there were deep gashes on her right thigh and buttock where she had been pinned by the metal of the car.

had been lost in the crash. "Gently, he removed the other earring and laid it on a surgical dish." She was still wearing a bracelet that Dodi had recently given her, and some simple rings. The ring she would have had if Henri Paul had only taken the Champs Élysées instead of the Alma tunnel, was on the floor of the crumpled Mercedes.

PRINCE CHARLES, STILL at Balmoral with his sons, was awakened at 1:45 A.M., on Sunday morning (2:45 A.M. in Paris), and informed by Robin Janvrin, the Queen's deputy secretary, that the Princess of Wales had been in a serious car accident in which Dodi Fayed had been killed. At that time hope remained that Diana would survive. Charles immediately rang his mother but decided not to wake William and Harry until he had more news. He dressed and met the Queen a little over half an hour later in her private study along with Sir Robert Fellowes who, with Jane, was also at Balmoral. At 3:15 A.M. (4:15 A.M. French time), Fellowes rang the hospital. The Princess of Wales, he was told, had just died.

Charles was distraught. There is no way one can surmise what his thoughts were, but certainly his concern for his sons must have been uppermost. But shortly afterwards he called Camilla.

A "crisis centre" consisting of the British Ambassador, his wife, and members of the embassy staff, had been set up on the same floor of La Pitié Salpêtrière where Diana's body now rested in a sequestered room of the intensive-care unit. A statement had to be written and given to the press, but first the Ambassador wanted to be sure that all members of Diana's family had been notified and the two princes told of their mother's death. Charles asked that no release be circulated until 7 A.M.

Jane, from whom Diana had been distant over the last few years, rang Sarah first then their brother Charles in Cape Town. None of them could believe that Diana was dead. The shock was overwhelming. Jane was in great distress. Earl Spencer and Sarah were both prepared to fly to Paris. Fellowes had told his wife to ask them to sit tight until it was decided what the next step should be. The atmosphere at Balmoral was grim, bordering on frenzy. There was much walking up and down the tartan carpets of the long hallways. Servants had been awakened and trays of tea and coffee were being served to those whose lights were on. A general sense of disbelief spread throughout the castle.

Finally, at just past 7 A.M., Charles went to the boys in the small sitting room their bedrooms shared, and where they had been told he wanted to see them. There "he soberly explained to them that their mother had been in a very serious accident. He gently led into the fact that, in fact, Diana was dead," a royal source has said. It was a fairly private moment, only a few members of the two princes' personal staff were present to give support if it was needed. Both boys were too stunned by the news to react immediately. Charles placed his arms about their shoulders. Harry was the first to cry, an observer noted, but neither of them lost control. After a few minutes they joined their grandparents and other members of the household. William was heard to say, "I knew something was wrong. I kept waking up all night."

Kes Wingfield was at Dodi's flat when René Delorm received a call from the Paris police at one o'clock with the news of Dodi's death. Wingfield asked about the others and was told that "a blonde woman and a man identified as Trevor Rees-Jones had survived, but were in critical condition and were being taken to hospital." Wingfield called the head of Mohamed al Fayed's personal Paris security, who in turn notified al Fayed at his country house in Surrey of the horrible tragedy.

"I felt like somebody had shot both my legs away," al Fayed said. "I had lost my son, the closest person to me. It is impossible to describe how that feels to someone who has not experienced it. I asked about Diana and was told she was hurt. I desperately hoped that Diana was still alive." A short time later, his Paris informer called back to tell him that Diana was critically ill and undergoing surgery at La Pitié Salpêtrière Hospital. Al Fayed called Raine, who had been asleep at her house in London's Farm Street. Then he woke his helicopter pilot. Within half an hour al Fayed was on the landing pad at his estate to board his Sikorsky Sk-76 helicopter for Paris. He arrived eighty minutes later at Le Bourget airport, where he was met by Dodi's chauffeur Philippe Dorneau and Kes Wingfield, and driven the ten miles north to Paris. He asked to be taken to La Pitié Salpêtrière first for news of Diana, as Dodi's body had already been taken to a mortuary.

"When I walked into the hospital they told me that Diana had just died. I could not believe it—the situation was too desperate to take in." He claims that a French official he recognized approached and told him that a nurse wanted to speak to him in private. "This nurse said she recognized me and had something important to tell me. But she was insistent that nobody would know her identity because it was unethical of her to pass on confidential information from an operating theatre. I understood and agreed never to reveal who she was. She then said that Diana had been slipping in and out of consciousness, and her last words were, 'I would like all my possessions in Dodi's apartment to be given to my sister Sarah, including my jewellery and my personal clothes, and please tell her to take care of my boys.' "

Al Fayed either believed the woman or created a terrible fiction. For the members of the hospital medical team have stated that Diana was unconscious when she was wheeled into the operating theatre (she had been heavily sedated by the ambulance medics almost immediately upon their arrival at the scene of the crash), and that she never regained consciousness. He also averred that he was told Dodi had survived for five or ten minutes after the crash, a statement that was refuted by Romuald Rat, Dr. Frédéric Mailliez, and other doctors at the accident scene.

Al Fayed then went to the Institut Médico Légal where the bodies of Dodi and Henri Paul had been taken as soon as they had been freed from the wreckage. Dodi's body, covered in a white sheet, was wheeled into a private room. His father would not let them lower the sheet past his neck. "I could see he was at peace . . . He looked like a little boy again . . . His injuries were quite terrible. . . . I don't think I could have endured the pain of seeing his mangled legs and broken chest." Al Fayed then sent his representatives to cut through the French technicalities to have Dodi's body released, for in the Muslim faith the dead must be buried within twenty-four hours. This took some doing as the French police had begun the investigation of the crash and the decision on whether or not to order an autopsy had not been made. However, protocol was bypassed. Dodi would be on his way back to England that night. So would Diana's possessions in the apartment on the rue Arsène Haussaye, which al Fayed ordered Delorm to pack. The ring he had paid for, undamaged in the crash, was turned over to him, as were the other valuables Dodi had had with him during his last ride. The thousand dollars he was known to have drawn from the cashier at the Ritz a short time before his departure were missing.

Father Yves Clochard-Bossuet, a small, grey-haired, middle-aged man, was the resident Catholic priest at La Pitié Salpêtrière. He was called at 4:05 A.M. to give Diana the Last Rites, which can be accorded to the dying of any Christian denomination. "There were so many people, police, the British Ambassador, doctors and, outside, journalists and crowds were all gathering," he recalled. "They had taken her to a private room [in the intensive-care unit]. I went to her bedside and prayed for her soul. I was alone with her for four hours. I was very aware of the Princess's position in the Anglican Church, and although I was never frightened by my task, I was very discreet." He did not give the Last Rites to Dodi. "That would have been against his religion as a Muslim." He added, "Even as a priest, you never get used to death, especially when it's someone young like Princess Diana."

The following morning, a Sunday, Britain awoke to the tragedy. Plans were being made to bring Diana home. The

Queen agreed with Prince Charles that he should accompany the coffin, and Sir Robert Fellowes suggested that Jane and Sarah should represent the Spencer family, for it would take too long for Earl Spencer to arrange a flight from South Africa. It does not seem that Diana's brother was consulted on this decision, but later that morning he booked a flight to London so that he could institute immediate arrangements for the funeral.

Three hours later, Prince Charles, his sons, the Queen, the Queen Mother and Prince Philip went to church. Charles looked exhausted, the boys in shock. Both were devastated and, once the truth had taken hold, burst into floods of tears. However, they were in control as they entered the small, nineteenth-century Crathie church that the Royal Family had attended while at Balmoral since the reign of Queen Victoria. Curiously, no mention of Diana's death was made during the hour-long service, nor were prayers said in her memory. This might have been omitted because of the Queen's edict at the time of the divorce that in church services Diana's name was no longer included in the prayers made for the Royal Family, or it might have been by direct request of the Queen that day.

If the latter is true, this was the first of many disastrous mistakes she made in the aftermath of the tragedy. Some in Crathie church were horrified that the sermon, called "Moving House," contained jokes by a well-known Scottish comedian. It set the tone for the public reaction to the Queen's attitude during this terrible time of their grieving. The Queen was out of touch, and seemingly unaware of the great love her subjects felt for her former daughter-in-law. And so were the courtiers upon whom she relied for advice: they had advised that the Royal Family should simply soldier on.

Paul Burrell, Diana's faithful butler, the man she called "my rock," was *en route* to Paris. He had been asked by Sarah to select clothes that would be suitable for Diana to be dressed in when her family arrived to view her body. In the small suitcase he placed in the care of the stewardess was a black cocktail dress that Diana had not yet worn, makeup from her dressing-table, a pair of black pumps and the rosary that had been given to her by Mother Teresa. On his arrival he was driven directly to the hospital and taken to her room. Diana had been washed and her hair brushed lightly. With a nurse's assistance Burrell dressed her, applied light makeup to her face, and placed the rosary in her hands across her chest.

"The valet was very dignified, very sad, very calm," the assisting nurse said. "He stayed with her a long time, putting on her makeup and making her look like a princess again . . . The dress [he had brought] was black, coming to just below her knees. It looked truly beautiful, but simple and sober. It was a wrap-around dress with long sleeves and a collar and delicate belt. The front of it crossed over, forming a V-neck." After the nurse left, Burrell sat by Diana's side, waiting for her sisters and Prince Charles.

It was three o'clock when BAe 146 aircraft of the Royal Squadron touched down at Villacoublay, a military airfield just outside Paris. The flight had been chaos. *En route* Charles had been informed that, as Diana was no longer a member of the Royal Family, her body would have to be taken to Fulham mortuary in west London. He was greatly distressed. "No! No!" he was heard to cry. "It won't do!" Then, almost all the time they were airborne, he was on the radiophone to Tony Blair and others making plans to bring Diana to the Chapel Royal at St. James's Palace.

The sun was fading when Burrell's vigil ended, although in the semi-darkness of the room, with the shutters closed, a single wall lamp lit, votive candles burning on a bedside table, he would not have been aware of it. Nor did he know that the press had rented balcony and window space across from the hospital room, cameras poised in the event that the shutters were opened.

Accompanied only by the Reverend Martin Draper from the Anglican cathedral in Paris, Charles, Sarah and Jane entered the room together. After a few minutes of prayer, Charles asked if he could have some time alone with Diana.

He remained with her for almost half an hour. In the past year, they had mended some of the acrimony between them and attended a few family gatherings together, such as the boys' birthdays. ("Daddy, hold Mummy's hand," Harry had said on one occasion. And Charles had.) But Charles is not an insensitive man, although he had seemed so during the years of his marriage. He had a great deal of forgiveness and considerable guilt to work through for himself. When he emerged from the room, it was evident that he had been crying.

President Chirac stood in the anteroom with the medical team who had lost their battle to save Diana's life. Charles pulled himself together with his usual fortitude and royal demeanour and walked over to thank them for having done the best that was possible.

Jane and Sarah now went back into the room, tightly grasping hands. When they left a few minutes later, their eyes were red and for a few moments they stood with their arms about each other.

Diana was placed in a coffin, which was draped with the Royal Standard. Borne by four pallbearers dressed in black, the cortège moved down the hospital corridors, the coffin and its bearers followed by Prince Charles, Sarah, Jane, Monsieur and Madame Chirac, Ambassador Jay and his wife. They left the hospital through a side entrance where a hearse was parked directly behind the Ambassador's grey Jaguar in which Charles would ride, and a black limousine that would carry Jane and Sarah. Twelve Gardes Républicaines stood at attention as the coffin was lifted into the back of the hearse. Charles then shook hands with the Chiracs and got into the rear seat of the Jaguar with the Ambassador. There was a pause as a British embassy aide, unable to control his tears, placed a plastic bag, containing Diana's possessions on her arrival at the hospital, in the boot of her sisters' car. President Chirac and the Gardes stood at attention saluting as the three-vehicle cortège drove out through the hospital gates. It was 6:15 P.M. A pale pink, twilight sky reflected a soft, almost ethereal light.

A large crowd lined the boulevard de l'Hôpital as the cortège turned into it. There were cries of "Diana! Diana!" and people were sobbing. Against the marble pillar bearing the hospital's nameplate, flowers and personal messages had been gathering since dawn. Even the people of Paris had felt a deep loss. It was an indication of what was to come.

Charles, pain still etched on his face, and Sarah and Jane, puffy and red-eyed, stood solemnly as British guards hoisted Diana's coffin aboard the royal aircraft. It was just after seven o'clock when the plane took off. It arrived at the Northolt Royal Air Force base forty-five minutes later where it was met by Prime Minister Tony Blair and other members of the cabinet. Charles spoke with them briefly. The coffin, topped with a large floral wreath, was placed in a hearse to be driven to London. Charles reboarded the aircraft with Diana's sisters for the short journey back to Balmoral, where no one had yet realized the extent of grief that cloaked the nation—indeed, the world.

The streets of Britain were eerily silent. Most people were seated, still in shock, before their television sets watching the same film footage over and over again—replays of televised moments of Diana's life interspersed with the images of the crash site, the Prince of Wales and Diana's sisters as the coffin was taken on and off the aircraft, and one of Jane, in the midst of her grief, curtsying to Charles as she descended the plane after him. But by nightfall, a strange phenomenon began to occur in London. People by the hundred, carrying garden flowers, florists' bouquets, and single roses, almost all bearing notes of affection and prayers for Diana, began to gather at the gates of Kensington and Buckingham Palace. By midnight there were thousands. An impromptu memorial service at St. Paul's Cathedral could not contain all the mourners who had come there for solace. People clasped complete strangers in grief, for in that they were companions. And that grief spread across the world.

By morning the crowds were overwhelming but they

were growing increasingly angry with the paparazzi whom everyone now blamed for Diana's death. Crowds shouted at besieged lensmen, "Go away, go away! Leave her alone, for God's sake. Let her rest in peace." Others screamed, "Assassins! Assassins!"

Dodi, in accordance with Muslim tradition, was buried in a private ceremony in Surrey eighteen hours after his death. The famous twinkling lights that etched the full expanse of Harrods, "the crown jewel in Mohamed al Fayed's global empire," were turned off, leaving spotlights to illuminate the Union Jack flying at half-mast outside. It was an eerie sight.

Britain's Union Flag had never flown above the roof of Buckingham Palace. Only the Royal Standard is seen and only when the Queen is in residence. It is never lowered to half-mast because it symbolizes the continuity of the monarchy. When the Queen is away, as she was then at Balmoral, the flagpole is bare. Its starkness in contrast to London's other flagpoles, with the Union Flag at half-mast, made the Queen's subjects feel she was uncaring and out of touch.

Tempers flared when the media claimed there would be no state funeral as Diana was no longer a member of the Royal Family. "If it isn't a state funeral, a crowd of several hundred thousand people will invade Buckingham Palace and tear the Royal Family apart," Bill McLaughlin, a CBS news reporter based in London, warned.

On Monday afternoon, at al Fayed's request, Sarah, dressed in black, went to see him in his massive office at Harrods. The tension was heavy. The Spencer family had been distancing themselves from the al Fayeds. They and Prince Charles had been greatly disturbed by the statements al Fayed had made to the press about Diana having spoken before she had slipped into unconsciousness. No one wanted to believe that she had suffered pain from her injuries. Al Fayed handed Sarah Diana's shopping-bags. Inside were the gaily wrapped packages she had prepared for her family. Sarah returned to her waiting limousine, escorted by al Fayed's press secretary, Michael Cole. It was the last time that any of the Spencers were in touch with him, until the day of the funeral.

By Tuesday, 2 September, an autopsy had been performed on Henri Paul showing that the alcohol level in his body had been over the legal limit for a car driver. Ten photographers who had been arrested at the scene of the crash were placed under investigation on suspicion of voluntary homicide and non-assistance to persons in danger. From London images of the vast fields of floral tributes, the hundreds of thousands of mourners, were shown to the world round the clock by CNN and other television networks. Diana's death had created an impact that equalled, or even surpassed, that of John F. Kennedy's assassination.

The Queen was at Balmoral, publicly silent, unseen. No official statement had been issued by the Palace. She was adamant that protocol be maintained: no flag would fly at half-mast over Buckingham Palace, and Diana should have a private family burial. With perhaps better instincts than the Queen's courtiers, Charles, it was rumoured, became "involved in a furious row with the Queen's private secretary, Sir Robert Fellowes, over the funeral [and flag arrangements], during which Charles is said to have told him to 'impale himself on his own flagpole'!"

According to a close source, when Charles had spoken to Tony Blair *en route* to Paris "the two men agreed the funeral should be on a state scale at Westminster Abbey." But in these early days, the Palace was divided on the issue. Earl Spencer had arrived from South Africa and was at Althorp House, where his sisters had joined him. Their mother was one of the first people whom Jane had called in the early hours of that terrible morning when she learned of Diana's death. Frances, from Scotland, joined her family the following day.

Numerous factions and personalities were involved in the final arrangements.* Earl Spencer was adamant that Di-

*The main people concerned with the plans for the funeral were: the Queen; Sir Robert Fellowes; the Queen's deputy private secretary

ana be given a special service and that she be buried at
Althorp. The Queen, her representatives and advisers still
believed that protocol could not allow for a state funeral.
Prince Charles countered that it was the only right and honourable course to take, and that the Royal Family would
suffer a great loss of confidence and support if the funeral
was private. Tony Blair agreed with him.

What the prime minister understood, which the Queen
and the Palace did not, was the phenomenon of Diana's
popularity or, indeed, the idolatry she attracted. Diana had
matured, as so many other Britons, through eighteen years
of Tory government. In that time, the world had changed.
A new society had emerged, which could find no viable
political symbol or expression. As Andrew Sullivan, contributing editor for the *New York Times Magazine* wrote so
astutely: "The Tories were as culturally inept as they were
economically successful; they created the substance of the
new country but they couldn't articulate it. Diana, in contrast, reflected the new reality. Like many of her English
generation, she was an individualist trapped in an anach-
ronism . . . She was, for a while, the only figure of institution truly reflective of a country that had changed beyond
recognition but had still found no way to symbolize that
change."

Diana was beautiful, but she had also developed her own
individuality and style. She had been a princess, but was at
ease with people from all walks of life—gay men and
women, the elderly, the young, the sick and dying, movie
stars, rock stars, ballet performers, opera singers, people of
all races and creeds. She saw no cultural boundaries, and
felt constrained by no traditional mores, even when it came
to falling in love with a man from another culture and re-

Robin Janvrin; Stephen Lamport, former Foreign Office diplomat who
was acting as an adviser; the Lord Chamberlain; the Earl of Airlie;
Prince Charles; his assistant private secretary Mark Boland; Tony
Blair (who was liaising with Prince Charles); Philip Astley, Director
of Protocol at the Foreign Office; and Earl Spencer.

ligion. She had shared pains that had plagued others and was not afraid to go public with them: an eating disorder, the betrayal of friends, a husband who loved another woman, diffident in-laws, divorce. She could moan and cry and admit her vulnerability and her bad behaviour. But Diana cared; she understood; she was loved for her faults as well as her virtues. She fought for those people who could not fight for themselves, and brought comfort to those who might otherwise have known none. And through all of it, she smiled.

Diana's smiling face had been a beacon to many. Her death had prompted "a shock wave of fear that this new cultural dawn could suddenly be a dusk."

Tony Blair, who had admired Diana, knew the extent of her power over the emotions of the people. In a way, so did Prince Charles. But he was also motivated by his love for his sons, his need to expiate his guilt, and perhaps to make some things up to Diana.

Blair, who had chosen a Saturday for the funeral so that working people would be free to stand along the route or watch it on television, was also aware that if the Queen did not return to London from her Scottish retreat, the people's animus would accelerate. This was not an easy thing to convey to her or to her Palace guard. She was a grandparent as well as a queen. It made good sense that the princes, having lost their mother, would find solace with their grandparents in the familiar setting of Balmoral. For them to return to Kensington Palace would be wrenching, and either Buckingham or St. James's Palace would feel strange. Charles had called Alexandra "Tiggy" Legge-Bourke back to work. He had hired her after the divorce, when Harry was only eight and William eleven, to help him with his sons when they were staying with him. Diana had been unhappy about this arrangement, believing that Tiggy was taking her place in their lives. Tiggy had since left Charles's employ but the boys liked her and she was an affectionate woman of their mother's age, who would help them through those first difficult days.

The Queen, under pressure, relented and by Wednesday morning the Union Flag flew at half-mast over Buckingham Palace for the first time in its history. There was a tumultuous cheer from the crowds below as they saw it fluttering in the rising September wind. Blair and Charles had also convinced the Queen that Diana must have a state funeral, and things began to happen with great speed. She was only the second person outside the Royal Family ever to be so honoured; the first was wartime leader Sir Winston Churchill.

Outside Buckingham Palace placards were raised reading "WHERE IS OUR QUEEN WHEN WE NEED HER?" With antipathy to the Queen's silence gathering momentum among the public mourners, the decision was now made for her, Prince Philip, Prince Charles and his sons to return to London on Thursday, 4 September. Walkabouts were planned. The boys would stay with Tiggy in the former nursery at Buckingham Palace. From their windows they could see the ocean of colourful flowers that seemed ready to envelop all London. A seemingly endless queue of people waited to enter St. James's Palace to sign one of the Books of Condolence.* It was a moving tribute to the love people had for Diana.

Late that afternoon, Charles, William and Harry, the boys in dark suits, their faces pale and drawn, walked among the crowds at Kensington Palace, stooping to read the messages written on cards attached to bouquets. There was a touching moment when Harry reached out for his father's hand, and held it tightly in a rare public display of intimacy. The Queen and Prince Philip walked among the flowers at Buckingham Palace, stopping to speak briefly with the people. The Queen wore a sombre, squat black hat and coat. One could with some squinting see vestiges of her great-great-grandmother Queen Victoria in her dowdy outfit, grey hair and round face. Where had the once gay,

---

*Mourners' names would fill forty-seven Books of Condolence at St. James's Palace in tribute to the Princess of Wales.

smiling, young Elizabeth who so charmed Winston Churchill and had given her country a sense of rebirth four decades earlier, gone? Those old enough to have witnessed her televised coronation could well wonder if the weight of a crown turned one ashen.

There were Palace meetings throughout Thursday. By nightfall a decision had been reached. The following day the Queen would make a televised address expressing her grief to the nation. Only once before during her forty-four-year reign had the Queen addressed the nation other than at Christmas; that had occurred during the Gulf War. She gave a short speech on Friday afternoon from a front room of Buckingham Palace. Over her shoulder viewers could see mourners placing flowers and tributes on the vast pile between the Victoria Memorial and the Palace gates. She called Diana "an exceptional and gifted human being," and added how greatly she would be missed. But there was no deep expression of true emotion or detailing of why she would be "so greatly missed." Nevertheless, it appeased her subjects to some degree. The press announcements of the arrangements for Diana's funeral, which had been printed that day, further soothed their earlier anger.

The usual military trappings of a state funeral were to be kept to a minimum, in keeping with Diana's humanitarian spirit. Invitations to leaders of foreign countries were issued only on the basis of their personal relationship with the Princess. The organizers, with Lieutenant Colonel Malcolm Ross in command (Earl Spencer was constantly consulted), were searching for "an imaginative response . . . to reflect Princess Diana's modern approach." This was no easy task, considering the Palace's reliance on tradition and protocol. But some of this was overcome when Elton John was asked to sing (as he had at Versace's funeral). He rewrote the lyrics to "Candle In The Wind," originally composed several of years earlier in tribute to Marilyn Monroe who also had died suddenly at thirty-six. With Paul Burrell's help, invitations were sent to many disabled and elderly people

whom Diana had befriended and with whom she had corresponded. Loudspeakers were installed outside the Abbey.
Giant screens were set up in Hyde Park so that the throngs
who had been gathering all week would feel they were part
of the service.

The night before the funeral, thousands of mourners
slept in London's parks, surrounded by the floral offerings.
Most florist's shops had placards in their windows stating
that they had sold out. Clean-up crews were ordered to pick
up dead flowers to make room for the new, but officials
vowed that the cards would not be destroyed. The messages
were deeply personal, telling often of how Diana had affected the giver's life.

A stillness fell over central London as the vigil moved
into the small hours of the funeral day. In Kensington Gardens hundreds of candlelit shrines had been made, with
smiling photographs of Diana from magazines and newspapers propped among them. At four in the morning,
thousands were walking slowly, arm in arm, threading their
way between the shrines. At St. James's Palace, the police
estimated over 10,000 people were still queuing to sign a
Book of Condolence before Diana's coffin was moved to
Kensington Palace where the funeral procession would start
out at 9:08 that morning. The weeping and hysterical outbursts had ceased. A new mood had set in: people were
exchanging memories of Diana.

As dawn came to the city, the twelve members of the
First Battalion of Welsh Guards, clad in crimson and wearing their black bearskins, began to prepare themselves for
their part in the funeral. They would flank the gun-carriage
carrying the coffin from Kensington Palace to Westminster
Abbey along a three-and-a-half-mile route. The carriage
would be drawn by three pairs of horses from the King's
Troop, Royal Horse Artillery, which could trace its history
to the Napoleonic Wars in the reign of King George III.
From St. James's Palace, Prince Charles, Prince William,
Prince Harry, Prince Philip and Earl Spencer would walk
behind the gun carriage.

Much of the nation had come to a halt. Most businesses, museums and shops were closed. Crowds were lining the path of the funeral procession even before dawn. This farewell was to be quite different from past state funerals. There was an air of modernity about it, a sense of colour and beauty. Many mourners wore jeans and T-shirts. Buildings were not hung with black bunting but flowers were everywhere, and it was a day of brilliant sunshine.

Earlier that morning, the coffin, covered with the Royal Standard, was secured to the gun-carriage as Charles and his sons stood beside it. Flowers from Diana's family covered it. Prominent were two wreaths: pink roses from William, white roses from Harry with a large MUMMY written on the card.

At 9:08 the muffled tenor bells of Westminister Abbey tolled, as they would at every minute during the procession. There seemed no other sound in all London. The cortège started on its way down Palace Avenue and turned left into Kensington High Street.

Onward it went, past quietly weeping mourners. There was an eerie keening as the gun-carriage progressed out of their sight. The procession entered Hyde Park at Queen's Gate, passed the Albert Memorial along Carriage Road, the tree-shaded avenue on the southern edge of the park. The Queen led members of the Royal Family on to the pavement in front of Buckingham Palace and, in a unique gesture, bowed to the coffin as it made its slow passage on to the Mall. All eyes were now on the two princes, sombre in their grey suits who had joined the procession at St. James's Palace. Harry, having to step a bit wider to keep up with the pace of the others, bravely walked between his father on the left and Earl Spencer on the right. William, head bowed, kept an even pace between his uncle and his grandfather, slimmer but equal in height and in solemn composure to both these good-sized men. For the first time there was music: someone played "Abide With Me" on the bagpipes. Harry soldiered onward with incredible fortitude and William glanced sideways at him in a caring way that brought his mother to mind. These were the boys who had been the joy of her life, as she had been theirs. William had been protective of his younger brother from when they had learned of their mother's death. He had always seemed older than the two years and three months that separated him from Harry. He had been his mother's confidant, and often her protector too. They had shared a strong bond, an understanding that went beyond words.

A group of about 500 mourners, casually dressed, *sans* medals, braid or bands, formed ragged lines and joined the procession behind the princes and Earl Spencer. These were charity workers, their clients and patients, nurses, artists and performers from the causes Diana had supported. One commentator noted, "They seemed far closer to the spirit of the Princess than the expressionless guardsmen . . . in their bearskins. Workers from the homeless charity Centrepoint wore yellow sashes; mothers bore young children; a man in a wheelchair sat ready to push himself up on to his crutches. In sweatshirts [and] T-shirts, they did not look casual but dignified and restrained."

The 1,900 invited guests began to arrive at Westminster Abbey at 9:30. If Diana and Charles had not broken with tradition, and the Queen had had her way, it would have been the scene of their wedding. Since the eleventh century English monarchs had been crowned there; and many English kings and queens had been buried there. The interior, with its French Gothic style, was awe-inspiring. That morning the sun poured through its great rose windows. At 10:15 the special guests—former prime ministers Margaret Thatcher and John Major, Prime Minister Tony Blair, stopping to examine the wall of tributes as he passed them, President Chirac and his wife, and First Lady Hillary Rodham Clinton entered. They were followed by celebrities from the worlds of film, dance, theatre and music. Then at 10:35 the Spencer family entered through the West Door. Everything had been timed to the minute, so that when the cortège arrived the congregation would be seated. In contrast to those outside, the invited guests wore ritual attire:

men in dark suits, women in black with hats.

Mohamed al Fayed entered alone. He walked down the long nave, "a proud, broad-shouldered man, his face crumpled in pain." When he was seated, he glanced over at the Spencers, but his overture was not acknowledged. The seating had been arranged so that the Spencers and the Windsors faced each other across the Abbey. Al Fayed sat in the section that separated them.

Within the next ten minutes the Royal Family arrived, each group in a black limousine—Princess Margaret and her two children, Prince and Princess Michael with theirs, the divorced Duke and Duchess of York with their daughters. Lastly, at exactly 10:50 the Queen's Daimler pulled up at the West Door bearing the Queen, the Queen Mother and Prince Edward.

As the bells tolled eleven, the procession reached the West Door. Charles stood ramrod straight next to Harry, William beside his grandfather as they paused to wait for the coffin. Harry suddenly broke down. Charles scooped him close and held him tightly. William laid his hand on his brother's shoulder. Harry muffled his tears and continued with the rest of the men in his family.

Slowly the honour guard lifted the 560-pound, steel-lined coffin, draped in the Queen's colours and decked with flowers, from its carriage, rearranging the Royal Standard as they went cautiously up the stone steps and bore it down the centre of the nave. Almost unbearably, the seated mourners now saw the card, balanced carefully on the first wreath of the coffin, which read simply "Mummy."

The service had been closely supervised by Earl Spencer. Lady Jane Fellowes gave a short reading. Sarah then spoke. The hymn, "The King of Love My Shepherd Is" was sung, followed by "I Vow To Thee My Country," which Diana had chosen for her wedding and which William had asked to be included in the service, 'because it was Mummy's favourite.' Tony Blair read from Corinthians: "Though I speak with the tongues of men and of angels, and have not love, I am become as sounding brass, or a tinkling cymbal." Then Elton John went to the piano. "Goodbye, England's Rose," he began, his rewritten version of "Candle In The Wind." With the moving lines "Your candle burned out long before/Your legend ever will," both William and Harry broke down.

Then Earl Spencer walked to the podium, his face etched with grief. No one knew what his eulogy for his sister would be, but they expected something tender and loving. They braced themselves for the emotion they believed would surely wash over them. And then came his assault on the Royal Family. "I stand before you today," he began, "the representative of a family in grief, in a country in mourning before a world in shock ... Diana was a very British girl who transcended nationality, someone with a natural nobility who was classless and who proved in the last year that she needed no royal title to continue to generate her particular brand of magic ..."

Although by prearrangement the television companies were not allowed to film the reactions of the Royal Family during the service, those close enough saw the Queen, Earl Spencer's godmother, stiffen, as did Prince Philip.* He alluded to the danger that Princes Harry and William would become "simply immersed by duty and tradition," and promised his nephews that "we, your blood family, would forestall such a fate."

His five-minute address electrified the world, but it was eloquent and moving too. He spoke of how Diana had "mothered him as a child, endured those long train rides between our parents' homes ..." He spoke of her eating disorder, her insecurities, how she was hounded by the press: "Of all the ironies about Diana, perhaps the greatest was this. A girl given the name of the ancient goddess of

---

*Later that day the Palace discussed restoring the title Her Royal Highness to the Princess of Wales, so that she might be referred to as such in written reports or in any books to be published in the future. Earl Spencer declined, saying his sister would not have wanted it after her death.

hunting was, in the end, the most hunted person of the modern age." And he managed somehow to bring her briefly back to life: "There is a temptation to rush to canonize your memory. There is no need to do so: you stand tall enough as a human being of unique qualities not to need to be seen as a saint. Indeed, to sanctify your memory would be to miss out on the very core of your being—your wonderfully mischievous sense of humour with a laugh that bent you double, your joy for life transmitted wherever you took your smile, and the sparkle in those unforgettable eyes, your boundless energy, which you could barely contain. But your greatest gift was your intuition, and it was a gift you used wisely."

"When he finished there was a silence. Then you heard this roar coming from outside the Abbey," said Elizabeth Emanuel, who had co-designed Diana's wedding dress. "The crowd was clapping and it just swept through the Abbey."

Diana's seventy-seven-mile journey to Althorp took her through the heart of England. People lined the roadways all along the route, tossing flowers at the black hearse that carried her coffin. Her final resting-place, consecrated in great secrecy the previous day, was to be a simple grave on an island in the centre of the ornamental lake known as the Oval, which as a teenager she had gazed at from the bank opposite while she wondered what the future might hold. The decision not to bury her in the village church was taken so that "the grave can be properly looked after by her family, and visited in privacy by her sons."

Tony Blair had named her the People's Princess. The poet Maya Angelou called her the "Sunshine Princess." Both are apt. Diana had left an indelible legacy. She had touched people in a way few others in our time have. She never did anything that seemed memorable at the time—she wrote no great books, painted no masterpiece. She was not a discoverer of a breakthrough medical cure. She was the most photographed woman of all time, but she never starred in a movie. Her achievement was that she could make people feel better. She somehow connected in a dysfunctional world of short-circuited people and for a time she lit our lives.

POST MORTEM

MORE THAN TWO billion people had watched the funeral on television. For weeks after, the world mourned and Britain was engulfed in grief. Diana's engaging smile, captured on endless news footage and luminous on the many magazine covers that followed her death, was a haunting reminder of her presence over her sixteen years in the spotlight. She had touched many lives, and her sudden death brought sharp winds of change to Britain and its monarchy.

The Queen, who had seemed so dispassionate at the time of Diana's death, had heard the angry voices of her people and listened to the advice from Downing Street. Her misjudgment of Diana's hold on the people had caused the most serious crisis the monarchy had suffered since Edward VIII's abdication. Now, if it was to survive, the Queen knew she must move with the times. She does not easily take to change, but there has been a cosmetic reshaping and a willingness to embrace 'the generation that will decide the future of the House of Windsor.'

A year after Diana's death, Simon Lewis, at thirty-nine the youngest voice in Palace politics, was employed by "the firm" (as Prince Philip likes to call the members of the Royal Family) as the Queen's communications director. But the Queen had already shown signs of easing into a more contemporary style: she smiled whenever she knew a camera was upon her, rode for the first time in a taxi (to promote environmentally friendly liquefied gas fuel), visited a Devon pub (holding a sealed bottle of ale in a gloved hand at the bar), and chatted easily with rock singer Julie Thompson at a Buckingham Palace function, seemingly unfazed by the young woman's shocking pink hair.

She accepted the changes to ceremony and procedure

that Tony Blair's Labour government put into effect. Primogeniture, an eldest son's right to succeed to the throne before his older sister, was abolished. This was followed by the Queen's ending compulsory bowing and curtsying to members of the Royal Family—which included the bow formerly demanded of Philip for the Queen, of Charles for his mother, and of those in the Royal Family junior to Charles for him.

Voices were raised over the need for constitutional reform, and accusations that "the system is an ancient briar rose, never pruned of pricks and suckers, impenetrable, obstructive, creaking with age." The government promised that in the near future hereditary peers would be expelled from the House of Lords.

Although no date was given the Queen agreed that Kensington Palace be transformed into a museum, housing art in the Royal Collection never before placed on public display. She would undertake the expense of rehousing its inhabitants. In November 1997, on her golden wedding anniversary, the Queen broke with tradition again to address the nation and reassure it "that the monarchy is in touch with its government and people."

But the most evident change was not in her words and actions but in the attitude of the people towards her and members of her family. Her subjects had become "a lot less reverential and a lot less deferential," author Brian Hoey concedes. "People no longer believe royalty walks on water."

It was Tony Blair who had popularized the phrase "the People's Princess" when he spoke movingly to newsmen that August morning after Diana was known to have died. His active role in bringing the Queen back to London and his stand throughout this time of public mourning secured his hold on the country. The Tories accused him of using the tragedy for political gain, but Blair had his finger on the pulse of public opinion and he knew how to use the media to get his message out to the people.

Once Henri Paul's alcohol intake was ascertained by autopsy, some of the heat was off the paparazzi who had been arrested at the crash site and later released. Romuald Rat and Christian Martinez were accused of "ravenously snapping pictures instead of trying to help," and of being "excessively aggressive, fighting with police, blocking access to the victims." Although later exonerated, their press cards and driver's licences were confiscated and they were forbidden to leave France. For Rat, the first to comfort Diana, this was ironic. Photographs of the victims, Diana included, were circulated to foreign markets, but publishers feared a backlash if they were printed. Rumours circulated that British intelligence had conducted secret raids on the homes and laboratories of some of the photographers to make sure that such pictures were not made public. Only those taken of the crumpled car after the victims were removed ever saw publication.

A new but voluntary press code was initiated by the Press Complaints Commission in Britain. It was more specific than the one in the United States which says only that newspapers "should respect the individual's right to privacy." Now British editors must justify the behaviour of their staff and of any freelancer whose material they use. If they expose someone's private life they must show that there is an "overriding public interest." Lord Wakeham, the commission's chairman, stated: "Motorbike chases, stalking and hounding are unacceptable—and editors who carry pictures obtained by them will be subjected to the severest censure." But as long as paparazzi can sell their photographs abroad for high figures, it will be hard to enforce this code.

The public temperature towards the paparazzi remained feverish. There was a modified global cooling of the kind of posse tactics that Diana endured. No other person, with the possible exception of Monica Lewinsky, the woman at the centre of the Clinton impeachment, has emerged whose image could command such prices.

Almost immediately after the crash conspiracy scenarios began to circulate. On the Monday after the funeral Libya's

Colonel Gaddafy in a speech on Libyan national television claimed that the accident had been an "arranged crash" plotted by British "anti-Islamic and anti-Arab" forces, "to make sure that a member of the Royal Family did not marry an Arab." He added that it was "naïve of people to believe otherwise." Ten days after the funeral, the lead story *Who Killed Diana?*, subtitled *Order From the Palace: Execute Emad Fayed*, appeared in Egypt's *Al Ahram* newspaper claiming that Diana had been "killed by British intelligence to save the monarchy." Newspapers in Jordan and the Gulf suggested the same scenario. And not long after Mohamed al Fayed began a vigorous investigation of his own and would claim rather wildly that there had been a conspiracy led by Prince Philip.

Diana's tragic death was met with such disbelief that people had the desperate need to find a reason for it that was as momentous as her death. First it was the paparazzi who had hounded her. That so beautiful and vital a young woman could have been the victim of an accident perpetrated by a drunk driver was too simple an explanation to be an acceptable idea to many.

Yet, the circumstances of the crash negate the theories that the death of the three people in the Mercedes was caused by anything other than a tragic combination of no seat-belts, and a drunk driver in an unfamiliar car travelling at great speed and losing control. It was hinted that Henri Paul might have been poisoned before he sat behind the wheel of the Mercedes—perhaps the yellow liquid he had consumed at the Ritz bar had contained some lethal substance; perhaps the car had been tampered with, or the mysterious white Fiat Uno had set up Paul for the crash. It was even suggested that an unidentified motorcyclist, cloaked in black leather, had swerved in front of the Mercedes causing it to crash.

These theories were all proven by the French investigation to be unfounded. They were also illogical. After twenty-three months of diligent inquiry led by Judge Hervé Stéphan, one of the most powerful judicial figures in

France, it was concluded that the accident had been caused by the speed of the vehicle and the driver's drunkenness. Even with the tremendous impact that crushed the front of the car, Diana and Dodi might have survived, albeit seriously injured, had they been wearing seat-belts.

The only survivor, Trevor Rees-Jones, returned to his home in Oswestry, England. After a year he was well enough to take a part-time job in a sports shop a short distance from his home. He has intense therapy for his left arm, which was crushed in the crash, and will have more surgery on scars. He can eventually sue the Ritz, but whatever he might receive will not erase the trauma and pain he has experienced. He is quieter, more reticent than his friends and family recall him before the crash. His memory has not fully returned, and may never do so.

On the day of Diana's funeral the Spencer family appeared united and Earl Spencer's speech caused speculation that his star was in the ascendancy, that the days of Champagne Charlie were behind him. Within a year, though, he was maligned from all quarters. An acrimonious divorce from his wife in November 1998 again splashed his name across the front pages of the British press: he was attempting to prove that she was not a fit mother due to her emotional problems, and was offering a settlement of less than half a million pounds. A former mistress, Chantal Callopy, supported Victoria in her sensational suit, which exposed his bad behaviour and his flagrant womanizing.*

In August 1998, Earl Spencer opened the Princess of Wales Museum at Althorp and was accused of profiteering by charging an exorbitant £10 entry fee (visitors to Buckingham Palace pay £8). It allowed visitors to tour the museum, which contained many of Diana's clothes and personal mementoes, but to view Diana's island grave they had to stand a hundred feet back from the banks of the water that surrounded it. His vow to his nephews in his

---

*Countess Spencer won a settlement of $3.2 million and her Cape Town house; and retained joint custody of their four children.

famous eulogy to his sister to be active in their lives was
difficult for him to uphold: he was, after all, living in South
Africa for most of the year, and had his own four children
to look after, while the princes had their own routine in
Britain. There was also some resentment on their part for
the way he had spoken against the Royal Family at their
mother's funeral. His time with his nephews has been limited. Sarah had been very close to Diana in the last years
of her life. They had spoken almost daily and Diana had
called her "the only person I can trust." Sarah was still slim
and a ravishing redhead as she approached her mid-forties
but Diana's death took a great toll on her. Her job with the
Diana, Princess of Wales Memorial Fund had placed her
under great stress but she and Jane found time for Diana's
beloved sons, attending school events, writing and tele-
phoning them frequently. Prince Charles has invited Frances Shand Kydd for several overnight visits to
Highgrove, and the princes and she have spent time together in their father's beloved Highgrove gardens.

Prince Charles spent more time at Highgrove where he
felt the most comfortable, and where he and Camilla could
be alone together. He told friends he needed her "now more
than ever before." For many months after Diana's death
Camilla was justifiably terrified to appear in public. There
were even fears that she might be assassinated: Charles employed bodyguards for her protection, and as she had lost
a great deal of money in recent investments, helped to cover
her expenses.

His grief, publicly displayed in the days after Diana's
death, was truly felt. Charles, as one close friend observed,
was "totally at a loss, torn in different directions by his
family's natural reserve and the public's frightening wave
of emotion." He was paralysed by a profound sense of guilt
about her and a desperation that he might now lose Camilla
for ever. He could hardly blame her if she turned away
from him rather than spend her life in hiding, loathed by
the world, denied a normal life with the man for whom she
had already, as he saw it, sacrificed so much. He knew he

could count on her discretion and loyalty, but she was entitled to a respected place beside the man she loved. He was not sure that he could give her that. Camilla did not turn away from him. She was there whenever he called and never complained. Her support paid off.

Within ten months the world had regained compassion for Charles, who had shown a more human side of his personality, kissing his sons for the first time in public, placing his hand easily on their shoulders, taking them to a rock concert. People felt the sincerity of his grief and the honesty of his love for Camilla. They felt, as had Diana after the divorce, that he should be allowed dignity in his private life, which meant accepting Camilla at his side. As the first year of mourning neared its end, she had virtually become mistress of Highgrove and accompanied Charles, ever discreetly, on many of his travels. On 12 June 1998, Prince William was introduced to Camilla in his father's apartments at St. James's Palace. Harry met her three weeks later, also over tea, at Highgrove.

These test meetings went well. Camilla is a jolly sort, with a good sense of humour, and there was no doubt that their father was happy in her company. Sensibly, the princes did what they could to mend fences. One important step was a party they gave for Prince Charles's fiftieth birthday, in which Camilla was an active participant.

In 1998 Charles and Camilla finally were seen together as they left a birthday celebration for Camilla's sister. The press had been notified that they would leave together and the photographs taken by them were widely published. By the summer of 1999 a holiday that included Charles, Camilla and William and Harry was approved.

The Queen still regards Camilla as a "non-person," but there is strong public sentiment that Charles and Camilla should be allowed to share a life openly.

In accordance with Diana's wishes, Harry joined William at Eton. Their mother's death brought both boys much closer to their father. Outwardly Harry seemed to have the greatest difficulty in coping with his loss: during the first

year he often seemed lost in thought and clung to his father.
William, always the more serious of the two, has grown
into young manhood. He looks more like his mother with
each passing year, and has her quick sense of humour and
the ability to laugh at himself. His recent style has become
more imitative of Charles—he's seldom seen in the sports
caps and jeans that he wore when he was younger. His
father spends more time with him preparing him to be king,
as does the Queen, whose eyes light up whenever he visits.

Both boys have bonded closely with the Windsors.
When the Spencer family gathered at Althorp for a private
ceremony on the first anniversary of Diana's death, William
and Harry opted to remain with their father and grandparents at Balmoral where they also had the companionship of
Peter and Zara Phillips. There they went shooting and fishing with Charles, or biked with their cousins.

Former Prime Minister John Major was appointed as a
special guardian to the princes to look after their interests
in sensitive negotiations over Diana's will. The problem
arose because she had neglected to update it following her
divorce and the receipt of her £20 million settlement (£17
million plus £3 million interest on it.) The final decision
was to split Diana's assets between her sons, the money to
be held in trust in an interest-bearing account until they are
twenty-five. (Much of Prince Charles's wealth is in trust
for Harry because William will eventually succeed to the
Duchy of Cornwall, which currently generates an after-tax
income of about £2 million a year.) In a moving clause in
her will, Diana gave her sons first choice of her personal
possessions, "including her stuffed animals," which they
prize as an intimate reminder of their mother. William also
took her Cartier tank watch, which he almost always wears.
Diana's intellectual property rights were, and still are,
worth tens of millions of pounds. These include the use of
her name or photograph on souvenirs and commercial products. A large part of this income was to go to the memorial
fund set up in her name.

The manner of Diana's death was so terrible that it will

not be forgotten, but her person and life will be immortalized. Unlike those historical figures of past centuries who stare blankly at us from portraits and photographs, she was born into the age of technology where her image, smiling, speaking, crying, elegant, funny, sexy, will always be available. Her story was an amazing welding of fairytale and soap opera. She was, as Bryan Appleyard wrote in *The Times* shortly after her death, "a kind of one-woman rainbow coalition of every imaginable trauma from infidelity to marriage breakdown, from domestic humiliation to global conflict."

In exchange for glory she traded, sometimes reluctantly, sometimes not, her privacy. Both her life and death were representative of an epoch "when celebrity obsession seems as out of control as a hurtling Mercedes on a late summer night in Paris." Diana's celebrity was such that when Mother Teresa died in the same week the saintly nun's death was given short shrift in a media preoccupied with the Princess. And why was Diana's death such a major story? For all the reasons listed above, but more importantly because her life and her death instituted changes that affected society. Diana changed the monarchy and the British attitude towards grief. The House of Windsor was almost brought down by the tears of their subjects, who demanded their democratic prerogatives and insisted that the Queen act as their subject, sharing their emotion, when for centuries British monarchs were held up as role models for public behaviour despite their own improprieties.

The synchronicity of Diana's death and Mother Teresa's also points up the complex nature of Diana's ability to survive in vivid memory, for she combined two unlikely components: glamour and spirituality. She talked to the poor, the disenfranchised, visited the homeless, the maimed, the dying and brought them hope.

There is a fascinating duality about Diana: she was a saint with mortal passions, a fairytale princess who encapsulated all the problems faced by women of her time. She was the most famous woman in the world who publicly confessed to adultery, attempted suicide, an eating disorder, and was loved even more for doing so. She died young, at the height of her beauty and popularity in a ghastly car crash. The tragedy was of ancient Greek dimension.

Her radical message will never be forgotten: "You don't need a palace to be a princess. You may even need to leave it to become one."

LADY DIANA SPENCER, HRH THE PRINCESS OF WALES,
DIANA, PRINCESS OF WALES
1961–1997

BIBLIOGRAPHY

BOOKS

Anderson, Christopher, *The Day Diana Died*, Morrow, New York, 1998.

Arnold-Brown, Adam, *Unfolding Character, The Impact of Gordonstoun*, Routledge & Kegan Paul, London, 1962.

Barry, Stephen, *Royal Service*, Macmillan, New York, 1983.

Battiscombe, Georgina, *The Spencers of Althorp*, Constable, London, 1984.

Benson, Ross, *Charles, The Untold Story*, Gollancz, London, 1993.

Blundell, Nigel and Susan Blackhall, *Fall of the House of Windsor*, Contemporary Books, Chicago, 1992.

Boyd, William, *School Ties*, Penguin, London, 1985.

Braithwaite D., *Savage of King's Lynn*, Cambridge, 1978.

Brown, Ivor, *Balmoral Castle—The History of a House*, Collins, London, 1955.

Bruch, Hilda, *Eating Disorders*, Vintage, New York, 1973. *The Golden Cage—The Enigma of Anorexia Nervosa*, Vintage, New York, 1979.

Bryant, Arthur, *A Thousand Years of British Monarchy*, Collins, London, 1975.

Burchill, Julie, *Diana*, Weidenfeld & Nicolson, London, 1998.

Campbell, Lady Colin, *Diana in Private: The Princess Nobody Knows*, St. Martin's Press, New York, 1992.

Cannadine, David, *The Decline and Fall of the British Aristocracy*, Yale University Press, New Haven, 1990.

Claude-Pierre, Peggy, *The Secret Language of Eating Disorders*, Times Books, New York, 1997.

Clayton, Michael, *Prince Charles: Horseman*, Stanley Paul, London, 1985.

Crawford, Marian, *The Little Princesses*, Cassell, London, 1953.

Davies, Nicholas, *Diana: The Lonely Princess*, Birch Books, New York, 1996. *Diana: The People's Princess*, Carol Publishing, New Jersey, 1997.

Dean, John, *HRH Prince Philip: A Portrait by His Valet*, Robert Hale, London, 1968.

Dimbleby, Jonathan, *The Prince of Wales*, Little, Brown, London, 1994.

Douglas-Home, Margaret, *A Spencer Childhood*, Autograph Books, Suffolk, 1994.

Duncan, Andrew, *The Reality of Monarchy*, Heinemann, London, 1970.

Edwards, Anne, *Matriarch: Queen Mary and the House of Windsor*, Hodder & Stoughton, London, 1984.

Royal Sisters: Elizabeth and Margaret, HarperCollins, London, 1991.

The Grimaldis: Centuries of Scandal—Years of Grace, HarperCollins, London, 1993.

Finch, Mary E., *Five Northamptonshire Families*, Northamptonshire Record Society, 1958.

Fincher, Jayne, *Diana, Portrait of a Princess*, Callaway, London, 1998.

Frere, J. A., *The British Monarchy at Home*, Gibbs & Phillips, London, 1963.

Graham, Tim, *Diana: HRH Princess of Wales*, Michael O'Mara, London, 1988.

Green, David, *Queen Anne*, Collins, London, 1970.

Hall, Philip, *Royal Fortune: Tax, Money, and the Monarchy*, Bloomsbury, London, 1992.

Haseler, Stephen, *The End of the House of Windsor*, Tauris, London, 1993.

Heald, Tim, *The Duke: A Portrait of Prince Philip*, Hodder & Stoughton, London, 1981.

Hepworth, Philip, *Royal Sandringham*, Wensum, London, 1978.

Hoey, Brian, *Monarchy: Behind the Scenes of the Royal Family*, St. Martin's Press, New York, 1987.

Holden, Anthony, *Charles, Prince of Wales*, Weidenfeld & Nicolson, London, 1979.

Charles, Weidenfeld & Nicolson, London, 1988.

The Tarnished Crown, Bantam Press, London, 1993.

Diana: A Life and Legacy, Ebury Press, London, 1998.

Charles: A Biography, Bantam Press, New York, 1998.

Hooke, B., *Sarah, Duchess of Marlborough, An Account of the conduct of the Dowager Duchess of Marlborough*, London, 1742.

Howard, Philip, *The Royal Palaces*, Hamish Hamilton, London, 1978.

Hudson, Derek, *Kensington Palace*, Cox & Wyman, London, 1968.

Junor, Penny, *Charles*, St. Martin's Press, New York, 1987.

Charles and Diana: Portrait of a Marriage, Headline, London, 1991.

Charles: Victim or Villain?, HarperCollins, London, 1998.

Kronenberg, L., *Marlborough's Duchess*, Weidenfeld & Nicolson, London, 1958.

Lacey, Robert, *Majesty: Elizabeth II and the House of Windsor*, Hutchinson, London, 1977.

Leapman, Michael, *Treacherous Estate*, Hodder & Stoughton, London, 1992.

Levin, Angela, *Raine & Johnnie*, Weidenfeld & Nicolson, London, 1993.

Llewellin, Philip, and Ann Saunders, *Book of British Towns*, Drive, London, 1979.

Mattingly, Dr. Stephen, *Aspects of Brington*, Mattingly, Northamptonshire, 1997.

Mackenzie, Compton, *The Queen's House*, Hutchinson, London, 1953.

Milward, Richard, *The Spencers in Wimbledon 1744–1944*, London, 1996.

Moore, Sally, *The Definitive Diana*, Contemporary Books, Chicago, 1991.

Morton, Andrew, *Inside Kensington Palace*, Michael O'Mara, London, 1987.

Diana: Her True Story, Michael O'Mara, London, 1992.

Diana—Her New Life, Michael O'Mara, London, 1994.

Diana: Her True Story—In Her Own Words, Michael O'Mara, London, 1997.

Mount, Ferdinand, *The British Constitution Now*, Heinemann, London, 1992.

Nairn, Tom, *The Enchanted Glass: Britain and Its Monarchy*, Picador, London, 1990.

Paget, Guy, *The History of the Althorp and Pytchley Hunt*, Collins, London, 1937.

Pasternak, Anna, *Princess in Love*, Bloomsbury, London, 1994.

Pearson, John, *The Selling of the Royal Family*, Simon & Schuster, New York, 1986.

Peel, J. Stuart, *John and Sarah, Duke and Duchess of Marlborough*, London.

Pimlott, Ben, *The Queen*, HarperCollins, London, 1996.

Plumb, J. H., and Huw Weldon, *Royal Heritage: the Treasures of the British Crown*, Harcourt, Brace & Jovanovich, London, 1977.

Richards, Paul, *King's Lynn*, Phillimore, West Sussex, 1990.

Sampson, Anthony, *The Changing Anatomy of Britain*, Hodder & Stoughton, London, 1982.

Sancton, Thomas, and Scott Macleod, *Death of a Princess: The Investigation*, St. Martin's Press, New York, 1998.

Shute, Nerina, *The Royal Family and the Spencers: 200 Years of Friendship*, Robert Hale, London, 1985.

Spencer, W. E. K., *A Short History of Althorp and the Spencer Family*, 1949.

Van Geirt, Jean-Pierre, *Diana: Enquête sur une Tragédie*, Éditions Ramsay, 1997.

Whitaker, James, *Diana vs. Charles: Royal Blood Feud*, Penguin Books, London, 1993.

MAGAZINES

Country Life, Royal Wedding Number, 30 July 1981.

Daily Telegraph, Royal Wedding issue, 17 July 1981.

Dennis Oneshots, "Diana's World" (Diana's Charity Work), Fall 1997.

Genealogists', June 1981: "The Ancestry of Lady Diana Spencer," David Williamson.

Historic Houses, Castles & Gardens, London, 1992.

New York Times magazine, 21 February 1998.

New Yorker, 15 September 1997.

News of the World Tribute, 7 September 1997.

Newsweek, 8 September 1997; 15 September 1997; 20 October 1997.

People, "Diana Her Life, Her Style, Intimate Memories," Fall 1997, special issue; "Diana's World One Year Later," 31 August 1998.

Royalty, "Forever In Our Hearts," Fall 1997.

Sunday Times Magazine, 5, 12, 19 July, and Royal Wedding issue, 28 July 1981; 16 and 23 November; 7 and 14 December 1997.

Time, 8 September 1997; 15 September 1997.

Vanity Fair, "The Princess Rebuilds Her Life," Cathy Horyn, July

1997; "Princess Diana's Last Love," Sally Bedell Smith, December 1997.

TELEVISION
ABC: *20/20*, Barbara Walters, 6 September 1997.
ABC: *Prime Time*, Mohamed al Fayed's security men, 10 September 1997.
ABC: Interview with Earl Spencer at Althorp, 12 August 1998.
A&E: *Biography*, 15 September 1997.
A&E: *Princess Diana: Person of the Year*, 31 December 1997.
BBC: *The Death of a Princess*, 31 August 1997.
BBC: All-day coverage of the funeral, 6 September 1997.
CBS: *Prime Time*, 3 September 1997.
NBC: *Dateline*, 3 September 1997.
PBS: All-day coverage of the funeral, 6 September 1997.
PBS: *David Frost*, 15 September 1997.

RADIO
BBC: *Diana, Princess of Wales, A Radio Tribute*.

ARCHIVAL MATERIAL
British Library, Rare Books: *Letters at Madresfield Court*, 1875. The British Library also has an exceptional collection of Spencer family letters in connection with their long relationship with Wimbledon, especially those of the second Earl, his wife Lavinia and their eldest daughter, Sarah; Churchill Archive Centre (for the Windsors); Research Department Public Library, Chillicothe, Ohio (for the Work family); Northampton Studies Collection, Central Library, Northampton (for Althorp); Spencer House (guidebooks).

NOTES

Full details of works mentioned in the notes that follow appear in the Bibliography (see pages 343–7).

CHAPTER 1
Diana's early childhood years and this first journey to Althorp were reconstructed though a combination of interviews conducted by myself in Great Brington with long-time residents and former staff members at Althorp, present staff at St. Mary's, Great Brington. The Spencer family history was drawn from numerous sources: *The History of the Althorp and Pytchley Hunt*, Guy Paget; *The Spencers of Althorp*, Georgina Battiscombe; *A Short History of Althorp and the Spencer Family*, W. E. K. Spencer; *A Spencer Childhood*, Margaret Douglas-Home.

CHAPTER 2
Books that were used for the information in this chapter were: *Marlborough's Duchess*, L. Kronenberg; *King's Lynn*, Paul Richards; *Aspects of Brington*, Stephen Mattingly; *Spencer House* (published by the estate). Interviews were granted me by the people of King's Lynn, Great Brington, former staff at Sandringham, and Janet Filderman.

"his more conventional neighbours . . .": Mattingly.
"never to turn his head . . .": *Raine & Johnnie*, Angela Levin.
"the wedding of the year:" *Daily Mail*, 28 May 1954. Other resources for this coverage: *Daily Telegraph*, 2 June 1954; *The Times*, 2 June 1954; *Daily Mail*, 2 June 1954.

Background on the Work family: archives at the public library, Chillicothe, Ohio; also, *Genealogists,*' June 1981, vol. 20, no. 6.

CHAPTER 3
Books used for this chapter: *Royal Sandringham*, Philip
Hepworth; *Royal Sisters*, Anne Edwards; *Matriarch: Queen
Mary and the House of Windsor*, Anne Edwards; *The Spen-
cers of Althorpe*, Battiscombe; *Diana, Her True Story*, Mor-
ton.
Much of the material for this chapter was drawn from in-
terviews with former staff at Park House and residents of
King's Lynn.

"crying in his bed . . .": *Diana: Her True Story—In Her
Own Words*, Andrew Morton.
"Lady Di," three-part series by Alison Miller, *Sunday Times
Magazine*, part I, 5 July 1981.
"crammed full . . .": *The Spencers of Althorp*, Battiscombe.

CHAPTER 4
My appreciation to the people of Diss for their recollections
of the years that Diana was at Riddlesworth Hall, to members of St. Margaret's Church, former and present employees of the Duke's Head Hotel in King's Lynn. Books used
for reference were: *King's Lynn*, Paul Richards; *Savage of
King's Lynn*, D. Braithwaite.

"in the school hall . . .": Miller, part 2, 12 July, 1981.
"in mid-air . . .": ibid.
"I ate and ate and ate . . .": Morton.
"Well, of course . . .": interview with former ladyfriend of
Earl Spencer, Diana's father.

Background material on Raine Dartmouth: *Raine & Johnnie*, Levin.

CHAPTER 5
Books used for reference for this chapter were: *The Spen-
cers of Althorp*, Battiscombe; *Queen Anne*, David Green;
The British Monarchy at Home, J. A. Frere; *Royal Family*

and the Spencers, 200 Years of Friendship, Nerina Shute;
*Spencer House; Diana in Private, The Princess Nobody
Knows*, Lady Colin Campbell; *Raine & Johnnie*, Levin; and
Diana, The True Story, Morton.

"accidentally find us . . .": Morton.
"Lord Spencer is in bed . . .": Levin.
"I'd sooner take residence . . .": ibid.
"It was such a quiet wedding . . .": *Daily Mail*, 16 July
1976.
"My sister [Sarah] was all over him . . .": Morton.
"He came up to me . . .": ibid.

Also my thanks to Great Brington's residents for their co-
operation.

CHAPTER 6
Books used for reference in this chapter were: *Eating Dis-
orders*, Hilda Bruch; *The Golden Cage—The Enigma of
Anorexia Nervosa*, Hilda Bruch; *The Secret Language of
Eating Disorders*, Peggy Claude-Pierre; *The Prince of
Wales*, Jonathan Dimbleby; *Charles, Prince of Wales*, An-
thony Holden; *Raine & Johnnie*, Levin (Lord Spencer's
stroke and illness; the sale of Althorp's treasures); *The
Royal Palaces*, Philip Howard; *Royal Sisters*, Edwards.
Archival material: The Spencer Family Archive, British Li-
brary.

"Next day the telephone rang . . .": Morton.

CHAPTER 7
Books used for reference in this chapter were: *A Thousand
Years of British Monarchy*, Arthur Bryant; *Majesty: Eliz-
abeth II and the House of Windsor*, Robert Lacey; *The Tar-
nished Crown*, Anthony Holden; *The Prince of Wales*,
Dimbleby; *H. R. H. Prince Philip, Duke of Edinburgh: A
Portrait by His Valet*, John Dean; *Monarchy: Behind the
Scenes of the Royal Family*, Brian Hoey; *The Reality of*

Monarchy, Andrew Duncan; *The Duke: Portrait of Prince Philip*, Tim Heald; *Royal Sisters*, Edwards; *School Ties*, William Boyd; *The Selling of the Royal Family*, John Pearson.

"For me, by far . . .": Dimbleby.

CHAPTER 8
Books used for reference in this chapter were: *The Prince of Wales*, Dimbleby; *Diana: In Her Own Words*, Morton; *Balmoral Castle: The History of a Home*, Ivor Brown.

"I still can't believe . . .": Charles's journal entry, quoted in Dimbleby.

Both Charles and Diana later discussed their early meetings with the press and with BBC Television interviewers during their engagement. Some of their quotes "bouncy, young teenager . . ." etc. come from those interviews.

CHAPTER 9
Books used for reference in this chapter were: *Royal Service*, Barry; *The Prince of Wales*, Dimbleby; *Charles, Prince of Wales*, Holden; *Raine & Johnnie*, Levin; *Diana: In Her Own Words*, Morton. Also *The Times*, 5 February 1981.

"I must call Mummy . . .": Morton.
"Can I marry . . .": Levin.
"Such exciting news . . .": ibid.

It is also based on conversations I had with Stephen Barry, Prince Charles's valet at the time of his engagement and marriage to Diana, when we were both on tours in the US in 1984 promoting our recent books. Some of these conversations were in the form of taped interviews for a book I was then beginning (*Royal Sisters*). Barry was very anti-Diana and pro-Camilla: he felt his situation would be endangered by the Prince of Wales taking a wife.

CHAPTER 10

Books and reference material used for this chapter were: *The Prince of Wales*, Dimbleby; *Royal Sisters*, Edwards; *The Queen's House*, Compton Mackenzie; *The Little Princesses*, Marion Crawford, also interviews I had with Miss Crawford for *Royal Sisters; Charles, Prince of Wales*, Holden; *Diana: In Her Own Words*, Morton; *Diana in Private*, Campbell.

"just pushed . . .": Diana, BBC *Panorama* Interview, November 1995.
"You are not going to hunt . . .": Morton.
"Don't worry, it will get a lot worse . . .": *The Grimaldis*, Edwards.
"I don't think . . .": Morton.
"You understand . . .": *Daily Mail*, 24 July 1981.
"Prince Andrew tied one . . .": Campbell.
"Everybody got terribly drunk . . .": guest at ball.

Diana and Charles's public appearances in the last days before the wedding were reconstructed with the aid of daily reports in several of London's newspapers—*The Times, Daily Telegraph, Daily Mail*, and *Evening Standard*. Also interviews with one of Diana's close friends at the time of her engagement, as well as one of her cousins.

CHAPTER 11

Some observations in this chapter were taken from my own notes when I covered the wedding for the Gannett Newspapers in July 1981. Tiered banks of seats had been built for the press in the north-east and south-east aisles of the cathedral. Press had to be in their seats by nine a.m. (the service started at eleven), other guests by ten (with the exception of the Royal Family, wedding party and Royal guests from other countries).
Articles and interviews (Barbara Daly, the Emanuels, Doris Welham, Kevin and Claire Shanley) in the *Sunday Times*,

The Times, Daily Telegraph, Observer, Guardian, Daily Mail, Mail on Sunday, and *Country Life Royal Wedding Number* (30 July 1981) enabled me to chronicle the days just before the wedding, the day of the wedding and the wedding itself.

"Father was so thrilled . . .": Morton.

CHAPTER 12
The opening paragraphs of this chapter owe much to an interview with one of Diana's closest friends. The memory of her wedding night and the next morning were recalled several years later.
Stephen Barry's *Royal Service* was extremely helpful in writing the paragraphs dealing with the honeymoon cruise. Additional assistance was given by members of the personal staff.

CHAPTER 13
Tour to Wales re-created with the help of articles in *The Times, Sunday Times, Time* magazine, and reports in Dimbleby and in *Charles,* Penny Junor. My appreciation as well to the confidential conversation about the tour and several other matters with a former member of the Princess of Wales's staff.

"I saw something . . .": private interview.
"she stooped . . .": Dimbleby.
Stair incident: private interview; also *Diana: In Her Own Words,* Morton.
"things had degenerated . . . :" *Diana in Private,* Campbell.
Kensington Palace: *Royal Sisters,* Edwards; *Kensington Palace,* Derek Hudson; *Inside Kensington Palace,* Andrew Morton; also interview descriptions, Anthony Holden, Janet Filderman.
"felt extremely . . .": Dimbleby.

CHAPTER 14
The major sources used as reference in this chapter were: *The Secret Language of Eating Disorders,* Claude-Pierre;

Prince Charles: Horseman, Michael Clayton; *The Reality of Monarchy*, Duncan; *Charles at Fifty*, Anthony Holden; *The Prince of Wales*, Dimbleby, *Sunday Times Magazine*, "Highgrove," *The Changing Anatomy of Britain*, Anthony Sampson; *The End of the House of Windsor*, Stephen Haseler.

CHAPTER 15
My thanks to Janet Filderman and Anthony Holden for their informative interviews.
Books and press coverage used for reconstructing the Australian tour were: *The Prince of Wales*, Dimbleby; *Charles, Prince of Wales*, Holden; *Diana, Portrait of a Princess*, Jayne Fincher; Australian and British newspapers covering the dates of the tour.

"It does seem about time . . .": private interview.
"Outdoing . . .": ibid.
"Then suddenly . . .": *The Wyatt Diaries, Sunday Times*, 4 October 1998.

CHAPTER 16
Books and press used as reference in this chapter were: *The Tarnished Crown*, Holden; *The Prince of Wales*, Dimbleby; *Raine & Johnnie*, Levin; *Princess in Love*, Anna Pasternak; to reconstruct the Washington and Palm Beach tour, *Washington Post, New York Times, Newsweek, Time, Daily Mail, Sunday Times, Telegraph, Miami Herald* for these dates.

"There is no doubt . . .": Holden.
"I don't believe . . .": private interview.
"her fingers . . .": Pastemark.

CHAPTER 17
Books and press used as reference for this chapter were: *The Definitive Diana*, Sally Moore; *Diana: In Her Own Words*, Morton; *Daily Mail; The Prince of Wales*, Dimbleby; *Wyatt Diaries; Raine & Johnnie*, Levin.

"I never saw . . .": private interview.
"The Princess of Wales . . .": ibid.
"that woman . . .": ibid.
"This created . . .": ibid.
"You won't need me . . .": Moore.
"Frequently, I feel . . .": Dimbleby.
"With steps . . .": Levin.

CHAPTER 18

Books consulted and quoted about Queen Elizabeth II were: *A Thousand Years of British Monarchy*, Bryant; *Fall of the House of Windsor*, Nigel Blundell and Susan Blackhall; *The Decline and Fall of the British Aristocracy*, David Cannadine; *The Tarnished Crown*, Holden; *The Queen*, Pimlott.

"She seemed not to smell . . .": *People*, fall (Special Issue) 1997.
"I know how he feels . . .": Prince Charles's housekeeper, Wendy Berry.
"Wills had elected . . .": ibid.
"[From that point] . . .": ibid.
"Boys . . .": Morton, *Diana: Her True Story*.
Also news articles in the *Washington Post, New York Times, Daily Mail*, and the *Sun*.

CHAPTER 19

Books used for this chapter included: *Raine & Johnnie*, Levin. The Squidgy tape: published transcript, numerous newspapers.
My extreme appreciation to Andrew Morton for the section on his writing of *Diana: Her True Story*. He generously answered many queries, adding a new insight.

"I'm not saying . . .": private interview.
Camillagate tapes: published transcripts, numerous newspapers.

CHAPTER 20

Radio and television coverage was an important aid to the work on this chapter. Quotes regarding Prince Charles's relationship with Camilla Parker Bowles from BBC transcript, 19 June 1994, conducted by Jonathan Dimbleby. Diana's quotes 21 November 1994, are also from a BBC transcript of her interview with Martin Bashir. Other comments come from the full reports in *The Times* and the *Evening Standard* of these interviews.

"Over the next few months . . .": BBC broadcast.

CHAPTER 21
"At first, I wasn't sure . . .": private interview.
"There was a young boy . . .": "Diana's World," *Dennis Oneshots.*
"[Charles and I] could have . . .": *New Yorker*, 15 September 1997.
"Diana was greatly disturbed . . .": private interview.
"All that blood . . .": *Diana: A Life and Legacy*, Anthony Holden.
"I'd really like to go to China . . .": ibid.

Also, my many thanks to Anthony Holden for his long hours of detailed recollections of his meetings with Diana and his years of documenting Charles's life that might not have been previously included in his publications.

CHAPTER 22
Much of this chapter was reconstructed with the generous help of staff in the al Fayed household in St. Tropez and people with whom Diana came in contact outside the household while in St. Tropez (press, disco staff).

"Hey! Diana!" exchange: *Time*, 23 July 1997; *Newsweek*, 15 September 1997.
"I am in love . . .": *Daily Telegraph*, 1 November 1997 (Rosa Monckton).
"a man whose idea . . .": *Sunday Times Magazine*, 2 November 1997.
". . . for most of his life . . .": *Sunday Times Magazine*, 16 November 1997 (Dodi Fayed).

"Something told me to save myself . . .": AE interview with Janet Filderman.
"Well never forget . . .": Rosa Monckton.

CHAPTER 23
Books by Dodi Fayed's butler, René Delorm, and Christopher Anderson, and abundant newspaper coverage were used to construct this chapter, along with some personal interviews with on-the-spot witnesses.
The descriptions of the cruise on the *Jonikal* were aided by accounts in *Newsweek*, 1 and 8 September 1997, *Time*, 1 September 1997, and the memories of René Delorm who was also on the cruise.

"Dodi was very cautious . . .": *Sunday Times Magazine*, 16 November 1997 (Dodi Fayed).
"She cried one night . . .": *The Daily Telegraph*, 1 November 1997 (Rosa Monckton).
"Och, there goes the Princess of Wales . . .": *Daily Telegraph*, 1 November 1997 (Rosa Monckton).
"That's it. All over the front pages . . .": ibid.
"That's not what I want . . .": ibid.
"and had the most beautiful eyes . . .": *Sunday Times Magazine*, 2 November 1997.
"a visible oneness . . .": private interview.
"If you don't speak to us . . .": *The Day Diana Died*, Christopher Anderson.

CHAPTER 24
Books used in this chapter were: *The Day Diana Died*, Christopher P. Anderson; *Diana & Dodi: A Love Story*, René Delorm; and *Death of a Princess: The Investigation*, Thomas Sanction and Scott Macleod.
Personal interviews were conducted at the Ritz Hotel by the author on 5 December 1997.

CHAPTER 25
Books as in Chapter 24.
On 4 December 1997, I made a careful journey through the

Alma tunnel arriving there via the same route as that taken by the Mercedes. A visit was made to La Pitié Salpêtrière Hospital that same day. Newspaper coverage appearing in London, Paris and New York publications from 1 September 1997 to 28 February 1998, was used to reconstruct the day of the crash and the crash, correcting any errors that were made, or suspicions that were later found to be groundless, that had appeared in early press reports or published in previous books.

CHAPTER 26
This chapter was drawn from the dozens of publications (magazines and newspapers) that carried the story of Diana's funeral. The author also drew from personal recall and notes made at the time of Diana's death and conversations with many members of the press, who covered the story, and of some of those who were witness to it.

CHAPTER 27
This chapter was helped with the daily news coverage in London and New York from 15 September 1997 to 28 February 1998, and from the transcripts of numerous television interviews with close observers and Spencer family members during that same period.

INDEX